Cinematic Cold War

Cinematic Cold War

The American and Soviet Struggle for Hearts and Minds

TONY SHAW AND DENISE J. YOUNGBLOOD

UNIVERSITY PRESS OF KANSAS

© 2010 by the University Press of Kansas
All rights reserved

Published by the University Press of
Kansas (Lawrence, Kansas 66045), which
was organized by the Kansas Board of
Regents and is operated and funded by
Emporia State University, Fort Hays
State University, Kansas State University,
Pittsburg State University, the University
of Kansas, and Wichita State University

Library of Congress Cataloging-in-Publication Data
Shaw, Tony, 1965–
Cinematic cold war : the American and Soviet struggle
for hearts and minds / Tony Shaw and Denise J.
Youngblood.
   p.   cm.
Includes bibliographical references and index.
Includes filmography.
ISBN 978-0-7006-1743-2 (cloth : alk. paper)
1. Cold War in motion pictures. 2. Politics in motion
pictures. 3. Motion pictures—Political aspects—United
States. 4. Motion pictures—Political aspects—Soviet
Union. I. Youngblood, Denise J. (Denise Jeanne), 1952–
II. Title.
PN1995.9.P6S525   2010
791.43'6582825—dc22
2010018067

British Library Cataloguing in Publication Data
is available.

Printed in the United States of America

10 9 8 7 6 5 4 3 2 1

The paper used in this publication is recycled and contains 30 percent postconsumer waste. It is acid free
and meets the minimum requirements of the American
National Standard for Permanence of Paper for Printed
Library Materials z39.48-1992.

Contents

Acknowledgments

I would like to record my thanks to the institutions that supplied financial and logistical support for this project. The Leverhulme Trust provided a grant and a year's leave via a Research Fellowship. The British Academy and the Scouloudi Foundation at London's Institute of Historical Research both helped with travel expenses. A Senior Fellowship at the Rothermere American Institute in Oxford enabled me to complete the project in a wonderfully stimulating environment.

The following scholars and friends seemingly never tired of answering questions, reading drafts, or asking when the book would be finished: Dave Bannerman, John Bell, James Chapman, Nick Cull, Jo Fox, Ifan Hughes, Pete Kind, Ray Ryan, Giles Scott-Smith, and Hugh Wilford. Andy Woods was an indefatigable research assistant.

The book is dedicated to Shirley and Isaac, and to the memory of my dad, Ernest Shaw (1933–2008).

T. S.

I am pleased to acknowledge the many institutions and individuals who have supported this project. My home institution, the University of Vermont, provided a one-year sabbatical leave and a grant from the Faculty Development Fund of the College of Arts and Sciences. Other grants came from the Kennan Institute for Advanced Russian Studies of the Woodrow Wilson Center, Washington, D.C., and from the Summer Research Laboratory at the University of Illinois, Urbana-Champaign. Thanks to Vladimir Padunov, I was able to travel to the University of Pittsburgh to use the library's extensive collection of Russian and Soviet films. The librarians in the European Reading Room of the Library of Congress were especially helpful, as were the librarians in the Slavic Reference Division of the University of Illinois Library. Interlibrary Loan at UVM's Bailey-Howe Library was indispensable. In Russia, I would like to thank Gosfilmofond for providing access to archival materials for chapters 2 and 3 and the Scientific Research Institute of Cinema Art (NIIK) for providing stills. In Hungary, the Hungarian National Film Archive offered a welcoming venue for viewing some of the rarer films from the late 1940s.

A number of individuals gave generously of their time and expertise to read various drafts of the manuscript, and I warmly thank Peter Kenez, Anna Lawton, Sudha Rajagopalan (who also allowed us to use one of her interviews), Oksana Sarkisova, Marsha Siefert, Richard Taylor, and Sergei Zhuk for their comments and criticisms. Joshua First, Emily Johnson, and Andrey Shcherbenok answered my queries at various points. Sergei Kapterev shared valuable unpublished work with me. Finally, special thanks go to Aleksander Deriabin for his unstinting assistance.

This book is dedicated to my devoted reader and critic, Kevork Spartalian, and to the memory of my father, James D. Young (1927–2009).

D. J. Y.

Grateful acknowledgment is made to the following sources for permission to reproduce material and film stills in this book. Every effort has been made to trace copyright holders, but if any have been inadvertently overlooked, the authors will be pleased to make the necessary arrangements at the first opportunity.

Photograph of Sin Sang-ok and Choe Eun-hui by Tim Clary, May 1986. Bettmann / Corbis.

Invasion U.S.A. (1952). Columbia / Photofest.

How to Marry a Millionaire (1953). Twentieth Century-Fox / Photofest.

The Manchurian Candidate (1962). M.C. Prods / United Artists / Photofest.

Top Gun (1986). Paramount Pictures / Photofest.

Russkies (1987). New Century / Vista Film Company / Photofest.

Man on a Tightrope (1953). Twentieth Century-Fox / Academy of Motion Pictures Arts and Sciences.

Roman Holiday (1953). Paramount Pictures / Academy of Motion Pictures Arts and Sciences.

Fail-Safe (1964). Columbia Pictures / Photofest.

Bananas (1971). MGM / United Artists / Photofest.

Rambo: First Blood Part II (1985). Tristar Pictures / Photofest.

Note on Transliteration and Translation

The transliteration in the source citations is according to the Library of Congress system for the benefit of Russian speakers. Transliteration in the text, including text in the notes, has been modified to facilitate pronunciation for non-Russian speakers: "y" instead of "ii," "ye" instead of initial "e," "yu" instead of "iu," and so on. The soft and hard signs, ' and ", have been omitted altogether. Well-known Russian names are rendered in the standard English spelling, for example, "Eisenstein" instead of "Eizenshtein."

Translations from the Russian are Denise Youngblood's, unless otherwise indicated.

Introduction: Culture, Film, and the "New" Cold War History

It had all the elements of a blockbuster—a sensational story of political intrigue, cross-border abductions, dangerous dictators, and love, capped off with a breathtaking escape.

It began in early 1978.

Lured to Hong Kong by an offer of a lucrative contract, the beautiful South Korean actress Choe Eun-hui is kidnapped by agents acting at the behest of Kim Jung-il, son of North Korea's communist dictator Kim Il-sung. Sin Sang-ok, Choe's estranged husband and one of South Korea's most famous film directors, travels to Hong Kong to investigate, only to suffer the same fate. His car is stopped at gunpoint and a sack put over his head. Sin is then drugged with chloroform and secretly bundled off to North Korea, where he soon learns that he is to make propaganda movies to persuade a world audience of the righteousness of the Korea Workers' Party, under Kim Jung-il's direct supervision. Unbeknownst to Sin, Choe is held under house arrest and brainwashed twice weekly by being forced to watch Marxist films and listen to lectures on the evils of the West.

At first, Sin bravely resists Kim Jung-il's blandishments. After two failed escape attempts from the barren republic, however, he is tortured and thrown into the notorious Prison No. 6, a concentration camp outside Pyongyang. For the next four years, Sin barely survives on a daily diet of grass, salt, a bowl of rice, and Party indoctrination. His spirit broken, Sin is then reunited tearfully with Choe in 1983, after which the couple live a bizarre double life: by day working on increasingly lavish communist film productions, by night living as "state guests" in a luxuriously furnished, heavily guarded compound, where a clearly insane Kim Jung-il tries to impress them with his private collection of 20,000 movies from Hollywood and other filmmaking capitals. This culminates in 1985 with the release of *Pulgasari,* a socialist version of the 1950s Japanese monster classic *Godzilla,* with Choe later named Best Actress at the Moscow Film Festival for her role in another of Sin's productions, *Salt,* about the 1930s Japanese occupation of Korea.

Washington, D.C., 16 May 1986: Choe Eun-hui and Sin Sang-ok smile after telling reporters of their escape from North Korea. ©Bettmann/Corbis.

By this stage, the North Korean regime deems Sin and Choe to be ardent communists, true believers. Consequently, they are allowed to travel abroad together for the first time in March 1986, in order to make a film in Hungary about the founder of the Mongol empire, Genghis Khan. This is the chance the couple have awaited for eight years. When they stop in Vienna en route to Budapest to source exhibition venues, Sin and Choe elude their North Korean handlers after a nail-biting taxi chase and are given sanctuary in the U.S. embassy. They then relocate to Hollywood, where, under the protection of the Central Intelligence Agency, Sin devises a highly successful martial arts film series, *Three Ninjas.* Meanwhile, the North Korean Ministry of Culture denies the kidnapping allegations and retaliates by accusing the couple of embezzling more than $2.3 million. When Kim Jung-il succeeds his father as North Korean leader in 1994, the *Los Angeles Times* reports that one of his first acts is to place a bounty of $1 million on Sin and Choe's heads.

Is this unique tale of Cold War double-border crossing the work of fiction or a harrowing real-life episode? We cannot know for sure, largely because North Korea remains one of the most isolated states in the world, but it is likely that the story is at least half true. Choe Eun-hui and Sin Sang-ok are certainly real people. They did mysteriously disappear from Hong Kong in 1978 and go on to make a series of movies in North Korea before "re-defecting" in 1986 and enjoying success in Hollywood. But whether they were kidnapped, as they claimed in their best-selling memoirs, or went to

North Korea voluntarily is open to debate. Sin Sang-ok's career in South Korea had ground to a halt in 1977, when the repressive government of General Park Chung-hee revoked his filmmaking license for breaking censorship regulations. Afterward he apparently told at least one friend that he had received offers of work in the North. According to Western observers, neither Sin nor Choe behaved like brainwashed prisoners when they traveled overseas to promote their North Korean productions in the mid-1980s. And Sin admitted to having made off with a lot of North Korean money when he fled to the West in 1986, cash he then used to rebuild his career in Hollywood.

Stranger than fiction Sin Sang-ok and Choe Eun-hui's story may well be, but the fact is just about everyone who read or heard about their ordeal seems to have believed it was true. Why? Part of the answer lies in North Korea's widespread reputation for political debauchery. Part of it lies in Kim Jung-il's well-known passion for cinema. But there is something else, too. The credibility of Sin Sang-ok and Choe Eun-hui's tale was strengthened by numerous other examples of governments coercing or cajoling filmmakers throughout the twentieth century and during the Cold War in particular.[1]

Between 1945 and 1990 the Cold War was a hotly contested and often financially lucrative subject for filmmakers. No cinema—from the East, West, North, or South—could fail to be touched in one way or another by a conflict that spanned more than four decades. During the war politicians of all stripes recognized the value of cinematic images and realized the need to intervene in the filmmaking process. Their interventions took a variety of forms, some better known than others. In the United States during the McCarthy era, numerous Hollywood leftists were jailed or blacklisted for allegedly conducting "un-American" activities.[2] In the Soviet Union during the same period, Joseph Stalin issued strict instructions to revered directors such as Vsevolod Pudovkin on how to make films that showed "the superiority of the Soviet order over bourgeois democracy."[3] In Canada in the late 1940s the federal police force ran an intensive campaign aimed at purging the national film board of suspected communists. And in Britain in the 1950s the foreign office went to great lengths to advise filmmakers secretly on how to construct plausible anti-Soviet images.[4]

That filmmakers could be blacklisted, jailed, submitted to loyalty tests, given "constructive guidance" by state agencies, and, if we are to believe Sin Sang-ok and Choe Eun-hui, even kidnapped and tortured testifies to cinema's power as a vehicle of entertainment and propaganda during the Cold War. A combination of the twentieth-century communications revolution and the Cold War's intrinsically ideological character rendered the clash between the East and the West a propaganda conflict par excellence. The key protagonists in this historic battle for hearts and minds were the mass media. The press, radio, cinema, and television devised and disseminated a barrage of words, sounds, and images the scale and ingenuity of which had never been seen before. This barrage played a critical role in helping to frame the Cold War for millions of ordinary people, not to mention public opinion makers and politicians. It told them why it was necessary to wage this new kind of seemingly permanent war, what the conflict was (and was not) about, and whose opinion they should trust.

Cinema's potency during the Cold War derived principally from its purported ability from the very outset to show audiences the "reality" of what was for most people a peculiarly abstract, "virtual" conflict. Through feature films, documentaries, and, before their place was taken by regular television broadcasts, newsreels, millions could watch "their boys" in action in Cold War hot spots like Korea and Vietnam, Taiwan and Afghanistan; see the terrible dangers implicit in nuclear research, powers most dramatically unleashed by hydrogen bomb tests; and witness with their own eyes the dangers posed by enemy spies. Seeing did not necessarily amount to believing, of course, but these countless, persistent images left no one in any doubt that their country was at war. For some people these images were the war. They served to underline the totality of the Cold War, to blur the old-fashioned distinction between soldier and civilian, and to simplify and shed physical light on what was, in reality, a diplomatically opaque and morally complex conflagration.

This book is the first comparative study of Soviet and American film during the Cold War. Scholars, journalists, and statesmen alike have shared a fascination with the politics of filmmaking in general for decades. Over the past thirty to forty years, Western historians in particular have constructed an impressive body of work focusing on wartime cinema. The bulk of this material has concentrated on the two world wars and, especially, on how the American, British, German, and Japanese film industries, among others, operated within a sophisticated network of state-run propaganda machines between 1937 and 1945.[5] Our study extends this field of scholarship, taking us beyond the 1940s and into the contemporary sphere. It looks at how the foundations were laid in the late 1940s for an intensive, multidimensional battle of images between the Soviet and American film industries that lasted well into the 1980s. This work, therefore, explores cinema's continuing propaganda role even after the birth of television, and examines how that role evolved along with the Cold War itself over a period of more than forty years. Given that its "hot" battles were often fought through surrogates, the Cold War was qualitatively different from most other conflicts of the twentieth century, and as a result had different propaganda demands. Explaining these demands, and analyzing how the two cinemas coped with them, is one of the book's chief aims.

As well as contributing to the historiography of film propaganda, our study also seeks to add substantially to the "new history" of the Cold War that has blossomed since the fall of the USSR and Soviet satellite states in the years 1989–1991. The study of the Cold War has undergone what might be described as a mini-revolution since the early 1990s. Two features of this revolution stand out. The first has been driven by new evidence excavated from previously inaccessible former Eastern bloc archives (Party records, Stasi files, and so on). This evidence has helped reshape or complete many aspects of what we know, or thought we knew, about the conflict, whether it be about high-profile episodes like the 1962 Cuban missile crisis or the complex triangular relationship between the USSR, China, and Albania.[6] *Cinematic Cold War* itself could not have been written without access to Soviet film archives, most of which are housed in Moscow and St. Petersburg.[7] Because of the integrated nature of the USSR's propaganda infrastructure, the book provides an insight into Soviet filmmaking and augments our understanding of Moscow's propaganda policies as a whole during the Cold War.

The second, more innovative feature of "the new Cold War history" is a determination to look at the conflict from the bottom up rather than from the top down. This development can be attributed to an increased interest in the role ideology played in the conflict,[8] and to the fact that the end of the Cold War brought together scholars from the East and West able to elucidate the comparative societal impact of the conflict. Twenty years after the fall of the Berlin Wall, most academic and mainstream accounts of the Cold War, as well as university courses, continue to focus first and foremost on diplomatic and military matters. In recent years, however, many scholars have rightly recognized that the Cold War was not fought solely between desk-bound politicians and generals with their fingers on the nuclear triggers. Like the world wars (if not more so, because of its duration), the Cold War was a people's war, too, and therefore a conflict that had important social and cultural dimensions.

Work on the cultural dynamics of the Cold War in particular over the past decade is part of a wider cultural turn recently taken by practitioners of diplomatic history.[9] This imaginative work has encompassed the literary and artistic endeavour of high culture, as well as popular culture and general mentalities. It has also included cultural diplomacy, conducted either between or within the blocs, predominantly by state bodies. Most of this scholarship has focused on the first Cold War (circa 1947–1962) and on the

West (principally the United States), partly due to funding and a greater access to documentation for that period in the West.[10]

As a result, we now know a great deal about, for instance, the Central Intelligence Agency's secret patronage of the arts, about how the Cold War affected the artistic and intellectual life of Italy perhaps more than any other West European nation, and about the traumatic impact that the atomic bombings of Hiroshima and Nagasaki had on postwar Japanese culture.[11] Thanks to more recent scholarship about the other side, we are also beginning to learn about "socialist consumerism" in Hungary, about anti-Western jokes in the Polish press, and even about the cultural appropriation of the North American Indian in Czechoslovakia.[12] The world awaits a comprehensive, definitive overview of the cultural Cold War, but some historians have at least started to grasp the nettle by comparing one side's output and performance with the other's.[13]

Though also transcending it, *Cinematic Cold War* is a logical extension of the "cultural Cold War" recently applied to international relations and international history. It looks inward at U.S. and Soviet Cold War society and at popular culture on the home front, seeking to compare how cinema reflected and shaped everyday Cold War mentalities and values. Relatively little in-depth work has been conducted as yet on Russian society during the Cold War or on Soviet propaganda of the era, making a study of these subjects well overdue.[14] *Cinematic Cold War* also extends the chronological boundaries of most existing scholarship on Cold War cultural affairs by covering the whole of the conflict instead of just the first two decades. Moreover, it seeks to do more than merely graft culture onto conventional Cold War historiography, a trait common to some diplomatic historians. Rather, it aims to demonstrate that culture, interpreted both as a way of life and a range of products (including paintings, television programs, and films), was a critical determinant of the Cold War, not an adjunct to diplomacy and military affairs, but a factor that shaped the meaning and nature of the conflict for millions of people from beginning to end.

The cinema of the Cold War itself is not uncharted territory for historians and film studies scholars. Excellent scholarship on the Hollywood anticommunist witch hunts of the late 1940s and 1950s dates back over thirty years.[15] One of the present authors has written detailed accounts of the relationship between filmmakers and the government in Britain and the United States during the Cold War.[16] The Australian historian Mick Broderick has spent two decades analyzing the cinema of nuclear war,[17] while Kyoko Hirano has examined how the United States used film as a means of creating a Cold War ally during its post–World War II occupation of Japan.[18] Other scholars have recently brought communist cinemas more clearly into the picture. We now have authoritative accounts of East German film, of Cuban cinema under Fidel Castro, and of Soviet cinema during the thaw that followed the death of Stalin.[19]

Cinematic Cold War builds on the above work in several important ways. The United States and the Soviet Union were the chief architects of the cinematic Cold War and its leading players. This is the first book to provide a detailed analysis of the ways in which these two cinematic superpowers covered and contested the conflict. As such, it not only delves deeply into one of the Cold War's key propaganda battle zones, but does so systematically from both sides. Second, unlike most other analyses of Cold War cinema, which focus on the period between the Truman Doctrine and the Cuban missile crisis, our book examines American and Soviet film output during the entire conflict. By taking this long view, we are able to provide a fuller and more sophisticated account of the visual dynamics of what many came to call "the long peace." By examining cinematic output over such a long period, we also explore the nuances of positive as well as negative propaganda, and incorporate pictures that move well beyond those commonly regarded as canonical.

Third, by going against the grain in this way, Cinematic Cold War stretches conventional definitions of what a Cold War film is and thus looks afresh at how millions of ordinary spectators might have comprehended the East-West conflict. Too many accounts of Cold War cinema have concentrated on the conflict's headline events and issues—espionage, the arms race, the Red Scare, the Vietnam War, and so on. This can leave the impression that filmmakers largely fought the war either transparently or, as in the case of Hollywood science fiction directors of the 1950s, in a crudely allegorical manner.[20] The truth is that filmmakers on both sides of the Iron Curtain engaged with the Cold War on a variety of levels between 1945 and 1990: implicitly and explicitly, wittingly and unwittingly, across a variety of genres, with some regarded as more political than others. This is not to say that every film made in the United States and the Soviet Union between 1945 and 1990 was about or can be linked to the Cold War in one way or another. Rather, certain films (or even film types) that are ordinarily dismissed as irrelevant have had a significant bearing on the conflict, especially if one defines the Cold War as a social phenomenon or traces its transnational contours.

Fourth, and of equal importance, Cinematic Cold War is explicitly comparative. Contrary to received wisdom, the American and Soviet film industries had culturally specific stories to tell during the Cold War and told them in culturally specific ways. Instead of presenting these stories separately, however, the book is structured such that differences and similarities in the two industries' output can be explored directly and in full. Moreover, by comparing and contrasting the two film industries' propaganda techniques and messages via this route, our study can, in turn, point to significant similarities and differences between U.S. and Soviet Cold War cultures as a whole.

Finally, *Cinematic Cold War* blends history with film and communication studies. Our book is interested not only in what people saw on the screen, but also in what went on behind it. It therefore offers close content and contextual analysis of how and why the cinematic superpowers covered the Cold War in the ways they did.[21] This means looking at the filmmaking process from the inside as well as the outside and entails examining cinematic propaganda from an economic, industrial, and cultural perspective. It requires us to consider the various meanings audiences might have ascribed to particular movies and, when possible, to make critical judgments on how people responded to films.

Some might argue that propaganda can only be understood fully when examined within the context of the polity that created it, and that to compare Soviet and American film propaganda during the Cold War is therefore conceptually problematic. While recognizing that propaganda can assume very different characteristics and roles in different sociopolitical systems, we believe that a comparative perspective on Soviet and American cinematic propaganda activity allows for a deeper understanding of the broader processes, functions, themes, and execution of propaganda in authoritarian and democratic states, not only during the Cold War but in general. This comparative perspective also poses some intriguing questions, not only for this study, but for future research on the comparative history of the Cold War. Among these are the following: What, if anything, was distinctive about film propaganda during the Cold War? What was the relationship between commerce, entertainment, and political persuasion during the conflict? How potent or influential was film during the Cold War? Did cinematic propaganda, especially enemy stereotyping, deepen or even prolong Cold War hostilities? Who won the cinematic Cold War (if there was a winner at all) and why?

In order to suggest answers for these and other questions, *Cinematic Cold War* is divided into two parts. Part 1, comprising chapters 1 and 2, provides a chronological and thematic overview of the ways in which the American and Soviet film industries treated the Cold War between 1945 and 1990. Each chapter looks at the political economy of filmmaking, who ran the film industry, the size of the cinema audience, and what reach that industry had internationally. Each explores the industry's overarching ideological stance, together with its real and perceived political role. Each explains the relationship that developed between the industry and government during the Cold War, and considers the scope that existed for exerting or resisting official influence on the filmmaking process. Each, finally, sets out the main thematic contours of the two industries' Cold War output, delineates which Cold War issues were addressed over others, and establishes the key propaganda messages conveyed.

Part 2, the core of the book, is given over to five case-study chapters, analyzing the following pairs of films: *The Meeting on the Elbe* (*Vstrecha na Elbe*) and *Man on a Tightrope*; *Spring on Zarechnaya Street* (*Vesna na Zarechnoi ulitse*) and *Roman Holiday*; *Nine Days in One Year* (*Deviat dnei odnogo goda*) and *Fail-Safe*; *Officers* (*Ofitsery*) and *Bananas*; and *Incident at Map Grid 36-80* (*Sluchai v kvadrate 36-80*) and *Rambo: First Blood Part II*. These pairs are arranged chronologically, beginning with the formative phase of the Cold War in the late 1940s and early 1950s, and ending with the second Cold War phase of the 1980s. Together these five chapters span the whole of the conflict and demonstrate the evolution of Cold War ideology as expressed cinematically. This is not a genre study, so each chapter's pair of films—one Soviet, the other American—relates either to a key propaganda theme or a seminal Cold War issue.[22] The origins, production, content, and reception of each of these paradigmatic films are examined in detail via a range of sources, including, as available, unpublished scripts, censors' reports, government documentation, reviews, and box office returns. Each film is also placed within its cultural, social, political, and, if relevant, diplomatic context.

Although each chapter refers to other films of the same type to provide the necessary cinematic context, the book eschews the catalogue-and-digest style of analysis that is the bane of many film histories. Rather, by identifying "model" movies—variously defined by genre, propaganda theme, Cold War subject matter, the type of audience targeted, extent of government input, and the year of production—*Cinematic Cold War* digs deeply into the mechanics of cinematic political persuasion during the Cold War. It identifies both the different and similar forms and styles that film propaganda took across the ideological blocs and across the decades.

Choosing "model" movies was not easy, and many readers will undoubtedly miss such films as Leo McCarey's classic Hollywood Red-baiter *My Son John* (1952), Andrei Tarkovsky's subversive *Andrei Rublev* (1966, released in 1971), or Yury Ozerov's officially commissioned *Liberation* (*Osvobozhdenie*, 1968–71). One could surely argue that Stanley Kubrick's *Dr. Strangelove or: How I Learned to Stop Worrying and Love the Bomb* (1964) warrants analysis when it comes to assessing Hollywood's vision of nuclear war. And what of Aleksander Alov and Vladimir Naumov's *Tehran-43* (*Tegran-43*, 1980), which casts the 1943 Tehran Conference as a spy thriller?[23]

All these are important Cold War artifacts, but they have dominated historiography for too long at the expense of other equally, or in some cases more, significant movies. *Cinematic Cold War* combines the canonical with a selection of movies that have either been marginalized, often by cineastes more interested in "art" than "power," or have not hitherto been categorized as Cold War films. Grigory Aleksandrov's military drama set in postwar Germany, *The Meeting on the Elbe* (released in 1949), is one of Soviet cinema's bona fide early Cold War classics, whereas *Man on a Tightrope* (1953) is a relatively unknown drama-carnival, despite being made by one of Hollywood's all-time great directors, Elia Kazan. These two movies form the basis of our first comparative case study in chapter 3, because they exemplify the thematic and ideological strategies of Soviet and American filmmakers in their demonization of the new enemy during the Cold War's formative phase.

Chapter 4 focuses on two movies that would not ordinarily register on the Cold War radar, but which give us a wonderful insight into how the American and Soviet film industries could subtly sell their side's way of life during the Cold War: William Wyler's stylish romantic comedy *Roman Holiday* (1953) and Marlen Khutsiev and Feliks Mironer's grungy melodrama *Spring on Zarechnaya Street* (1956). This form of "soft," "positive" propaganda was an essential weapon in the two film industries' arsenals, and was especially pronounced in the 1950s for a mixture of political, economic, and diplomatic reasons.

As the world entered what would soon be labeled in the West the "Swinging Sixties," a minority of filmmakers on both sides of the Iron Curtain started to balk at the seemingly inevitable road to Armageddon that nuclear science was taking them down. Two films that capture this dissent better than any are the cult movies analyzed in chapter 5: Mikhail Romm's pathbreaking laboratory drama *Nine Days in One Year* (1962) and Sidney Lumet's chillingly claustrophobic thriller *Fail-Safe* (1964). These two films were remarkably similar aesthetically, further illustrating the degree to which our two industries converged during this phase of the Cold War.

In the 1970s, Soviet and American cinema took quite different political paths: the former to the right, in line with the Brezhnev Doctrine and cinema's "period of stagnation," and the latter to the left, encouraged by the Vietnam and Watergate imbroglios. Chapter 6 looks at this critical cleavage through two very different but richly representative films from 1971: Vladimir Rogovoy's extraordinarily popular family saga *Officers,* and Woody Allen's enormously inventive though ultimately flawed madcap comedy *Bananas.* Film historians often claim the Cold War disappeared from the big screen during the 1970s, a reflection of that decade's thaw in East-West relations. *Officers* and *Bananas* illustrate nicely how Cold War cinema in fact largely went underground during this period, with filmmakers continuing to comment on the conflict, but indirectly.

In contrast, our final chapter looks at how explicitly Cold War movies returned with a vengeance during the 1980s, many of them topping the box office. Here the focus is on two films that symbolized the hatred the Soviet Union and United States felt for each other at the height of the second Cold War: Mikhail Tumanishvili's *Incident at Map Grid 36-80* (1982) and George P. Cosmatos's *Rambo: First Blood Part II* (1985). Both highly successful adventure combat movies, the most popular Cold War genre of the 1980s, they serve to remind us how influential cinema could still be even during the latter stages of the four-decade conflict.

Taken together, these case studies seek to demonstrate that the best-known Cold War films were not necessarily the most representative or politically effective. The unorthodox choice of case studies also makes it possible that *Cinematic Cold War* will be read as a study of film and the culture of the Cold War, as opposed to just Cold War cinema. Finally, the choices also reflect our wish to examine how the Cold War encompassed battles within as well as between societies. These battles—over science versus nature, public space versus private space, city versus province, militarism versus pacifism, freedom versus authority, old world versus new world—should encourage us to think of the Cold War as a geostrategic conflict and an international civil war, in both of which culture played a central role.

PART ONE

Industry, State, and Cold War Contours

Introduction

The Cold War forged the longest and most sophisticated cinematic conflict in history. The American and Soviet film industries traded blows not over a period of six years—merely the length of the Second World War[1]—but over more than four decades. This they did by competing for hearts and minds on the international stage as well as at home. To catalogue each and every feature film, documentary, and newsreel that contributed to this gargantuan battle of images is well nigh impossible. The USSR, for its part, saved copies of most of its films (including the banned ones). And while many American films from the era have not survived, in some cases without even a record to prove their existence, the number of those extant today is absolutely daunting.

Nevertheless, in Part 1 we construct a clear outline of how the American and Soviet film industries represented the Cold War from beginning to end. By tracing the main contours of the industries' treatment of the Cold War between 1945 and 1990, we can also identify both the key phases of their coverage and the core propaganda themes that emerge from thousands of hours of screen output. This is vital if we are to understand fully the case studies that lie ahead in our book. By delineating the industries' Cold War trajectories at this stage, we can also flag the chief similarities in and differences between their coverage, pinpointing, for instance, when negative and positive propaganda came to the fore and showing how both industries took direct and indirect approaches toward the conflict.

Part 1 also provides the reader with an overview of the political and economic context in which filmmaking took place in the United States and the Soviet Union during the Cold War. This includes the informal versus formal modes of censorship, how the film industries were owned and operated, and the relationship between cinema and the state. On the face of it, the American and Soviet film industries were two quite different animals during the Cold War. Whereas the former was known to be highly politicized and to operate as part of a tightly structured government propaganda machine, many people, especially in the West, regarded Hollywood as an apolitical "dream factory" that focused entirely on making money via escapist entertainment. The reality, as we show in the next two chapters, was somewhat different. Throughout the conflict both industries interacted with their state's information apparatus in various, often subtle ways, sometimes openly and on other occasions covertly. As a result, to call one industry's output "propaganda" and the other's "entertainment" is highly misleading. As we shall see, the two terms were often interchangeable during the Cold War. Indeed, Cold War cinema might be said to have blurred them in unprecedented fashion.

The final aim of Part 1 is to establish for whom Cold War films were made and to determine whether their audiences changed as the conflict progressed. Over the course of the Cold War, both Soviet and American cinema suffered a marked decline in the size of their domestic audience, due not least to competition from television.[2] It is important to take note of this, as well as to appreciate why, despite the drop in cinema attendance, film continued to play an important role in the cultural Cold War. One key difference, however, is Hollywood's greater international reach compared with Soviet film, a fact that can be tied predominantly to the broader appeal of American movies. This meant that whereas Moscow concentrated reluctantly on using film mainly for domestic and bloc purposes during the Cold War, Washington was able to place a stronger emphasis on wooing neutrals and subverting the enemy's sphere of influence. Washington's wider parameters indicate how much better equipped the American film industry was to fight a long, drawn-out propaganda conflict compared with its Soviet rival. This, in turn, gives us a clue as to which of the two cinemas would prove to be the more dominant and why, therefore, we should start by looking at Hollywood.

CHAPTER ONE

American Cinema and
the Cold War

*Pictures give an idea of America which is difficult to portray in any other
way, and the reason, the main reason, we think, is because our pictures are not
obvious propaganda.*

> Eric Johnston, president of the Motion Picture Association
> of America, testifying before the U.S. Senate Committee on
> Foreign Relations, June 1953[1]

For over a century now, America's film executives have habitually prided
themselves on creating harmless, feel-good, apolitical entertainment. We
give the people what they want, they say: the chance to laugh, cry, be thrilled,
and, above all, to escape. "If you want to send a message, call Western
Union," mogul Sam Goldwyn famously told one of his high-minded producers in the 1930s. Hollywood is a business, in other words, whose purpose is
to make a profit, not propaganda.[2]

The truth is that American film—just like the nation's theater, radio,
newspapers, and television—has always been political in one way or another. In particular, the big screen has traditionally been hostile to what it
loosely defines as extremism. This helps account for the dozen or so explicitly anticommunist films that appeared in the immediate aftermath of the
1917 Bolshevik Revolution. Made during the first Red Scare of 1918–1920,
these silent movies were no less hysterical than the classic Hollywood Red-
baiters of the McCarthy era. Bristling with titles like *Dangerous Hours* (Fred
Niblo, 1920) and *Starvation* (George Zimmer, 1920), they depicted Bolsheviks as the bringers of murder, rape, chaos, and destruction.[3]

Communists continued to be portrayed negatively on the American
screen intermittently throughout the 1920s and 1930s, though in a more
gentle and thus arguably more effective fashion politically. In comedies like
Trouble in Paradise (Ernst Lubitsch, 1932) they came across as wholly lacking
in humor or style. In melodramas like *Little Man, What Now?* (Frank Borsage,
1934), they were exposed as selfish phonies unconcerned with the genuine poverty many Americans were experiencing during the Great Depression. In Ernst Lubitsch's big-budget and seminal romantic satire *Ninotchka*
(1939), audiences watched Greta Garbo's female Soviet commissar defect
after falling in love with the material wonders of Western capitalism.[4]

17

The American government played no direct part in the making of these early "Cool War" movies. It had no need to, for Hollywood shared Washington's ideological worldview. "Hollywood"—the place and the way of doing business—came into being in the 1920s, when the geographically scattered array of small and medium-sized producers, distributors, and exhibitors that had characterized the American filmmaking industry since the early 1900s was supplanted by an increasingly oligarchic, vertically integrated studio system with production centered in Los Angeles and business offices in New York. By the end of the 1920s, eight major studios controlled over 90 percent of the films made and distributed in the United States. The executives who ran MGM, Paramount, Warner Bros., Twentieth Century-Fox, RKO, Columbia, Universal, and United Artists were hostile to communism, owing to political conviction and economic self-interest, not because they felt beholden to officialdom. Men like Louis B. Mayer at MGM and Joseph Schenck at Twentieth Century-Fox instinctively equated patriotism with capitalism. Throughout this period and beyond, the major studios' films consistently reinforced the reigning cultural ethos and political-economic order in the United States, abounding with what many in the industry saw as the quintessentially American ideals of democracy, social mobility, capitalist consumption, justice, and cross-class harmony.[5]

By the time of the Second World War, cinema had become the prime entertainment medium in the United States and across large parts of the world. Talkies had taken over from silent movies, and cinema admission figures in the United States had reached almost 100 percent of the population. During the war, American filmmakers, like their Soviet counterparts, played an enthusiastic, imaginative, and vital role in the struggle against fascism. In accordance with guidance from one of the government's propaganda arms, the Office of War Information (OWI), a small number of movies sought to transform the Soviet Union from an erstwhile enemy into a valuable wartime partner. These films—*Mission to Moscow* (Michael Curtiz, 1943), *Tender Comrade* (Edward Dmytryk, 1943), *The North Star* (Lewis Milestone, 1943), *Song of Russia* (Gregory Ratoff, 1944)—would come back to haunt the studios when the Cold War proper started in the late 1940s, providing spurious evidence that Hollywood was infested with communists. Meanwhile, the links established between the film community and the OWI during the Second World War would help facilitate cooperation between Hollywood and the government once the renewed but now more pressing propaganda battle with Soviet communism got under way.[6]

The following overview of Hollywood's Cold War output divides the years 1947 to 1990 into five periods: 1947–1953 (dominated by hard-line negative propaganda); 1953–1962 (soft-core, positive propaganda mixed with the beginnings of negotiated dissent); 1962–1980 (pro-détente propaganda); 1980–86 (New Right propaganda); 1986–1990 (a call for peace). None of these dates is definitive, and there is scope for considerable overlap between some of the sections. More space is allotted to the 1940s and 1950s due to film's role in the development of America's early Cold War consensus and because this period also marked the high point of the state's involvement in Cold War filmmaking.

DECLARING WAR, 1947–1953

Having challenged and ridiculed communists (usually as pathetic individuals) for the better part of three decades, Hollywood went several steps further in the late 1940s by declaring full-scale war on international communism. As would be the case for the next forty years or so, Hollywood followed rather than led political and public opinion during this era. Its first full-fledged Cold War movie, for instance, *The Iron Curtain,* a fact-based exposé of Soviet espionage in postwar Canada directed by William Wellman for Twentieth Century-Fox, appeared in May 1948, fourteen months after the announcement of the Truman Doctrine.[7] Nevertheless, once it got into its Cold War stride, the American film industry pretty much hit Soviet communism with all it had. Many historians have tended to belittle this campaign by suggesting it amounted to little more than a cycle of crudely made box office flops.[8] Evidence indicates otherwise.

Hollywood came under tremendous pressure to establish its anticommunist credentials once U.S.-Soviet diplomatic relations froze soon after the defeat of fascism in 1945. The chief turning point came in October 1947, when the House Un-American Activities Committee (HUAC) arrived in Hollywood to root out those who had turned the American film industry into, as its chairman J. Parnell Thomas put it, a "Red propaganda center." HUAC failed, both in 1947 and again in the early 1950s, to uncover any hard proof of communist infiltration or Marxism on celluloid. Nevertheless, the blacklisting of real or suspected communists was introduced, spreading like a tapeworm throughout the industry into the 1960s. The climate of fear induced by the blacklist put an immediate end to the hopes of some in the film industry during the Second World War that Hollywood would shift to the liberal left. The wounds left by HUAC's inquisition would be felt across Hollywood for decades, not least by those such as the Hollywood Ten, who were jailed for actively opposing the committee, and the relatives of actor Philip Loeb, whose persecution helped drive him to suicide.[9]

As we shall see in chapter 2, in the earliest years of the Cold War strict controls over the Soviet film industry were issued from the very center of government. In the United States, HUAC's investigations were part of an uncoordinated yet ferocious campaign fought by conservative forces inside and outside the government in the late 1940s and 1950s designed to draft the media into the Cold War. Five organizations played an especially important role in ensuring Hollywood acted in the national interest during this period.

First, the Catholic Legion of Decency, a militant right-wing group established in the 1930s, acted as guardian of the big screen's moral and political rectitude. It was quick to categorize any politically or sexually dubious film material as potentially "subversive." The Legion of Decency enjoyed an especially close relationship with Hollywood's own Production Code Administration (PCA), a second highly conservative censorship body, which had been set up in 1934 and run until the mid-1950s by the Catholic intellectual Joseph Breen. The PCA selected stories, examined scripts, and approved the final cuts of movies. During the early phases of the Cold War, it managed to control the content of nearly all films shown in the United States, domestic and foreign.[10]

Third, the Motion Picture Alliance for the Preservation of American Ideals issued regular advice to filmmakers on how they should best express their patriotism in the Cold War's battle for hearts and minds. Established in Hollywood in 1944 to vanquish "the growing impression that this industry is made up of, and dominated by, Communists, radicals, and crackpots," the Alliance was headed by, among others, Eric Johnston, who was president of the Motion Picture Association of America (MPAA), Hollywood's main trade body, and Roy Brewer, leader of the most powerful film labor union, the International Alliance of Theatrical Stage Employees. In 1948, the Alliance published a highly influential booklet by novelist and conservative ideologue Ayn Rand, *A Screen Guide for Americans,* which warned studios against, among other things, smearing the free enterprise system or deifying "the common man."[11]

Fourth, the American Legion, a veterans' organization founded in 1919, on the one hand campaigned against those identified as suspect by the Alliance, the Legion of Decency, or HUAC, and on the other hand organized boycotts of films it deemed subversive or that featured actors labeled as communist sympathizers. With over 17,000 posts and nearly three million members nationwide in the 1950s, the Legion, like the numerous other established social organizations of the right such as the Daughters of the American Revolution, carried considerable economic and political weight in the film industry. During the 1970s, Legionnaires were more than willing to put a stop to movies criticizing America's presence in Vietnam by tearing up theater seats.[12]

Finally, and perhaps most important, the Federal Bureau of Investigation (FBI), run between 1924 and 1972 by one of the nation's most ardent anticommunists, J. Edgar Hoover, operated its own triangular-shaped film strategy. First, the bureau ran a comprehensive surveillance operation in Hollywood, pinpointing communists with the aid of secret informers and identifying those movies that were being used as "weapon[s] of Communist propaganda." Second, the FBI secretly laundered its intelligence through HUAC, thereby helping to pressure the industry into establishing, then strengthening a blacklist. Third, the bureau helped produce movies that fostered its image as the protector of the American people. It provided script material, editing expertise, production consultation, and even special agents as actors for at least eight feature films between 1945 and 1959.[13]

Given this measure of policing, it is hardly surprising that the content of American movies in the late 1940s and early 1950s lurched decisively to the political right. We should also take into account the numerous film artists who voluntarily contributed to the anticommunist onslaught on screen, some because they were conservative Catholics, others because they were liberal anticommunists, others still due to their strong links with the government or military. These are often overlooked, but they include the world's preeminent animator, Walt Disney, Columbia Pictures' President Harry Cohn, the head of censorship at Paramount, Luigi Luraschi, big-name directors such as Leo McCarey and John Ford, the legendary producer-director Cecil B. DeMille, and A-list actors including John Wayne and James Stewart.[14]

Hollywood turned out approximately seventy explicitly anticommunist movies between 1948 and 1953, roughly 5 percent of the total film output for those years. This, the high point of the American film industry's full-frontal assault on the Soviet Union, took place when cinema attendance in the United States numbered roughly sixty million patrons per week (down from an all-time peak of eighty million patrons per week in 1945).[15] None of these films reached anywhere near the top of the annual box-office charts; indeed, many failed to recoup their costs. But some did not do too badly financially. Alfred E. Green's *Invasion U.S.A.*, for instance, which was distributed by Columbia in 1952 and foretold a Soviet atomic attack on America through Alaska, only cost $120,000 but grossed a respectable $1.2 million.[16] MGM's *Never Let Me Go* (Delmer Daves, 1953), a Clark Gable vehicle telling the story of an American journalist stationed in Moscow just after the Second World War who falls for a Russian ballet dancer, made $1.5 million.[17]

Critics justifiably panned most of these movies for being poorly constructed and transparently propagandistic. Historians have since used the term "agit-prop" to describe this material, denoting its resemblance to the Soviet Union's highly politicized, often clumsy style of mass persuasion.[18]

Invasion U.S.A.: A publicity truck for the film encourages cinemagoers to sign up for the civilian auxiliary of the U.S. Air Force. Courtesy of Columbia/Photofest.

There were exceptions, however. Alfred L. Werker's *Walk East on Beacon,* for example, a Boston-set spy docudrama made by Columbia in association with the FBI in 1952, eschewed sensationalism in favor of a factual, no-frills portrait of communist fifth-columnism in the United States. The Central Intelligence Agency leased copies of this movie for showings overseas well into the 1970s.[19] George Seaton's *The Big Lift* (1950), a romantic drama that extolled the bravery of the U.S. Air Force during the 1948–1949 Berlin Airlift, was nominated for a Golden Globe. Made on location in collaboration with the Defense Department's public relations directorate, *The Big Lift* was an early example of the Pentagon-Hollywood axis during the Cold War.[20]

Other anticommunist movies of this era garnered Academy Award nominations. These include the Warner Bros.' drama *I Was a Communist for the FBI* (Gordon Douglas, 1951) and Sam Fuller's crime thriller *Pickup on South Street* (1953).[21] Dore Schary's *The Hoaxsters* won the Oscar for best documentary in 1953 and was endorsed by the FBI, the State Department, and the Psychological Strategy Board, the coordinator of the U.S. government's Cold War propaganda activities between 1951 and 1953. Narrated by a host of MGM actors, this thirty-six-minute film likened the lure of communism to "that of the old-time medicine man whose phony brew promised to cure everything, being swallowed cheerfully by the gullible until rigor mortis set in."[22]

The overriding theme to emerge from Hollywood's Cold War material in this early phase of the conflict is the fear of communist subversion. This is hardly surprising because international communism had long been known to favor underground takeovers rather than open military invasion. The theatrical trial of Julius and Ethel Rosenberg in 1951 on atomic espionage charges—they were executed in 1953—then provided strong evidence for many people that the Reds really were under Americans' beds. What is striking, however, is Hollywood's versatility in depicting subversion, and the film industry's ability to incorporate this and other Cold War themes across the full range of genres. This ability helps set the American film industry apart from its Soviet rival throughout the Cold War and was one of its main strengths in propagandistic terms.

Communists were shown to be infiltrating the United States from all directions—east, west, north, and south. They were sabotaging military installations, controlling labor unions, twisting the minds of university students, and masquerading (though not very successfully) as Christians on church pews. Film fans could watch them doing all this in dramas, comedies, documentaries, espionage thrillers, science fiction shockers, crime capers, and even westerns. To an extent, many of these movies simply amounted to a retooling of Second World War plot lines, in which communists played the new Nazi infiltrators with identical personality flaws, false idealism, and brutal methods. In some cases the "Red-fascist" totalitarian link was made explicit. RKO's *The Whip Hand* (William Cameron Menzies, 1951), for example, focused on a former Nazi scientist since converted to communism who was carrying out germ warfare experiments in sleepy Wisconsin.[23]

Just as important, communist subterfuge appeared merely in passing or as minor subplots in films that otherwise had no bearing at all on the Cold War, indicating how commonplace but no less real the threat was to America. Paul Guilfoyle's *Captain Scarface* (1953), an adventure story set in the United States' backyard, Panama, is one example. Alternatively, Russian agents popped up in historical movies such as Lew Landers's *California Conquest* (1952), where they manipulated indigenous Mexican nationalism in a nineteenth-century plot to take control of Los Angeles. Some viewers, like the critics, may well have seen these images as clumsy didacticism. Many others might have been alerted—subconsciously or otherwise—to the need for vigilance.[24]

Hollywood was not just concerned with its own front- and backyards, however. Other films showed communism to be spreading across the world, thereby emphasizing the global, total dimensions of the Cold War and calling upon the American people to support Washington in its duty to defend the cause of freedom. Sometimes Americans were depicted as fighting the scourge of communism as private individuals (as in Fred T. Sears's 1953 drama *Target Hong Kong*), on other occasions as professional spies (as in Robert Parrish's 1952 *Assignment—Paris*). Established Hollywood stars added to the general picture of American Cold War heroism. Thus the Indian-born actor Sabu and former Tarzan star Johnny Weissmuller (now the hunter Jungle Jim) fought communist insurgencies in tropical islands in *Savage Drums* (William Berke, 1951) and *Savage Mutiny* (Spencer Gordon Bennet, 1953), respectively.[25]

Wherever Americans were countering the threat from the new enemy, communists were usually portrayed according to a set of easily identifiable conventions. While their American (read democratic and capitalist) adversaries were innocent, courageous, clever, and law-abiding freethinkers, communists were evil-doing, cowardly, mentally unstable, heartless automatons who worked for the Party. Sporting cheap suits and murdering opponents in cold blood, they looked and acted like gangsters. The Communist Party did not stand for anything in these films, only against sacred American principles: God, motherhood, and love for one's family and country. Communism's political and economic principles might receive token expression in crudely distilled comments and speeches, but Hollywood's overall attitude toward ideological matters during these years can be summed up in a line from R. G. Springsteen's *The Red Menace* (1949). "I don't know what communism is," says a Party member's mother to a recent convert, "but it must be bad if it makes you do the things you do."[26]

Perhaps those movies that spelled out the bankruptcy of communism more starkly than any other during the late forties and fifties are those that purported to depict the reality of life behind the recently installed Iron Curtain. Relatively few such movies were made in this period, partly because much of what was actually happening in the Eastern bloc was a mystery at the time and partly because the threat to the United States from communist fifth-columnists was hogging the headlines. One notable B-feature was Felix Feist's *Guilty of Treason* (1949), which, like Columbia's more prestigious *The Prisoner* (Peter Glenville, 1955), accused the communist government in Hungary of torturing and brainwashing the nation's Catholic Primate, Cardinal József Mindszenty, after his highly publicized real-life arrest in 1948.[27] As information about the degradations faced by many living under communism began to leak into the West, especially after Khrushchev's famous Secret Speech of 1956, Hollywood went more on the attack by alleging widespread human rights abuses behind the curtain. One film, Elia Kazan's *Man on a Tightrope*, set in Czechoslovakia and released just after Stalin's death in 1953, anticipated this enduring portrait of communist dictatorship; it is analyzed in depth in chapter 3.

Hard-line, negative cinematic propaganda continued to appear beyond the era dominated by HUAC and Senator Joseph McCarthy. Hollywood made over fifty films about the 1950–53 Korean War throughout the 1950s, for instance, many of which stressed the expansionist teamwork of Beijing and Moscow.[28] In the early 1960s, the American government was still sponsoring documentaries like *The Challenge of Ideas* that used scare tactics to spell out the dangers posed to civilization by godless communism.[29] When the perceived threat of domestic subversion reemerged in the late 1960s and early 1970s, sparked by civil rights protests and opposition to the Vietnam War, conservative business organizations and civic and educational institutions adopted similar tactics.[30]

In the mid-1950s, a small number of American filmmakers started to question cinema's role in this Cold War propaganda campaign. As the perceived threat from the communist enemy within receded and McCarthy's own witch-hunt tactics were famously exposed on television in 1954, space opened for liberals within Hollywood to challenge aspects of the Cold War consensus. The result was what can be termed the beginnings of negotiated dissent on the screen in the United States, of images that offered an alternative perspective on the Cold War, but which, at this stage of the conflict at least, were still largely contained by long-standing industrial constraints and contingent political pressures. Any filmmaker who went too far in subverting the Cold War consensus in the 1950s still had to reckon with the blacklist and the American Legion. His projects also had to get past the Production Code Administration.

Two particular movies led the field in questioning American Cold War orthodoxy in the mid- to late 1950s. In Daniel Taradash's 1956 melodrama *Storm Center,* Bette Davis played an elderly small-town librarian who is hounded out of her job for refusing to remove from her shelves a tome, *The Communist Dream,* which local officials deem to be subversive "garbage." *Storm Center* made only a small impression at the box office but represented Hollywood's most direct assault on McCarthyism until the mid-1970s.[31] Stanley Kramer's star-studded drama *On the Beach,* released three years later in 1959, was the first American movie to challenge seriously the feasibility of nuclear war survival. Set in Melbourne, its plot followed the fates of the crew of a U.S. atomic submarine and their Australian hosts who are helplessly awaiting the cloud of radioactive fallout that is drifting south, after having already killed everyone in the Northern Hemisphere.[32]

As significant as these films were, what really characterized so much of Hollywood's output of the 1950s and early 1960s was its promotion of "American" ideals. The roots of this lay in the studios' often unconscious support for individuality, freedom of choice, material abundance, cultural vibrancy, and political moderation dating back to the 1920s. These quintessential features of the American Way of Life took on greater ideological currency during the Cold War. Film executives in particular were acutely aware of their role in selling what both they and official propagandists called "people's capitalism" at home and overseas, showing that the fruits of American free enterprise could be enjoyed by all, not just by the rich. In 1951, MPAA head Eric Johnston announced in the film press that Hollywood was on the front line in the Cold War. It was a role "that we can fill with credit and distinction as we have with every call in the past," he declared, "with ingenuity, with a large dash of daring and a large helping of the sauce of wholesome showmanship."[33]

Hollywood celebrated America's material prosperity like never before in the 1950s. There was a good reason for this: the nation's economic boom during that decade, partly driven by the defense industry, brought unprecedented growth and consumer spending power. Movies reveled in presenting the United States as a land of unbridled opportunity, fun, and get-ahead spirit in the 1950s. The musical—arguably the quintessential American genre, offering utopian images of social harmony, affluence, and material well-being—thrived.[34] Walt Disney's films reverberated with tried-and-true Americanism even more than usual during this period. Having declared in 1947 that Hollywood's communists ought to be "smoked out," Disney, an FBI informant, proclaimed a year later that the time was ripe to "renew acquaintance with the American breed of robust, cheerful, energetic, and representative folk heroes." Hits like *Davy Crockett, King of the Wild Frontier* (Norman Foster, 1955), *Johnny Tremain* (Robert Stevenson, 1957), and *The Light in the Forest* (Herschel Daugherty, 1958) followed.[35]

Historical heroes, religion, and the Cold War came together in one of the defining genres of this era, the biblical epic. The very splendor of mega-budget epics like *Quo Vadis* (Mervyn LeRoy, 1951) and *Ben-Hur* (William Wyler, 1959)—with their fantastic special effects, rich colors painted on spectacularly large canvases, and international stars—testified to America's capitalist-based creativity and advertised the superiority of democracy's freedom of spirit. At least one of these epics, Cecil B. DeMille's multi-million-dollar-grossing extravaganza *The Ten Commandments* (1956), was designed to give scriptural authority to the ideology of America's Cold War.[36] On a very different note, Marilyn Monroe, one of the biggest female stars of the 1950s, came to symbolize American glamour, sexiness, and the pursuit of happiness—all things many Soviet propagandists publicly rejected as decadent but privately admired.[37]

Fueling so much of Hollywood's creativity during the 1950s was a relentless pursuit of the international box office. Hollywood had dominated the

How to Marry a Millionaire: Marilyn Monroe, Betty Grable, and Lauren Bacall in Jean Negulesco's 1953 romantic comedy, a paean to American glitz, prosperity, and free-spiritedness. Courtesy of Twentieth Century-Fox/Photofest.

international film market since the 1920s but after 1945 found those areas under communist control effectively closed off. American cinema attendance was in marked decline in the 1950s, which meant that it was vital to expand Hollywood's interests in regions such as Western Europe, Asia, and Latin America. If Hollywood could also offset the growing costs of filmmaking in the United States by making movies in these regions (so-called "runaway productions"), where labor and studio costs were far cheaper, so much the better. Making films on foreign locations would also be a way for American studios to spend their blocked funds, money they had accumulated in unconvertible currency in those countries. The State Department was more than happy, for commercial and diplomatic purposes, to help Hollywood in this respect by breaking down tariff and tax barriers. Put simply, Washington believed that the more people saw Hollywood movies, the more Americanized the world would become.[38]

The U.S. government worked in other ways to bolster Hollywood's "Americanization" and Cold War programs in the 1950s. The CIA camouflaged its cinematic activities by secretly paying for a British animation company, Halas and Batchelor, to adapt one of the Cold War's greatest anti-totalitarian fables, George Orwell's *Animal Farm,* for the big screen in 1954.[39] The United States Information Agency (USIA), coordinator of the American government's overt propaganda activities after 1953, sponsored documentaries extolling the virtues of "people's capitalism," celebrating America's racial "melting pot," and promoting the peaceful nature of nuclear weapons.[40]

Simultaneously, the State Department, CIA, and USIA all worked to penetrate the Iron Curtain cinematically. In 1960 this bore fruit when, among other movies, William Wyler's 1953 romantic comedy *Roman Holiday* was exhibited in the Soviet Union. Chapter 4 focuses on this film, a prime example of the feel-good, "runaway" Hollywood production of the early Cold War era.

FEAR AND LOATHING: 1962–1980

In contrast with its Soviet counterpart, the American government never had the power to ban films from the other side.[41] Nor could it entirely dictate to the nation's filmmakers how they should cover the Cold War. It never wanted that power, however, for all its occasional criticisms of Hollywood's disloyalty. After all, the United States' claim to have the freest media in the world lay at the heart of Washington's propaganda strategy during the Cold War, and it was one of the simplest and most powerful ways for Americans to distinguish democrats ("Us") from communists ("Them").

As it was, in the first decade and a half of the Cold War, very few filmmakers either desired or dared to challenge the super-patriotic, pro-nuclear, anticommunist consensus in the United States. Once the 1960s got into full swing, however, this began to change. The subsequent shift in Hollywood's treatment of the Cold War can partly be attributed to Cold War events and partly to the wider political mood within the United States. The 1960s was arguably the most turbulent decade of the twentieth century for Americans (the 1962 Cuban missile crisis, civil rights marches, political assassinations, Vietnam, the feminist movement, drugs, and rock 'n' roll) and was quickly followed by one of the most dispiriting decades (Watergate, energy crises, economic recession, and international terrorism).

Aside from terrorist atrocities, the Cold War remained at the top of the geopolitical agenda during this period. But to many Americans the conflict, which was now twenty to thirty years old, looked far less politically and morally clear-cut. If Moscow and Beijing really were the twin centers of evil, some asked, why was the U.S. president going there? Could the U.S. military ever be justified in burning a Vietnamese village, as one officer notoriously put it on television, in order to save it? Did the existence of a "missile gap" really matter when the United States already had enough nuclear warheads to blow the world to kingdom come?

An equally important cause of greater Cold War dissent on screen is the structural changes Hollywood underwent in the 1960s and 1970s. These in fact started in the early 1950s, when anti-cartel legislation triggered the dismantling of the old studio system. Though most of the majors remained, their relative weakness opened up greater opportunities for independent filmmakers to make movies that were artistically avant-garde and politically experimental. Many of these filmmakers were liberals who, once black-listing disappeared, felt more able to push for, among other things, a re-consideration of Cold War shibboleths. In the late 1960s, the concept of a New Hollywood began to take shape, centered on a generation of younger directors who had cut their teeth in the faster-moving television industry and who were less beholden to both the old, conservative-minded studio chiefs and to many of the film industry's conventions. At the same time, Hollywood's old-fashioned censorship system was relaxed. This allowed for greater sexual, social, and political license on the big screen.[42]

Hollywood's treatment of the Cold War tracked these political and indus-trial changes closely in the 1960s and 1970s. Anxieties and doubts about the direction in which U.S. foreign policy was heading characterized the first decade's coverage, a sense of bewilderment and anger the second. Overall, movies gave a distinct if uncoordinated impression that America had lost its way in the Cold War, that the West and the East were playing a cynical game of power politics, and that peaceful coexistence was now essential.

Between 1962 and 1965, five movies were released that, together, her-alded a sea change in Hollywood's attitude toward the Cold War. Two were political conspiracy thrillers directed by the thirty-something John Frank-enheimer, *The Manchurian Candidate* (1962) and *Seven Days in May* (1964). Two were nail-biting anti-nuclear dramas made, again, by young directors, *Fail-Safe* (Sidney Lumet, 1964) and *The Bedford Incident* (James B. Harris, 1965). The fifth was a brilliant black comedy about the madness of nuclear deterrence, made, like *The Bedford Incident,* in Britain, by the thirty-five-year-old Hollywood exile Stanley Kubrick, *Dr. Strangelove or: How I Learned to Stop Worrying and Love the Bomb* (1964).[43]

Each film, in its own way, took a scalpel to the Cold War consensus. Each also aroused deep controversy, thereby encouraging filmmakers, politi-cians, and the public to question received wisdom about the conflict. *The Manchurian Candidate* starred Laurence Harvey as Raymond Shaw, a brain-washed Korean War hero programmed as a communist "mole" to assassi-nate an American presidential candidate. A complex, sophisticated movie, it

The Manchurian Candidate:
Eleanor Iselin (Angela Lansbury),
a communist agent masquerading
as a McCarthyite, torments her
brainwashed son, Sergeant
Raymond Shaw (Laurence Harvey).
Courtesy of M.C. Prods/
United Artists/Photofest.

launched a powerful assault on the American Right and on the media's role in fostering political paranoia.[44] *Seven Days in May* depicted an attempted coup d'état by the U.S. Joint Chiefs of Staff in order to prevent a dovish American president from signing a nuclear disarmament treaty.[45]

Fail-Safe, analyzed in chapter 5, was the first Hollywood movie to propose seriously that nuclear Armageddon could be brought about by accident due to the flaws within the machinery of deterrence. *The Bedford Incident,* focusing on a chase between a U.S. Navy destroyer and a Soviet submarine, showed that World War III could result from fatigue and miscommunication.[46] *Dr. Strangelove,* a richly textured film now widely regarded as one of the finest of all Cold War movies, satirized the theory of Mutual Assured Destruction by depicting America's political and military leaders as criminally insane sex maniacs.[47]

Another important movie of the era, though one far less well known today, is *The Russians Are Coming, The Russians Are Coming.* Directed by the forty-year-old Canadian-born Norman Jewison for United Artists and released in 1966, it told the story of a Soviet submarine crew that, after accidentally running aground in U.S waters off the coast of Massachusetts, causes a communist invasion scare when it goes ashore to look for help. The islanders and sailors eventually come together to save a young boy from falling from a church steeple. The movie humanizes the Russians by de-communizing them, rendering the "enemy" just like "us."

Jewison managed to enlist some minor help from Soviet film officials in making *The Russians Are Coming* as part of his efforts to encourage peaceful coexistence. A gentle, slapstick satire on East-West relations, the movie tapped into a rich vein of U.S. opinion in the mid-1960s, becoming the fifth highest grossing movie in the nation in 1966. The movie also enjoyed a series of special screenings in the Soviet Union, where audiences reportedly cried with joy and were amazed that the Americans were allowed to make such a funny and optimistic film about the Cold War. In a small way, this reaction helped pave the way for co-production talks between Soviet and American filmmakers in the late 1960s and 1970s, resulting in George Cukor's family fantasy *The Blue Bird* in 1976 (discussed in chapter 2).[48]

With one or two exceptions, the sunny optimism exhibited by Hollywood in *The Russians Are Coming* failed to last beyond the 1960s. The 1970s kicked off with a number of films evincing deep cynicism about the Cold War and particularly about America's role in it. Many of these were designed to appeal especially to those Americans between the ages of fifteen and twenty-five, who were not born when the Cold War started but now made up a disproportionately high percentage of filmgoers. In 1971, U.S. cinema attendance reached an all-time low of sixteen million patrons per week, after which it recovered slightly. By 1990, it stood at roughly twenty-five million patrons per week.[49]

A large number of the anti–Cold War films of the early 1970s were, like some of their 1960s counterparts, complex dramas highlighting diplomatic intrigue and political skullduggery. Gone were the simple, black-and-white images of the McCarthy era, with their easily identifiable, ugly "baddies" and well-dressed, honorable "goodies." Audiences had to work harder, both to follow the plots and to work out who was on whose side (or indeed if there were any clear-cut sides anymore). John Huston's espionage thriller *The Kremlin Letter* (1970) was in this mold, centering on a proposal from the United States to the Soviet Union that the two superpowers collaborate in the annihilation of Mao Tse-tung's China.[50] Sydney Pollack's *Three Days of the Condor* (1975) was equally challenging (plot-wise and politically), based on a best-selling novel suggesting that the CIA acted as a law unto itself within the United States and overseas. Hollywood quickly capitalized on the paranoia induced by press revelations of U.S. secret service dirty tricks in the early 1970s, featured most prominently in the Watergate scandal. A flurry of taut, popular, liberal conspiracy thrillers was the result, including *Executive Action* (David Miller, 1973), *The Parallax View* (Alan J. Pakula, 1974), *All the President's Men* (Pakula, 1976), and *Twilight's Last Gleaming* (Robert Aldrich, 1977).[51]

This last film focused on the Vietnam War and was soon joined by others in the late 1970s that explored the ways in which that conflict had ripped apart Americans, physically and psychologically. Three of them—*Coming*

Home (Hal Ashby, 1978), *The Deer Hunter* (Michael Cimino, 1978), and *Apocalypse Now* (Francis Ford Coppola, 1979)—attracted immense popular and critical acclaim in 1978–1979.[52] Jane Fonda, who picked up an Oscar for her role in *Coming Home,* was one of the most creative and influential liberals working in Hollywood during this period. James Bridges's 1979 thriller *The China Syndrome,* which told the story of safety cover-ups in a nuclear power plant outside Los Angeles, was funded by her company, IPC Films, part of a long-running campaign Fonda had been conducting on- and offscreen to expose economic and corporate power elites in the United States.[53] Some commentators have since argued that such films represented an unprecedented liberal assault by Hollywood on the political and economic status quo, encouraging a short-term national shift to the left. Others claim the movies helped foster the New Right in the United States by depicting big government and large institutions as conspiratorial and dangerous to a free and libertarian community.[54]

Not everything was doom and gloom on the American Cold War screen in the 1970s, however. Nor was every film so didactic or straightforwardly propagandistic, either. Antidotes to this sort of material were movies that cast a skeptical eye on the Cold War but did so indirectly and humorously. One such film is analyzed in chapter 6—Woody Allen's *Bananas,* the story of a New York nerd who gets enmeshed in Latin American politics in order to spice up his love life. Released in 1971, *Bananas* was part of a whole series of movies, many made on Hollywood's left-wing fringes, that played around with the idea that the CIA was the new American "enemy within."[55] More important, it also ridiculed the liberal left. In sum, the movie reflected and projected the view held by many Americans in the 1970s that the Cold War was an absurd anachronism.

BACK TO BASICS, 1980–1986

Ronald Reagan's sweeping victories in the 1980 and 1984 presidential elections marked a powerful reaction to the notion that the Cold War did not matter anymore. The Great Communicator's eight years in the Oval Office saw the United States take a decisive shift to the right, based in large part on a revitalization of the ideological and strategic conflict against the communist bloc. As a former movie actor and FBI informant within the film community, Reagan instinctively looked to the media, including Hollywood, to do his political bidding. This explains why he launched an impassioned assault on the cultural "liberal elite" that in his view had led the United States astray in the 1960s and 1970s, and why he appointed the former Hollywood impresario Charles Z. Wick to the directorship of the USIA. Movies (both old and new) played a key role in shaping Reagan's thoughts and actions in the White House. In turn, his rhetoric and policies had a significant influence on Hollywood output.[56]

American Cold War cinema of the 1980s was not as one-dimensionally anticommunist as some would have us believe. Though Reagan might have liked to see an informal blacklist initiated, there was no equivalent of that from the McCarthy era, nor any HUAC-style investigations designed to root out that corrosive "liberal elite" in the entertainment industry. Oppositional films of the type made in the 1970s continued to appear, albeit in smaller numbers, most of them plowing a similar "what's-it-all-about" furrow. Few of these attracted much attention.[57]

Notable exceptions were Warren Beatty's Oscar-winning epic *Reds* (1981), about as even-handed an account of the Bolshevik Revolution that Hollywood was ever likely to produce during the Cold War and that was based on a book written by the legendary left-wing American journalist John Reed, and Constantin Costa-Gavras's *Missing* (1982), an Oscar-winning drama about the CIA's role in the 1973 Chilean coup that deposed socialist president Salvador Allende. *Reds* took a generally sympathetic view toward its main characters, most of whom were American communist activists, but ultimately not toward their cause. Reed's pathetic death in a communal hospital in Moscow underscored the Bolsheviks' betrayal of his dreams. Such was the controversy caused by *Missing* that Secretary of State Alexander Haig felt it necessary to issue a categorical denial of U.S. complicity in the Chilean coup and concurrent death of Allende.[58]

Two other prominent films reflected the fears engendered in the early 1980s by Reagan officials speaking of a "winnable nuclear war." John Badham's *WarGames,* the fifth highest grossing movie of 1983, presented a new Cold War threat to world security—the possibility that unauthorized users might gain access to the computer systems controlling the superpowers' arsenals. Centered on a teenager who inadvertently gains access to the U.S. nuclear defense system through his computer modem, *WarGames* soon acquired cult status among American youngsters.[59] Jayne Loader, Kevin Rafferty, and Pierce Rafferty's *The Atomic Café* (1982) was an independently produced feature-length documentary ridiculing civil defense information and training films from the 1950s. Distributed across the nation, where it was especially popular in colleges, the documentary drew attention to cinema's use as a government propaganda tool in the early phases of the Cold War. It also challenged the sort of claims ridiculed by Robert Scheer in his book *With Enough Shovels* (published in 1982) that most Americans could survive a nuclear attack.[60]

"His is a kind of 1952 world," one of Ronald Reagan's advisers told a journalist in 1980. "He sees the world in black and white terms."[61] Much the

Top Gun: Hot pilots for a new, hot war: Anthony Edwards (as Goose) and Tom Cruise (as Maverick). Courtesy of Paramount Pictures/Photofest.

same could be said about Hollywood's rejuvenated attack on Soviet communism in the early to mid-1980s. During this period, virulently xenophobic movies once again appeared warning of communist landings on U.S. soil: *Red Dawn* (John Milius, 1984) and *Invasion U.S.A.* (Joseph Zito, 1985). Films about Soviet defectors were back in vogue at the cinema and on television: *Sakharov* (Jack Gold, 1984), *Moscow on the Hudson* (Paul Mazursky, 1984), *White Nights* (Taylor Hackford, 1985).[62] The Soviet secret services were up to their old tricks: *KGB: The Secret War* (Dwight H. Little, 1986), *No Way Out* (Roger Donaldson, 1987). U.S.-Soviet relations were an ongoing battle between men (the Americans) and machines (the Russians): *Firefox* (Clint Eastwood, 1982), *Rocky IV* (Sylvester Stallone, 1985). And the Soviet Union was once again flexing its imperialist muscles, notably in Afghanistan: *The Beast of War* (Kevin Reynolds, 1988).[63]

Of course, even the Hollywood Reaganites knew they could not simply erase a critical part of the Cold War by rewinding to the good old days of Dwight Eisenhower, Cecil B. DeMille, and John Wayne. The U.S. military had to demonstrate that it had moved on since the 1950s and 1960s and that it was now capable of vanquishing its Soviet foe: *Top Gun* (Tony Scott, 1986). The American people had to rekindle their love affair with the U.S. military—*An Officer and a Gentleman* (Taylor Hackford, 1982)—and with the nation's get-ahead spirit—Philip Kaufman's *The Right Stuff* (1983), which focused on the early years of the East-West space race.[64] The shame and humiliation of Vietnam had to be exorcised: *Missing in Action* (Joseph Zito, 1984), *Heartbreak Ridge* (Clint Eastwood, 1986), *Good Morning, Vietnam* (Barry Levinson, 1987). And a scapegoat had to be found for the defeat in Southeast Asia, a pusillanimous government bureaucracy: *Uncommon Valor* (Ted Kotcheff, 1983).[65] One outstanding movie that fused all these themes was George P. Cosmatos's *Rambo: First Blood Part II* (1985). A gung-ho action-adventure movie par excellence, *Rambo* represents the apotheosis of the politics of Reaganite entertainment; it is analyzed in chapter 7.

PEACE AND VICTORY, 1986–1990

Hollywood's second Cold War reached its frenzied climax in 1985–1986, when *Rambo, Rocky IV,* and *Top Gun* headed the U.S. and international box office charts. Had anyone predicted at this point that the Cold War would be over within a mere five years, and the Soviet Union consigned to history within six, they would have been given very short shrift. No American diplomat, let alone filmmaker, was making any such prediction in 1986 or even in early 1989, just months before the collapse of the Berlin Wall.

Yet a careful look at Hollywood's output in the late 1980s does at least hint that a meaningful Soviet-American rapprochement was on the horizon. A number of filmmakers adjusted quickly and positively to the policies of glasnost (openness) and perestroika (restructuring) initiated by Mikhail Gorbachev, who became the Soviet leader in March 1985. Some of the resulting movies harked back to the 1960s, demonstrating how few differences there really were between ordinary people on either side of the Curtain. Thus *Russkies* (Rick Rosenthal, 1987) told a touching tale, not dissimilar to *The Russians Are Coming, The Russians Are Coming,* of the friendship that develops between three American boys and a forlorn Soviet sailor washed up on the coast of Florida.[66] Other films depicted the long-time enemies now fighting as allies in new wars, against narcotics smugglers—Walter Hill's *Red Heat* (1988)—and Middle East terrorists—Sidney J. Furie's *Iron Eagle II* (1988). *Red Heat* was glasnost in action—the first entirely American produced movie that incorporated scenes shot on location in the Soviet Union.[67]

The political climate was changing rapidly. In early 1988, Moscow hosted its first major American film festival. Among the movies screened in the Soviet Union for the first time was *Kings Row* (Sam Wood, 1942), starring Ronald Reagan, and a film that in the early eighties Soviet film critics had labeled "reactionary," Irvin Kershner's sci-fi blockbuster *The Empire Strikes Back* (1980).[68] In 1989, two American films appeared, one at the cinema (Andrew Davis's *The Package*) and the other on television (Lawrence Gordon Clark's *Just Another Secret*), depicting Americans preventing Gorbachev from being assassinated by renegade factions within his own spy establishment.[69]

Russkies: Joaquin Phoenix, Peter Billingsley, Stefan DeSalle, Whip Hubley, and Susan Walters in Rick Rosenthal's plea for peaceful coexistence. Courtesy of New Century/ Vista Film Company/Photofest.

Hollywood's last major contribution to the Cold War was John McTiernan's $30-million blockbuster *The Hunt for Red October.* Made with the assistance of the U.S. Navy in 1989, the movie was the paradigmatic pro-détente American production: the story of a Soviet naval commander (played by Sean Connery, the original James Bond onscreen) who defects with his country's latest hi-tech nuclear submarine. His goal is to avert a first strike on the United States by the communist old guard and to establish the grounds for a lasting peace between the Russian and American peoples. By the time *Red October* was released, in March 1990, it had become an instant period piece. The Eastern bloc had disintegrated, Gorbachev had declared peace with the United States, and Americans could watch the movie knowing they had effectively won the Cold War.[70]

CHAPTER TWO

Soviet Cinema and the Cold War

> *Soviet society is organized not for happiness, comfort, liberty, justice, personal relationships, but for combat.*
> Isaiah Berlin, 1957[1]

Cinema occupied a place of honor in Soviet culture.[2] Lenin was famously quoted as saying that "cinema is for us the most important of the arts," a testament not to the Bolshevik leader's fondness for films but rather to the mass character of the movies. This comment, whether apocryphal or not, also reflects Soviet recognition of cinema's enormous potential as a weapon for agitation and propaganda. The film industry was nationalized in 1919 and put under the authority of the Commissariat for Enlightenment. In 1922 the state film trust, Goskino, was established, replaced by Sovkino in 1924. Cinema immediately demonstrated its propaganda value as agit-trains toured Bolshevik-held territories, showing the short propaganda films known as *agitki*. Yet the Soviet cinema did not always enjoy the degree of state support and unity that nationalization implies.

In the Golden Age of the 1920s, for example, there was considerable diversity in film studios and in the film press; there was little censorship, although that changed by the end of the decade, as Sergei Eisenstein and others learned. According to the tenets of the New Economic Policy (NEP, 1921–28), which advocated a mixed economy, the industry was required to pay for itself; hence the reliance on foreign, and especially American, pictures that Soviet audiences flocked to see.[3] Indeed, the Soviet people loved Hollywood movies to the extent that the director and film theorist Lev Kuleshov coined a word to describe the phenomenon: *amerikanshchina* (Americanitis).

Profits from these foreign films, and Soviet popular films made in the Western style, funded the production of noncommercial, revolutionary avant-garde masterpieces, like Eisenstein's *The Battleship Potemkin* (*Bronenosets Potemkin*, 1926) and Vsevolod Pudovkin's *The End of St. Petersburg* (*Konets Sankt Peterburga*, 1927), for which the era is famous. Although "capitalist encirclement" was a source of grave concern to the state, there are few feature films from this earliest stage of the Cold War, unlike what we have seen in the United States. Two exceptions, Kuleshov's *The Extraordinary Adventures of Mr. West in the Land of the Bolsheviks* (*Neobychanie prikliucheniia mistera Vesta v strane bolshevikov*, 1924) and Yury Zhelyabuzhsky's *The Cigarette Girl from Mosselprom* (*Papirosnitsa iz Mosselproma*, 1924), utilized Americans as major characters. They were not, however, villains but objects of humor, satirized in tongue-in-cheek fashion.[4] In the first film, set in Moscow, Mr. West, the president of the YMCA, learns to put down his little American flag and appreciate the vigilance of the Soviet state security police in bringing to justice the criminals who have plagued him. In the second film, Oliver MacBride, a deluded but ultimately kindly American businessman who wants to trade with the Soviet Union, finds that his wealth cannot buy the love of the cigarette girl turned movie star. (She falls for a Soviet cameraman instead.)

By the time the NEP ended early in 1929, the cultural climate was rapidly chilling, away from the decentralization that prevailed and toward hypercontrol. After the Cultural Revolution of 1928–1932 (the cultural and social corollary to Stalin's collectivization and industrialization campaigns), cinema became highly centralized, with a single aesthetic, Socialist Realism,[5] and a film press that spoke with one voice.[6] Sovkino, the beleaguered state film trust, was abolished, replaced in 1930 by Soiuzkino, an organization deeply unfriendly to foreign and Western-style films as well as to avantgarde cinema. There were three major studios—Mosfilm, Lenfilm, and the Kiev Studio. The chief censorship body, Glavrepertkom, established in 1923, became extremely active at this time.[7] Public screenings of foreign movies essentially came to a halt, although occasional exceptions were made, especially for films deemed to show the West in an unfavorable light. Filmmakers were now "in the service of the state," and they received more attention than they desired in the 1930s, as Stalin's interest in film became increasingly obsessive and intrusive, to the point of revising scripts, supervising casting, and titling film projects in which he was particularly interested. Not surprisingly, the numbers of banned films rose, and in 1933 Soiuzkino was deemed unsuccessful as cinema's governing body and so was replaced by the Main Administration of the Movie-Photo Industry, which at first reported directly to the Council of People's Commissars.[8]

The cinematic repertory was not entirely bleak, however, and was more diverse than Cold War anti-Soviet rhetoric allowed. Mixed in among the "enemy" films like *The Party Card* (*Partinyi bilet*, Ivan Pyriev, 1936) were popular historical films, revolutionary films, adaptations from literature, and, most of all, the entertaining musical comedies of Grigory Aleksandrov and Ivan Pyriev.[9] Foreign cinematic enemies were fewer than internal enemies, and the foreigners were Germans or Japanese, two obvious threats to the USSR, rather than the Americans, who had become socialist brethren with the rise of the American Communist Party and the policy of the united front.[10] (German enemies, including the Teutonic knights of Eisenstein's *Alexander Nevsky* [*Aleksandr Nevskii*, 1938], had to disappear from the screen after the signing of the Molotov-Ribbentrop pact in 1939.)

The outbreak of war in June 1941 offered challenges and opportunities to the film industry, which was relocated to Soviet Central Asia as part of the evacuation of equipment and personnel from industries deemed essential to the war effort. Mosfilm and Lenfilm operated from Alma-Ata, and the Kiev studio from Tashkent.[11] Under the aegis of the Central United Film Studios and the Committee on Cinema Affairs (established in 1938), filmmakers devoted themselves wholeheartedly to supporting the war effort. As was true for other segments of Soviet society, filmmakers enjoyed slightly more autonomy during these terrible years.[12] The degree of independence should not, however, be exaggerated. As recent research has demonstrated, the heavy hand of the state continued to weigh on filmmakers, and some films were banned for being insufficiently patriotic or for not presenting the model Soviet citizen.[13] Unlike the United States, where a few pictures about the Russian war effort were made, Soviet movies about the war ignored the Allies, in keeping with the Soviet belief that the delay in opening a second front resulted from Churchill's desire to destroy the USSR.[14]

War films, which constituted about 70 percent of production, focused initially on partisans, with a special emphasis on women, and only later (after Stalingrad) on the heroism of the Red Army. A number of these films featuring women, including Fridrikh Ermler's *She Defends the Motherland* (*Ona zashchishchaet rodinu*, 1943) and Mark Donskoy's *The Rainbow* (*Raduga*, 1943), were shown in the United States.[15] Ermler's film, which was retitled *No Greater Love* for American consumption, did not make much of a mark on American consciousness and was seen as fairly primitive by Hollywood's standards. *The Rainbow,* however, found a fan in Franklin Roosevelt, who commented that the film was so powerful he did not need a translation.[16] Any hopes that Soviet filmmakers had for the relaxation of cultural restrictions after the war faded as Stalin quickly moved to reassert stringent control over the industry. Signs of this had been apparent by the end of 1944, when some pompous films about Soviet heroes, in full Socialist Realist style, began to appear. Marking another trend, Ermler's *The Great Turning Point* (*Velikii perevorot*, 1945), a film about the Battle of Stalingrad in which the generals appear as concerned about the failure to open the second front as they are with fighting the battle, was a harbinger of the Cold War around the corner.

The fragile peace of 1945 was, of course, broken almost immediately by the Cold War. The following overview of the relationship between Soviet cinema and the Cold War divides the years 1946–1988 into four periods:

1946–1953 (hard-line propaganda); 1953–1978 (the beginnings and devel-opment of soft propaganda); 1978–1986 (a return to harder propaganda, but a return that bears hallmarks of softer times); and 1986–1988 (the glas-nost era). After 1988, with cinematic glasnost in full swing, filmmakers no longer cared about the Cold War.

THE EARLY COLD WAR, 1946–1953

Between 1946 and 1953 the Cold War received the most focused atten-tion from filmmakers and cinema bureaucrats throughout the whole con-flict. The early Cold War years coincided with the final, tumultuous years of Stalin's long rule. Because of the importance of the late Stalin era in laying the foundations for the cinematic Cold War, a foundation that later genera-tions sought either to undermine or to bolster, special attention is paid to it here. During this period Soviet films directly engaged the Cold War enemy and are classic examples of hard-core negative propaganda.

On 20 March 1946, less than a year after the end of the war, the Com-mittee on Cinema Affairs became the Ministry of Cinematography, giving film a considerably elevated status among the arts, but also drawing cinema even closer to the bosom of the state.[17] Indeed, historian Vladislav Zubok sees the "Cold War rationale" of cultural competition as the force behind the continued tight control over the arts.[18] Ironically, the ministry presided over a collapse in production. Production during this period averaged twenty feature films per year (compared with 150 by the late 1920s). By 1949, the numbers were so low—eighteen films in 1949, ten in 1950, nine in 1951—that by 1950 a large number of copies (1,800–2,000) of each film circulated just to fill the screens.[19] (In later years the norm for most films was 100–400 copies.)[20] This situation also helps us understand the popularity during this period of the foreign "trophy films" that were the "cinematic spoils of war."[21]

This collapse in production was due in part to other pressing needs, no-tably the necessary investment in postwar reconstruction. More important, however, were the propaganda demands of the brewing Cold War and the concomitant "freeze" in Soviet culture signaled by the rise of Andrei Zhda-nov and the *zhdanovshchina,* primarily an attack on Western influences in Soviet culture. The *zhdanovshchina,* which focused on alleged "formalism" as well as the alleged negativism and inferiority complexes of Soviet artists, was followed in 1949 by an onslaught against the Jewish cultural intelligent-sia known as the anti-cosmopolitan campaign, closely linked to the founding of the state of Israel the previous year.[22] Among numerous charges, "cos-mopolitans" were accused of "groveling before the West," "aiding American imperialism," "slavish imitation of bourgeois culture," and "bourgeois aes-theticism."[23]

Another factor that paralyzed filmmakers was Stalin's obsessive interest in the movies, apparent since the early 1930s. So many projects were axed at the script stage that directors retreated to hagiographical historical biographies intended to reinforce traditions of Russian national might. Yet it did not take long for even these "safe" subjects to become problematic, as Pudovkin found with his Crimean War epic *Admiral Nakhimov* (1946).[24] Additionally, Stalin declared that the film industry should abandon "mass production" to make four to six films per year of high quality ("good ones, remarkable ones").[25] Talk about abandoning "mass production" in cinema served as a justification for maintaining the political status quo during the "film famine."

Filmmakers faced the daunting task of shoring up a sagging propaganda campaign that its creators already saw as defensive, rather than offensive, as Vladimir Pechatnov's research on early Soviet Information Bureau (Sovinform) propaganda has shown.[26] Pechatnov recounts Soviet propagandists' "enormous respect [for] and jealousy" of Western propaganda and their pronounced inferiority complex.[27] Particularly germane to the themes of Soviet Cold War films was the concern about "the wave of slanderous reporting about Red Army 'brutalities' in the occupied countries, 'rapes' being one of these."[28] As a result, Soviet propagandists were exhorted to "take urgent countermeasures, such as obtaining information about the bad behavior of Allied troops."[29] It was deemed essential to counter those who questioned the wisdom of rejecting the Marshall Plan by painting the plan's connections to and support of American imperialism and capitalism in garish colors.[30] Additionally, and paradoxically given the seeming inevitability of the Cold War turning hot, propagandists needed to underscore the "peace-loving nature of Soviet foreign policy" in order to give the USSR higher moral ground than the bellicose, warmongering Americans.[31]

As critical as these issues were, it is important to remember that most Soviet films in the early Cold War did not deal with the conflict directly. Only eight major Cold War films appeared, a "whole bloc" of "artistic documentaries" devoted to linking the former Allies with the Nazis, denouncing the Marshall Plan, and generally attacking the Americans.[32] These were *The Russian Question* (*Russkii vopros*, Mikhail Romm, 1948), *The Meeting on the Elbe* (*Vstrecha na Elbe*, Grigory Aleksandrov, 1949, discussed in chapter 3), *The Court of Honor* (*Sud chesti*, Abram Room, 1949), *The Conspiracy of the Doomed* (*Zagovor obrechennykh*, Mikhail Kalatozov, 1950), *The Secret Mission* (*Sekretnaia missiia*, Romm, 1950), *They Have a Motherland* (*U nikh est rodina*, Aleksander Faintsimmer, 1950), *The Dawn over the Neman* (*Rassvet nad Nemanom*, Faintsimmer, 1952), and *Silvery Dust* (*Serebristaia pyl*, Room, 1953).[33] Such was the prominence of these films that 45.6 percent of screen villains in Soviet films from 1946 to 1950 were American and British, compared with just 13 percent British from 1923 to 1945.[34]

To be sure, some historical epics, like Pudovkin's *Admiral Nakhimov* (1946) and Mikhail Romm's *Admiral Ushakov* (1953), used these heroes' naval exploits to comment on the perfidy of the West. Films about the glories of Russian science—*Academician Ivan Pavlov* (*Akademik Ivan Pavlov*, Grigory Roshal, 1949)—or Russian music—*Mussorgsky* (*Musorgskii*, Grigory Roshal, 1950)—could also be considered part of the Cold War effort because they sought to bolster national pride at a time when pride was sagging in the face of American anti-Soviet attacks. Finally, hyperbolic films about the Great Patriotic War—such as *The Fall of Berlin* (*Padenie Berlina*, Mikhail Chiaureli, 1949)—more often than not focused on Stalin, magnifying his role in the victory and downplaying that of the Allies. However, none of these films, important as they were, contributed to the core concerns of early Soviet Cold War propaganda, which were to demonize the new enemy and to emphasize the Soviet struggle for peace. *The Fall of Berlin,* for example, is central to the evolution of the Stalin Cult, *Admiral Ushakov* to the emphasis on Great Russian nationalism that began in the 1930s.

Like most of the American Cold War films of this period, the foundational eight films are almost totally lacking in nuance. Each responded to a particular theme of anti-Soviet propaganda and inverted the West's view of events.[35] No freedom of the press in the USSR? Neither was there freedom of the press in the United States, where corporations, the government, and the likes of William Randolph Hearst and his ilk reigned. Honest journalists who were open-minded about the Soviet Union saw their careers ruined (*The Russian Question*). Did the Red Army engage in the mass rapes of German women and pillage German art treasures, factories, and forests? In Soviet cinema the opposite was true. American soldiers molested German women. The U.S. Army and government presided over a vast plan to strip Germany of her treasures. Haggard German civilians in the American zone bartered their last possession for a cigarette and a bite to eat (*The Meeting on the Elbe*). Were the Soviets attempting to steal scientific material to cover up the failures of their own scientific research programs? Not likely. Under the guise of free exchange of ideas and friendship, the U.S. government, arm in arm with the pharmaceutical companies, sought to dupe naïve Soviet scientists into giving up their formula for a painkiller (*The Court of Honor*).[36]

Had the USSR made a deal with the devil in 1939 with the Molotov-Ribbentrop Pact? The United States and Great Britain were responsible for much worse: near the end of the war, they attempted to conclude a separate peace with the Germans, collude to defeat the Red Army, and negotiate valuable trade agreements (*The Secret Mission*). Were the Soviets accused of

The Court of Honor: The scientist's actions are judged by his peers. Courtesy of the Scientific Research Institute of Cinema Art (NIIK).

forced repatriation of citizens unwilling to return to the motherland? For their part, the Americans and British refused to repatriate Soviet children captured by the Germans, giving them over to West Germans in bondage as unpaid household and workplace help (*They Have a Motherland*). Had the Soviet government deported minority citizens like the Chechens and the Crimean Tatars from their historic homelands to places east for reasons that seemed as much based on racial bias as national security? The Americans were surely in no position to cast stones. They kept black Americans in virtual slavery, using them as human guinea pigs in scientific experiments (*Silvery Dust*). Were the Soviets accused of rigging elections? In fact, it was the Americans who were phony democrats completely uninterested in elections (*The Meeting on the Elbe*), and the Soviets who were building democracy in Central and Eastern Europe (*The Meeting on the Elbe* and *The Conspiracy of the Doomed*). In addition, the Vatican, in collusion with American business and government, sought to unseat freely elected people's democracies through arms smuggling and agricultural sabotage (*The Conspiracy of the Doomed* and *The Dawn over the Neman*).

Unlike in the United States, many of these early Cold War films were very popular with audiences. *The Meeting on the Elbe* led the box office in 1949, as did *The Secret Mission* in 1950. Although it is true that Soviet film production had fallen dramatically, giving viewers few Soviet films from which to choose, this is still noteworthy considering the competition from the trophy films, many of them American, captured from the Germans. The release of American movies from the 1930s at a time of official anti-Americanism is the kind of paradox common in Soviet history. Initially there had been an effort to restrict the distribution of the American films, but sixty were shown at the House of Cinema (*Dom kino*), the filmmakers' club, in 1946.[37] From these showings, it became clear that the trophy films could fill the empty screens and satisfy the audience's pent-up desire for entertainment, thereby raising much-needed money for the film industry.[38]

The Cold War films' popularity does not necessarily imply that Soviet moviegoers were particularly anti-American. By the standards of Soviet cinema, these were first-rate pictures, with invariably high production standards. They drew upon the best scriptwriters, directors, actors, cinematographers, and composers that the Soviet Union had to offer. Furthermore, as film scholar Evgeny Dobrenko has argued, the content was fresh, the political message was subsumed in a detective or detective-like tale, and the overall effect was a "balm" that quieted fears. By showing that the USSR was ready to confront any threat, "the films of the cold war brought a feeling of deep satisfaction; they removed the trauma of the new global order."[39]

As satisfied as Soviet viewers may have been, the members of the Artistic Council of the Ministry of Cinematography were usually dissatisfied. The council served as a major organ of censorship during the production of a film. The minutes of the many long meetings held before, during, and after the production of these films are highly revealing of the cinema bureaucrats' goals and insecurities. Their concerns dovetail neatly with the problems Sovinform propagandists confronted. The discussions were rarely related to artistic goals or achievements, except in the area of casting, but rather to political aims.[40]

Three key political goals were central to the making of the Cold War canon. The first was the importance of making an "accurate" film, particularly in its depiction of Americans, their warmongering, their capitalism, and their imperialism. This was deemed especially significant because most of these films would be shown in the people's republics and, it was hoped, in France, which was considered a sympathetic Western country.[41] The awareness that these films would be seen—and judged—abroad was a constant refrain in the discussions. Even though the council members knew the pictures would not be shown to the U.S. public, they worried that egregious errors would provide more fuel to the humiliating American chatter about an "Iron Curtain."[42] When judging accuracy, it is important to remember, as

Andrey Shcherbenok has noted, that "the Soviet concept of the enemy was anything but paranoid."[43] To cite but one example, in real life the Vatican proved its enmity time and again.[44] Even though Roman Catholic priests were almost certainly not smuggling arms (*The Conspiracy of the Doomed*), they were openly opposed to communist regimes.

Sometimes the council members expressed praise for particular parts of the movies they supervised. For example, *They Have a Motherland,* the film about the plight of "lost" Soviet children languishing in the British sector of West Germany, was commended for showing the "bestial character of imperialism," as well as for its clarification of "Anglo-American imperialism."[45] It was also praised for demonstrating the continued strong alliance between the British and the Americans against the USSR.[46] "What feelings and thoughts should this film call forth?" one commentator asked, then answered approvingly, "Hatred toward the English and the Americans."[47] But even though *They Have a Motherland* was further extolled for showing that the "enemy is still strong, he is still dangerous," the picture was also criticized for failing to demonstrate the opposing strength of the USSR in its full glory.[48]

Directors and scriptwriters could rarely win, and no film ever received unqualified praise. Council members sought to outdo one another in finding errors so that they could prove themselves the most vigilant among their peers. As an example, *The Russian Question,* one of two films set in the United States and a scathing attack on American newspapers and reporters, was criticized for showing only the anti-Soviet side of American capitalism, and for failing to expose the "economic bankruptcy of the capitalist system."[49] Mikhail Romm's *The Secret Mission,* about a spy who has infiltrated the German SS, generally considered the most scurrilous of the Soviet Cold War films from the Western perspective, was nonetheless deemed so problematic that some council members thought Andrei Vyshinsky, then the foreign minister, should look the script over to approve it.[50] The council believed that the role of the British in the film was overplayed and the Americans underplayed. Nevertheless, the American government seemed exaggeratedly mighty, calling the shots for the British.[51]

The second major political goal for these films was to contrast the "two worlds": aggressive, capitalist-imperialist America with the peace-loving, socialist-internationalist Soviet Union.[52] This was difficult to achieve, given that six of the eight pictures, save *The Court of Honor* and *The Dawn on the Neman,* were set outside the USSR (and *The Dawn on the Neman* takes place in newly occupied Lithuania). The perfidy of the Americans, and their allies, the British, the Vatican, and unrepentant Nazis, was vividly depicted, but its opposite, the rightness of the Soviet way of life, could only be shown

The Secret Mission: Churchill with his bust of Napoleon and bottle of whiskey. Courtesy of the Scientific Research Institute of Cinema Art (NIIK).

indirectly, in terms of rebuilding Germany (*The Meeting on the Elbe*) or east-central Europe (*The Conspiracy of the Doomed,* which takes place in an un-named country that resembles Czechoslovakia).

The conundrum was how to present the power and determination of the enemy and ridicule them at the same time. The aim was to explain and justify the present situation to the Soviet people and their allies, and jolt them to awareness, if not action. It was not to terrify them into a state of paralysis. *The Secret Mission,* for example, succeeded in painting a negative picture of American intentions toward the end of the Second World War, but at the same time it was censured for making the United States seem "al-mighty," as if it were the "alpha and omega."[53] Absent from the picture was a counterbalance: "the strength of Stalinist power, the power of the Soviet Army, the power of our country, and the power of progress."[54] *They Have a Motherland,* as noted above, was lauded for its negative depiction of the Brit-ish and Americans and their association with "bad" Germans, but the char-acter of the Soviet motherland was nowhere to be seen. The council feared that viewers might be tempted to view the film's core dilemmas in purely emotional terms: heart-warming when the children were returned to their parents, heart-wrenching when they were not.[55]

The two Cold War movies set in America, *The Russian Question* and *Silvery Dust,* provided sharp contrasts and sharper paradoxes. The portrayal of black

Americans as sub-humans kept in laboratory cages was deemed to be crude, even given what was known of southern racism (*Silvery Dust*). The film was therefore considered "politically accurate," but not accurate in terms of "artistic truth."[56] That an American reporter, even one being bribed to write against the Soviet Union, would be able to live in a magnificent country cottage, with a large and sparkling kitchen, lovingly rendered, might have been hard to believe, but it was oh so enticing a dream (*The Russian Question*).[57] With regard to *The Russian Question,* which was somewhat freely adapted from Konstantin Simonov's play of the same name, the council also expressed concerns that the "America" in the film was that of 1945, not 1947 or 1948. Given that the United States was supposedly changing so rapidly for the worse, this became an important issue.[58] How could directors possibly cope with these multiple and often competing demands?

The third of the three major goals for these films, as expressed in council meetings, was the need to portray the Soviet state as fundamentally peaceful, in contrast to the war-crazed American leadership. Furthermore, the USSR had to be shown aggressively promoting peace: "The Soviet Union is an active fighter for peace, gathering around itself all the democratic forces in the world."[59] Only two of the eight Cold War films were believed to be successful at doing this: *The Russian Question* ("The picture underscores that the USSR does not want war")[60] and especially *The Meeting on the Elbe,* which is discussed in the next chapter. At the same time, however, the films also needed to stress military and civilian preparedness for war should the American provocateurs strike (*The Secret Mission*).[61]

The drawn-out discussions at the council meetings indicate that members did not believe that their goals were being achieved with any consistency. For their part, directors and scriptwriters expressed frustration at the constantly moving targets and mixed messages they were receiving; productions dragged on for two years or more. The apparent failure of anti-Americanism to take hold in the moviegoing population further indicates that this first wave of Cold War cinematic propaganda, entertaining though it may have been, was not successful in achieving its stated aims. Indeed, given the popularity of American trophy films, it might be argued that moviegoers were the segment of the population most likely to admire Americans and American culture.

The Era of "Positive Legitimation," 1953–1978

On 5 March 1953, Stalin died.[62] Ten days later, the Ministry of Cinematography was abolished and replaced by a Main Administration of Cinema Affairs located within the Ministry of Culture.[63] This was a welcome move. Since it took cinema out of the direct line of Party and government fire, filmmakers might feel less fearful of possible repercussions and more encouraged about new productions.

Apart from this shift, the impact of Stalin's death on cinematic politics was not immediately obvious as Nikita Khrushchev battled Lavrenty Beria and Georgy Malenkov for the succession, exacerbating the insecure mood within the country. In 1954, the writer and journalist Ilya Ehrenburg, a regime bulwark who was also staunchly (and apparently genuinely) anti-American, published a startling novel, *The Thaw* (*Ottepel*), which suggested corruption and bureaucratic obstruction in the factory system and gave its name to a cultural era. The Thaw in culture was a time of genuine diversity, although the break with the Stalinist past was not—and could not be—complete, not even after Khrushchev's Secret Speech in 1956. Censorship and self-censorship relaxed as well, and, as Alexander Prokhorov has noted, "this relaxation led to the fragmentation of the unified, hierarchical universe of Stalinist culture."[64] The major characteristics of Thaw cinema include new cultural institutions, new (mainly young) talents, new genres, and a turn away from the monumentalism of Stalinist film.[65]

The film industry sought to return cinema to the apex of Soviet culture, as it had been in the 1920s, "making it a major element of the 'peaceful' contest with the West."[66] Film production increased dramatically and by the late 1950s Soviet studios were turning out more than 100 films annually; in 1959, the number was 137, up from 9 in 1951.[67] Ivan Pyriev, director of rural Stalinist musical comedies like *The Kuban Cossacks* (*Kubanskie kazaki*, 1949/50), made his most valuable contributions to Soviet cinema at this time, as the energetic head of the Mosfilm studio, the country's largest. Under Pyriev, Mosfilm was rebuilt and expanded and became the home of many bright young talents.[68] Pyriev was also adept at bending the numerous rules that still existed, in order to benefit his filmmakers.

This was an era of artistically revolutionary pictures such as Mikhail Kalatozov's *The Cranes Are Flying* (*Letiat zhuravli*, 1957), Sergei Bondarchuk's *The Fate of a Man* (*Sudba cheloveka*, 1959), Grigory Chukhrai's *The Ballad of a Soldier* (*Ballada o soldate*, 1959), and Andrei Tarkovsky's *Ivan's Childhood* (*Ivanovo detstvo*, 1962), films that were making history in the Soviet Union and in the West. The fact that they were hailed abroad and won prizes at international film festivals was a special point of pride for filmmakers and the Soviet public. The majority of the most artistically renowned films "revisioned" the Great Patriotic War, moving away from generals, maps, and complaints about the perfidy of the Allies and toward the human cost of the conflict.

Nevertheless, as Julian Graffy has shown, negative Cold War filmmaking that showcased foreigners as threats to the USSR continued to be popular with audiences in the 1950s, even as artistically innovative pictures drew accolades from the critics. The biggest box office draws among the negative Cold War films in the decade after Stalin's death was *Ch.P.: An Extraordinary Event* (*Ch.P.: Chrezvychainoe proisshestvie*, 2 parts, Viktor Ivchenko, 1958/59, 72 and 98 million viewers); *The Fort in the Mountains* (*Zastava v gorakh*, Konstantin Yudin, 1953, 44.8 million, released after Stalin's death); and *The Blue Arrow* (*Golubaia strela*, Leonid Estrin, 1958, 44.5 million).[69] The genres were either the detective-adventure or the suspense-adventure, in which lay their primary appeal for audiences, but it is important to note a few key differences from the films of the early Cold War.

First, the negative Cold War films made during the Thaw (unlike those made in the first period) mainly took place within the Soviet Union, showing foreign spies and saboteurs, suggesting that the country's heavily guarded borders were more porous than they seemed. (This becomes important in *Officers*, a film discussed in chapter 6.) Second, more often than not, the nationality of the foreign villains remained obscure, although there was an occasional American among them.[70] Third, internal enemies, as they had in the 1930s, appeared as saboteurs and collaborators in cahoots with the foreigners. And finally, big-name and art film directors no longer participated in the enterprise; makers of popular films beloved by the mass audience (but not the critics) rose in prominence.

The spirit of the Thaw era is better exemplified by the positive films that provided guides to the Soviet good life. These came to the forefront, as they had been in the 1930s. Given the new freedoms of the Thaw, however, the definition of the "good life" changed. It could not be achieved through vigilance and denunciations, but rather by developing one's personal life and relations. Family, friends, and romantic love were now positioned at the center of the collective society. Individualism was a hallmark of the Thaw, and we see directors attempting to put an individual stamp on these films, mostly without breaking wholly from the conventions of Socialist Realism.[71]

It was very important to show that Soviet life, modest though it may be compared with material life in the West, was still preferable. The best examples of this type of soft propaganda came from early in the era: *The Big Family* (*Bolshaia semia*, Iosif Kheifits, 1954), a sentimental but surprisingly realistic look at the loves and lives of a working-class family, and *Spring on Zarechnaya Street* (*Vesna na Zarechnoi ulitse*, Marlen Khutsiev and Feliks Mironer, 1956), the latter discussed in detail in chapter 4. *The Big Family* and *Spring on Zarechnaya Street* were followed by more "this is how we live" pictures such as Stanislav Rostotsky's *It Happened in Penkovo* (*Delo bylo v Penkove*, 1957) and Aleksander Zarkhi's *Heights* (*Vysota*, 1957), among many others.[72] Balancing the tensions that existed between the old and the new aesthetics grew increasingly difficult as it became clear that Socialist Realism's tenet of purposeful and socially engaged art had deep roots. Breaking completely with the artistic past was just as impossible as breaking with the political past.

American culture became particularly important at this time, especially to urban populations.[73] Cultural exchanges increased access to books, movies, and music, making it difficult for the Soviet government to persuade citizens of the evils of the Western system.[74] In film scholar Yana Hashamova's words, "The more Soviet ideology demonized the West, the more fictional and imaginary this demonization became,"[75] too "fictional and imaginary" to be believed.

Indeed, the generation that defined the Thaw had spent their formative teen years watching Hollywood trophy films from the 1930s. The popularity of Johnny Weismuller's Tarzan series in particular among Soviet youth of this era is legendary. Joseph Brodsky, the Nobel Prize–winning poet who was expelled from the USSR in 1972, wrote that the "Tarzan series alone did more for de-Stalinization than all Khrushchev's speeches at the Twentieth Party Congress and thereafter."[76] Brodsky, who was born in 1940, continues: "We took all those papier-mâché, cardboard props for real, and our sense of Europe, of the West, of history, if you will, always owed a great deal to those images."[77] For these youth, the purpose of going to the movies was not for love of cinema, but to learn about the West.[78] The state made an effort to draw a distinction between "good" Western culture and "bad," but this distinction was hard to delineate and communicate to a generation chafing from the strictures of the postwar Stalinist regime.[79] Conservatives attempted to provoke a backlash against Westernism; an example from cinema is Eduard Zmoiro's zany satire of youth infected with "Americanitis," *Foreigners* (*Inostrantsy*, 1961).

The influx of trophy and Western cultural exchange films had an impact on filmmakers as well. Soviet directors took inspiration from the American style, given that they were able to see the "films received as part of Hollywood's insistent attempts to infiltrate the Soviet market," including films never officially released to the public at large.[80] "Active assimilation" of such pictures, even if never acknowledged, contributed to the revitalization of Soviet moviemaking in the 1950s.[81]

However, by the early 1960s, even before Khrushchev's ouster, the cultural climate was beginning to chill. To give one example, Andrei Tarkovsky's darkly subversive movie about the tragedies faced by children in wartime, *Ivan's Childhood* (*Ivanovo Vetstvo,* 1962), ran into censorship trouble because of its "negativism" and unorthodox style, although it was eventually released. The same can be said of Mikhail Romm's *Nine Days in One Year* (*Deviat dnei odnogo goda*, 1961/62), discussed in chapter 5, in which the physicist hero sacrifices himself in the name of science, a martyrdom that harks back to the

Foreigners: The shenanigans of Soviet youth corrupted by Western values. Courtesy of the Scientific Research Institute of Cinema Art (NIIK).

revolutionary martyrs beloved in prewar Soviet cinema. The film's "pessimism" and "negative" second lead, Ilya Kulikov (played by Innokenty Smoktunovsky), raised serious alarm bells. The chilling cultural climate was also signified by a series of crude and forgettable spy films.[82]

Leonid Brezhnev, who came to power in 1964 and ruled for the next eighteen years, was known as a hard-liner, but the Thaw in cinema did not truly end until 1968. Indeed, the Thaw and détente effectively inhibited neo-Stalinist efforts to turn the cultural clock all the way back to Stalinism.[83] An important step in the hardening of the cinematic "line" occurred in 1963, when the Main Committee of Cinema Administration was abolished within the Ministry of Culture and ministerial status was restored to film by the (re)creation of Goskino as cinema's administrative body, headed by Aleksei Romanov.[84] Goskino was answerable to the State Council of Ministers on economic matters, and to the Party's Central Committee on ideological matters.[85] By the time Filipp Yermash took over Goskino in 1972, it had become a mighty conglomerate, overseeing Soveksportfilm (film export), Sovinfilm (co-productions), Sovinterfest (film festivals), the journals *Art of the Cinema* (*Iskusstvo kino*) and *Soviet Screen* (*Sovetskii ekran*), VGIK (the state film institute), and Gosfilmofond (the central state film archive).[86]

Dead Season: The faces of the police state. Courtesy of the Scientific Research Institute of Cinema Art (NIIK).

Goskino quickly began to assert its authority. From 1966 to 1968 the cinema bureaucrats banned and heavily cut a number of films, signaling "a major manifestation of the new cultural policies in the film industry."[87] State and Party once again became intensely interested and involved in the minutiae of filmmaking, especially in the union republics where filmmaking had revived and developed.[88] A few negative Cold War films appeared, including *A Game without Rules* (*Igra bez pravil*, Yaropolk Lapshin, 1965), an overtly anti-American spy thriller, and *Neutral Waters* (*Neitralnye vody*, Vladimir Berenshtein, 1969), which portrayed American might more impersonally (as a ship harassing a Soviet ship).[89] The most interesting film to appear at this time was Savva Kulish's *Dead Season* (*Mertvyi sezon*, 1968), a drama about a spy exchange set in an indeterminate Western European country.[90] Nevertheless, the "near absence [in Soviet Cold War films] of strong propaganda effects" is noteworthy.[91]

Regardless, the interest in and influence of American films continued to be intense, as even a cursory reading of the mass fan magazine *Soviet Screen* (circulation two million)[92] shows. In issue after issue, one finds discussions of American films that would likely never be shown in the USSR, as well as stories on American stars like "Who Killed Marilyn Monroe?" ("Kto ubil Merilin Monro?").[93] By the end of the 1960s, *Soviet Screen* was running an annual survey to determine its readers' favorite films and actors. The poll carefully distinguished between Soviet and foreign films (doubtless to prevent foreign films from taking first place), but films from the bloc and the capitalist countries (*kapstrany*) were usually lumped together. There were some exceptions. In 1967, for example, *Spartacus* (Stanley Kubrick, 1960) took top honors among the imports from the *kapstrany*, but one would have to guess at its place in the box office as a whole.[94]

Official tolerance of this interest in foreign films may be explained by the cinema bureaucrats' desires to ramp up profits from cinema, especially in the wake of growing competition from television.[95] Comedies, adventures, and domestic melodramas began to dominate the box office, along with a steady diet of foreign films, most from the satellite states and India, which constituted about 50 percent of the repertory. Even though importation of American films increased, the types of American films imported did not always satisfy audiences, especially when they were "B" pictures or tendentious fare or "old" films shown a decade or more after their making. In response to readers' queries about the principles for selection of Western films, signifying their dissatisfaction with the repertory, *Soviet Screen* published the justification that films appropriate for import were those made by "progressive," left-leaning directors who were not hostile to the Soviet Union (these remained unnamed).[96]

To make up for the relative absence of Hollywood films on the screen, some Soviet directors began to compensate through imitation by the late seventies. Among the biggest box office hits of the decade were Soviet movies that were distinctly "Hollywood" in terms of style. Two well-known examples are *The Crew* (*Ekipazh*, Aleksander Mitta, 1980, 70 million viewers), an airplane disaster film, and Vladimir Menshov's *Moscow Does Not Believe in Tears* (*Moskva slezam ne verit*, 2 parts, 1979/80, 68 and 82 million), the fairytale story of an upwardly mobile middle-aged factory director finding love with a ruggedly attractive worker. In 1981, *Moscow Does Not Believe in Tears* won the Oscar for Best Foreign Language Film.[97]

Another form of substitution for Hollywood and Western films was the co-production, and Sovinfilm aggressively sought partnerships. Among the best known are Mikhail Kalatozov's *The Red Tent* (*Krasnaia palatka*, 1969, Mosfilm/Vides Cinematografica), about Umberto Nobile's disastrous Arctic expedition of 1928, starring Sean Connery as Roald Amundsen, Peter Finch as Nobile, and Claudia Cardinale as the misplaced love interest;[98] and Sergei Bondarchuk's *Waterloo* (1970, Mosfilm/Dino di Laurentis), starring Rod Steiger as Napoleon, Christopher Plummer as the Duke of Wellington, and Orson Welles as King Louis XVIII. Both films were made in English, a nod to the dominance of English as the international language of the movies, with primarily Italian crews. The most successful film among the co-productions in artistic terms was rather different: Akira Kurosawa's *Dersu Uzala* (*Derusu Uzara* in Japanese, 1975, Mosfilm/Daiei/Atelier 41), which was filmed in Russian with a Soviet cast and primarily Soviet crew.[99] A soulful tale deeply rooted in the Russian romanticization of the Siberian wilderness and its indigenous peoples, *Dersu Uzala* deservedly received the Oscar for Best Foreign Language Film in 1976.[100]

The most notorious example of the co-production is George Cukor's *The Blue Bird,* the sole Soviet-American co-production (Lenfilm/Twentieth Century-Fox).[101] A screen adaptation of Maurice Maeterlinck's symbolist play, the film was made in English and starred Elizabeth Taylor and a host of British and American stars in the main roles. After taking nearly two years to complete, *The Blue Bird* was finally released, to neither critical acclaim nor box office success, in 1976. The Americans and British on the cast and crew were hit hard by the culture shock of living in Leningrad and dealing with the slow pace of Soviet life and work; for their part, the Soviets must have resented the obvious condescension they met, although they were too polite to say so. They did, however, object to Jane Fonda's attempts to talk about communism with them. *The Blue Bird* provides a textbook case of culture clash and the potential problems with Soviet co-productions, given that Soviet film technology was not as advanced as Hollywood's. It is a shame, however, that Cukor did not utilize the skills of the Kirov Ballet dancers in the film better than he did or draw on the deep reservoir of superb Soviet actors for the cast.[102]

The cost of this fascination with America (and, to a lesser extent, other Western countries), however, was high. By the late 1960s, according to Eric Shiraev and Vladislav Zubok, "the United States was becoming an important cultural symbol. . . . For most representatives of Russia's new middle class, America became the antipode of the inefficient, bureaucratic, and backward Soviet Union. . . . Soviet patriotism quickly waned."[103] To bolster this waning patriotism, the Brezhnev regime began to expand the nascent cult of the Great Patriotic War.[104] Films about the war had been popular with audiences and directors alike since 1945 but especially since Stalin's death, and they joined monuments, rituals, anniversaries, and Victory Day ceremonies in commemorating the war. A particularly notable example is Yury Ozerov's five-part film *Liberation* (*Osvobozhdenie,* 1968–71), which was commissioned as part of the ongoing celebrations of the twenty-fifth anniversary of Victory Day.

Brezhnev was interested in strengthening the military in order to ensure parity with the West, even as he sought détente with Nixon, successfully, and Jimmy Carter, unsuccessfully. Parity was achieved by the mid-1970s,[105] but mere parity was not enough. Reviving the Soviet Army's reputation and attracting first-rate officers and soldiers to careers in the military was essen-

The Blue Bird: An international cast, led by Elizabeth Taylor as the Queen of Light, on the Leningrad set. Courtesy of the Academy of Motion Picture Arts and Sciences (AMPAS).

tial. Of course, the many Great Patriotic War films of this period succeeded in bringing the heroism and sacrifices of the population to life for the post-war generation.[106] It is nevertheless important to remember that during the war the Red Army was more a civilian army than a professional one, and so films about the peacetime military intended to enhance its status also appeared during the 1970s.

The rewards of lifetime military service got a particular boost in 1971, with the release of *Officers* (*Ofitsery*, Vladimir Rogovoy, 53.4 million viewers), discussed in chapter 6. This deceptively simple film—about how a man who wanted to be a teacher is transformed by military service—became a huge hit, taking first place at the box office that year. Given the reality of the shortcomings in the military that the government sought to suppress, the film serves as an example of positive legitimation in the face of eroding respect and increasing suspicion about the authenticity of military accomplishments.[107]

Positive reinforcement did not only concern war and military films. During détente there were a few films that went so far as to portray Americans positively, such as Aleksander Stefanovich's *Dear Boy* (*Dorogoi malchik*, 1974), with a script by Sergei Mikhalkov. The film follows the adventures of two boys, American and Soviet, who eventually escape from the gangsters who have kidnapped them.[108] But although there were some anti-American films made in the 1970s, as Sergei Dobrynin points out, "care was taken to differentiate between the 'imperialists' and the 'ordinary Americans': children, 'progressive' journalists, scientists working for the good of all humanity."[109]

By the late 1970s, the Brezhnev regime was in steep decline. Some Soviet directors were not surprisingly drawn to make "social problem" films, productions that treated real-life problems, like bureaucratism or workplace corruption, seriously but cautiously.[110] Other Soviet directors, such as Aleksei Gherman, Kira Muratova, Aleksander Sokurov, and especially Andrei Tarkovsky, became ever more daring, resulting in subversive films that were banned or received curtailed distribution. (Tarkovsky felt the constraints binding filmmakers so keenly that he went into exile in 1982; he died in Paris in 1986.)[111]

THE LATE COLD WAR, 1978–1986

Any feeling of equanimity toward the United States that existed under the Nixon and Ford administrations was badly disrupted by the late 1970s, first by Jimmy Carter, then more forcefully by Ronald Reagan. The refusal of the United States to participate in the 1980 Moscow Olympics was a slap in the face of national pride, of course, but Reagan's bellicose rhetoric genuinely dismayed the leadership of the "evil empire," as did his announcement of the Strategic Defense Initiative (SDI, dubbed "Star Wars") in 1983.[112] Reagan's aggressive anti-Sovietism came at a time of political upheaval and economic decline in the Soviet Union, which saw three Party secretaries—Brezhnev, Andropov, and Chernenko—die in less than three years, from November 1982 to February 1985, not to mention the ongoing, unpopular war in Afghanistan.

By 1978, the number of articles in *Soviet Screen* that were sharply critical of specific Hollywood films had increased.[113] Even before that, concerns were expressed about the large number of films Hollywood made compared to the production of any European country, strongly implying that the Hollywood juggernaut was well on its way to destroying European cinemas.[114] At this time, the USSR was making up to 150 films a year (and importing about 150 more), the United States more than 300 annually.

The early 1980s marked a newly aggressive anti-American campaign, but one that was still principally oriented toward positive legitimation.[115] Yet in 1983, the same year SDI was announced, anti-American attacks increased in the cinema press. In *Art of the Cinema,* a high-brow journal (circulation 50,000), the violence, "anti-humanism," and explicit anticommunism of American films were lambasted.[116] This coincided with an article in *Soviet Screen* complaining about the *Star Wars* films, among others, and declaring that recent Anglo-American film displayed a "class hatred for socialism."[117]

The anti-American rhetoric in the film press became almost as shrill as it had been in the late Stalin era. Hollywood was "anti-democratic."[118] Americans were "uncultured" (*nekulturnyi,* a serious insult in Russian) and ignorant of their own culture and history.[119] (Ironically, concerns were growing about the historical literacy of Soviet youth, especially about the Great Patriotic War.) The "reactionary power of imperialism" was evident in James Bond films, whether American-made or not (by this time no distinction was drawn between films in the American style and "Hollywood"). According to this rhetoric, Hollywood was playing cinematic war games for "mis-entertainment."[120] Hollywood films were further charged with being "filled with hatred, brutality, and professions of militarism and anti-communism."[121] We must remember, however, that most of this was a reaction to anti-Soviet American films, which only became worse as time went on: *Red Dawn* (John Milius, 1984), the Rambo series, especially *Rambo: First Blood Part II* (George P. Cosmatos, 1985; discussed in chapter 7), *The Year of the Dragon* (Michael Cimino, 1985), and others. (The heat of the response also probably reflected the plummeting popularity of Soviet films within the USSR.) Soviet critic Nikolai Savitsky undoubtedly spoke for many when he opined in 1986: "It's hard to imagine that a viewer with developed aesthetic tastes could like *Rambo II* . . . or that *The Year of the Dragon* could appeal to a serious lover of cinema."[122]

Most Soviet films in this period continued to be apolitical. The biggest hit of the 1980s, the blockbuster *The Pirates of the 20th Century* (*Piraty XX veka,* Boris Durov, 1980), drew 87 million spectators, a truly colossal number for a Soviet film, especially for this late date when movie attendance had sunk so low.[123] A few anti-American films were, however, made at this time.[124] The major Soviet response to the wave of anti-Soviet American films can be found in two pictures by the Georgian theater and film director Mikhail Tumanishvili, both discussed in chapter 7. The first, *Incident at Map Grid 36-80* (*Sluchai v kvadrate 36-80,* 1982), about an American nuclear submarine accident, continued the Soviet practice of carefully distinguishing between "good" and "bad" Americans, laying the weight of the crisis on the U.S. military command, not ordinary sailors.[125] The second film of this pair, *Solo Voyage* (*Odinochnoe plavanie,* 1985/86), which features a crazed Vietnam War veteran taking over a secret underground missile command post at the behest of the CIA, is a much more extreme form of propaganda. Here the Americans, with two exceptions, are extremely bad characters, and one of the good Americans is initially highly suspicious of the intentions of Soviet marines who only want to help him and his wife to safety.

Another particularly interesting Cold War film from this period, *Flight 222* (*Reis 222,* Sergei Mikaelian, 1985), treated the anti-American theme

Flight 222: Jolly Soviet citizens sequestered on the plane. Courtesy of the Scientific Research Institute of Cinema Art (NIIK).

from an unusual perspective, that of a Soviet husband and wife who are well-known sports figures. Based on the events surrounding the real-life defection of Soviet dancer Alexander Godunov in August 1979,[126] the husband defects without telling his wife, which leads to a major international incident. The woman emphatically does not want to stay in the United States, but the American authorities cannot believe it. They hold her plane in New York for several days, inflicting terrible conditions on the Soviet passengers, who loyally refuse to disembark so that they can support their compatriot. Eventually, of course, the Americans relent, understanding that they will never win in the face of Soviet patriotism. Soviet critics considered this a very fair-minded treatment of an ever-embarrassing issue.[127]

THE END OF THE COLD WAR
IN CINEMA, 1986–1988

At the same time, Gorbachev's cultural thaw (glasnost) was clearly making headway. Filipp Yermash was unceremoniously removed as head of Goskino in 1986 and replaced by a reformer, Aleksander Kamshalov. Rapid decentralization of the industry followed. In 1989, Sovinfilm was abolished, with co-production authority now residing in the studios; in 1990 Mosfilm began offering its films to international distributors independently of Soveksportfilm.[128] The Union of Filmmakers, founded in 1965, began to take a leading role in perestroika under the leadership of director Elem Klimov.

Change could not come fast enough for movie audiences. Near the end of 1986, *Soviet Screen* published two pages of angry letters from filmgoers dissatisfied with the state of the repertory and what they saw as the hypocrisy of Soviet cultural politics. Svetlana Sheltsova from Kaliningrad complained: "We discuss the negative problems of Western cinema from all sides. But less often [do we] discuss our own shortcomings." Olga Glukikh from Perm observed: "We have good films, but few. And every year, there are fewer and fewer." As a final example, the teens in a tenth grade class in Vladivostok asked: "What is there to see, if not foreign films?"[129]

Filmmakers also began critiquing the past with impunity, while critics could now discuss a previously criticized twenty-year-old film, *The Russians Are Coming, The Russians Are Coming* (Norman Jewison, 1966), with equanimity.[130] Censorship, such as it was, was merely "bureaucratic" and focused on taking banned films "off the shelf."[131] But at the same time, Soviet critics chafed under the humiliation of a Hollywood season filled with macho, often explicitly anti-Soviet films like *Top Gun, Rambo,* or Chuck Norris pictures.[132]

In 1988, however, Arnold Schwarzenegger, who had just finished the Soviet-friendly film *Red Heat*, visited Moscow (to a reportedly lukewarm reception), a delegation of American filmmakers from the American-Soviet Film Initiative arrived, and Elem Klimov attended Hollywood's Academy Awards ceremony with considerable enthusiasm.[133] (There were plenty of snapshots of Hollywood stars from the latter's visit; one might say Klimov was left star-struck.) A film reporter traveling to the United States for the first time for the First International Film Festival in New Orleans was quite impressed by the scale and budget of the operation, the fact that this was a minor festival notwithstanding.[134] The American people were suddenly reported to be friendly, not hostile. After decades of excoriation, Hollywood cinema had now become a "new model" to be emulated, at least in technological terms.[135] How times had changed—and how quickly! Glasnost had permeated Soviet cinema so thoroughly that the cinematic Cold War effectively ended in 1988, a year before the Berlin Wall came down.

Conclusion

American and Soviet cinema were truly engaged in a form of asymmetric warfare during the Cold War. American cinema was an international juggernaut, churning out several hundred pictures a year and dominating box offices worldwide. Soviet cinema, in contrast, struggled to make enough pictures to fill its own screens, and, despite its dislike of the West, the country was forced to import motion pictures to satisfy domestic demand. Despite Soveksportfilm's campaigns to sell Soviet films abroad, they only occasionally found an audience, except in the captive market in Eastern Europe or at rare moments of artistic flight, such as during the Thaw.

These differences in the relative size and popularity of American and Soviet cinema may be traced to the differences in the structures of the two industries. Soviet cinema had been nationalized since 1919; after a period of qualified diversity in the 1920s, it was rigidly centralized and vertically constructed. The belief that cinema was the "most important of the arts" was a bane as much as a blessing because of the level of scrutiny and control exercised by the state and Party. The loss of autonomy meant that filmmakers had to realize the state's vision, which rarely coincided with their own, and banned or heavily censored films became fairly commonplace, despite the efforts of filmmakers to self-censor. After Stalin's death, however, strictures loosened enough so that some remarkable films were made, including two that are discussed in later chapters, *Spring on Zarechnaya Street* and *Nine Days in One Year.*

American cinema, on the other hand, was comparatively freer of political influences, although very much constrained by commercial imperatives. It is true that U.S. government agencies and political actors at various moments influenced or tried to influence Hollywood, and that Hollywood's interests seemed to coincide with the interests of the state. However, the number and variety of studios, filmmakers, distributors, exhibitors, and trade papers combined to create an industry that demonstrated breadth and depth, as well as an uncanny instinct for what audiences liked, whether they were in Des Moines or Sverdlovsk.

Yet despite the considerable contrast in the very essence of the two film industries, there were surprising similarities as well as understandable differences in Cold War filmmaking. Comparing Soviet and American films at similar junctures during the Cold War can elucidate the reasons behind these similarities and help us answer the questions posed in the introduction about who won the cinematic Cold War and why.

PART TWO

Sites of Conflict

CHAPTER THREE

Justifying War

If a nation is taken to war, its people must have a clear picture of the enemy. They need to know and see—even if it is only in mediated form—who and what they are fighting against. During the Second World War, Americans and Soviets had few difficulties demonizing and "visualizing" fascism. After all, Hitler's widely publicized speeches and actions clearly identified him as a brutal, racist megalomaniac. The Japanese, for their part, had ruthlessly occupied large parts of China, a country that shared a border with the Soviet Union, and brazenly attacked American territory at Pearl Harbor.

The deepening tensions between the American and Soviet governments after 1945 were marked by no such dramatic, clear-cut acts of military aggression. Instead, the two slid gradually, messily, and often invisibly into a strange sort of war, one that was undeclared and yet, due to the arrival of nuclear weapons, more dangerous than any other in history. Getting the public's support for such a war would be difficult at the best of times. It was going to be particularly difficult in the wake of the Second World War, not least because trying to picture the enemy risked causing double vision. How, for instance, could one go about presenting the communist Soviet Union as a direct threat to the United States, as anathema to American values, when it had been, arguably, Washington's most valuable antifascist ally? Equally, how could one portray the capitalist United States of America as an inveterate imperialist bully, after all the good will generated from the Lend-Lease program? In any case, both countries were mentally and physically exhausted after four years spent struggling to defeat fascism, especially the Soviet Union, and were in no mood to engage in another global conflict.

This chapter looks at the role the Soviet and American film industries played in defining the new enemy and justifying what quickly became known as a "cold war" in the wake of World War II. It focuses on the years 1948–1953, the darkest period of the cinematic Cold War, demonstrating the marked convergence between U.S. and Soviet propaganda goals and methods. We analyze two films made at either end of this formative period, bringing out the sharp contrasts in resources for the cinematic propaganda campaign as well as the different ideologies and styles that the two film industries adopted.

In the Soviet Union during this period, as noted in chapter 2, only eight major Cold War films appeared: one in 1948 (*The Russian Question*), two in 1949 (*The Meeting on the Elbe* and *The Court of Honor*), three in 1950 (*The*

Conspiracy of the Doomed, The Secret Mission, and *They Have a Motherland*), one in 1952 (*Dawn on the Neman*), and one in 1953 (*Silvery Dust*).[1] These films framed the Cold War enemy carefully, distinguishing between the "good" citizens of the capitalist/imperialist states—usually, but not always, members of the working class—and the nefarious representatives of the political, military, and intellectual elites. Of these films, Grigory Aleksandrov's immensely popular *The Meeting on the Elbe* (1949) best exemplifies the main attributes of early Soviet Cold War cinema. A cautionary tale of the new world order, it charts American perfidy at the end of the Second World War, particularly U.S. efforts to shelter "useful" Nazis, and the depravities of American culture, even as reconstructed in occupied Eastern Europe. The focus on a divided Germany allows for a direct confrontation between Americans and Soviets, with the former portrayed as Germany's new fascist leadership.

The American films of the period provide many more choices for analysis. In surveying the scores of anticommunist movies made in the late 1940s and early 1950s, one quickly gravitates to such obvious examples as *The Red Menace* (1949) or *The Whip Hand* (1951), sensationalist, heavy-handed productions that best capture the era's paranoid fear of communist subversion. However, the vast majority of these classic Red-baiters failed at the box office and had little real influence, and thus are unsuitable for comparison with a film such as *The Meeting on the Elbe.* Our attention focuses instead on Elia Kazan's *Man on a Tightrope* (1953), a movie that, though largely forgotten today, was highly regarded at the time for the measured yet powerful fashion in which it exposed the destructive qualities of Soviet "totalitarianism." *Man on a Tightrope* is set, like *The Meeting on the Elbe,* in post–World War II Europe, the story of a Czechoslovakian circus troupe fleeing from the East to the West. An entertaining mixture of two genres, drama and carnival, Kazan's movie contains all the trademark Hollywood features of life under communism: violence, fear, forced politicization, poverty, and the systematic manipulation and distortion of everyday things, even entertainment. *Man on a Tightrope* helped serve as a model for later American films that purported to open a window on life behind the dreaded Iron Curtain.

New Allies, New Enemies:
The Meeting on the Elbe

The Meeting on the Elbe, the canonical early Soviet Cold War film, is a masterpiece of negative propaganda that tells us most of what we need to know about the construction of Soviet cinematic anti-Americanism. It makes two major points. First, it dramatically demonstrates that the nation's Second World War ally had now become the enemy. Since the revival of the film industry in the early 1920s, but especially since the advent of Stalin's cultural revolution at the end of that decade, Soviet directors had had much experience defining the "Other" for the screen.[2] Three basic types of foreign adversaries populated the early Cold War films: lingering Nazis and other unrepentant Germans, scheming Roman Catholic priests or Vatican officials bent on corrupting Soviet rule in the Roman Catholic territories of the new empire,[3] and the Americans. Without doubt, the most powerful and therefore most dangerous Cold War enemy is American: the American government, the American military command, American industrialists, and American racists, but not Americans as a whole. Director Grigory Aleksandrov emphasized that his film was not about the "American people (*narod*)"; rather, it concerned a "specific group of monopolists and allies of American imperialism."[4] (Likewise, he argued that he did not want to demonize Germans "in general," but only those "estates and classes" that had supported the Reich and refused to support Soviet democracy.)[5]

Second, *The Meeting on the Elbe* may also be seen as a justification for the emergence of the new "empire" in east-central Europe. This kind of justification or rationalization propaganda had two audiences: the domestic—Soviet—audience and the audience in the people's republics, where Soviet films became a mainstay of the cinematic repertory. *The Meeting on the Elbe* is the only important film of the period to focus entirely on postwar reconstruction in a satellite state.[6] It takes place in an imaginary German town divided by the Elbe River, of great symbolic significance for both sides given that the river is where the U.S. and Soviet armies met in April 1945.

The Meeting on the Elbe is the only Cold War film from this period in which Soviets directly confront Americans.[7] It graphically depicts the corruption, materialism, decadence, and racism of American culture transplanted into the American sector, on one side of the Elbe, in the charming medieval town of Altenstadt. On the river's other side, the Soviet regime works tirelessly to rebuild the shattered town, set up elections, heal the psychic wounds of war, and so on. Altenstadt is therefore divided not only physically but also spiritually. *The Meeting on the Elbe* became the model film for formulating the Cold War enemy while vindicating the Soviet empire.

Its cast and crew represented the best that Soviet cinema had to offer. Aleksandrov had started in cinema as an assistant to Sergei Eisenstein and accompanied the legendary filmmaker on his 1929–1931 sojourn to the West, which included time in Hollywood. After his return to the USSR in 1931, Aleksandrov joined the ranks of the most popular Soviet directors, a favorite of Stalin who became best known for his entertaining American-style musical comedies.[8] Eduard Tisse, who came to fame as Eisenstein's cameraman, was Aleksandrov's cinematographer. The Tur brothers, well-known journalists, wrote the script for *The Meeting on the Elbe* based on their play *The Governor of*

the *Province* (*Gubernator provintsii*),[9] with the assistance of Lev Sheinin for political protection. (The politically well connected Sheinin had been a henchman
of state procurator Andrei Vyshinsky during the Great Terror and an assistant
prosecutor at the Nuremberg trials.)[10] Dmitri Shostakovich composed the
score, with a rousing theme song titled "Peace Conquers War."[11] The popular and ruggedly handsome Vladlen Davydov starred as Major Kuzmin, com-
mandant of the Soviet sector.[12] Lyubov Orlova, one of the best-loved stars
of Soviet cinema, played against type as the perfidious American spy Janet
Sherwood.[13] Ostensibly a journalist and a German expatriate looking for her
father in Altenstadt, in reality she is "Miss Collins" of the American "Federal
Intelligence Sevice," trying to smuggle an infamous Nazi war criminal out of
Germany into the United States.

The result is a handsome, highly entertaining film, if one sets aside political and historical accuracy. As Peter Kenez has noted, it is almost a textbook case for psychological transference.[14] Although Aleksandrov grandly
proclaimed that "life was the demanding fact-checker of our work [and] international reality was our editor,"[15] he has taken actual Soviet and American behaviors in the occupied territories and switched them. Americans
pillage, Soviets rebuild; Americans abuse German women, Soviets respect
and protect them. It is doubtful, however, that many Soviet viewers cared a
lot about any of this; rather, they wanted to see the popular stars, especially
Orlova swathed in furs and jewels, and listen to the snatches of forbidden
jazz in the American officers' club. *The Meeting on the Elbe* took first place at
the box office in 1949 (24.2 million viewers), tying *Secret Mission* (1950) as
the fourth most-seen film of the late Stalin era.

Driven by its complicated cast of characters, *The Meeting on the Elbe* has
a convoluted plot with lots of loose ends. It opens in the war's last chaotic days. Both the American and Soviet armies have reached the Elbe. Nazi
sympathizers pile onto a boat called the *Adolf Hitler* to escape from the Soviets to the Americans. Soviet tanks arrive and we see the faces of the Red
Army soldiers, open and honest. This is in sharp contrast to the American
soldiers. Already drunk, they swim across the river to the strains of "The
Battle Hymn of the Republic" and "Yankee Doodle Dandy," bottles high in
their hands, to meet their Soviet counterparts in friendship.[16] The "Allied"
generals, however, greet each other cautiously. The American thinks that the
Soviet's binoculars are so superior they must be German-made; the Soviet
general then makes a gift of them to his American counterpart, both to demonstrate Soviet quality and as a show of his generosity.

Altenstadt, now a divided city, is itself a Janus-faced character in the film.
On one side of the Elbe, it is ruined but reviving, thanks to the ministrations
of Major Kuzmin and a local teacher, Kurt Dietrich. They work to restore

The Meeting on the Elbe: Mrs. MacDermott gets her portrait painted. Source: British Film Institute (BFI).

not only the buildings but also the social and moral order of the town. On the other side of the Elbe, Altenstadt is ruined and decaying even further thanks to the dirty deeds of the Americans, most prominently General Mac-Dermott, his wife, Senator Wood, and a host of drunken officers.

Although most of the villains are male, it gradually becomes clear that American villainy is gendered female, initially through the person of Mrs. MacDermott, and later through Janet Sherwood. The whiskey-swigging, cigar-chomping General MacDermott and Senator Wood pretend to believe that they are in charge, as evidenced by their bluster and swagger, but Mrs. MacDermott is definitely calling the tune. The implication is clear: even an American general is not man enough to control his woman.

A biting caricature of Eleanor Roosevelt, Mrs. MacDermott was played by the well-known Soviet Jewish actress Faina Ranevskaya (an interesting choice considering the anti-cosmopolitan campaign). Mrs. MacDermott is mannish: loud, arrogant, and uncultured, shot so that she appears to dwarf the men. She is seen having her portrait painted in a style that can only be called imperial. A black marketeer and speculator, Mrs. MacDermott brings in truckloads of cigarettes and canned food to barter for valuable German paintings and other personal family artifacts, trading on the misery of destitute Germans. (The American flag is prominently displayed.)

Not only does she seize Germany's cultural heritage; she also seeks to destroy the vestiges of its natural beauty. She orders her husband to send his soldiers out to raze a virgin forest so that the MacDermotts can sell the timber to fuel-deprived Britain, thereby seizing control of the market and making a huge profit.

As it turns out, however, it is not Mrs. MacDermott to whom the general answers. Mrs. MacDermott too is a front—for another female villain. The MacDermotts and Wood report to Janet Sherwood, an aging but flirtatious beauty whose mission is to spirit the Nazi war criminal Schrank out of the country to the United States. Schrank's task is to steal a set of valuable patents from a local scientist; the implication is that the United States is uninterested in prosecuting Nazis for war crimes so that they can utilize them for their own dirty deeds. Sherwood appears in the Soviet sector as a German American journalist looking for her father, from whom she was separated during the war. This "father" is Schrank, posing as "Krauss," a former political prisoner. Richly dressed, long-stemmed rose in hand, Sherwood attempts to beguile Major Kuzmin into a state of paralysis on a romantic nighttime cruise. He appears tempted but only slightly, put off by her materialism and decaying beauty, in contrast to the wholesomely attractive wife we see in a photograph that reminds him of what he has at home.

The two good Americans—Major Hill and his Ukrainian American orderly from Poltava, who dreams of his homeland—do not stand much of a chance against Sherwood and the MacDermotts. Hill, according to Aleksandrov, comes "from the ranks of those Americans who retain friendly feelings and respect toward the Soviet Army."[17] Hill immediately trusts Kuzmin, so when Kuzmin informs him that "there will be no Soviet Reich established in Germany," he is reassured. At the end of the film, when Kuzmin notifies Hill of Sherwood's plot to smuggle a Nazi war criminal, Hill naturally attempts to arrest her. In the end, Sherwood eludes capture, reveals herself as "Miss Collins" (flinging off her fur coat to show her uniform underneath), and returns to the United States, doubtless to hatch other nefarious plots against the Soviets. Poor naïve Hill is stripped of his rank and awaits his return to the United States to face charges of anti-American activities. He had actually believed that American justice meant something, but we see that good Americans cannot win.

Villainy cannot be truly understood without reference to heroes. *The Meeting on the Elbe* has the perfect Socialist Realist hero in Major Kuzmin. In the Soviet sector, under his control, everything is different. Major Kuzmin's authority is uncontested; he is the sole named representative of Soviet power, and the occupying Red Army has magically faded away. (Curiously, there is no mention of Stalin at all; Lenin's is the only portrait in Kuzmin's

The Meeting on the Elbe: Glamorous Janet Sherwood with upright Major Kuzmin. Source: British Film Institute (BFI).

office.) As tireless as he is kind and good-looking, Kuzmin quickly wins the loyalty and admiration of the inhabitants. He sees to it that people are fed and complaints are heard—even nuns walk away happy, with oil for their lamps. He frees political prisoners from the local jail (including the evil Schrank) and befriends one of them, the teacher Kurt Dietrich, whose communist sympathies landed him in jail under the Nazis.

Kurt is the estranged son of the town's most famous citizen, the anti-Nazi scientist Professor Dietrich, whose house Kuzmin has commandeered for his living quarters. Professor Dietrich hates and fears communists as much as he did Nazis, but the kind and patient major still permits the professor, his daughter Elsa, her young son Walter, and her covert Nazi husband to maintain their previous lifestyle in their home. Kuzmin appears to occupy only an upstairs bedroom rather than commandeering the entire house, which is large, light, and well decorated, the kind of home most Soviet citizens could not even imagine.

Kuzmin's first big initiative is to reopen the local school with Kurt as the principal. At the convocation, Nazi leaflets, distributed by the child Walter, appear on the pews. Kuzmin calmly and gently persuades the children that it is the Nazis, not the Soviets, who have turned Germans away from their heritage. He informs the children that they are the "future of the New Germany," at which they spontaneously tear up the leaflets. Gradually, he

The Meeting on the Elbe: The old and the new: Professor Dietrich and Major Kuzmin.
Source: British Film Institute (BFI).

wins over Walter, explaining that the Soviets fought so hard during the war because the Germans had no business invading the Soviet homeland. In this spirit, he adds, he hopes to create a "Germany for Germans, not fascists." To prove that Soviet power will not diminish German culture, he orders the restoration of the statue of the great German Jewish writer Heinrich Heine, Kurt's literary idol and a poet whom the cultured major can recite by heart.

Kuzmin has not, however, succeeded in winning over Professor Dietrich. Dietrich is angry because the laboratories in the optical plant where he worked are being dismantled and taken to the USSR. He has trade secrets hidden from the Soviets in his home safe. Eventually, Dietrich warms to the upright Kuzmin, especially when the major decides that Dietrich should run for town mayor as a "non-party" person who will be able to bring all factions together in the new German democracy. After the election, however, Dietrich's cringing son-in-law, still a Nazi sympathizer despite seeing all the good the Soviets are doing in their sector, steals the patents and passes them on to the war criminal Schrank. The guileless Dietrich is convinced that Kuzmin stole them and crosses over to the American sector to carry on his work with the aid of the Marshall Plan.

Professor Dietrich is, however, quickly disillusioned when he sees the sharp contrast between the American and Soviet ways of life. In one five-minute sequence, he wanders disconsolately down a street ringing with the raucous laughter of drunken officers and soldiers, witnesses the beating of a black GI whose girlfriend is then dragged off to be raped,[18] sees his compatriots standing in a long line at the barter center, observes Mrs. MacDermott up to no good, and is nearly hit by a truck carrying a load of Lucky Strike cartons, which tumble out the back. It quickly becomes obvious to Dietrich that it is the Americans, not the Soviets, who are as corrupt and dissolute as the Nazis. German honor and the German soul will not be restored in the American sector. Dietrich humbly returns to beg Kuzmin's permission to reenter the Soviet sector, bringing three other like-minded German scientists with him. He will devote his life to working with the Soviets to rebuild his homeland. "Two worlds met on the Elbe. We have made a choice," he says. This is no occupation, but a partnership.

The overt message of the film would certainly have been clear to Soviet and bloc audiences of the time. *The Meeting on the Elbe* was shown in the satellite states and reportedly received enthusiastically.[19] In a discussion at the filmmakers' club, the House of Cinema, in March 1949, the film was widely praised, but in rote fashion as if to a script. One commentator, A. I. Poltorak, described it as showing the "contemporary political situation in Germany" and how American occupation politics were mobilizing the "most reactionary" elements in Germany in preparation for a new war.[20] The Soviets, Poltorak argued, have occupied East Germany to rebuild and restore; the Americans to feed their insatiable appetite for money and material goods. The Soviets, in his view, represented democracy and peace; the Americans, imperialism and the desire for permanent war. Poltorak praised the depiction of the "two worlds": democratic, anti-imperialist East Germany and anti-democratic, imperialist West Germany.[21]

Whether or not this message mattered to Soviet moviegoers is a different question. Based on what we now know of Soviet postwar disillusionment,[22] it is doubtful that many Soviet viewers much cared about whether or not the film portrayed life in postwar Germany believably. It is not clear that they were persuaded of American villainy; the fact that American culture enjoyed forbidden popularity in the USSR from the late 1940s on indicates they were not. Indeed, the "cognitive dogmatism and narrowness" of anti-American propaganda in the Soviet Union completely undermined people's trust in it.[23]

The Meeting on the Elbe may sound clichéd now, but it did not seem so in 1949, which partly explains its reception at the time. Like the equally popular *The Secret Mission,* it is a spy thriller. For all its propagandistic message, Soviet power does not entirely triumph: Schrank is captured but Sherwood escapes, indicative of the menace of American might. Furthermore, this was a Soviet film that on a small scale attempted to compete with the trophy films seized from the Germans, both in terms of entertainment and production values. It gave Soviet viewers the opportunity to glimpse the glamour lacking in Soviet postwar life. Audiences could gaze at one of their favorite actresses, Lyubov Orlova, in a role somewhat reminiscent of her turn as the American vaudeville performer Marion Dixon in *The Circus* (1936), except that Marion was the heroine rather than the villain. They could watch the sparkling, spinning neon lights of the American nightclub and enjoy the jazz music in the American officers' club, catching glimpses of the frenetic modern dancing that was frowned upon at home.[24]

Aleksandrov faced both praise and criticism during the entire filmmaking process, and in the end the production was released through Stalin's intervention ("The film is shot with great knowledge of matters," opined the Great Leader).[25] As discussed in chapter 2, the Ministry of Cinematography's Artistic Council spent a great deal of time over every Cold War film's "accuracy." As a result, considerable energy was expended to make sure the actors playing American characters in *The Meeting on the Elbe* looked American, rather than Russian or even British.[26] Aleksandrov may have been too successful in this regard, however; some council members complained that Major Kuzmin appeared weak by comparison, arguing that he needed to be "strong and authentic." They also complained that the Americans—exemplified by the villainous MacDermotts—seemed to be much better prepared for the occupation than Kuzmin, though it is unclear what aspect of occupation is intended here.[27]

Nevertheless, industry professionals seemed to agree with Aleksandrov's own assessment that the finished picture was "a weapon in the battle for peace."[28] Such ironically combative language became a leitmotif of the House of Cinema discussion. Prominent actor Nikolai Cherkassov approvingly noted that the film demonstrated "the Party's order that all Soviet citizens should fight for peace."[29] Screenwriter Georgy Mdivani remarked that "*The Meeting on the Elbe* strikes a sharp blow against the Anglo-American anti-Soviet reaction and against growing fascism in America." Mdivani also noted that the "film shows that the Soviet Union thinks only of peace."[30] Journalist M. N. Dolgopolov liked the accuracy of the depiction of the Americans—all the Americans he had personally met were completely "uncultured"—and praised the film for stirring "profound patriotic feelings."[31] Director Leo Arnshtam declared it Aleksandrov's "biggest and most successful" work.[32] Aleksandrov himself closed the session by emphasizing several times that the film was not about war, but the "struggle for peace," hoping that the film might mitigate "anti-Soviet falsification about the Iron Curtain" (although he disingenuously stressed that he would not "dirty his hands" by responding directly to such propaganda).[33]

Published reviews were likewise favorable, making the same points as those from the House of Cinema screening.[34] For example, the Party newspaper *Pravda* devoted six columns to Vsevolod Pudovkin's canned review of the film as a struggle for peace and against world war. The reviewer for the newspaper *Evening Moscow* proclaimed that this "new victory of Soviet cinematography" demonstrated the struggle for peace and the safety of the Soviet people (*narod*).[35] *Leningrad Pravda* praised the film as "interesting, intelligent, and politically sharp," but also stressed the "two worlds" theme.[36]

On the surface, *The Meeting on the Elbe* is a straightforward piece of unvarnished propaganda. Looking deeper, however, one may find that it is not quite so simple.[37] The film also has what may be a highly subversive subtext. Many years later, Aleksandrov recalled that he was concerned that the film would not get past the censors, citing its depiction of "good Germans."[38] He may well have been concerned, but not necessarily for that reason.

Much has been made of the movie's inversion of Soviet and American behaviors in the first stages of the occupation. Film historian Maya Turovskaya writes, for example, that "the filmmakers were scarcely conscious that they were displacing their own 'moral climate' to an imaginary American."[39] Could the filmmakers have really been "scarcely conscious"? After all, the Tur brothers had served on the Western front as correspondents with the Red Army in 1945 and saw much that they did not report. Director Aleksandrov traveled to Berlin in 1947 to check out the scene there, so that he could re-create it in Riga, where most *of The Meeting on the Elbe* was shot.[40] Aleksandrov was also quite familiar with Americans and American culture, having spent, as noted above, nearly three years in the United States between 1929 and 1931.[41]

Aleksandrov was a gifted filmmaker whose considerable abilities have been overlooked in part because of his commercial success, the less serious genres with which he typically worked, and the favor his films enjoyed with Stalin. We see his gifts in evidence here, particularly in the film's structure and editing. The inversions in this film are so perfect that it is hard to see them as accidental or subconscious. The horrors of the Soviet occupation of the liberated territories are so well known today that the parallels need not be spelled out; Russian directors have in recent years filmed exposés on the painful subject of Soviet atrocities in the occupied zones.[42] (There were, of course, problems associated with the American occupation as well, but the situations were completely different.)[43]

Had the Turs forgotten what they saw? To the contrary, it may be argued that they remembered it all too well. The film's depiction of the occupation in Germany is accurate enough—if we reverse the agents. Instead of drunken Red Army troops, we see drunken Americans lurching down a shattered street, one to leer and paw at a frightened young girl standing in a barter line, marking an "X" on her back in chalk to indicate that, like the stolen art, she is property to be exported. We see Americans capitalizing on the misery of the German people; as a friend of Professor Dietrich's tells him, while waiting in a barter line, "We're trading German culture for a pack of Lucky Strikes and a can of pork and beans." We see Americans stealing technical secrets and luring unsuspecting German scientists. They crate art work that they clearly do not value as they chalk their "X's" on the front of the paintings, oblivious to the damage they might be doing. Americans chop down a forest, take all the best food for themselves and for their lavish parties, and give no thought to the restoration of basic social services. The American sector of Altenstadt has been degraded to a colonial outpost.

On the other hand, it is the Soviets, not the Americans, who command the respect of the citizenry, reopen schools, restore cultural and historical artifacts, and hold free elections. Kuzmin persuades the reluctant Professor Dietrich of their righteousness to the extent that he turns over the patents; Kuzmin does not have to expropriate them forcibly. Although Kuzmin is in important ways a model Socialist Realist hero, in other ways he is not. His political stance, to name one example, is expressed quite indirectly for a film of this period. (Contrast him to the upright communist Hannah in *The Conspiracy of the Doomed.*) He neither spouts the Party line nor privileges Party membership or political cronyism, instead bypassing the proletariat in favor of that representative of the old German intelligentsia, Professor Dietrich. Dietrich is, after all, openly hostile to Soviet power and so anti-communist that he has disowned his son Kurt.[44] Kuzmin does not attempt to punish Walter, the child who distributed the Nazi flyers, nor does he attempt to expose him. Furthermore, Kuzmin holds meetings in churches, not attempting to transform the edifices for more useful social purposes. He declares the love of the Soviet people for Americans; he is learning English to better communicate with them. ("We love America—the home of brave and honest people.")

Of course, the East Germans or Hungarians or Czechs or Poles who were encouraged to watch this film knew full well that it was absurd and did not reflect their experiences with the Soviet regime in any respect. (According to Norman Naimark, East Germans complained that Soviet films were in general "too heavy" and that "poor-quality copies of films and inaccurate and clumsy dubbing also gave Soviet films a bad reputation in the zone.")[45] Therefore, even if they had had no direct contact at all with the Americans, they would likely have inferred that if the film was wrong about the Soviets it was wrong about the Americans, too. Nevertheless, Soviet authorities appeared to have believed that *The Meeting on the Elbe* would serve a useful purpose in justifying their new empire to its citizens—for example, they reported the supposedly highly positive reactions of the German audiences with pride.

But what about the Soviet mass audience, the millions that made the picture the number one box office draw? Propaganda is, of course, intended to persuade. In some respects, this film was a balm. It reassures Soviet citizens that Soviet behavior, despite rumors they may have heard from returning veterans, was above criticism in the occupied territories. It is accurate in showing that not all Germans welcomed the Soviets, but that German suspicions could be overcome. It explains the split between the Soviets and the Americans by displaying American behavior and hostility toward the Soviets, hostility that Major Kuzmin does not reciprocate.

Reception is the thorniest aspect of film research. We tend to accept critical opinion as if it reflected that of the general audience. Audience reactions were always reported for important Soviet films like this one, but they always sounded the same. Soviet citizens well understood the perils of speaking their mind. However, through memoirs and historical studies of the World War II generation, we have a much better idea of the extreme disaffection of the educated Soviet population with the postwar regime.[46] It appears that many were inclined to discount public pronouncements just because of the source (the Party and the government), preferring to rely on rumors instead. Certainly the war veterans knew this rosy picture was not true—even though they were not about to broadcast the negative aspects of their wartime experiences.

In fact, many aspects of the portrayal of the Soviet regime, as embodied by Major Kuzmin, that look so wrong to the Western eye may have looked wrong to Soviet spectators, too. Of course there were Major Kuzmins. There were many—and some of them ended up disgraced for being "too sympathetic" to the Germans, the Hungarians, the Poles. But Major Kuzmin does not act the way a "stalwart communist" (*krepkii kommunist*)—or any Soviet citizen—would be expected to act. He should have known not to trust Professor Dietrich and Janet Sherwood, both foreigners, one openly anticommunist, the other with the notoriously anticommunist occupation of journalist. Nor would any Party member consort so openly and in such a friendly fashion with an American, not to mention the exchange of affectionate mementos, as Major Hill and Major Kuzmin do at the end of the film.

There is much more about the film that would have seemed wrong to Soviet eyes, regardless of whether they had firsthand experience in what was happening outside the country's borders. They knew what life was like within. Children who engaged in sabotage—like Walter, who spread the

The Meeting on the Elbe: Major Hill and Major Kuzmin raise a glass in friendship. Source: British Film Institute (BFI).

Nazi leaflets—did not receive a pat on the head. (And if they were being treated that way in Germany, why there and not here?) Why were the Dietrichs not immediately ejected from their spacious house or relegated to one room so that it could be redistributed to workers, or at least to other Soviet officers? This had happened in the USSR. Where were the investigations of the Nazis who were hiding in plain sight? Where were the trials of those who opposed the new regime? Why was East Germany being rebuilt with Soviet funds when the USSR remained in a state of collapse?

The Cold War pictures that followed *The Meeting on the Elbe* scored mixed success as propaganda, even though their genres made them popular with the audiences. *The Secret Mission,* for example, which featured a Soviet spy named Masha (Marthe, in her German incarnation) doubling as a member of the SS, had a production history that belied its box office standing in 1950. The Ministry of Cinematography's Artistic Council criticized the film from a variety of angles. It felt the lack of potent opposition minimized Masha's achievements as a spy, which included self-annihilation, the ultimate in Soviet heroism.[47] It thought that the very "adventure" and "detective" characteristics that viewers enjoyed diminished the film's political impact. It criticized the portrayal of Hitler as too hyperbolic, despite the precedents set by *The Fall of Berlin*'s Hitler.[48] Council members even fretted that the actor

cast as Martin Bormann had an unsuitably "Russian face," to which director Romm responded in exasperation that the real Bormann did too.[49] Any
director would have had difficulty reconciling such contradictory demands,
and Romm's frustration with the council was palpable. The finished film is
choppy, and the propaganda message is often disconnected from the action,
but it is nevertheless a suspense-filled action picture, a rarity for Soviet cinema at this time.

Of the remaining Cold War films of the period, only *The Court of Honor*
may be said to have a clear message, successfully transmitted, without contradictions. The brilliant but vain Soviet scientist, Dobrotvorsky, is tricked
into thinking that the United States believes knowledge has no boundaries,
when all it wants is to steal his formula for financial gain. After public de-
nunciation and repentance at the court of honor, Dobrotvorsky is redeemed
and allowed to continue at his laboratory, prestige intact, but his naiveté
about Americans is gone.

For other films, the propaganda message is partly obscured. In *They Have
a Homeland,* set in Germany, many Soviet children are not rescued from the
villainy of the British and Americans, leading to a worrisome question about
the strength of Soviet power. In *The Conspiracy of the Doomed,* set in one of
the newly emerging "people's democracies," the native communist and antifascist fighter Hannah is a model citizen and good friend of the Soviet Union,
but the persistence of Western culture among other members of the government is marked. The modernist buildings and avant-garde art offer a thrill-
ing contrast to shoddy postwar Soviet building projects and the ubiquitous
portraits of Stalin.

Clearly a new path to political persuasion was much needed. After Stalin's death, it became possible. Although negative propaganda continued,
positive propaganda came to the forefront, as we see in the next chapter
with *Spring on Zarechnaya Street.*

Beware! It Might Happen Here:
Man on a Tightrope

Out of the mire on the edge of the fir forest, the trucks and caravans, the
elephants and menagerie begin to move. "Roll! Let 'em roll!" shouts the manager, waving frenzied arms at the lumbering vehicles. Pom-pom-pom go the
trombones as the circus follows the brass band through the Bavarian valley.

All that is tawdry and garish, yet somehow indomitably brave and cheerful, is on the move. The clowns in their exploding car; the Chinese juggler;
the "Duchess" on her *haute école* horse; the dwarf in the pram smoking a
cigar; the performing dog walking on its front legs.

Man on a Tightrope: Disguised as a communist border guard, roustabout Joe Vosdek leads Cirkus Cernik to freedom at the climax of the film. Courtesy of the Academy of Motion Picture Arts and Sciences (AMPAS).

But it is no ordinary circus parade that takes the winding road through the valley . . . on toward the bridge across the river, on to the barbed-wire barricades and machine-gun posts on the frontier.

Under the banner proclaiming "Cirkus Cernik" on the front of the heaviest truck is a battering ram; under the wet-white grin of the clowns are lines of anxiety. For every member of the circus knows what is at stake. They are trying the greatest bluff of their lives. They are making a dash for freedom out of communist-controlled Czechoslovakia into the American zone of Germany.

Few American movies of the 1940s and early 1950s could better this, the nail-biting, suspenseful climax to Elia Kazan's *Man on a Tightrope.* Fewer movies still, at the same time, offered viewers a more compelling case for why America needed to stand up to Soviet "extremism." In contrast with *The Meeting on the Elbe, Man on a Tightrope* does not depict a direct confrontation between the U.S. and Soviet armed forces. In this sense, it is actually more representative of both the Cold War itself—the definitive proxy war—and how American cinema portrayed the conflict. Instead, Kazan's movie takes cinemagoers behind the Iron Curtain to show what communism holds in store for them. If *The Meeting on the Elbe* stands out as the only important Soviet film of the postwar period to focus on reconstruction in a satellite state, then *Man on a Tightrope* was one of the first Hollywood exposés of life in one of those states. By depicting the transplantation of a stultifying and repressive Soviet culture into a once democratic, open, modern, and rich Czechoslovakia, Kazan's movie mimicked Aleksandrov's depiction of the transplantation of American corruption and materialism into a once quaint, civilized Altenstadt.

Like *The Meeting on the Elbe, Man on a Tightrope,* too, accuses the new Cold War enemy of perfidy and imperialism—not at the messy end of the Second World War, however, but shortly afterward, by subjugating a country it claimed to have liberated from the Nazis. That country, Czechoslovakia, was not just any Soviet satellite. It was the most Westernized of them all, with a vibrant capitalist economy prior to the Second World War. Czechoslovakia had been the last of the countries under Red Army occupation to turn communist, in 1948, and had been depicted as a center of U.S.-Vatican intrigue in Mosfilm's *The Conspiracy of the Doomed* (1950). In the West, Czechoslovakia also symbolized the bankruptcy of a policy of appeasing dictators, courtesy of the notorious September 1938 agreement struck between Adolf Hitler and Neville Chamberlain in Munich—the city where, as luck would have it, Kazan's film was shot.

Compared with *The Meeting on the Elbe, Man on a Tightrope* focuses less on the direct threat that the Soviet Union poses to U.S. security and more on why Soviet communism represents America's ideological Other. In this sense, it builds on the foundations established by Hollywood movies of the interwar years, like *Ninotchka,* referred to in chapter 1. That said, *Man on a Tightrope* constructs the Cold War enemy less dogmatically than either Aleksandrov's film or many other American movies of the era. *Man on a Tightrope* was consequently more likely to be believed.

As noted in chapter 1, Hollywood wasted little time in declaring war on communism once relations between Washington and Moscow broke down in the mid- to late 1940s. The industry's first Cold War movie, William Wellman's *The Iron Curtain,* was released by Twentieth Century-Fox in May 1948, two months after the USSR's *The Russian Question.* Other studios soon followed suit, the titles of their films—*Walk a Crooked Mile* (Gordon Douglas, 1948), *Conspirator* (Victor Saville, 1949), *Spy Hunt* (George Sherman, 1950), for example—clearly signposting their Red-baiting credentials. Such movies helped get HUAC investigators off producers' backs and served to underscore the super-patriotic consensus developing across the United States during the McCarthy era. By the mid-1950s, Hollywood had made upward of a hundred movies that explicitly attacked either communism or the Soviet Union. Soviet communism remained the chief enemy thereafter, with China, North Vietnam, Cuba and others given occasional walk-on parts.

Few of these early Hollywood movies were direct equivalents of *The Meeting on the Elbe* in terms of boasting a top-notch cast and crew. Warner Bros.' *Big Jim McLain* (Edward Ludwig, 1952), which starred John Wayne as a HUAC investigator rooting out communists in Hawaii, and MGM's aforementioned *Never Let Me Go* (Delmer Daves, 1953), a romantic adventure set in the Soviet Union and starring Clark Gable, perhaps came closest in this regard.[50] In terms of sheer volume, Hollywood's early Cold War salvos far outgunned their Soviet counterparts, at a ratio of about ten to one. They amounted to only 5 percent of all the U.S.-made films released during the period, however. It is therefore possible to argue that the Soviet Union's Cold War films were more influential, or were at least seen by proportionately more people, because they amounted to double that—10 percent—of the industry's output.

As we saw in chapter 1, the vast majority of Hollywood's early Cold War material was of a negative, crude nature that focused on the threat of domestic subversion. Communists were shown to be undermining the United States in a variety of devious ways, ranging from acts of sabotage, espionage, and drug smuggling to infiltrating labor unions, atomic laboratories, university faculties, and even churches in order to spread the Party line.

Though it would continue to raise the specter periodically right through the end of the Cold War, Hollywood's obsession with the ideological "enemy within" soon passed. What took its place was an important subgenre of Cold War films that focused on political subversion—defined as dissidence or resistance—within the Communist bloc. Making such movies made good sense commercially and politically. They could be based in mysterious, even exciting locations; they shed light on the mysteries of life on what quickly became known as the Other Side; they normally contained highly charged dramatic elements, centering on the theme of defection and escape; and, like *The Meeting on the Elbe,* many of them could be bracketed within the popular spy thriller genre.

Typically, Hollywood presented communist subversives in the United States either as gullible, dysfunctional loners, hysterical fanatics, or power-hungry, treacherous snobs. In contrast, anticommunist rebels in Eastern Europe were characterized as reluctant heroes fighting to liberate their families or countries from totalitarianism. By exposing the brutality of life behind the Iron Curtain, and detailing the extraordinary lengths people would go to escape it, these movies underlined audiences' perceptions that the world was divided into two sub-universes: a free and open West and an enslaved and closed East. Moreover, films depicting conditions on the Other Side were able to show in a graphic, semi-documentary style what America itself or other Western countries might look like if communists took power.

Like *The Meeting on the Elbe* to some extent, *Man on a Tightrope* was based on real-life events. In the summer of 1950, Western newspapers were awash with accounts of ingenious or dramatic escapes from Eastern Europe, including one by a German circus troupe, Circus Brumbach, from East to West Berlin. (The Berlin Wall would be built in 1961.)[51] In January 1952, a novelette based on the Brumbach story appeared in the British monthly magazine *Lilliput,* penned by an English soccer player-turned-writer, Neil Paterson. A few months later, Twentieth Century-Fox paid Paterson $50,000 for the rights to his story, then hired playwright and Oscar-winning scriptwriter Robert E. Sherwood to adapt it for the screen.[52]

Unlike the script for *The Meeting on the Elbe,* Sherwood's work on *Man on a Tightrope* was not filtered through a complex, official bureaucracy. Given his gift for political material and nose for propaganda, however, this was probably unnecessary. Sherwood had won the Pulitzer Prize in 1940 for his anti-Stalinist play *There Shall Be No Night,* about the Soviet invasion of Finland. After Pearl Harbor, he had worked as a speechwriter for Franklin D. Roosevelt before serving for a time as Director of the Office of War Information. His Oscar-winning screenplay for *The Best Years of Our Lives* (William Wyler, 1946) had demonstrated a real empathy for the differences experienced by veterans returning to civilian life.[53]

Drafting the script for *Man on a Tightrope,*[54] Sherwood kept close to Paterson's outline but sharpened the novelette's anti-Soviet, pro-Western messages in key areas. Most important, perhaps, Sherwood stuck with Paterson's idea of turning the German-based Brumbach Circus into the Czech-based Cirkus Cernik. Traditionally, Hollywood features depicting political affairs overseas had been geographically nonspecific, for fear of upsetting foreign censors. Setting *Man on a Tightrope* explicitly in present-day Czechoslovakia—an early caption gives us its locale—lent the movie a semi-documentary appearance and dramatized recent events in the one Soviet satellite the American public probably knew best. The communist coup in Prague in early 1948 had been widely covered in the American media, with newspapers condemning the death of Czech foreign minister Jan Masaryk, whom the communists claimed had fallen from a window, as early proof of the Soviets' predilection for state-sanctioned murder. Sherwood rewrote Paterson's escape route, taking the circus troupe from Czechoslovakia into the American zone of West Germany rather than Austria. This had the twin benefits of drawing American audiences more directly into the plot and rationalizing U.S. intervention in Europe.

Next, Sherwood fleshed out the political and cultural motivations for escape. This was, of course, critical. A large part of the reason Gustav Brumbach had fled East Berlin in 1950 was in fact to save his property from government expropriation. In Sherwood's script, Cirkus Cernik leaves Czechoslovakia not for financial reasons but in order to save its soul or, in the case of its leader, Karel, his very life. The communist government is blackmailing the circus into making its performances ideologically correct. In particular, the Propaganda Ministry is insisting on the circus portraying America as racist. America's racial divide was Washington's Achilles heel during the early decades of the Cold War and, as we saw in the nightclub scene in *The Meeting on the Elbe,* a theme that Soviet propagandists constantly played up. Karel Cernik interprets the ministry's orders as a form of mind control that runs entirely contrary to the circus spirit of free-flowing entertainment.[55]

Sherwood then beefed up the role played by a U.S. Army deserter called Joe Foster in Paterson's novelette and radically changed the character's backstory. In the script, Joe is turned into a Czech expatriate called Vosdek who escapes Hitler by migrating to the United States in 1939 and then enlists in the U.S. Army to help rescue his native country from Nazism. Toward the end of the war in Europe, Vosdek then absconds from the U.S. military, not, as was the case in the novelette, because his American wife has filed for divorce, but in order to search heroically for his missing father. (Unlike Janet Sherwood's in *The Meeting on the Elbe,* therefore, Vosdek's desire to be reunited with his father is genuine.) Finding himself trapped behind Red lines after peace is declared in 1945, Vosdek's consuming ambition is to escape Czechoslovakia's newest jailors and, after that, rid Europe of Nazism's natural successor, communism. During this stage of the Cold War in particular, the U.S. government and media constantly linked the two "isms" like this, often under the usefully elastic umbrella term "totalitarianism." Numerous other references to the Second World War in the film further underlined this overlap between Nazism and communism.[56]

Finally, Sherwood added a more exciting climax to the whole story, one that he believed audiences would crave and that also underlined both the circus troupe's heroism and America's liberationist strategy. In reality, Circus Brumbach had escaped gradually and by stealth, its only viable option. Even in Paterson's story the circus had fled quietly under cover of darkness. In the film, however, Cirkus Cernik crosses the armed Czech-German frontier dramatically en masse in broad daylight while being fired upon by border guards. Vosdek leads from the front, bravely using a homemade bomb to scatter the guards and a gun to keep them at bay. Tragically, Karel, the stoic circus manager, dies at the hands of a communist spy.

Twentieth Century-Fox originally penciled in one of two consummate Hollywood professionals to direct *Man on a Tightrope.* The first, Russian-born Anatole Litvak, had been in charge of combat photography and motion picture operations during the 1944 D-Day landings. The second, Henry

Hathaway, had pioneered the postwar trend of shooting features on actual exterior locations in semi-documentary style, and had just finished the Cold War espionage thriller *Diplomatic Courier* (1952). However, the job eventually fell to Elia Kazan, for $100,000 plus 10 percent of the profits. What initially looks like an odd choice of director can be explained by the politics of the second Red Scare.[57]

Kazan was perhaps the most gifted theater and movie director of his generation, a man who had helped revolutionize acting via the Method, and who, through boldly liberal social problem films for Fox like *Gentleman's Agreement* (1947), personified Hollywood's brief shift to the left in the mid-1940s. Kazan's fame and his membership in the Communist Party in the 1930s made him a valuable target for HUAC. As a consequence, despite having defended the Hollywood Ten in the late 1940s, in April 1952 Kazan presented HUAC with a list of communist "names" in the film industry in order, as he saw it, to save his career. Kazan also bought space in the *New York Times* for a statement urging others in his position to do the same. After his testimony, however, he was not restored to favor within the industry. Indeed, Kazan became known as a "rat," despised by many on the Hollywood left until his dying days. Thus when the chance of directing *Man on a Tightrope* came up, he took it. As Fox's head of production, Darryl Zanuck, told Kazan, the movie would prove the sincerity of his HUAC statement.[58]

When Kazan started work on *Man on a Tightrope* in May 1952, he hated the first outline delivered by Sherwood, pronouncing it unbelievable and crude: "all-black and all-white characters, typical propaganda stuff." The director took a somewhat different view, however, after spending weeks filming *Man on a Tightrope* in and around Munich in the West German state of Bavaria in the summer of 1952. Members of the Brumbach Circus had been recruited to appear in or work on the movie, and Kazan was moved by their accounts of communist oppression. Kazan was further shocked to hear from a visiting State Department official how one of the East Germans among the film crew had been burnt escaping to the West under a car hood. Communist-controlled Radio Leipzig then threatened to harm the families of East German crew members, forcing one of them to quit. Kazan's visits to the heavily fortified East German border turned what hitherto had been an abstraction to him, the "Iron Curtain," into reality. These experiences, some of which were used in the publicity for *Man on a Tightrope,* plus the need to hire a bodyguard to protect his family in New York from communists angered by his HUAC testimony, convinced Kazan that his movie needed to be hard-hitting yet credible in its condemnation of Stalinism.[59]

Man on a Tightrope benefited greatly in this regard by being shot in Bavaria using an all-German crew. This level of German technical assistance was unprecedented for a major American production and lent the movie a European authenticity. Location work in Munich and near Fall in the Bavarian Tyrol country, where the River Isar was used as a fictional line of delineation between Germany and Czechoslovakia, added to the verisimilitude. On the back lot of the Bavaria-Filmkunst Studio in the Munich suburb of Geiselgasteig, the West German film capital, the unit constructed an entire Czech village, complete with a huge Stalin Works nationalized factory.[60]

Staff of the Munich-based Radio Free Europe also acted as advisers on *Man on a Tightrope*, in order, as Fox put it, "to insure technical accuracy of the Czech scenes." RFE's headquarters were situated in the beautiful surroundings of Munich's Englischer Garten, where, ironically given *Tightrope*'s subject matter, the rehabilitated Nazi spy chief Reinhard Gehlen helped provide base security. Funded secretly by the CIA, and publicly supported by Hollywood stars such as Frank Sinatra and Rock Hudson, RFE provided surrogate home radio services, alternatives to the Party-dominated domestic media in the "captive nations." The broadcasters sought to create anarchy in the Eastern bloc by pointing to the moral, spiritual, and economic emptiness of communism and, in association with President Harry Truman's Escapee Program, launched in March 1952, by encouraging flight from the East. RFE tried to ensure its output was not overtly polemical or preachy, which may help to explain the relatively moderate tone taken by *Man on a Tightrope*.[61]

Meanwhile, back in Los Angeles, Darryl Zanuck, a vastly experienced film executive who had served as a lieutenant colonel in charge of a documentary film unit during the Second World War, and who had recently made *The Desert Fox* (1951) with Henry Hathaway partly to promote German-American reconciliation, toned down those parts of the script he believed were clumsily political. If the movie was too propagandistic, he warned, it risked being branded a "message" picture, which would be counterproductive commercially and politically. Zanuck therefore cut an opening sequence that showed a bunch of gaunt slave laborers standing beside incongruously cheerful propaganda posters. He also excised a scene at a shoe factory showing downtrodden workers being bribed with gasoline coupons and harangued by a Party orator to increase productivity for "our great march forward to world revolution."[62] (This self-imposed control contrasts with the conflicting demands of censorship for Soviet films of this era.)

Together, Zanuck and Kazan cast *Man on a Tightrope* with care. Kazan rescued prominent Hollywood liberal Fredric March from the blacklist to play the lead role of Karel the circus manager. March was a mature stage and screen actor whose forte was portraying characters in mental anguish. Gloria Grahame, with whom Kazan had worked on *Crossfire* (1947), played Karel's flirtatious wife, Zama. Kazan indulged in a private joke by casting

Man on a Tightrope: Fesker confronts Karel Cernik. Courtesy of the Academy of Motion Picture Arts and Sciences (AMPAS).

Adolphe Menjou as the evil communist propaganda official Fesker. Menjou was among the founders in 1944 of the Motion Picture Alliance for the Preservation of American Ideals and a well-known supporter of the Hollywood blacklist.[63]

Shot in black and white, colors that reflected the monochrome world it portrays, *Man on a Tightrope* opens on a slightly mysterious note. A ramshackle array of circus vans is quietly traveling along a road, when a convoy of troops in armored vehicles brutally forces it into the ditch. Wagons full of what look like emaciated slave laborers pass through. Where is this, and why do the circus people look so tired, as if their maltreatment is a day-to-day occurrence? Is it a war zone? Is it a contemporary documentary, or a fictional representation of the past—Nazi-occupied Europe, perhaps?

The answer, we soon learn, is present-day Czechoslovakia, a country experiencing an even more insidious form of occupation than what it had endured under the Nazis, with its people held captive not for military or racial reasons but for the sake of a false, utopian ideology. That ideology, Soviet communism, is turning Eastern Europe into one vast prison, surrounded by barbed wire, watchtowers, and guards zealously poised over automatic weapons. Communism, like every "system" (the word is used regularly in the movie's dialogue), deprives people of their individuality and robs them of their self-respect. It claims to be efficient but is choked by internal contradictions and economic sclerosis. It even politicizes entertainment. Ultimately, the film tells us, communism drives everyone to despair. For those who are willing to risk their very lives, the only way out is to seek sanctuary in the West.

All this would be too complex, too abstract to comprehend, were we not to see and experience it through the eyes of a small group or one person in particular. By focusing on a circus troupe—typically care-free outsiders with an internationalist outlook—*Man on a Tightrope* teaches us that communism brooks no "deviant" minorities. It wants to engineer a society of automatons, by force if necessary. At the same time, by concentrating on the commonplace troubles faced by the troupe's leader, who is also a loving father and jealous husband, the film both humanizes political dissidence and makes it easier for the audience to put itself into the picture.

Karel Cernik (March) is a proud, mild-mannered, once vibrant circus man eking out an increasingly drab and colorless existence in communist Czechoslovakia. Karel is struggling to keep together his beloved circus, which belonged to him before being nationalized by the communist government. The government has allowed Karel to manage Cirkus Cernik, but, under a regime that distrusts spontaneity and would like to bureaucratize fun as part of a Five Year Entertainment Plan, this is an almost impossible task. He is losing his best workers to forced factory work. Worse, he is constantly being hounded by the secret police, the SNB, and the Propaganda Ministry, which wants him to incorporate anti-Western themes into the show.

Karel, who performs as a clown and tightrope walker, must also contend with a willful daughter, Tereza (Terry Moore), who is a bareback rider in the show. Tereza is in love with a roustabout, Joe Vosdek (Cameron Mitchell), who Karel fears might be a police spy. On top of all this, Karel's marriage is on the rocks. He suspects his flirtatious wife (Grahame) of having an affair with another member of the troupe but is too weary to do anything about it. Karel's lassitude is highly significant. *The Meeting on the Elbe* suggested that capitalism distorts sexuality, in the shape of the "manly" Mrs. MacDermott. *Man on a Tightrope* shows us that communism emasculates, sapping real men such as Karel of their passionate instincts.

When Cirkus Cernik puts on a show its bedraggled condition is blindingly obvious. Its flea-bitten tents have holes and its ropes are rotten—"like everything else in this country," mutters one circus hand. Despite this, the crowds, clapping along to the American big-band song "Chattanooga Choo Choo,"[64] enjoy themselves enormously, laughing hysterically as if this is their only respite from the ennui brought on by communism. At the same time, the cameras linger on the anguished desperation behind the painted smiles and feigned merriment of the show's performers. The low-key photogra-

Man on a Tightrope: Zama Cernik and other down-trodden circus members betray the true face of communism. Courtesy of the Academy of Motion Picture Arts and Sciences (AMPAS).

phy, masterminded by George Krause, an East Berliner with bitter personal experience of the Russian secret police, accentuates communism's gray, featureless landscape.[65] Shops are nonexistent, people's clothes are plain and inexpressive, and the mangy circus lion survives on slops and sawdust.

One day, just before another show, SNB officers dressed in dark Gestapo-esque leathers frog-march Karel away to police headquarters in Pilsen. This is a key scene. The headquarters look like a dungeon. In reality, it was a centuries-old wine cellar, housed in the partially bombed Bavarian Royal Residence in Munich's city center. The residence provided exactly the atmosphere Kazan felt necessary for his purpose: cold, wet, seemingly endless underground chambers—"foreboding and bare enough to chill the marrow of a Spanish Inquisitor," Fox's publicity boasted.[66]

Here, the police chief interrogates Karel, asking him why he is not performing a government-dictated act in which he is to portray an American "Negro" being abused by a Wall Street tycoon. Karel sheepishly explains that such anti-capitalist jibes always fall flat. Pointing his finger menacingly at Karel, the chief tells him that unless he resumes the required act within forty-eight hours his circus will be turned over to a rival, Barovik (Robert Beatty). On the water-dripping walls hang large photographs of Stalin and Lenin, flanking a smaller likeness of Czech president Klement Gottwald. The visible tab names on the files behind the chief's desk are those of actual anticommunist Czechs, starting with the imprisoned Archbishop Josef Beran.

Karel is about to be dismissed when Fesker (Menjou), a slimy official from the Propaganda Ministry, casually asks him about the radio in his caravan. Karel nervously states that the radio cannot receive shortwave transmissions, and after he is sent out, the SNB officials are angered that Karel's dossier did not contain information about the radio. Although the police chief believes that Karel poses no threat, Fesker disagrees with his "comrade" and declares that he will watch the troupe personally from now on. Piqued, the chief orders his subordinates to investigate Fesker, a suspicious-looking "intellectual," as well as Karel. Clearly, information is highly controlled in a communist state. Listening to Western radio broadcasts is a crime. And no one trusts anyone in a surveillance society. Even the government's security and propaganda apparatus are at loggerheads.

Unknown to the officials, Karel does listen to Western shortwave transmissions and, inspired by news of a recent spate of escapes from the Iron Curtain, has decided to move his circus over the border to Bavaria. That night, he discloses his plan to escape into the American zone and tells his more reliable associates there must be a spy in the circus who reported the information about the radio and clown act. Meanwhile, Karel's chief suspect, Joe, is telling Tereza of his own escape plan. It transpires that Joe is an entirely innocent character, a U.S. Army deserter who slipped across the German-Czech border into the Russian zone after VE-Day to search for his Czech-born father, who had been arrested by the Nazis during the war. After discovering that his father had died in a concentration camp, Joe found himself trapped inside its Soviet equivalent and joined Cirkus Cernik in the hope of making it back to the West when it reached the border of the American zone.

The next morning the burly Barovik, an apparent collaborator, arrives and reveals that he knows all about Karel's plan to escape. Barovik's information came from a dwarf called Kalka (played by Hansi, a real-life Brumbach member), who had eavesdropped on Karel after being fired by him. Barovik assures Karel that although they are rivals, they are both circus men, and that he will not betray him to the communists. Karel agrees to leave behind some tent wagons that Barovik will "ambush" at the nearby town of Mikulov, thereby distracting the police. The scene ends with the pair staging a fake fight to keep the SNB from guessing the truth about their conference.

Karel prepares to make for the frontier at once. His plan is a daring one. The troupe is to be dressed for its usual pre-performance parade. As it approaches the military checkpoint near a river bridge, across which lies the American zone, the circus hands will release the wolves to create a diversion, throw a handmade bomb among the Red sentries, and crash the bar-

Man on a Tightrope: Karel, Joe, and Tereza plan their escape. Courtesy of the Academy of Motion Picture Arts and Sciences (AMPAS).

rier with the leading truck. Zama, admiring her husband's new-found courage and the fact that he has slapped her in the face like a "real man," kisses him passionately. However, Krofta (Richard Boone), who is in charge of the equipment, demands an explanation of the change of route and reveals himself as an ideologue and the police spy. Karel, having knocked out and bound Krofta, goes to the police headquarters for the necessary travel permit for Mikulov. There, Fesker authorizes the permit, with the objective of pouncing when the circus manager makes his fatal, treacherous mistake.

The troupe moves off. A rural, civilized idyll—the wide-open space of free Bavaria—beckons. As the troupe approaches the checkpoint, Joe overcomes a sentry, dons his uniform, and prepares to escort the circus to safety. In Pilsen, meanwhile, Fesker is about to pursue the circus when he is arrested by an SNB sergeant for exceeding his authority in issuing Karel's travel permit. He is dispatched to Prague, presumably to be shot.

As the cavalcade comes closer to the bridge, Krofta loosens his bonds and mortally wounds Karel before being killed himself by Kalka. The Red guards are taken completely by surprise when the trucks belonging to this innocent-looking procession ram the barricades. Joe then lobs the bomb at the barrier and uses his pistol to hold off the soldiers while the others run and drive the caravans across the bridge, to the bemusement of the American soldiers on the other side. Zama's former love interest, the once cowardly

Man on a Tightrope: Karel sees the light of freedom moments before dying from a communist bullet. Courtesy of the Academy of Motion Picture Arts and Sciences (AMPAS).

lion tamer Rudolph (Alex D'Arcy), sacrifices himself on the bridge while providing cover for the troupe.

In the final scene, the circus people are stunned by the news that they have won freedom at the cost of their leader's life. Just like Moses, he led his people to the Promised Land but died before reaching it. The show must go on, however. Zama and Tereza issue orders for a performance to be given that night, just as Karel demanded in his last breath. In the time-honored tradition of real troupers, Cirkus Cernik, now safely in the West, lines up in formation and prepares to set up the Big Top.

Man on a Tightrope enjoyed a more than timely release in April 1953. The Western press had recently been gripped by the "show trial" and execution of Czech communist leader Rudolf Slánský on charges of fomenting a counterrevolution. The sudden news of Joseph Stalin's death in March 1953 then sparked the first Eastern bloc uprisings of the Cold War. In East Berlin, workers' demonstrations turned into a general strike, an eruption that soon spread to other parts of East Germany before the Red Army crushed it. In Pilsen, large-scale riots at a Skoda car factory, which quickly spread to other Czech cities, saw demonstrators trampling portraits of Stalin and Gottwald underfoot. These events were greeted with considerable excitement in the American press and encouraged some official U.S. propagandists to believe that the Czech Communist regime was about to collapse.[67]

In light of these incidents, plus press reports gleaned from U.S. government sources that the Soviet Ministry of Culture had recently started cleansing Russian circuses of ideological impurities,[68] it is not surprising that the overwhelming majority of American reviewers thought *Man on a Tightrope* had great box office potential and that its plot was extremely believable. The film "captures the terrible terror that blankets all people behind the Iron Curtain," proclaimed the *Los Angeles Examiner.*[69] There was an element of playing to the politically fashionable gallery here, just as there was in the Soviet Union with regard to *The Meeting on the Elbe.* Many U.S. newspapers and film trade journals made a habit of praising anticommunist pictures during this period—the height of McCarthyism—lest they appeared "Un-American." What sets the reviews of *Man on a Tightrope* apart from many others, however, is their praise for its moderation. *Time* thought the film had a "nightmarish quality," while the *Hollywood Reporter* called it "inspiring" for "swinging a devastating wallop at the police state without requiring a single speech on the evils of Communism." One can imagine Darryl Zanuck's pride, and relief, on reading such plaudits. The same goes for the Radio Free Europe staff in Munich who had cautioned against crude Red-baiting.[70]

Like most explicitly anticommunist Hollywood movies of the early 1950s, *Man on a Tightrope* was designed predominantly for domestic consumption. It sought to strengthen the anti-Soviet consensus within the United States by building on the general anticommunist framework established by the government and media, and, in the case of Kazan's film, by dramatizing real-life tales of heroism behind the Iron Curtain. This helps explain why the movie's premiere in New York in June 1953 was heralded as a fund-raising event for the International Rescue Committee, an organization that provided emergency relief for escapees from the Eastern bloc. It is important to bear in mind how influential films like *Man on a Tightrope* could be during this early period of the Cold War, before the barriers between the East and West grew more porous from the late 1950s onward (as we see in the next chapter) and when the visual media were in a peculiarly strong position to determine the public's views of what life was like on the Other Side.[71]

In any event, *Man on a Tightrope* did not fulfill its U.S. box office potential. Despite being named as one of the ten best films of 1953 by the *New York Times,* it failed to appear on *Variety*'s year-end list of financial successes. One sign that the film had captured at least some part of the American imagination, though, is the fact that it was turned into a major radio play in December 1953, featuring Hollywood star Edward G. Robinson, who himself had recently "escaped"—from the blacklist.[72]

There are also indications the movie played well overseas, especially in Western Europe, where the threat from Soviet communism was felt most keenly. In Britain, while the communist *Daily Worker* newspaper predictably condemned *Man on a Tightrope* as "hate propaganda," the country's most prestigious paper, *The Times,* declared it "the best, most exciting, and most reasonable film with an Iron Curtain setting yet to be made." West Berlin's executive body, the Senate, then awarded it a special prize at the Berlin international film festival. And the International Broadcasting Service of the U.S. State Department adapted the movie for a forty-five-minute radio program to be transmitted in the Far East and Europe, including behind the Iron Curtain. Its reception there is unknown.[73]

In the years ahead, *Man on a Tightrope* was followed by a steady stream of Hollywood movies attesting to Eastern bloc tyranny. The majority of these focused on the issue of defection and the quest to escape to Freedom—media and official shorthand for the West. America, the fabled Land of Freedom, was nearly always the defectors' preferred destination. Some of these films, like *The Secret Ways* (Phil Karlson, 1961), fictionalized real-life incidents of Soviet military brutality, most notably in Hungary in 1956. Others, such as *Escape from East Berlin* (Robert Siodmak, 1962), focused on that most contested of Cold War cities. Others still—*White Nights* (1985), for example, which starred the Russian defector and renowned ballet dancer Mikhail Baryshnikov—highlighted the suppression of dissent within the Soviet Union itself.[74] Almost all owe at least something to the pattern established in the early Cold War years by movies such as *Man on a Tightrope.*

CONCLUSION

This comparison of *The Meeting on the Elbe* and *Man on a Tightrope* has demonstrated the value that Soviet and American filmmakers attached to hard-hitting, negative propaganda during the earliest phase of the Cold War. In particular, it has identified the ways in which the two movies turned an ally into an enemy and helped establish an easily comprehensible framework for conflict, despite the fact that the Soviet Union and United States—Korea notwithstanding—were not conventionally at war.[75] This last point needs to be reemphasized, for it underlines the importance of the cinematic threat conveyed. It is one thing for a set of movies to reinforce the hatred of an enemy that is actually shooting at you or your loved ones. It is quite another for films to help create that hatred or sense of threat when a military standoff exists.

Our analysis has brought out the remarkable similarities shared by *The Meeting on the Elbe* and *Man on a Tightrope*. Both films were carefully constructed, the product of an industry that recognized its place within the Cold War propaganda firmament. The state played a role in the making of both films: in everything from finance through scripting to distribution in the case of *The Meeting on the Elbe,* and by way of Radio Free Europe's advice about "accuracy" in the case of *Man on a Tightrope.* Inevitably, both films drew heavily on pre–World War II stereotypes of the Other: the grasping, exploitative capitalist versus the heartless communist automaton. Unsurprisingly, both films recycled images and rhetoric from the Second World War to portray the new (or at least now fully fledged) enemy as the new Nazis.

This is not all. Both Aleksandrov's and Kazan's films highlighted the ideological nature of the East-West conflict, but through the use of readily accessible human interest stories. Both fastened onto the significance of closed borders, through which people were either being smuggled or escaping. Both internationalized the Cold War by factoring third parties into the equation, Germany and Czechoslovakia. Both were shot in the superpowers' respective spheres of influence: *The Meeting on the Elbe* in Latvia and *Man on a Tightrope* in West Germany. Both acknowledged that there was now a clear division between the two sides. And both even used music as a propaganda tool: jazz in *The Meeting on the Elbe* to signify American decadence, and the Glenn Miller big-band sound in *Man on a Tightrope* to represent America's spirit of freedom.

The differences between the two films are less numerous but equally significant. First, *The Meeting on the Elbe* is more nationalistic than *Man on a Tightrope* in terms of highlighting the Soviet Union's role in "saving" postwar Europe and in emphasizing America's threat to Soviet communism, as opposed to the communist movement as a whole. By contrast, *Man on a Tightrope*'s democratic call to arms is painted in decidedly international shades and therefore looks less ideologically blinkered. Though Aleksandrov's movie would have been seen by more people than Kazan's, it is doubtful that it traveled as successfully overseas, reports of its success in East Germany notwithstanding. This did not augur well for an industry charged with promoting worldwide revolution.

Second, *The Meeting on the Elbe* spells out its message of fear and hate more crudely than *Man on a Tightrope.* Though plenty of Hollywood Red-baiters competed with *The Meeting on the Elbe* on this level, few, like Aleksandrov's film, did so with the state's approval. This Soviet dogmatism can be attributed to the political straitjacket imposed on filmmakers during the late Stalin era, but, as we see later in the book, it would resurface at the end of the Cold War. By comparison, Hollywood's output was generally less condescending toward its audience, and, as the conflict progressed, tended to be more believable because it was more in tune with public opinion.

Finally, *Man on a Tightrope* provides an early hint of Hollywood's greater resources than its Soviet counterpart. *The Meeting on the Elbe* is certainly an impressive production, its epic choreography fully deserving of the Stalin

Prize the film received. But *Man on a Tightrope*'s script, acting, and action sequences are equally impressive, and, because Kazan's movie was relatively cheap to make, an illustration of Hollywood's more efficient filmmaking practices. *Man on a Tightrope* also benefited from Hollywood's long-established links with overseas filmmakers, in Western Europe especially. These links, in turn, expanded Hollywood's distribution and exhibition networks during the Cold War, leading to increased profits and cultural penetration.

CHAPTER FOUR

Pleasure versus Progress

If some Soviet and American movies—like *The Meeting on the Elbe* and *Man on a Tightrope*—focused on what the nation was fighting against during the Cold War, far more films told audiences what they were fighting for. More often than not, they did this by projecting the virtues and benefits of their own side's way of life. The very phrase "way of life" was central to most people's understanding of the Cold War. It simultaneously implied normality and difference and could invoke a range of emotions from loyalty and pride to comfort and passivity. If images marketing one side's way of life happened to be screened on the other side of the political divide, they might elicit quite different reactions, among them anger, ridicule, or envy.

Despite the importance of this sort of public relations material in such a long and drawn out conflict, few people have bothered to analyze it. There are three main reasons for this oversight. First, most historians instinctively define wartime propaganda in narrowly negative terms and consequently focus on those press reports, radio broadcasts, films, and other material that explicitly target the enemy. Second, rather than make their way through the thicket of literally thousands of American and Soviet movies produced during the forty-year Cold War, most scholars have opted for a short cut and fastened on to those dramatic productions that accentuated hostility and crisis.[1] Finally, and perhaps most significant, there is a long-held belief in the West that the vast majority of Hollywood movies were free from political interference during the Cold War and generally apolitical in character. While some historians have recently begun to challenge this assumption,[2] the conventional view remains that of a one-sided conflict in which Soviet filmmakers clumsily tried but failed to indoctrinate their captive audiences in the values of Marxist-Leninism, while their American counterparts concentrated on making money and entertainment.

This chapter seeks to revise matters by exploring how both the Soviet and American film industries projected the benefits of their ways of life during the 1950s. This was a decade marked by a gradual yet distinct shift away from the production of crudely offensive Cold War propaganda in both countries to a more discreet form of cinematic salesmanship. In the case of both industries, this shift reflected political and cultural changes at home and overseas. On the Soviet Union's part, the shift can be linked to the Thaw that followed Joseph Stalin's death in 1953, and to cinema's assigned role in

97

refashioning what were perceived to be outmoded images of a communist workers' paradise. In the case of the United States, the shift can be attributed to an increased need to sell "American values" abroad, for commercial and diplomatic reasons.

The movies chosen for detailed analysis in this chapter—*Roman Holiday* (1953) and *Spring on Zarechnaya Street* (1956)—exemplify the two competing visions of Western Pleasure versus Eastern Progress, or materialism versus advancement. The films also reflect the two industries' different outlooks on where their target audiences lay: at home or abroad, within their own geopolitical bloc, or even on the other side of the Iron Curtain. *Roman Holiday* and *Spring on Zarechnaya Street* were among the most artistically creative and popular Cold War films the United States and Soviet Union produced in a period when the Cold War was becoming fully institutionalized across East and West. They can usefully be categorized as flexible, "soft" propaganda.

Selling the American Dream: *Roman Holiday*

Positive American cinematic propaganda came in various guises during the Cold War. Some films literally sought to teach viewers the benefits of capitalism and were designed entirely for domestic consumption. *Story of Enterprise* (1955), for example, a simple, twelve-minute short narrated by a handsome history professor, Clinton L. Ganus Jr., and circulated principally among American high schools and colleges, presented capitalism as a dynamic force for good that simultaneously promoted individuality and wealth for all. It told a typically American rags-to-riches story of how two adventurous entrepreneurs, Tom and Agnes Carvel, had used the United States' "wonderful incentives for enterprise" to build a multimillion-dollar ice cream business from scratch in the Depression, to the point where in the 1950s their company employed over 3,000 people. *Story of Enterprise* was part of the anticommunist National Education Program funded by fundamentalist Christian George S. Benson, president of Harding College in Searcy, Arkansas. The film's patriotic overtures encouraged viewers to consider capitalism, freedom, and the American way of life as synonymous.[3]

In contrast with *Story of Enterprise* and scores of other commercially sponsored shorts made during the genre's heyday of the 1950s, relatively few mainstream Hollywood features promulgated capitalism in a heavy-handed, strict economic sense during the Cold War. Rather than sell capitalism overtly, Hollywood instead promoted capitalism indirectly and largely unwittingly, by portraying it in lifestyle terms. In this way, capitalism was seen as laying the foundations for unprecedented levels of consumerism and what, through gritted teeth, Soviet filmmakers called "ordinary affluence."[4]

In the 1950s especially, American films reveled in the material pleasures associated with the postwar U.S. economic boom, presenting their nation as a new, classless consumer democracy. Even many movies that professed to show the dark underside of affluent American family life—epitomized by James Dean's delinquent Jim in *Rebel without a Cause* (Nicholas Ray, 1955)—effectively underpinned the Cold War national consensus by suggesting that acutely personal relations outweighed wider social, political, and economic concerns. Many of the biggest hits of the decade—romantic comedies such as *The Seven Year Itch* (Billy Wilder, 1955), documentaries such as *Cinerama Holiday* (Robert L. Bendick and Philippe De Lacy, 1955), breezy musicals such as *High Society* (Charles Walters, 1956)—were lavish productions that projected America as a prosperous land of opportunity and abundance.[5]

Well-made, feel-good entertainment of this sort had cultural and political influence far beyond America's own borders. Hollywood dominated the international film trade during the Cold War. In the wake of the Second World War, the Motion Picture Export Association (MPEA), Hollywood's international trade organization, systematically smashed foreign import quota barriers to American films in tandem with the State Department, especially in Europe. This process was driven by the studios' need for commercial expansion to combat the threat from television and by Washington's desire to use Hollywood as a propaganda tool. In turn, the State Department, CIA, and film industry chiefs worked hard to censor material that might be damaging to U.S. interests overseas by, for instance, depicting America as violent or racist.[6]

As a consequence of these actions, hundreds of American films poured into foreign countries, exporting idealized versions of American life and seducing audiences through the "soft power" of attraction. Images of U.S. skyscrapers and automobiles sold American modernity, pictures of spotless homes with all modern conveniences marketed mass American affluence, while stories of rebellious teenagers and loose women advertised individualism and freedom of choice. Hollywood's high production values, encapsulated in the million-dollar movie people could watch for a few pennies or centavos, projected a powerful image of American material plenty and helped to sell liberal capitalism. Most non-American movies, including those made in the communist world, seemed aesthetically impoverished by comparison, and therefore could barely compete in what Hollywood producer Walter Wanger called "the struggle for men's minds" between East and West.[7]

Hollywood's international reach even traversed the Iron Curtain on occasions, depending on the prevailing political climate. In the 1920s, hundreds of American films were distributed in the Soviet Union, mostly silent movies by the likes of Charlie Chaplin, Harold Lloyd, and Cecil B. DeMille. With the onset of a full-blown cold war in 1945, just about the only Hollywood material Russians were allowed to see were those found among the old "trophy" films the Red Army had brought back from occupied Europe.[8] In 1958, however, Washington and Moscow signed the first of what would become regular Cold War cultural exchange agreements. As part of this, American government propaganda officials and film industry executives selected an elite set of Hollywood films they believed would best serve U.S. interests behind the Iron Curtain. Among these movies was William Wyler's *Roman Holiday* (1953), a benign romantic comedy that acted as a messenger for that quintessential American ideal—the right to have a good time.

Now considered a classic of its genre, *Roman Holiday* on the face of it has nothing whatsoever to do with the Cold War. With hindsight, however, it is now possible to see why the movie was appropriated by a U.S. government keen to sell the Western way of life. *Roman Holiday* showed the West to be modern, glamorous, full of opportunity, and fun. It portrayed a cosseted and emotionally imprisoned European monarchy being temporarily "liberated" by classless consumerism and American democratic values. And its high production values, charismatic stars, and location work in an apparently economically resurgent Italy all advertised capitalism's popularity and success.

Roman Holiday's plot is straightforward and undemanding. Though she has dutifully executed her obligations as representative of her country, Coravia, on a European goodwill tour, the lovely, nineteen-year-old Princess Ann (Audrey Hepburn) is finding it wearing. By the time she reaches Rome she is sick of schedules and public appearances, and suffers a mild case of hysteria in the privacy of the state bedroom at her country's embassy. The royal doctor gives her an injection that will make her sleep, and advises the ambassador (Harcourt Williams) to cancel her engagements for the next day, including a press conference. A bulletin is issued that the Princess is temporarily indisposed with a cold. Ann, however, not yet affected by the sleeping drug, decides to have a little fun all by herself and manages to slip, unseen, out of the embassy in the back of a van.

Joe Bradley (Gregory Peck), American correspondent for the ANS—a news service in Rome—happens upon the princess, now in a sleepy daze. Thinking she is drunk, he is faced with the choice of either turning her over to the police or letting her sleep it off in his modest apartment. Being soft-hearted, he opts for the apartment. It is not until Joe drops in at his office the next morning, where he gets a bawling out from his boss, Hennessy (Hartley Power), for being late and sees a newspaper picture of the

Roman Holiday: Unaware of his overnight guest's identity at this stage, Joe wakes up Princess Ann in his apartment. Courtesy of the Academy of Motion Picture Arts and Sciences (AMPAS).

princess, that he realizes the identity of his overnight guest. Since Hennessy, or any other news service, would pay big money for an exclusive story on Princess Ann, Joe decides to capitalize on his incredible good luck and get that exclusive interview with Her Highness. But he doesn't breathe a word to Hennessy about having the princess stashed away.

Meantime, Princess Ann's disappearance from the embassy has thrown the place into an uproar. No word of her running away must get out. Dozens of Coravian secret agents, dressed comically in identical dark suits and hats, are hastily dispatched to conduct a quiet search for her. And while all this is going on, Princess Ann, awake now, decides to prolong her stolen holiday for a few hours more. She gaily window-shops and has her long hair cut fashionably short. Joe, not wanting to lose his story, tags along and finally persuades her to let him show her Rome, during which he happily grants all her simple wishes. Needing pictures to go with his story when he writes it, Joe shares his secret with his photographer pal Irving Radovich (Eddie Albert), who trails them with his tiny lighter-camera. Ann suspects nothing.

Princess Ann has a wonderful time and loves every minute of it, even when a runaway scooter they are riding lands her and Joe temporarily in the police station. That evening they attend a lively dance on a Tiber barge and almost get caught by the secret agents searching for Her Royal Highness. By now Joe and Ann know they are in love—but each, deep inside,

Roman Holiday: Joe and Ann charm the police after their arrest for scootering recklessly around the Eternal City's streets. Courtesy of the Academy of Motion Picture Arts and Sciences (AMPAS).

knows nothing can come of it. Joe takes Ann back to the embassy after a tender farewell, and then proceeds to infuriate Hennessy by insisting he has no story on Princess Ann. Guessing how Joe feels, Irving backs him up. The next day, when the princess receives the press, Irving slips her the pictures he took along with the negatives—and she and Joe take a silent, moving goodbye to each other.

There are two main levels on which one can assess *Roman Holiday*'s public relations value. The first is the film's whole look. What made most American movies of this era stand out above their foreign competitors was their high-quality film stock. Color films especially brought a luster and aura to the gray surroundings in which many of them were viewed. William Wyler opted to shoot *Roman Holiday* in black and white due to the technical difficulties of using color stock on the city's street corners and piazzas. However, by employing as skilled a cinematographer as Henri Alekan, a Frenchman who was an expert in capturing the essence of a location, allied to his own meticulous craftsmanship, Wyler brings a vibrancy and freshness to the picture. *Roman Holiday* has a magazine-like layout—candid, immediate, and realistic—somewhat akin to Italian Neorealist cinema of the late 1940s and early 1950s.

Despite being shot in black and white, *Roman Holiday* oozes glamour. In Edith Head, Paramount had arguably the best costume designer in the world.

Over a career spanning half a century, Head fashioned outfits for some of the screen's most illustrious stars, including Bette Davis, Grace Kelly, and Paul Newman. In *Roman Holiday,* Head helped turn Audrey Hepburn, a Belgian-born twenty-three-year-old who had previously appeared only in tiny roles in British pictures, into an instant film star and an enduring international fashion icon. Hepburn developed a lengthy association with Paris fashion designer Hubert de Givenchy, the epitome of Western style and luxury, for both her on- and offscreen wardrobes. Her roles in, among others, *Funny Face* (Stanley Donen, 1957), *The Nun's Story* (Fred Zinnemann, 1959), and *Breakfast at Tiffany's* (Blake Edwards, 1961), together with her later work for UNICEF, made her the perfect role model for Western goodness.[9]

Instead of trying to hide Hepburn's waif-like physique, Head turned these into assets, making her stylish and elegant, equally attractive but different from buxom, voluptuous stars like Marilyn Monroe. When dressed as a princess, Hepburn looks for all the world a regal, fragile, bejewelled young lady. When masquerading in the plain skirt and blouse of a commoner, she appears even more beautiful—"free" and literalizing the postwar department-store mannequin look. Everyone can afford to look and feel this good, the film seems to be saying, no matter what their station in life. The fact that Hepburn was a relative newcomer when she starred in *Roman Holiday* made her appear all the more like the girl next door, as a person everyone in the audience (especially women) could relate to and with whom they could share their emotions.[10]

Rome itself—ostensibly merely the location but in reality every bit one of the movie's stars—is a picture of prosperity in Wyler's hands. As the camera takes us on a Cook's Tour of the city, we might be forgiven for thinking the Italian "economic miracle," which came into effect in the late 1950s, had already happened. We should not expect a Hollywood fairy tale, no matter how modern, to have dwelt on the penury many Italians were experiencing in the early 1950s. And, true, Joe's apartment is a little cramped (Ann initially thinks it is an elevator). But the picture of abject Czech poverty painted in *Man on a Tightrope* stands in brutal contrast to the images of "ordinary affluence" seen in *Roman Holiday:* well-dressed couples on scooters, a vibrant cafe culture, shops full to the brim with shiny goods. The political effect of this distortion was twofold. It helped rehabilitate a former enemy, one that, like Germany as noted in the previous chapter, was fast becoming a valuable Western ally in the Cold War. And it vindicated the Marshall Plan, through which Washington had been economically reconstructing Western Europe since 1948, by showing Italy back on its feet, a place of free-living fun where everyone can enjoy themselves or subsist on even a small amount of money.

So much for *Roman Holiday*'s bright and alluring look. How did its plot help sell Western virtues? Since the 1920s, American filmmakers had regularly turned out fantasies of love, consumption, and harmony among the classes. Cross-class fantasy films invariably stressed individualism over collective action, acceptance rather than change, and contentment with one's class position rather than aspirations to something more. Such material taught audiences that all problems, personal and societal, could be solved through love, and that true love was strong enough to break down any class barriers.[11]

Roman Holiday updated the cross-class love story, partly by giving it an international twist. Overall, the movie manages to spirit away class by taking the two lead characters out of their natural environment—Princess Ann out of Coravia, Joe out of America. Yet the film also pities the aristocracy for its social constraints. Ann has all the wealth and privilege she needs, but none of the ordinary freedoms she wants. At the end of the film she is obliged to put duty before love, her country before Joe. Ann remains a prisoner of European conservatism, albeit a conservatism that has dignity and therefore deserves respect.

For a period in the film, however, Ann escapes her constraints—and who better to act as her guide to the simple pleasures of the people than an American like Joe Bradley? *Roman Holiday* was by no means the only Hollywood movie to focus on the relations between Europeans and Americans in the aftermath of the Second World War. One of the first and most controversial was Billy Wilder's *A Foreign Affair* (1948), the story of a U.S. Army captain's secret relationship with a sirenic cabaret singer (played by Marlene Dietrich) in occupied Berlin. *A Foreign Affair* attracted heated opposition from Congress and the U.S. government's overseas cultural agencies for its negative portrayals of both Germans and Americans. More in tune with Washington's thinking was Nunnally Johnson's 1956 *The Man in the Gray Flannel Suit,* a drama about an ex-GI (Gregory Peck again) who jeopardizes his family and livelihood to help care for a son he belatedly learns he fathered while stationed in Rome during the war.[12] *Roman Holiday* stands apart from both of these films by highlighting the romance and "marriage" of U.S. and Western European values. Instead of being seducers or victims, the two parties share the same interests and dreams. They also come across almost as equals: while America ultimately plays the liberator, Europe is far from powerless.

Gregory Peck's Joe Bradley is the model American suitor-cum-ambassador. Peck was the archetypal screen nice guy of the 1950s, famous throughout large parts of the world. Tall and handsome, Peck projected moral and physical strength, intelligence, virtue, and sincerity.[13] We first meet Joe play-

Roman Holiday: Joe and Ann, the epitome of style, share a moment next to the Italian capital's "Wall of Wishes." Courtesy of the Academy of Motion Picture Arts and Sciences (AMPAS).

ing poker with his buddies, the clever score by French composer Georges Auric quoting the opening lines to "The Star Spangled Banner" in sly chromatics. However, it soon becomes clear that Joe is no inveterate gambler obsessed with money. He is willing to put many things above it, demonstrated by his chivalrous act at the end of the picture, when he relinquishes the $5,000 he could have made from selling Princess Ann's story.

Joe's decency is combined with a free spirit. He plays cat and mouse with his boss, knows how to show a girl a good time, is entirely unencumbered by class deference or prejudice, and looks as fashionable as the princess despite being on a journalist's salary. Moreover, Joe's democratic outlook on life liberates Ann. Acting, script, and camerawork combine to project a moving portrait of a princess's discovery of the joys of life: the freedom felt by a sheltered girl suddenly able to go where she wants, the exhilarating disobedience of nibbling a *gelato* on the street, or the sinful fun of having her hair done. Joe leads her by the hand through most of this. Look how easy it is to enjoy life, the movie is saying, when pleasure is not circumscribed. How lucky we are—us ordinary folk—not to carry the burden of royal responsibility in a world of limitless opportunity.

It is richly ironic that such a powerful showcase for Western virtues as *Roman Holiday* had originally been penned by a fully paid-up member of the Communist Party, Dalton Trumbo. In fact, *Roman Holiday*'s protracted production history offers us a fascinating insight into the political and diplomatic complexities that could lie behind even the most anodyne Hollywood movies during this era.

Dalton Trumbo was America's best-paid screenwriter—on $3,000 weekly (or $75,000 a script, as his MGM contract stipulated)—before being imprisoned as one of the Hollywood Ten in 1950.[14] Shortly before his incarceration, Trumbo wrote a gently irreverent comedy that would form the basis of *Roman Holiday,* hoping the proceeds would help support his family while he was in jail. English-born scriptwriter Ian McLellan Hunter then fronted for Trumbo, selling his friend's story for $35,000 in late 1949 to Frank Capra's Liberty Films production company based at Paramount. Hunter then worked on turning the story into a screenplay. Capra arranged for Cary Grant and Elizabeth Taylor to star in the picture, but shortly afterward backed out of the project after warnings from Britain, one of Hollywood's prime markets, that censors would refuse *Roman Holiday* an exhibition permit if it appeared to be based on Princess Margaret, Queen Elizabeth's sister, whose romantic flings, particularly on a trip to Italy, had recently aroused controversy in the press.[15]

When Frank Capra left Paramount in 1951, *Roman Holiday* was passed on to his one-time partner at Liberty Films, William Wyler. Already a two-time Oscar winner for Best Director with *Mrs. Miniver* (1942) and *The Best Years of Our Lives* (1946), Wyler, who both produced and directed *Roman Holiday,* had by the early 1950s built a reputation as one of the most inventive stylists of the American screen. Wyler was a high-profile liberal who had incurred the anticommunists' wrath in 1947 by helping to form the Committee for the First Amendment to support the "unfriendly" witnesses who appeared before HUAC. He escaped the blacklist but only by the skin of his teeth.[16] Meanwhile, from 1950 to 1952, *Roman Holiday*'s script passed through the hands of a number of Hollywood luminaries, partly due to Ian McLellan Hunter's own blacklisting in 1951. These included the Oscar-winning Ben Hecht, the veteran satirist Preston Sturges, and Lester Koenig, Trumbo's long-time collaborator, who was himself blacklisted in late 1952.[17]

It is interesting to speculate how different *Roman Holiday* might have turned out had Frank Capra directed it. Capra was not known as Hollywood's champion of the common man for nothing, and it is possible his version would have targeted aristocratic greed more than Wyler's. As it was, Hunter's and Hecht's attempts to add a little diplomatic and political spice to the movie did not get very far. In Hunter's first script Princess Ann was to be kidnapped by Mafia gangsters. This storyline was cut after Wyler received complaints from the Italian Ministry of Enlightenment and Tourism, whose permission to use Paramount's blocked funds in the country was needed if the movie was to see the light of day.[18] Ben Hecht wanted to portray Princess Ann less angelically, as a manipulator using her aristocratic charms to persuade wealthy Europeans and Americans, including U.S. Secretary of State George Marshall, to bail out her financially bereft country. To even things up, most of Hecht's American characters were uncouth, hard-nosed business types enjoying the hold the United States had over Europe via the Marshall Plan. On the whole, the political spin Hecht lent *Roman Holiday* suggested postwar Europe was Janus-faced. On the one hand, it was a temptress America ought to avoid at all costs. On the other hand, Europe resembled an orphan being seduced by American dollars.[19]

Roman Holiday's connections to the Marshall Plan went deeper than Hecht's scripts. Since 1947, when Marshall announced his European Recovery Program (ERP), Washington, with Hollywood's assistance, had been conducting a multimillion-dollar propaganda campaign combating communism in Western Europe. Italy, where the Communist Party was especially strong, was the focus of intense activity. "Positive" American films—Hollywood features like *Ninotchka* (1939) and government documentaries—had flooded into Italy for the pivotal 1948 elections, which the pro-American Christian Democrats won. "Negative" pictures, like John Ford's Oscar-winning drama about homelessness in the Great Depression, *The Grapes of Wrath* (1940), were held back from distribution. The ERP established its own film unit in Europe, producing and distributing dozens of documentaries aimed at selling the United States as the model for mass-consumption modernization. "You Too Can Be Like US" came to be the central message of the Marshall Plan, especially in Italy, which saw one of the largest publicity offensives of its kind in any European country.[20]

America's cultural drive into postwar Europe was prompted by economic as well as political considerations. Hollywood films had been exported to Europe en masse since the 1920s. After 1945, American producers, who were squeezed between the rising costs of filmmaking and falling domestic cinema attendance, pressed especially hard for access to European markets and to the continent's cheaper facilities. Heavy lobbying by Hollywood kept State Department pressure on European negotiators, and agreements to allow entry for U.S. films formed part of every major bipartite deal or loan agreement reached by the United States and its European allies in the first postwar decade. When European governments after 1949 took to taxing cinema receipts in order to subsidize domestic film production, American producers reacted by investing directly in foreign productions. By 1953, when *Roman Holiday* was released, 50 percent of the U.S. film industry's revenue was generated overseas, most of it in Europe. As the decade progressed, Hollywood's studios expanded their access to the increasingly sophisticated but still relatively inexpensive filmmaking facilities in Britain, Italy, and other countries.[21]

All of this, plus Paramount's investment in Europe dating back to the twenties, helps to explain why *Roman Holiday* was the first Hollywood movie to be shot and processed entirely in Italy, between June and October 1952. Studio interiors were filmed at the Cinecitta facilities in southeastern Rome, founded in 1937 by Benito Mussolini and bombed by the Allies during the Second World War.[22] Wyler exploited the Eternal City's beautiful, historic landmarks to the full. Palazzo Barberini and Palazzo Colonna were used for the embassy scenes, for example, while the movie's comical motor-scooter race was filmed in Piazza Venezia. Bribes were distributed to the authorities to divert traffic and rope off public monuments in order to facilitate filming, but even then difficulties and delays occurred. Gregory Peck was constantly mobbed for autographs in the city's streets. Filming was also punctuated by pitched battles between supporters of the ruling Christian Democrats and their communist opponents.[23]

These delays, combined with Wyler's notorious perfectionism, meant that *Roman Holiday* went $700,000 over budget. Its final cost of approximately $2.1 million amounted to a significant investment for a studio that was feeling the financial pinch. Paramount's chief executives, however, were fully aware of *Roman Holiday*'s potential value, both commercially and diplomatically. The studio's president, Y. Frank Freeman, was a staunch anticommunist, while production head Barney Balaban had signaled Hollywood's ambassadorial role at the very start of the Cold War. "We recognize the need for informing people in foreign lands about the things that have made America a great country," he told his industry colleagues in 1946, "and we know how to put across the message of democracy." Luigi Luraschi, head of foreign and domestic censorship at Paramount, worked for the CIA and, like the agency, believed Hollywood had a crucial part to play in exporting positive "American values."[24]

In August 1953, *Roman Holiday* opened at the American movie industry's most prestigious showcase, New York's 6,000-seat Radio City Music Hall, to rave reviews and instant fame.[25] A month later, Audrey Hepburn appeared on the cover of Henry Luce's flagship magazine *Time*, illustrated by Boris Chaliapin, who had studied art under the Soviet regime before moving to Paris in the mid-1920s. This coverage caused a sensation, giving a major boost to the profile of both Hepburn and *Roman Holiday*. At the end of 1953 a host of influential newspapers and august bodies in the United States rated *Roman Holiday* one of the best pictures of the year. A young Democratic senator by the name of John F. Kennedy demonstrated an early but sure touch for public relations by declaring it his favorite film. *Roman Holiday*

Roman Holiday: Brazilians wait in line in São Paulo in 1954. "The Princess and the Peasant," says the poster. Courtesy of the Academy of Motion Picture Arts and Sciences (AMPAS).

was then nominated for ten Academy Awards, more than any other movie of 1953; Edith Head, Audrey Hepburn, and Ian McLellan Hunter each took away Oscars in their respective categories.[26]

Roman Holiday grossed roughly $5 million at the U.S. box office, putting it among the top twenty Hollywood earners of 1953. Significantly, though, the movie made another $12 million worldwide over the next four decades. This testified both to the movie's international appeal and to Paramount's muscular marketing and distribution strategy overseas. In March 1954, Luigi Luraschi cabled Wyler from São Paulo to congratulate him on the "outstanding smash success" *Roman Holiday* had enjoyed at the Brazilian Film Festival. A few months later Wyler's film was named Best Picture of the year in Argentina.[27]

Roman Holiday enjoyed similar success in Britain and France, and in Sweden actor William Holden reported the movie was doing "a tremendous job for American public relations."[28] Italian women especially were enchanted with Audrey Hepburn's elegant, demure image. Within a few years, Elsa Martinelli, dubbed "Italy's Audrey Hepburn," had helped to usurp the model of the *maggiorata*—the "physically well-endowed woman" like Sophia Loren—on the Italian screen.[29] *Roman Holiday* enjoyed an extraordinary reception in Japan, where the film soon earned back a third of its costs alone. In the summer of 1954, Audrey Hepburn haircuts were all the rage

Roman Holiday: The movie gets the front-window treatment at Poulex Department Store in Manila, the Philippines, in 1954. Courtesy of the Academy of Motion Picture Arts and Sciences (AMPAS).

for young Japanese women. In 1990, the year after the collapse of the Berlin Wall, a survey conducted by two Japanese television companies found that *Roman Holiday* was the nation's favorite foreign film of all time.[30]

Given *Roman Holiday*'s popularity in Asia, Western Europe, and Latin America, it comes as no surprise to learn that U.S. Cold War propaganda officials thought the film might usefully be deployed as a weapon of subversion behind the Iron Curtain. In mid-1954, *Roman Holiday* appeared on a list of thirty-seven Hollywood movies the USIA's Motion Picture Service wanted to show in Eastern Europe, if the opportunity arose.[31] Four years later, the watershed U.S.-Soviet Cultural Exchange Agreement, which incorporated everything from athletes to agricultural experts, marked a breakthrough in the long diplomatic impasse on film trade between the two superpowers.[32] Brokered on the American side by MPEA president Eric Johnston and USIA film chief Turner Shelton, the film agreement allowed for the sale and purchase of features and documentaries, film delegation visits, week-long film festivals, and even the joint production of movies. In the first instance, the Americans agreed to market seven Soviet feature films,[33] while the Soviets began distributing ten Hollywood products. Each government played a part in ensuring their country's movies were ideologically correct and the other's material was devoid of propaganda (at least in an overt sense). In 1959–60, the first American movies to be exported officially to the Soviet Union in more than twenty years were the musicals *Oklahoma!* (Fred Zinnemann, 1955), *The Great Caruso* (Richard Thorpe, 1951), *Rhapsody* (Charles Vidor, 1954), and *Lili* (Charles Walters, 1953); a love story, *Marty* (Delbert Mann, 1955); a drama, *All About Eve* (Joseph L. Mankiewicz, 1950); a biopic, *Man of a Thousand Faces* (Joseph Pevney, 1957); the adventure-dramas *The Old Man and the Sea* (John Sturges, 1958) and *The Seventh Voyage of Sinbad* (Nathan Juran, 1958); and *Roman Holiday.*[34]

A paucity of records means we can only really guess how *Roman Holiday* was received by Russian cinemagoers. We know that Russia's mass circulation film magazine, *Soviet Screen*, publicized *Roman Holiday* more than the other Hollywood imports of 1959–60, though it is not clear why. The USIA must certainly have been pleased with the response to *Roman Holiday*'s previews in the capital. "30,000 in Moscow Warm to US Film," reported the *New York Times* in March 1960. *Roman Holiday* was then showcased across the Soviet Union.[35] Wyler's movie might have caused at least some of those who saw it to have doubts about Nikita Khrushchev's recent promise that the Soviet Union would overtake the production capacity of the United States in the 1970s, especially in terms of consumer goods. Some women in the audience presumably compared their own dreary lifestyles under communism highly unfavorably with Audrey Hepburn's image of West European feminine chic.[36] To a degree, *Roman Holiday* also belied stereotypical Soviet images of Western vulgarity, superficiality, and decadence and definitely revised the image of the American journalist, reviled in films such as *The Russian Question* and *The Court of Honor*. The Americans in the picture come across as rather cultured and kind, not overly materialistic.

Notwithstanding these positive interpretations, *Roman Holiday* scored something of an "own goal" by failing to live up to Hollywood's customary high standards of production in Moscow. Reports in the American press that Russian cinemagoers were being shown poor quality prints of the film indicate that Hollywood executives and the USIA failed to get their act together. When William Wyler himself got wind of this, he was so angry that he accused Paramount's bosses of failing their country. "Our Government is spending hundreds of millions on the 'Voice of America' and on centers of information designed to reach the people behind the Iron Curtain and to impress them with American achievements," he told Barney Balaban. "Sending 'scratched and broken films showing signs of overuse and old age' to the millions of people we have been trying for years to reach, is tantamount to sabotage and contrary to the national interest." Jack Karp, Paramount's new head of production, responded by accusing the Russians of distributing stock prints intended only for the Kremlin's selection process.[37]

Whoever was to blame for this blunder, *Roman Holiday* seems not to have lived up to the hopes of at least some American cultural diplomats. From

1960 onward it never registered as one of Russia's favorite American films. This distinction fell instead to sexually tinged comedies such as *Some Like it Hot* (Billy Wilder, 1959), *The Apartment* (Billy Wilder, 1960), and *Tootsie* (Sydney Pollack, 1982). Despite this, Wyler must have been pleased that by the time of his death in 1981 another five of his films had been released in Soviet cinemas, a number bettered only by the films of director Stanley Kramer.[38]

Roman Holiday's strange political afterlife continued even after Wyler's demise. When Gregory Peck was invited to communist China to celebrate the movie's official debut there in the mid-1980s, he was amazed to see "little Audrey Hepburns everywhere." In 2000, the noteworthy Russian writer Andrei Gelasimov published a prize-winning story entitled "A Tender Age" ("Nezhnyi vozrast"), which purports to be the diary of a hostile, alienated teenager. The boy's life is transformed when his piano teacher gives him a copy of *Roman Holiday*. "Wow! There are simply no words." He becomes obsessed with *Roman Holiday*, watching it again and again. He falls in love with Audrey Hepburn and searches everywhere for an Audrey look-alike.[39]

"WORKERS' PARADISE" REDEFINED:
Spring on Zarechnaya Street

It is hard to imagine two films less alike on the surface than *Roman Holiday* and *Spring on Zarechnaya Street*. *Spring on Zarechnaya Street* certainly does not ooze glamour like *Roman Holiday,* and it was not designed to impress an international audience. Yet both films served the same political purpose: through the plot device of a cross-class romance, they presented people and lifestyles in an uplifting, believable way that might persuade audiences of the values inherent in the American and Soviet systems.

Spring on Zarechnaya Street is a classic of early Thaw cinema. As we saw in chapter 2, during the 1950s "positive legitimation" showcased the advantages of Soviet life in preference to direct anti-American attacks. Soviet cinema focused on positive propaganda to present warm, affirming, but reasonably realistic images of Soviet life for the benefit of the Soviet people and its allies. These new "human-scale" films were down-to-earth melodramas (with a few comedies) that focused on the ordinary lives of ordinary people facing ordinary challenges.

Although most of these films were stylistically less adventurous and artistically less important than a film like Mikhail Kalatozov's canonical *The Cranes Are Flying* (*Letiat zhuravli*, 1957), they marked a change in style and content from the heyday of Socialist Realism and drew moviegoers in droves. If they occasionally won prizes or other recognition at international film festivals, all the better. Once again, Soviet cinema was making waves as it had in the glorious 1920s. Even if Khrushchev was not fully conscious of the persuasive power of art, the Soviet cultural intelligentsia basked in the acclaim. As far as the native audience was concerned, a victory in the Cold War had already been scored on the cinema front.

As noted in chapter 2, the most famous Thaw films abroad revisioned Soviet experiences in the Great Patriotic War. However, the *bytovoi* film (a film that examines daily life and its challenges) also deeply resonated with domestic audiences, particularly those who had come to adulthood during the war, and remained enduringly popular. Such films had not been made in the USSR since the late 1920s, when movies by Boris Barnet and Fridrikh Ermler had engaged Soviet audiences with provocative, sometimes satirical depictions of contemporary social issues.[40] *Spring on Zarechnaya Street* is a landmark film in the rebirth of that genre.

It also represents a revisioning of the reeducation film, a genre that Russian critics see as truly their own. As the filmmaker and theorist Vitaly Troyanovsky writes, "This genre is our native invention, as the Western is American."[41] *Spring on Zarechnaya Street* combines a Neorealist quasi-documentary style with elements of Socialist Realism.[42] It is, therefore, a transitional film that demonstrates the "complex interaction between old and new aesthetic tendencies,"[43] and the sense of uncertainty and impermanence that are intrinsic to the Thaw.

Spring on Zarechnaya Street, the debut film[44] of the up-and-coming young directors Marlen Khutsiev and Feliks Mironer, from Mironer's screenplay, was released in late November 1956. The few contemporary reviews were mixed, some critics thinking the film a bit one-dimensional, and it was advertised in *Evening Moscow* (*Vecherniaia Moskva*) only once.[45] Despite this, audiences found their way to the movie and, according to one history of Soviet cinema, "met *Spring on Zarechnaya Street* very warmly."[46] Recent commentators on the film have been even more impressed. *Spring on Zarechnaya Street* "brought a new attention," film scholar Julian Graffy writes, "to everyday life visible in the settings, in the acting style (new actors replaced the stars of the 1930s and 1940s), even the way the characters looked."[47] Josephine Woll also notes its innovations: "At a time when totally remaking human beings dominated Soviet life, Khutsiev and Mironer refused to create model protagonists. . . . Moreover, with its gritty, textured details of muddy streets and crowded rooms, *Vesna* [*Spring*] reflects actual Soviet life far more truthfully than the lacquered pristine surfaces characteristic of earlier Soviet films."[48] ("Lacquered pristine surfaces" certainly characterize *The Meeting on the Elbe* and other early Cold War films such as *The Court of Honor.*) Finally, a recent Russian history featured the film as one of only three listed for 1956, characterizing it as "one of the warmest [and] most soulful films of its time."[49]

The similarities between *Spring on Zarechnaya Street* and *Roman Holiday* are subtle, while the differences between the capitalist and socialist dream-worlds they portray are obvious from the opening shots. *Spring* takes place in a grungy unnamed provincial Ukrainian steel town (it was filmed primarily in Zaporozhe, Ukraine).[50] It deals with the not very successful efforts of a prim and inexperienced young teacher from the city to teach Russian literature in night school to unmotivated, unruly, and often vulgar young adult students who are steelworkers by day. Their labors are hard, hot, and long; exhausted by evening, they often fail to see why they need to memorize Pushkin and to kowtow to this stuffy, green teacher.

This honest portrayal of the workers' paradise was new and refreshing in the Soviet context and struck a chord with audiences. It was a purely domestic product that valorized the characteristics that Soviet people considered their best traits, traits that are remarkably like the American self-image: simplicity, sociability, friendship, and love of country, traits they believed to be in opposition to Western materialism and elitism. To Western viewers, *Spring on Zarechnaya Street* would have likely seemed a clichéd and unremarkable romantic melodrama about how two young people, from different stations in life, learn from each other (not just from books) and fall in love, despite the interference of friends. The plot sounds clichéd in the Soviet context as well; reeducation had been a stock topic in Socialist Realist film and literature.[51]

As we shall see, however, the film goes much deeper than its surface impressions. It is, in fact, a reflection of the social disarray in Soviet postwar society and a prescription for how to overcome it. Unlike William Wyler, who is creating a Western fantasy world, Mironer and Khutsiev attempt to construct a believably positive version of Soviet life, complete with shortcomings and contradictions, to entertain and persuade audiences at home and perhaps in the "near abroad" of the East European satellite states. There was never an illusion that it would convert westerners to the Soviet way of life. It is not a fairy tale.

In contrast to Princess Ann, Tanya Levchenko (Nina Ivanova) is not a glamorous beauty, but, like the princess, she is very much an outsider, from a different class than the "ordinary people" who are like foreigners to her. Tanya arrives in this "everytown" on an unprepossessing day: continual heavy rain floods the muddy, rutted roads. She learns from Yura, the garrulous driver who gives her a lift to the school on Zarechnaya Street, that her predecessor quickly fled in horror from the lack of amenities in this quiet backwater: "It must seem uncivilized for you. No television, no fashion, the smell of factory smoke." Tanya cannot find a suitable place to live. She ends up renting a room for an exorbitant price at Maria Gavrilovna's house, which

Spring on Zarechnaya Street: Sasha presents his teacher with flowers. Courtesy of the Scientific Research Institute of Cinema Art (NIIK).

is fussily furnished with antiques and lace, clearly alien to the serious Tanya, as is Maria Gavrilovna's daughter, the petulant, voluptuous brunette beauty Zina, who is a clerk at the steel mill.

Tanya's students unsettle her even more. Yura makes sure to point out a group of workers drinking beer at a stand and announces, "Here are your students." At the first class meeting, they snicker at her tight bun and severely cut suit and enjoy mocking her self-conscious attempts to exert authority over them. "How long will *you* be here?!" one calls out. (Lapses in student discipline, in particular the heckling of teachers, were a common concern in the Khrushchev era.)[52] Tanya feels completely isolated—spiritually and physically—in this bleak place; "I'm alien [*chuzhaia*] here, and they are alien to me," she remarks dispiritedly at one of her lowest points late in the film.

Her most troublesome student is Sasha Savchenko (Nikolai Rybnikov), the handsome, popular young man who is the boyfriend of the landlady's daughter, Zina. Sasha attempts to flirt with Tanya at a party her first night in town. The next night, in a juvenile effort to charm the new teacher, Sasha deliberately arrives late to make a grand entrance to impress her and is so disruptive in class that even his friends chide him that "others want to learn." He is sent out into the hall. He continues to transgress the boundaries that Tanya believes should separate teacher from student, regardless of their closeness in age. He flirts with her every chance he gets; he waits for her after class, in order to invite her to a dance; he visits her in her room for special help, to Zina's seething anger. His romantic interest in Tanya becomes an open joke to his friends, who cannot understand what attraction the prim teacher holds for the strong and good-looking steelworker. (Sasha's easy-going manner and sexual self-confidence are reminiscent of Joe's in *Roman Holiday*.)

What Tanya does not know is that beneath Sasha's devil-may-care exterior is a man who, unlike Joe, is full of doubts. Sasha longs to study science but feels insecure about his prospects due to his working-class background. Tanya's friend from home, the young working-class engineer Kolya, who finished his secondary education at night school, tries to reassure Sasha that it really is possible, but to no avail. Tanya also does not know that Sasha is a loving parent to his young brother and sister and encourages their education; the three have apparently been orphaned by the war. Finally, Tanya also does not know until late in the movie that Sasha is a highly skilled foundry worker, much respected in the factory.

The turning point in the film occurs when Sasha has become increasingly frustrated with the subtleties of Russian poetry and the difficulty of learning Russian declensions—and especially with his failure to break through Tanya's icy exterior. He is constantly being taunted by his pal Yura, the driver who brought Tanya to town, about the hopelessness of this infatuation. (The gadfly Yura, who refuses to attend the night school, is a persistently annoying presence in the film who needles Sasha about studying and reports on Sasha's activities to Zina.) Sasha starts skipping class; when he returns, he arrives just as class is ending, because he wants to speak with Tanya, to declare his love and ask her to marry him. "We're grownups," he tells her; "I'll do anything for you," adding, "I'm just a factory worker, a worker, a regular guy." When Tanya orders Sasha to stand away from the door and allow her to leave, he draws what for him is the obvious conclusion: "Do you look down on me? Are you afraid to dirty yourself?" They sadly trudge home through the snow, Tanya to find that Zina has evicted her from Maria Gavrilovna's house in a fit of jealousy. Tanya eventually finds another place to live, not in a petit-bourgeois nest, but a clean, empty room in a communal apartment building. The class goes on without Sasha, who has dropped out for good.

But winter does not last forever, not even on Zarechnaya Street. With the spring thaw comes not only the birds, but also a new way of thinking for Tanya, who has found it harder to embrace the simple life than Princess Ann did. Tanya decides at last to visit the factory where her students labor. As she walks along the railroad tracks to the factory, in true Socialist Realist fashion it appears like a castle on the horizon: new, shining, enormous, dominating the field of vision. Inside, Tanya is impressed by the majesty of the foundry

Spring on Zarechnaya Street: Sasha at the foundry. Courtesy of the Scientific Research Institute of Cinema Art (NIIK).

(built *without* the Marshall Plan money that had reconstructed Rome). For the first time, she sees her students for the adults they are: mature, hard-working, self-confident, highly productive. But when she spies Sasha on the bridge, he deliberately avoids her gaze, leaving her downcast.

The thaw continues, and spring has truly arrived. The ugly town is transformed. The young factory workers stroll in the park by the river, their version of a "Roman holiday." Sasha has returned to Zina, who wears a pretty pleated skirt and an embroidered Ukrainian blouse that provide a stereotypically feminine contrast to Tanya's severe and unadorned light dress. When a massive thunderstorm forces everyone to take shelter in a gazebo, Tanya and Sasha see each other again. Confused by her emotions, she rushes off, the downpour notwithstanding, to avoid the mockery of the workers' clique crowded in the gazebo. When Sasha starts out after her, Zina realizes to her great dismay that he still harbors feelings for Tanya. Her mother, Maria Gavrilovna, does not sympathize; rather, *bourgeoise* that she is, she laments the loss of Tanya's rent money.

The film concludes in late spring. Tanya is at school grading final exams while her students are enjoying the lovely weather. Walking by the school, Sasha spies her through the window; she has loosened her bun in a gesture of freedom so that we can admire her curly hair. As he climbs through the window, a breeze catches her papers, which swirl around the room. In their first spontaneous interaction, he joins her in retrieving them, and she allows

Spring on Zarechnaya Street: Tanya with her test papers. Courtesy of the Scientific Research Institute of Cinema Art (NIIK).

herself to accept his help. As Sasha leaves, he gives her a small, embarrassed wave. Tanya stands by the window watching him go, deep in thought. Historian Tamara Eidelman writes about this famous scene: "Is it possible to build a love scene against the backdrop of test papers from a Russian language class? It turns out it is. And the scene is so full of purity, tenderness, and beauty, that it is quite difficult to forget once you have seen it."[53] The film ends with ellipses (*Konets* [The End] ...) , implying an indeterminate ending.

The most obvious and important theme in this film is its depiction of the class divisions in Soviet society and the conflicts that arose from them. It was essential to bridge this divide, not only from the domestic perspective but also internationally, to persuade others, especially in the bloc, of the rightness of the Soviet way of life. Class conflict was a motif in a number of Thaw-era domestic melodramas, but none portrays this sensitive, ideologically explosive question more honestly than *Spring on Zarechnaya Street.* Reviving a flagging ideology and restoring fading interest in Komsomol membership in the postwar generation was an abiding concern of the Soviet leaders who succeeded Stalin.[54] This film seeks to restore young working men and women to their rightful place in a socialist society, while recognizing that other social types are there to stay. They need not be branded enemies of the people.

Tanya is no proletarian, of course, but an unreconstructed Russian intellectual (*intelligentka*). Her surname may be Ukrainian, but culturally she is

Russian. Tanya is undeniably elitist and uncomfortable around the "lower orders," although she is not a bad person at heart. The self-absorbed young woman has no interest at all in her students' lives and the many family and work burdens that they carry. For Tanya, the fact that the students sometimes fall asleep in class and resist her authority signals their social and intellectual inferiority, rather than suggest that their lives are more complicated than her own. In one of the film's most famous scenes, Tanya forces a heavily pregnant woman to stand up as she calls roll. In another, she chides the woman's husband for sleeping at his desk, only to learn that the baby was born the night before. She assigns classic nineteenth-century Russian writers—Pushkin, Lermontov, Griboyedov—and delivers mannered formal lectures more suitable to the university than to a night school for factory workers. She goes to the factory dance at the Palace of Metallurgists but refuses all invitations to dance, standing aloofly to the side like a princess, watching the fun but never participating. "I don't dance," she tells a young man who dares to invite her. She tells an aspiring worker-poet that his ode to Sasha Savchenko is "not very good" when he recites his verses to her (but on seeing his dismay, adds that they are "very beautiful" nonetheless).

Her adversary Sasha is a revelation: a worker in the worker's paradise who is torn between his pride in his work and his clear, spoken understanding that many of his fellow citizens, including Tanya, consider him not as a prince of labor, but as a man with a toehold on one of society's lower rungs. It is hard to tell why he is attracted to cold and withdrawn Tanya. Of course, she is pretty in a classically Slavic way—blonde and slim, a complete contrast to the swarthy Zina. (Film historian Neya Zorkaya, however, finds Tanya "somewhat dull and not very attractive.")[55] It may be that Sasha is attracted to what she represents: a manifestation of his deep-seated longing for education and culture, even though he publicly scoffs at learning. He is certainly sensitive to the vulnerability that Tanya hides beneath her shell, and his passion drives the film. As Zorkaya ironically notes: "Today's viewer of *Spring on Zarechnaya Street* will probably be impressed most of all by the stormy and inspiring passion of Sasha Savchenko. . . . He reveals a love that makes one's bones crack."[56]

One of the film's best scenes takes place when Sasha has gone to Maria Gavrilovna's to see Tanya, ostensibly for help on an assignment. Tanya tells him that she is waiting for a Rachmaninoff piano concerto that she has requested to be played on a radio program and invites him to listen with her. Princess Ann was transported by her taste of the simple life; here, Tanya is transported by high culture. Listening to the beautiful music, she visibly relaxes, her face glowing with rapture, while Sasha watches in puzzlement. He quietly takes his leave; she is too engrossed to notice. Outside the door,

Spring on Zarechnaya Street: Sasha and Tanya listen to Rachmaninoff. Courtesy of the Scientific Research Institute of Cinema Art (NIIK).

in an evocative close-up, Sasha ponders what he has witnessed and leaves without speaking to the glowering Zina (who thought he had come to visit her) and her mother. In one of the reeducation melodramas of the thirties, Sasha would be given credit for saving Tanya from herself, as Joe saves Princess Ann; this film, however, while daringly posing the question as to who has improved whom more, leaves it unanswered.

The persistence of *meshchanstvo,* the petit-bourgeois philistinism endemic to America and the bane of Soviet social critics, is exemplified in the minor characters Maria Gavrilovna and her daughter Zina. As Elena Zubkova writes in her excellent history of Soviet postwar culture and society: "The fear of materialism, of philistinism, more characteristic of the revolutionary romanticism of the 1920s, revived in the 1950s, and in spite of its shrill character, nevertheless had a rational basis."[57] Maria Gavrilovna's home is warm and cozy in a cloying way, overstuffed with kitschy material possessions. The two women do not bother to clear them away when Tanya rents the room; she has to make space for her few personal items as best she can. Mother and daughter are also overstuffed, plump from indulging in Maria Gavrilovna's bountiful spreads of food and drink. Although Sasha has helped to provide for the lavish (by Soviet standards) party at the beginning of the film, where the rest of these goods come from is not clear. There is no husband (not surprising for a middle-aged woman ten years after the war), and

Maria Gavrilovna neither looks nor acts like a working woman, which suggests that she survives by dealing in the gray market, trading goods.

Sasha's sometime friend Yura, who cares only for "wine, women, and song," may also be said to represent *meshchanstvo*. Like Zina, Yura is fond of gossip and stirring up trouble. As a truck driver, he provides a service rather than a product, so he occupies a lower position than Sasha in the ranks of the proletariat. Sasha eventually jettisons Zina and Yura both, the latter dramatically by shoving him into the river after one too many taunts. (Tanya escapes overlong contamination with the petit-bourgeois "element" by being evicted.) In the end, the petit-bourgeoisie are pushed to the outer circle of society, while at the beginning of the film they were at its center, Maria Gavrilovna hosting a big party for the young people, with lots of food, drink, and merriment.

The road to the future is clear: a union (*smychka*) of the intelligentsia and the workers, but one that could not be achieved in Party meetings or through ideological hectoring about how "good" Soviets should behave. Rather, the film depicts how simple human interactions lead to understanding. By the film's end, Tanya has cast off her shell and has opened herself to the possibilities of her new life. Zarechnaya Street is no longer ugly; spring's promise has been fulfilled; and she just may find romance with an extremely worthy (and ruggedly handsome) young man. For his part, Sasha has been persuaded by the example of Tanya's friend Kolya that it *is* possible for a worker to achieve his educational goals, and that the night school, a benefit of Soviet society, is the all-important first step to achieving higher education at a technical institute.

Spring on Zarechnaya Street is also important for establishing a wholesome, though not too wholesome, model for youth culture in contrast to westernized models such as those seen in *Roman Holiday*. Zubkova dates to 1948 the beginning of a youth movement independent of state-sponsored youth organizations.[58] Quickly the *stilyagi* (the "style conscious" youth attempting to mimic Western fashions), whose heyday was 1949–1956, became notorious.[59] This youth culture was based not only on Western-style clothing, but also on Western music, specifically jazz. Although frequently under fire, jazz had been popular in the USSR since the 1920s. After D-Day, it was positively connected with the Americans and the opening of the second front.[60] Red Army bands were permitted to play jazz as a tribute to the American allies, a practice that continued into demobilization.[61] This all changed with the advent of the Cold War; by 1948 jazz was regularly being denounced as "cosmopolitan."[62] As noted in chapter 2, the importance of films captured during the war to this Americanized counterculture is also clear; in 1952, Johnny Weismuller's *Tarzan* films took first, second, third, and fourth place at the box office.[63] (Soviet youth who imitated Weismuller's slicked-back longish hair were known as *tarzantsy*.) Even before the 1958 cultural agreement, the penetration of American culture, especially music and dress, into elite youth circles was extensive enough that noted Russian writer Vasily Aksyonov referred to them as "stateniks" (*shtatniki*).[64]

How to prevent this particular infection from spreading? By the early 1950s, before the first new wave of American films was shown at the end of the decade, it was clear that Soviet youth were more or less immune to anti-American propaganda.[65] Soviet cinema therefore sought to depict viable alternatives on screen. The young working-class adults in *Spring on Za-rechnaya Street* have few luxuries at their disposal for entertainment ("no televisions"). They rely on their social network for fun, as well as the traditional Russian pastimes of strolling, music-making, and drinking (but beer instead of vodka—there was great concern about youth drinking and alcohol-fueled hooliganism at this time).[66] We see the night school students dancing on two occasions, first at Maria Gavrilovna's and then at the workers' palace; they dance some sedate old-fashioned dances, but the music is gay and the crowd is having fun. As noted in chapter 2, dance was as deeply politicized as everything else in Soviet society. Dances connected with Western music— the tango, the foxtrot, and the "slow waltz"—were part of the much-feared postwar "dance craze."[67] The simple joys of a non-materialistic lifestyle are presented as appealingly as possible, although even in provincial cities the lure of Western culture was irresistible, as recent research demonstrates.[68]

Finally, *Spring on Zarechnaya Street* is important for the ways it redefines Socialist Realism's promise of a glorious new life and for the subtle ways it deviates from the visual constraints of Socialist Realism. Of course, the gleaming mega-factory and the highly aestheticized foundry are reminiscent of the industrialization films of the late twenties and thirties, and Tanya's pristine room in a communal apartment is a far cry from the squalor and overcrowding of true communal apartments. These are the fantasy elements of this socialist dream world. Unlike a true socialist realist film, not to mention *Roman Holiday*, *Spring on Zarechnaya Street* also shows the ruts and potholes of Soviet life, literally as well as figuratively. Its message, therefore, is one of achievable aspirations, for better living conditions, a better education, a better job, a happier life.

The film indirectly reminds viewers that the country is still rebuilding from the devastation of the war without Marshall Plan funds. (The rejection of Marshall Plan money was a point of contention with some Soviet citizens.)[69] In this context, it seems logical that a new factory should precede, for example, a new building for the adult students who squeeze into desks at the middle school. The housing crisis is also treated. Tanya is told that a room will be very hard to find after she is ejected from Maria Gavrilovna's, but she does find one, indicative of the Khrushchev regime's efforts to redress the housing shortage through massive apartment-building projects. (The goal, however, was to provide each family with a separate, not communal, apartment.) *Spring on Zarechnaya Street* was therefore truly a sign of "spring," a turning away from the bombast and falsity of Stalinist fairy tales. The film created a new kind of "dream world," a dream world within the audience's grasp, rather than one that was forever out of reach.

As Soviet cinema production recovered from Stalinism, Soviet moviegoers once again had choices, and they chose to see this film even though, as noted above, it received very few reviews at the time, and none in major organs such as *Pravda* and *Art of the Cinema* (*Iskusstvo kino*).[70] Fittingly, the labor newspaper *Work* (*Trud*) reviewed it favorably, praising its depiction of the "poetry of love, youth, beauty, the joy of life."[71] It took first place at the 1957 Moscow Film Festival and ninth place at the box office in 1956, with 30.6 million viewers.[72] *Spring on Zarechnaya Street* would prove to have great staying power, becoming one of the most beloved films in Soviet cinema.[73] Twenty-five years after its release, in 1981, it was named by readers of *Soviet Screen* as one of the old films that they most wanted to see again.[74]

Spring on Zarechnaya Street launched a whole series of important and popular films about daily life. These were set mainly in cities, like Georgy Danelya's cheerful *I Walk around Moscow* (*Ia shagaiu po Moskve*, 1962), a beautifully filmed, upbeat day in the life of a Moscow teen. Occasionally such films were set in towns, such as Aleksander Zarkhi's reeducation film *Heights* (*Vysota*, 1957) and Khutsiev's *The Two Fyodors* (*Dva Fedora*, 1958/59). From time to time, they offered a (romanticized) glimpse of life on a collective farm, of which Danelya's *Seryozha* (*Serezha*, 1960) is a good example.

As a reeducation film, *Heights* provides a useful point of contrast with *Spring on Zarechnaya Street,* especially since Zarkhi considered it a "reply" to *Spring*'s dangerous focus on personal life.[75] It suggests the limits of the Thaw and points to the dissent within the film industry over the new course. *Heights* is set in a shipyard; one of the plots concerns the stumbling romance between two workers, Kolya (again, Nikolai Rybnikov) and Katya (Inna Makarova). Kolya, unlike Sasha, provides a model of upright proletarian behavior from beginning to end. Katya, unlike Tanya, has been infected with Western culture. She is a spunky little blonde tomboy, a bit off-color in terms of her manners and dress. She smokes in public; her name is tattooed on her hand. She tries to dress in the Western style, in a green pencil skirt and a red sateen blouse. Seeing this getup, Kolya notes that she looks like a traffic light, a remark that ruins his plans for the evening. He also tells her that the outfit looks "American," not a compliment coming from him. By the end of the film, having fallen in love with Kolya, she dresses in the Soviet style and happily gives up her dreams of America.

Marlen Khutsiev was not, however, content to stay within the boundaries of *Spring on Zarechnaya Street*, and his subsequent career was troubled. His next film, *The Two Fyodors*, a heartwarming but realistic tale of a returning soldier who adopts his namesake, an orphaned boy, was criticized as too pessimistic to be set in the immediate postwar period, at a time when "festivity reigned."[76] The adult Fyodor, who is trying to reintegrate himself back into his old life, was seen as "sullen, taciturn, unsociable. That's not what our people are like."[77]

The *bytovoi* film reached its limit during the Thaw with Khutsiev's brilliant *Ilich's Gate* (*Zastava Ilicha*, completed 1961), finally released in a bowdlerized form after considerable censorship difficulties in 1965 as *I Am Twenty* (*Mne dvadstat let*).[78] The "gritty, textured details" that Khutsiev and Mironer employed so successfully in *Spring on Zarechnaya Street* had become too gritty, too realistic in this movie that follows a trio of friends, perturbed by the banality of life, on their travels around Moscow. These travels famously include a marvelously chaotic May Day parade and a documentary sequence of a poetry reading with Yevgeny Yevtushenko, Bella Akhmadulina, and Bulat Okudzhava, among other famous Thaw poets. In 1963, the film was denounced by Khrushchev himself as reflecting "entirely unacceptable" standards of behavior and a disregard for the wisdom of parents and elders.[79]

CONCLUSION

This chapter has demonstrated that in order to appreciate Cold War cinema fully we must look beyond the images of fear and hatred, or the sounds of bullets and bangs, analyzed in chapter 3. We must look instead for those movies that accentuated the positive over the negative and that indirectly celebrated their side's way of life. In order to do this, it is necessary to look afresh at films that superficially have no relevance to the East-West conflict, but that on close examination might reveal complex political origins, hidden propaganda messages, or discreet government support. This is especially the case during the 1950s, when viewers' opinions on important aspects of the conflict were still being formed.

Despite coming from very different filmmaking traditions, and the fact that each film was made for quite different purposes, *Roman Holiday* and *Spring on Zarechnaya Street* were inextricably related from a Cold War perspective. Both movies promoted their side's version of modernity. Both films delivered their positive messages the most effective way possible—via the heart rather than the brain. Both movies received state assistance. Both highlighted the interconnection between the politics of domestic and international culture during the Cold War. And both demonstrated, through their afterlives, the long-lasting influence movies could have on the public's emotions, partly due to the power of the visual image. Taken together, and when coupled with the films examined in chapter 3, they demonstrate how oppositional Soviet and American cinema was between 1945 and 1960, in a negative and positive sense.

Our comparison of *Roman Holiday* and *Spring on Zarechnaya Street* also tells us something about the relative positions and aspirations of the United States and the USSR at this stage of the cultural Cold War. *Roman Holiday* shows that Hollywood was extremely confident in its ability to demonstrate to the world the superiority of the American way of life. Its power to do this was enhanced by using Western Europe as a base for film production. At the same time that *Roman Holiday* demonstrated the new glory of Rome, rebuilt with American foreign aid, it showed a softer side of American capitalism generally and of American journalism specifically, both excoriated or lampooned in Soviet films of the late 1940s. The fantasy quotient in *Roman Holiday* is very high. In this sense, it is a perfect example of American Cold War public diplomacy, Hollywood-style.

Soviet cinema was certainly interested in reaching the West, principally through art films—like the World War II drama *Peace to Him Who Enters* (*Mir vkhodiashchemu*, Aleksandr Alov and Vladimir Naumov, 1961)—that were not blockbusters but won international acclaim for Soviet artistic achievements. (Unlike *Spring on Zarechnaya Street, Peace to Him Who Enters* was distributed in the United States, receiving good reviews.)[80] More important in the 1950s, however, as Soviet society was destabilized by Stalin's death and then by de-Stalinization, was the effort to rebuild public confidence in the values of the Soviet way of life. In *Spring on Zarechnaya Street,* Khutsiev and Mironer demonstrated that it was possible to succeed in such an endeavor while remaining true to the ethos of the Thaw. Despite the serendipity at play in *Spring on Zarechnaya Street,* it is a much more realistic film than *Roman Holiday,* and its honesty is its charm.

The optimism for the future that characterized *Roman Holiday* and *Spring on Zarechnaya Street* would change by the 1960s, however, as concerns about the dangers of nuclear power grew and, in the Soviet Union, as Thaw films took a darker turn. These concerns are evident in the subjects of the next chapter, *Nine Days in One Year* and *Fail-Safe.* Once again we shall see a high degree of convergence in the overarching mission of these two films, just as we see contrasts in approach to the material.

CHAPTER FIVE

Deterrence and Dissent

We have seen how, in the late 1940s and 1950s, Soviet and American film-makers delineated what their countries were fighting for—and against—in the Cold War. During this early, formative phase, key cinematic propaganda themes emerged that would by and large prevail throughout the conflict. According to Hollywood, the United States was combating totalitarianism in the name of freedom. According to Soviet cinema, Russia stood for progress in the face of capitalism and imperialism. That the two cinemas occupied diametrically opposed ideological positions in this way is of course hardly surprising. Most filmmakers thought patriotically, many were put under political pressures of one sort or another, and the start of any war helps accentuate a them-versus-us mentality.

As the Cold War aged, however, some filmmakers on both sides of the geopolitical curtain began to ask questions about the conflict. These questions tended to focus less on whether it was right to fight, and more on how and at what cost. Most often, filmmakers who challenged aspects of Cold War orthodoxy in this way were following the lead of politicians, journalists, or broadcasters. On the rare occasion, movies might appear whose messages were more original or, even if not, nonetheless proved to be highly controversial. What is interesting to consider about such films is the sort of issues they highlighted, in what ways, and when. From our point of view, it is especially important to identify the similarities and differences between American and Soviet films in this regard.

This chapter concentrates on the changes Soviet and American Cold War cinema underwent in the early 1960s. This was a period during which the two cinemas converged in terms of offering a forum for Cold War dissent to a greater degree than at any other point of the conflict. Rather than continuing on the oppositional parallel paths they had established in the 1950s, we shall see that, in fact, Soviet and American cinema had a good deal in common by the mid-1960s. Responding to cultural, political, and diplomatic changes, a small number of filmmakers in both countries expressed deep concerns about one issue in particular—nuclear science.

No two movies illustrate this better than *Nine Days in One Year* and *Fail-Safe*. Released on either side of the October 1962 Cuban missile crisis, they show how communist and capitalist cinemas challenged prevailing wisdom about the inherent dangers of nuclear science in apparently very different

127

but actually quite similar ways. An examination of the two films offers us an insight into the scope that existed for political dissent or protest in Soviet and American cinema during the 1960s. It also points to a fusion of visual aesthetics during this era, and questions how far such films, now critically revered, could act as a catalyst for political change.

Science and Sacrifice: *Nine Days in One Year*

"We are shown nine days, only nine days—one of them long, the others short. But in them, the nine: our life, our people, our arguments, our joy, and of course, our struggle."[1] The well-known writer, scenarist, and critic Yevgeny Gabrilovich wrote this appreciation in 1967, five years after the release of *Nine Days in One Year* and on the cusp of the Thaw's end.[2] The same year, when *Soviet Screen* reported on its annual readers' survey, *Nine Days in One Year* made the list for readers' all-time favorite films, right after *Chapaev* (Sergei Vasiliev and Georgy Vasiliev, 1934).[3] Of all the Soviet Cold War films, *Nine Days in One Year* is arguably the only work of art. This deeply subversive film about a nuclear accident at a physics research institute came, ironically, from that master of Cold War propaganda, Mikhail Romm (*The Russian Question, The Secret Mission*).

Nine Days in One Year pays tribute to the role of the scientist in Soviet life. The depiction of scientists in Thaw cinema had its antecedents in the Stalin era, most notably in the biopics of well-known Russian and Soviet scientists such as Aleksander Dovzhenko's film about the horticulturalist Michurin (*Michurin,* 1948/49). The most important early Cold War science film was, as noted in chapter 2, Abram Room's *The Court of Honor,* the story of a gullible biologist who almost turns the results of his research over to an American scientist on the payroll of a large pharmaceutical company. This film illustrated the keen distrust Stalin felt for scientists given their allegedly close ties to the West because of the inherent "cosmopolitanism" of science.[4] Stalin's concerns about possible traitors within the ranks of scientists, and his belief that science must be centrally controlled, are understandable when we consider that, according to Ethan Pollock, the Great Leader "saw science as a sphere of Cold War competition in its own right."[5] Grigory Aleksandrov's hilarious comedy *Spring* (*Vesna,* 1947) provides a slightly subversive example of the early Cold War science film.[6] In this picture Lyubov Orlova (who played Janet Sherwood in *The Meeting on the Elbe*) doubles as a well-known scientist and the actress who will play the scientist in a film. *Spring* satirizes the stiffness and supposed lack of femininity of women in the sciences. Due to a case of mistaken identities, the scientist finds herself in the role of the actress, and discovers that she likes "being a woman"—dressing up, learning to flirt, and finding romance.

At age sixty and with a checkered record in filmmaking, Mikhail Romm seemed an unlikely director to make a path-breaking film. This was despite his evident talent, which could be seen in his first film, *Pyshka* (1934), one of the last silent pictures in Soviet cinema.[7] Romm survived the brutal 1930s as the maker of films like *Lenin in October* (*Lenin v Oktiabre*, 1937) and *Lenin in 1918* (*Lenin v 1918 godu*, 1939). His best-known World War II film was *Person no. 217* (*Chelovek no. 217*, 1944/45), a compelling story of Soviet prisoners being used as slave labor for the Germans.

During the war, Romm had acted as the conscience of the film industry, attempting to intercede with Stalin on issues of bureaucratic interference, censorship, and antisemitism. Despite this, Romm seemed to follow the Party line rather easily in the late 1940s and early 1950s. His results, however, often left something to be desired as far as the cinema administration was concerned; recall the conflict over *The Secret Mission* discussed in chapter 2. After Stalin's death, he was quiet, making only one fiction film in the 1950s—*The Murder on Dante Street* (*Ubiistvo na ulitse Dante*, 1956), about French wartime collaboration—which he disliked for its artificiality.[8] As Romm ruefully noted, the Stalin era had ruined "not only those who were not allowed to make films but also the chosen few who were."[9]

For most of the 1950s, Romm was running an experimental workshop in the Mosfilm studio and teaching at the VGIK, the All-Union State Institute of Cinematography, where he attracted a passionate following among younger filmmakers. There he met scenarist Dmitry Khrabovitsky, then in his late thirties, whom Romm chose as his co-writer for the script of *Nine Days in One Year*. In another key recruitment, Romm selected an inexperienced thirty-one-year-old cinematographer, Gherman Lavrov, for the crew. Rejuvenated by working with the next generation of filmmakers, including Grigory Chukhrai, Andrei Tarkovsky, and Georgy Danelya, Romm disavowed his previous compromises.[10] The result is a remarkable film at last worthy of his considerable ability.

Nine Days in One Year is structured as a series of linked episodes following the lives of three young nuclear physicists: the experimentalist Dmitry Gusev (Aleksei Batalov), his girlfriend and later wife Lyolya (Tatyana Lavrova), and their friend, the theorist Ilya Kulikov (Innokenty Smoktunovsky). Gusev and Kulikov are rising stars in the field of nuclear physics. Lyolya, however, puts any career goals she might have had to the side and dedicates herself to becoming Gusev's caregiver first and a physicist second.

The first of the film's nine days takes place in early autumn, beginning with a scene of rising panic. With alarm sirens blaring and a neon "Danger" sign flashing, people run about trying to find out what has happened. "It's Sintsov," they whisper. While working on a test, Gusev and his mentor

Nine Days in One Year: Kulikov and Lyolya in the hospital waiting for Gusev. Courtesy of Ruscico/Photofest.

Sintsov are irradiated by neutrons leaking from an experimental thermonuclear unit. (In his memoirs, published in 1990, the eminent Soviet nuclear physicist and dissident Andrei Sakharov called this a "remote possibility, then and now.")[11] Sintsov's dose will prove fatal, while Gusev's leaves him with a bleak future.

The second day takes place two months later, in a clinic in Moscow, from which Gusev is about to be released. Gusev's longtime girlfriend Lyolya arrives with Kulikov to pick him up; afterward, the three go to a chic restaurant to dine. Lyolya plans to tell Gusev that she has fallen in love with Kulikov and will marry him. She is understandably uncomfortable, and Kulikov's cowardice in helping her break the news does not calm her nerves.

Lyolya and Kulikov's plans for marriage are eventually derailed. In Moscow's central telephone exchange, where people would go to place long distance calls, often with poor connections, the uncommunicative and distant Gusev confesses to Lyolya that his prognosis is grim because this was not the first time he had been irradiated. He is determined nevertheless to hang on for a year to finish his research. Lyolya then announces to the startled Kulikov, who had stepped out to allow them privacy for what he thought would be an embarrassing and painful conversation, that she is marrying Gusev instead. Her decision arises from guilt over her desire for Kulikov and her betrayal of Gusev, as well as from compassion for Gusev's condition, his loneliness, and what she believes is his true love for her.

Gusev and Lyolya marry on day three, in an ironically festive celebration at the House of Scientists—ironic given that the groom is probably dying and the bride has married him out of pity. Yet the guests are clearly enjoying themselves, feasting and endlessly talking about physics, and even Gusev manages to break a smile. He dances with Lyolya to the beat of some tame jazz music.

Day four takes place in winter. Lyolya is horrified at what she has become, a dissatisfied housewife with a growing resentment toward Gusev, who only cares about his work. Around the kitchen table he pays her no attention as he reads the newspaper, eating the breakfast she has grudgingly prepared so that her husband can enjoy a few extra minutes of sleep. Gusev stays at work longer and longer, generally coming home after his wife has gone to bed.

The fifth day marks the arrival of spring. It is breakfast time again. Lyolya is absentmindedly oversalting the kasha (breakfast cereal) as she mulls over her unenviable situation. Gusev does not notice the saltiness, and when she asks how it is he pronounces the breakfast fine. He then rushes off to the institute, after complaining as usual that his wife is always too late to ride with him. When Kulikov unexpectedly arrives at their apartment, Lyolya is startled because she thinks it is her husband who has returned to fetch her. Having had no idea Gusev's work has reached a critical stage, she learns that he had invited Kulikov to the institute to witness the conclusion of his tests. The experiment is a success: they are able to chart and repeat what looks like a historic, thermonuclear reaction. Yet unbeknownst to members of Gusev's staff, who are literally jumping for joy at their victory, Gusev has again been irradiated, for the third time.

The sixth day starts at night. Gusev is discouraged by the results of his group's efforts to increase the neutron flux, which may mean that the reaction is not thermonuclear after all. He is especially depressed because his health is declining rapidly, a condition that he still attempts to hide from Lyolya. Finally he confesses to her: "It's the beginning of the end."

On day seven, Gusev takes Lyolya on a surprise visit to meet his family, who are, rather incongruously, villagers living in a world as far removed from the world of experimental nuclear physics as imaginable. (The first shot, of Gusev's sister or sister-in-law carrying pails, records a scene that could have taken place a century earlier.) Gusev is uncomfortable around his family; he clearly has not visited them often, and they did not attend his wedding. His illness is now obvious: his hands shake and there are beads of perspiration on his forehead. He looks unnatural against these natural surroundings (the only time we really see "nature" in the film), even stiffer and more standoffish than usual. In a conversation while Lyolya attempts to sleep, Gusev's father asks him point-blank if he was involved in making "the

Nine Days in One Year: Gusev alone with his machines. Courtesy of Ruscico/Photofest.

bomb." He admits that he was. The visit lasts one day, and on their return Lyolya is seen back in the laboratory. They are more at home there than in their real "home."

Day eight, the "most important day of his life," as the voiceover narrator intones, marks the return of autumn. After Lyolya has gone to work, Gusev leaves his bed to head for the lab on foot. He is gravely ill, and it has been a while since he was last there. Once at the lab, he discovers that Lyolya has secretly asked Kulikov to supervise Gusev's project, but to no avail. The experiment still will not work, even though there is a new installation. Gusev, recognizing that he has failed, is furious and shouts at everyone. He rushes away, and when Lyolya follows him he tells her that he needs to return to the Moscow clinic immediately.

The film's ninth and last day finds Gusev back at the hospital. He has persuaded his doctor to conduct a dangerous experimental operation on him—a bone marrow transplant—his only chance to survive a little while longer. This is against the doctor's better judgment, who tartly tells him, "I don't experiment on humans." (They have previously had a discussion about experimenting on dogs.) Lyolya and Kulikov are in the hospital lobby, waiting, just as they were on day two. The film ends without resolution, the three planning to dine out together as they had after Gusev's first hospital stay.

This remarkable film delineated the outer limits of Thaw cinema at a time when it was becoming clear that the end of the Thaw was near. Not only does it reject "positive legitimation" and decline to provide closure, but its severe visual aesthetic also sets it outside the Soviet mainstream. The characters are mainly shrouded in darkness; the sets are sparsely and functionally dressed; there is no music to soften the stark effect.[12] Technical and artistic accomplishments aside, *Nine Days* has multiple layers of meaning that a recitation of its plot can only suggest. We shall treat the most important here: the valorization of the scientist, particularly the physicist; the return of the martyr hero; the tensions between public and private life; and the collision of two competing worldviews about nuclear science.

That physicists were considered heroes at this time is not surprising. Although publicly the state extolled its scientific advances, privately Soviet officials were acutely aware of American superiority in physics, notwithstanding the Soviet detonation of the atomic bomb in 1949, which quelled some of Stalin's fears about his scientists' loyalties and abilities. Still, the Soviets' need to catch up was clear,[13] and the conditions for scientists began to change, especially for physicists. This process accelerated after Stalin's death, aided by Khrushchev's keen understanding of the function of science in the Cold War. The way to overcome Soviet backwardness, the Kremlin decided, was to give physicists more autonomy and privileges. The result was that under Khrushchev scientists became "elite members of Soviet society," a status derived from "their ability to innovate."[14] Major new research facilities were established to augment the older, secret sites. As Pollock notes, a "mutually beneficial relationship between physics and the Soviet government" began in 1949 and became a "powerful symbol of the Soviet sciences in the 1950s."[15] Many scientists also used their new prestige as a platform for talking about much needed changes in society.[16] It is this privileged life of Soviet physicists, with spacious apartments, first-rate health care, and private cars, that is very much apparent in *Nine Days in One Year*.

Romm's decision to make his scientists physicists and to situate the film in a secret research facility was, therefore, fraught with political meaning, especially after the successful detonation of the Soviet hydrogen bomb in 1955.[17] The fact that his hero, Gusev, admits to having worked on "the bomb" provides a source of tension with other characters in the film. For example, although Gusev emphasizes the positive uses of his work, particularly in terms of finding peaceful uses for nuclear energy, his father clearly disapproves of his son's involvement with atomic weapons.

But the choice of subject was more than merely topical. As film scholar Alexander Prokhorov notes, the older generation of filmmakers (to which Romm belonged) privileged the scientist as "the tragic visionary and potential redeemer" of society.[18] Even the official history of Soviet cinema saw larger meaning in Romm's choice of physicist-protagonists, because such individuals engaged with serious questions of "life and death and the future of mankind."[19]

The film's amalgamation of an old-style hero to the new aesthetics provides yet one more source of artistic tension. Gusev is in most respects a model scientist and a model Socialist Realist hero;[20] Andrei Sakharov believed at the time that the character was modeled after himself.[21] Although Sakharov may certainly have inspired Romm in part, it is likely that Gusev was also patterned after a lesser-known Socialist Realist hero, the film director Vladimir Skuibin. Skuibin had worked doggedly up to his early death at the age of thirty-four in 1962. According to Aleksei Batalov, who played Gusev, the Skuibin story had impressed Romm, especially Skuibin's desire to "live one more year" in order to finish his last project.[22]

Although Gusev is taciturn and glum (unlike a Socialist Realist hero), he is also brilliant, self-sacrificing, and self-effacing. He scoffs at the idea of naming the reaction he has discovered the "Gusev effect," claiming that his name, the root of which means "goose" in Russian, sounds too silly. He is so devoted to his work that Lyolya concludes that she is little more to him than a housekeeper.

Aleksei Batalov's persona as an intense leading man (established in *The Cranes Are Flying, My Dear Man,* among many others) reinforces Gusev's laconic heroism in the screenplay. But despite Gusev's obvious heroism, the film causes the viewer to question the value of his sacrifices on the altar of science, particularly when his alter ego Kulikov is on the scene. Indeed, the film's problem insofar as its depiction of Soviet scientists was concerned lay not in Gusev's characterization but in Kulikov's.

Innokenty Smoktunovsky, who played Kulikov as the "antipode" to Gusev,[23] was an especially charismatic actor and one of the leading heartthrobs of the Soviet screen. Smoktunovsky dominates every scene he is in, to the extent that his role seems much bigger than it actually is. His Kulikov is as silver-tongued as Batalov's Gusev is tongue-tied. He talks constantly, but everything he has to say is interesting, especially his tart and cynical observations about people and life. In the restaurant scene, for example, he refers to the other diners as "Neanderthals," and he scorns Gusev's idealism about science. Kulikov is, moreover, handsome and well dressed. (Romm wants us to understand that Lyolya's rejection of such a man is truly a sacrifice.) Yet he too is a brilliant and dedicated scientist, as well as a good friend; Lyolya and Gusev's marriage does not seem to bother him for long, and he endures their emotional ups and downs with bemused patience.

In a classic Socialist Realist film, a man like Kulikov would have either been exposed as a traitor or reeducated by Gusev. Neither happens. What Romm has accomplished through Kulikov, therefore, is to complicate the icon of the physicist in ways that disturbed the political watchdogs at the Mosfilm studio. Although the other scientists in the film are portrayed as eager, obsessed pedants, Kulikov stands alone, and above them, a cosmopolitan to the core.

Lyolya's role as scientist also complicates the story and reveals much about the condition of women in the USSR despite the vaunted equality of the sexes. Lyolya, arguably the film's most complex—and most irritating—character, is in certain respects a stock figure, the sidekick or the all-suffering helpmeet. There are three possible ways to understand her. The first is somewhat unsavory: that the young woman has failed to live up to her promise as a scientist and therefore has attached herself to two highly successful men in order to bask in their reflected glory. When she is at the lab, she seems more like a technician than a scientist, on the sidelines rather than at the center of the action. Much of the time, she is seen in the shadowy halls of the facility, clipboard in hand, without seeming to have any real purpose in the purposeful activity that swirls around her, her white lab coat the only sign that she belongs there.

The second possible and more subversive interpretation is that Lyolya reflects the double bind of women in science: the difficulty of reconciling being a full-time wife with the more-than-full-time demands of major scientific research. Why should she not be resentful? Although she is not a particularly successful homemaker, she has added another layer of duties to her busy schedule. The recurring breakfast scenes are a case in point. She has to drag Gusev out of bed in the morning, which she tries to do cheerfully in the tones of a perky housewife, before struggling over the preparation of a hot breakfast for her man. Yet Gusev cannot understand why she is not dressed and ready to leave when he is. "Well, *I'm* ready," he says in annoyance, completely self-absorbed and unaware of everything she has done to help him be ready on time. Very self-aware, Lyolya is also self-critical, as we hear from her interior monologues or when she is talking to herself. She does this frequently when she is alone, which is almost always. She is not, however, ready to break with society's expectations for her and sums her dilemma up this way: "I'm a bad physicist. I'm a bad wife."

The final and perhaps most subversive interpretation is that Lyolya has atrophied both as a wife and as a physicist because she married the wrong person. The supposedly honorable decision to marry Gusev was the wrong one for her. She represents a version of the Soviet female martyr, but there is no commendation for her in a society that values physicists, not women.

The return of the martyr-hero of Socialist Realism is closely linked to the valorization of Gusev as scientist. Gusev was not the only martyr-hero in Thaw filmmaking; two other prominent examples, the sharpshooter

Nine Days in One Year: Lyolya hurriedly dresses, late as always. Courtesy of Ruscico/Photofest.

Mariusya in Grigory Chukhrai's *The Forty-First* (*Sorok pervyi,* 1956), and the supply-master Gubanov in Yuly Raizman's *The Communist* (*Kommunist,* 1958), also put duty to the cause above life and love. In *Nine Days in One Year,* the cause has shifted from the Revolution to worship of a new god, science.

Gusev cares about his health and prospects for survival only in relation to the demands of science. His model was Sintsov, an aggressive scientist who put his experiment before his safety and dies as a result. After the accident, although Sintsov is completely aware that he is dying from radiation poisoning that cannot be seen, heard, or smelled, he is positively ebullient, chattering away. He refuses to lie down to allow the doctors to attend to him and brusquely demands his special pencil, the one he uses to write his "best thoughts." The "best thoughts" he needs to note in this instance are a record of the events leading to the accident, including a diagram of his and Gusev's positions relative to the reactor. When Sintsov's hysterical wife arrives on the scene, he bellows for her to go away. "Can't you see we're working?" Gusev watches silently the entire time, absorbing Sintsov's example.

Thus, even though one might have expected Gusev to withdraw from the laboratory after the accident to enjoy his last months of life, this is never an option for him. Like his mentor, his enjoyment of life lies only in his work and his expectations of discovery. In his complete devotion to science he is Sintsov's perfect heir. After the accident, when ordered to lie down, he immediately declares that he is "completely healthy." Only after he collapses as he walks up the steps of a plane does he accept help—but because he has no choice. After his release from the hospital, he tells Lyolya that no one besides her needs to know the true condition of his health, not just because he wants no pity, but also because he wants nothing to interfere with his work.

Gusev's belief that science is a worldview provides another clue to the reasons behind his martyrdom. We see that he is deeply dedicated to science as a means not only of progress, but also as a means of defense for his country. Working on the bomb was a way of ensuring the survival of mankind, following his belief that what was known as "mutual assured destruction" (MAD) was the only defense again nuclear holocaust. Gusev's own life is unimportant against the larger forces of history.

Even at the end, he is offering himself up as a guinea pig for an experimental operation, recalling the dying dog that disturbed him as he discussed experimentation on animals with his doctor on day two. At his wedding, Gusev is toasted as a "Soviet scientist, a simple Soviet man," an updated version of *homo sovieticus,* devoted with all his heart to the cause. Yet even this Soviet man can finally assert some self-interest. "I did not come to die," he says to the doctor, and later, when they are discussing the virtual impossibility of the operation succeeding, Gusev explains that he is willing to become part of an experiment because "I should live."

Lyolya is another kind of Soviet martyr. She recognizes that Gusev is a Great Man who needs her support, whether or not he knows it. She sacrifices her happiness with Kulikov to marry the dour Gusev, and gradually falls in love with him as she comes to value the straightforward quality of his character in contrast to the cynical Kulikov. She continues to work at the laboratory but presumably with half-hearted attention. She sets aside her career in order to focus on humdrum housekeeping chores, like learning to make a proper kasha, in which she takes neither pleasure nor pride. But unlike Gusev, she grumbles and whines to herself, filled with self-pity and self-loathing. She feels she should at least be able to take satisfaction in her sacrifice, but she cannot. Unlike Gusev, she longs for external reinforcement to validate her decision, but she never receives it from Gusev, and certainly not from Kulikov. That she is the only character whose thoughts we know from interior monologues and conversations aloud with herself is especially important. It seems that Romm wants to complicate the way that the public/private split has been structured in Soviet life. The viewer never hears Gusev's thoughts, however, which implies that he has no doubts. He is what he seems to be.

The theme of public and private life, always a problematic issue in Soviet society, takes a surprising turn in *Nine Days in One Year*. Gusev represents a reversion to the old Socialist Realist model of the hero who is essentially un-interested in a private life and privileges the public sector. Private life, with the demands of women, children, and home, will naturally sap a man of his strength. But unlike the classic, essentially upbeat Socialist Realist hero such as Chapaev or Alyosha in *The Fall of Berlin,* Gusev is a heavy-hearted character who takes no joy from life (apart from his science), despite his professed desire to live. It is important to keep in mind that Gusev was probably like this before his irradiation. After all, he had strung Lyolya along for six years without commitment to marry, hence her "defection" to Kulikov. The viewer may admire Gusev's dedication to his work but at the same time is likely to feel sorry for him (or annoyed with him).

Kulikov, on the other hand, is indeed Gusev's antipode. The essence of "lightness" (in Milan Kundera's definition), he is engaged with his work but not overly so. He takes what should have been a heavy blow—Lyolya's impulsive marriage to Gusev—with equanimity. Of all the characters he alone can smile in gloomy times, probably because he takes such a dim view of human nature.

The decline of Lyolya—her rapid slide into depression—represents the degradation of the Socialist Realist heroine. She is supposed to be a superwoman, able to juggle both public and private life—the demands of a career and home—efficiently and happily. But the viewer accepts her word that she is no better a physicist than she is a homemaker. The Gusev home is cold and under-furnished, devoid of homely knickknacks, and basically book-free, which would have startled contemporary viewers from the intelligentsia. Lyolya's desire to do good is strong, but she never succeeds. She knows it, too. As she says to Gusev during an outburst near the end of the film, "Why do you need me? Stupid question. It seems to me that I bother you." In bed, she tries to kiss him, with no response. (She initially interprets this as a rejection, then realizes when he runs out of the room how sick he is.)

Finally, Gusev's and Kulikov's worldviews on science need to be examined. By the early 1960s, there was a split among scientists on nuclear policy, with Andrei Sakharov calling for test bans and conservative scientists holding fast.[24] Kulikov and Gusev debate about the latter's firm belief in the ultimate humanity of science. Kulikov ticks off a list of harmful applications that have resulted from pure science, including the German development of poison gas from chemical discoveries and the American invention of the atomic bomb from nuclear fission. He finds scientific disaster inevitable, due to human curiosity and human greed, regardless of the potential costs to humanity. Note that Kulikov does not single out American science as a particular evil; his mention of the bomb and the Americans is strictly matter-of-fact. This is life according to Kulikov; if the Soviets could have made the bomb first, they would have.

Gusev, on the other hand, feels the need to justify himself when his father asks him about the bomb, presumably the hydrogen variant since Gusev would have been in school at the time of the atomic bomb. Like Gusev, his father is a laconic man. "Did you make the bomb?" his father asks him bluntly, staring at Gusev with penetrating eyes, clearly fearing the answer. "Yes," Gusev answers, adding, "If we hadn't made it we wouldn't be having this conversation—and half of humanity as well." Gusev obviously means that in the absence of a Soviet bomb, the Soviets would have been annihilated by the Americans. Well and good, but which character speaks for Romm? Is it Kulikov, who believes in the inevitable evil uses to which scientific advances will be applied, or Gusev, who can make even the bad (the bomb) seem good? Gusev's hurried rationalization to his father about the bomb seems to belie his general optimism about the beneficence of science.

The answer to this question lies in the film's visual style, which is integral to its message. As noted above, the film is dark and gloomy, with heavy reliance on shadows. The laboratory is abstracted, shrouded in foreboding darkness, filled with a twisting maze of large pipes and heavy lead doors and a welter of dials on control panels. Nothing is identifiable to the lay viewer as a particular type of apparatus. Apart from Gusev, Kulikov, and Lyolya (and to a certain extent Sintsov and Gusev's doctor), the other characters populating the film remain anonymous, abstractions of scientists rather than real people. Humans, in other words, seem to be dwarfed, even controlled, by machines, machines that leak invisible death. The film's most famous scene occurs on day eight. The camera tracks a tiny, very sick Gusev in extreme long shot as he trudges to the laboratory, traversing a seemingly endless, high, blank wall, which confirms the relatively minor position of humans compared to what they have built.[25] Gusev's discomfiture with his family, who as farmers are close to nature, and his reluctance to stay more than a day on the farm, reinforces his alienation from the natural world, even though working with the laws of nature is his calling.

It is not surprising that, according to Lev Anninsky, bard of the sixties generation, the "film aroused a furor,"[26] for the paradoxes presented by its central characters, for its scintillating dialogue, its strange beauty, and its uncomfortable ending, not to mention its forthright engagement with one of the burning issues of the day. Aleksei Batalov recalled: "Disputes and arguments raged, as much about physicists and poets as about the new morality, about Picasso's paintings, and so on."[27]

The experienced Romm had not, of course, been naïve about the dangers of the topic, and the script went through several iterations in 1960. He

Nine Days in One Year: A very sick Gusev walks to the laboratory. Courtesy of Ruscico/
Photofest.

was determined to ensure authenticity and, according to Andrei Sakharov,
met both with Vasily Emelianov, the director of a commission for the peaceful uses of atomic energy, and then with Igor Tamm, Sakharov's mentor, to
talk about the issues connected with magnetic thermonuclear reactors.[28] As
Josephine Woll notes, the topic was so sensitive that the script was sent to
the atomic energy division of the Council of Ministers for review to be sure
that it did not reveal scientific secrets. The official who read it was disturbed
that "the authors of the scenario turn this one case of irradiation into a law,
suggesting that the danger of radiation is inevitable."[29] (Sakharov too was
disturbed by the "artificiality of its plot.")[30] When the partly finished film was
screened for the Artistic Council of the Mosfilm studio, committee members were worried about the film's negativism and ambiguity.[31]

The unhappy ending was a particular sticking point, but as Romm wrote
about the film to actress Faina Ranevskaya (from *The Meeting on the Elbe*),
"There are no happy people in the world except for fools and also cheats."[32]
Fortunately, Romm found a powerful ally for the film in the person of math-
ematician Mstislav Keldysh, president of the Soviet Academy of Sciences,
who put in a good word with the minister of culture, Yekaterina Furtseva.[33]
The film was released in March 1962 after an unusual amount of pre-pub-
licity.[34]

Given the fissures evident in the Soviet Union under Khrushchev, it is
not surprising that reactions to the film were sharply divided. It was heavily

reviewed in publications major and minor from all around the country.[35] Liberal critics, recognizing that Kulikov was an extremely negative character in the Soviet context, self-censored their writing about the film as though it were solely about Gusev, his heroism, and his martyrdom. Such reviews were overwhelmingly laudatory (although even in these there are complaints about Lyolya's characterization).

Liberal critics also praised the realism of the film in fulsome, Socialist Realist terms. "The world of this film is populated with living, intelligent, thoughtful, reflective people. They are simple, but not simpleminded."[36] "Gusev and his comrades are first of all good people," not just hardworking but also humane, "good, honest, glorious people."[37] "Gusev! Our dear Gusev and your wonderful friends—Soviet people in the forefront of science."[38] The film was praised in Art of the Cinema (Iskusstvo kino) as a "decided step forward," and even in Pravda as a "talented film."[39] Pravda went on to note the importance of the subject: "It's very good that our cinema is engaging with complicated and important themes of contemporary life."[40] It was also lauded in the journal Science and Life (Nauka i zhizn) for emphasizing that science is a collective endeavor.[41] The film's obviously serious theme led critic Nik. Kruzhkov to warn viewers: "The film Nine Days in One Year [forces one to] worry, think, argue, experience. It's not the kind of cinema picture that one watches for entertainment or to pass the time."[42]

Conservative critics, exemplified by those writing in October (Oktiabr) and Young Communist Pravda (Komsomolskaia pravda), saw the film as a natural outgrowth of disturbing new trends that had begun with The Cranes Are Flying, trends that were linked with Westernism. Kulikov's blasé persona epitomized these trends, yet even Gusev was not immune from criticism because of his passivity.[43] (Why, for example, did he remain friends with Kulikov?) Pavel Strokov attacked the film: "Are there really such troglodytes among Soviet scientists, who are famous for their humanism and their struggle for peace [emphasis added]? . . . If art is true to life, this collective of scientists should be shown as true citizens of their Motherland, with a broad intellectual sweep, politically mature, and far-sighted. But the heroes of the film seem to live on some kind of little island, cut off from the whole country."[44]

In fact, scientists at the secret institutes did live on "some kind of little island," cut off from the cares of ordinary Soviet citizens and the woes of ordinary Soviet life, as the memoirs of Andrei Sakharov amply illustrate. Although in less vivid terms than Strokov's, M. Kvasnetskaia also countered the left's disingenuous claims that Kulikov was intended as a foil to Gusev, understanding the attractiveness of Kulikov to the disenchanted. She found all the characters, not only Lyolya, to be one-dimensional: "the audience wants more from these characters."[45]

Negative reviews notwithstanding (or perhaps because they helped raise interest), *Nine Days in One Year* was seen by 23.9 million viewers, an extremely high number for an art film.[46] (By comparison, another artistically significant film from 1962, Andrei Tarkovsky's *Ivan's Childhood* [*Ivanovo detstvo*], reached 16.7 million viewers.)[47] *Nine Days* was named Best Picture of 1962 by *Soviet Screen*'s cinephile readership; Aleksei Batalov was voted Best Actor by readers. It was exhibited at the Karlovy Vary, San Francisco, and Melbourne film festivals, and Artkino imported it for screening in the United States.[48] In 1967, it was listed among the top seventeen films from the previous decade, a decade that included many outstanding Thaw pictures.[49] *Nine Days in One Year* has become a classic of Soviet art cinema and has been written about more than any other Soviet film discussed herein.[50]

A film as original and troubling as *Nine Days in One Year* was unlikely to unleash a wave of imitators, especially in the chilling cultural climate of the early 1960s, a climate that had become icy by 1968. Yet *Nine Days*' influence may be seen in Frunze Dovliatian's *Hello, It's Me!* (*Zdravstvui, eto ia!*, 1965/66, 10 million viewers). Set in 1942, this is a film about two young physicists and the "class relations" between scientists and intellectuals on the one hand and "the people" (*narod*) on the other. Ilya Averbakh's first full-length film, *Degree of Risk* (*Stepen riska*, 1969, 16.9 million viewers), about a research surgeon, is another film considered to have drawn inspiration from *Nine Days in One Year*.[51]

An Accident Waiting to Happen: *Fail-Safe*

Variously described by critics on its release as "one of the most important films in our times" and "a sensational scareshow," Sidney Lumet's tense nuclear thriller *Fail-Safe* caused as much controversy in the United States in 1964 as *Nine Days in One Year* had two years earlier in the Soviet Union.[52] Indeed, it is remarkable how similar the two films are, both ideologically and stylistically, given the tendency of historians to portray American and Soviet cinema during the Cold War as akin to chalk and cheese.[53] Like *Nine Days in One Year*, *Fail-Safe* was politically a deeply subversive film, casting grave doubts on the sanity of nuclear science. This it did by depicting another set of nuclear experts, the political scientists who advise governments on nuclear strategy as the Cold War's new priesthood, alienated from and a potential threat to the rest of mankind. *Fail-Safe*, too, showed how the Cold War state trampled over people's private lives, demanding the ultimate sacrifice. Fundamentally, going a step further than *Nine Days in One Year*, Lumet's film argued that humans were in thrall to machines, with potentially devastating consequences not just for scientists but for everyone. All these messages, like those conveyed in *Nine Days in One Year*, were accentuated by thoughtful, minimalist filmmaking: via the use of sparse sets, stark black-and-white photography, and a conspicuous absence of music.

Both *Fail-Safe* and *Nine Days in One Year* used time as a dramatic device, but in very different ways. In the latter, the clock ticks slowly, marking a poisoned scientist's painful last months on earth. By contrast, in *Fail-Safe* we are invited to experience, in what seems like real time, what may be the last few hours *of* earth. The audience watches as an accident, caused not by human error (as in Romm's film) but by mechanical malfunction, sends a group of nuclear-armed U.S. bombers from their "fail-safe" positions outside Soviet air space to attack Moscow. When combined U.S. and Soviet efforts fail to stop the warplanes, the American president realizes he can forestall World War III only by ordering a nuclear attack on New York as compensation for the destruction of the Soviet capital. His anguish is even more acute because his wife will likely be killed in the process.

If the power of *Nine Days in One Year* was enhanced by its unwillingness to provide closure, *Fail-Safe*'s denouement was equally provocative for refusing to provide a final, upbeat twist. The result is one of the most stylish and thought-provoking endings of any American Cold War movie. As the bombs fall on New York, a series of swooping zoom-shots of one half-second each catch the final moments of moving, pulsating life on the city's streets before an almost instantaneous freeze-frame. A children's group at the Bronx Zoo, two arguing taxi drivers, and a Park Avenue doorman walking a poodle are, along with millions of others, gone.

Fail-Safe was part of a cycle of American anti-nuclear and anti-Cold War movies made in the early to mid-1960s. Hollywood was experiencing its own thaw during this period, for several reasons. The demise of the traditional studio system was opening up space for liberal, independent producers to make more politically conscious movies. The post–World War II baby boom was giving rise to a younger, more liberal audience that wanted more experimental films. Television was forcing filmmakers to think more creatively, both socially and artistically. And HUAC's grip on Hollywood had diminished, with blacklisting being discontinued.

Like all high-profile oppositional movies of this era (*On the Beach, The Manchurian Candidate, Dr. Strangelove, Seven Days in May, The Bedford Incident*), *Fail-Safe* was based on a best-selling novel. This is important, for it points to Hollywood's marked tendency to take the political lead from other public opinion makers during the Cold War, especially when it came to dissent. Written by two political scientists, Eugene Burdick and Harvey Wheeler, the novel was published the same month as the Cuban missile crisis, October 1962. It subsequently stayed at the top of the *New York Times* best-seller list for several months, and by late 1964, when the movie version appeared, it had sold upward of two million copies and been translated into ten languages.[54]

Fail-Safe's underlying premise—that a nuclear war could be triggered by a flaw in the United States' highly computerized military machinery—sparked heated debate in late 1962. Even though it was a novel, critics accused the authors of irresponsibility in exaggerating the risks of accidental war. By distorting the facts of the actual command procedures of the American nuclear forces, argued the philosopher and co-founder of the Congress for Cultural Freedom, Sidney Hook, *Fail-Safe* fomented hysteria and was "intellectually scandalous."[55] Burdick and Wheeler's "faction" tapped into the widespread anxiety about technology in the sixties. In 1960, Norbert Wiener, the father of cybernetics, publicly warned of the dangers of World War III being caused by the military's fascination with "push-button" programming. Later in the decade, the residents of Pomona, California, even worried that opening their garage doors might accidentally launch guided nuclear missiles, because the test launch of missiles near the city was causing them to fly open.[56]

Such speculative stories might now strike us as comical, but they were not fantastical. A full-scale nuclear alert was triggered at one U.S. Air Force base in Minnesota during the Cuban missile crisis when a lone inquisitive bear was mistaken for communist saboteurs.[57] Back in the early 1960s, these stories were, in Lumet's opinion, an inevitable result of the secrecy surrounding America's nuclear deterrence system. Lumet (who was born in 1924) was part of that new generation of youngish liberal directors who had started their careers in television in the early 1950s before breaking into movies via the collapse of Hollywood's studio system. "We're suddenly living with things that are out of control," he told *Newsday* in early 1963. "I'm not going to leave it to an IBM machine whether I'm going to be blown sky-high or not." Max Youngstein, *Fail-Safe's* independent financier and producer who bought the screen rights to Burdick and Wheeler's novel in January 1963 for $300,000, concurred. Youngstein was a member of SANE and other groups concerned about the possibility of accidental nuclear war, and believed the government was withholding critical information about the potential for failure of the nation's so-called safeguard system.[58]

Hollywood had subjected that system, and Washington's overall nuclear strategy, to little serious scrutiny since their inception in the mid-1940s. There was a spate of mutant movies in the 1950s—*Them!* (Gordon Douglas, 1954), *The Incredible Shrinking Man* (Jack Arnold, 1957), *Attack of the Crab Monsters* (Roger Corman, 1957), and others—which, much like the Soviet-made *Amphibious Man,* had clear psychological roots in fears of genetic damage from radioactive fallout.[59] At the same time, Hollywood had

Fail-Safe: Sidney Lumet (center, with glasses) directs Larry Hagman (Buck, left) and Henry Fonda (the U.S. president) in a stark and sparsely furnished mock-up of the White House bomb shelter. Courtesy of the Academy of Motion Picture Arts and Sciences (AMPAS).

made a host of documentaries and features that, like the immensely popular Jimmy Stewart vehicle *Strategic Air Command* (Anthony Mann, 1955), sought to assuage the public's anxieties about mutual assured destruction by showing that America's nuclear "umbrella" protected both the nation and world peace. Such films reflected the often close give-and-take relationship that existed between Hollywood and the Defense Department during the Cold War, with producers enjoying access to spectacular military hardware so long as the Pentagon was allowed to vet their scripts.[60]

The tight script for *Fail-Safe* was written by Walter Bernstein, a former communist whom Lumet had rescued from the blacklist in the 1950s by allowing him to collaborate without attribution on many of his television projects. Bernstein, who would later write the screenplay for Martin Ritt's satire on the communist witch hunts of the 1950s, *The Front* (1976),[61] made few substantive changes to Burdick and Wheeler's novel. Among the exceptions, however, were the words spoken by the U.S. president at the end and the greater emphasis the film places on the psychological and moral aspects of human crisis. Earlier in the Cold War, the Production Code Administration would have disapproved strongly of a project like *Fail-Safe* on moral and political grounds. In April 1963, however, the only change to Bernstein's script the organization requested was the deletion of a few expletives. This provides concrete proof of the cultural shift taking place in Hollywood during the early 1960s.[62]

Not surprisingly, after reading *Fail-Safe*'s script in early 1963, the Pentagon refused point-blank to cooperate on the movie's production. Military officials told Youngstein that the picture he was painting of the nation's safeguard system (called Positive Control) was wrong on several counts. A malfunctioning computer, for instance, would have automatically resulted in the recall of bombers and not in a signal to attack as presented in the novel and script. Youngstein countered by arguing that even if the film misrepresented certain details, it was essentially right in claiming that the fail-safe system's weaknesses rendered an accidental nuclear war possible. When Youngstein then found that even stock military footage from rental houses was off-limits to Lumet, and firms like IBM and General Dynamics refused to let the filmmakers see some of their machines involved in defense work, the producer accused the government of organized censorship.[63]

Lacking free actuality footage put a serious strain on *Fail-Safe*'s $1.3 million budget. Nevertheless, through a combination of thrift, clever improvisation, and sheer guesswork, the filmmakers succeeded in making a movie that most critics found highly realistic. In order to save money and to reduce what Lumet called "fakery," the film was shot "live" in a mere thirty-two days at an old Twentieth Century-Fox studio in New York, rather than in Hollywood where rental rates and manpower were more expensive. Lumet opted for black-and-white instead of color film, partly because it was cheaper, but also because he believed its darker tones accentuated tension when coupled with what he termed old-fashioned, Eisenstein-style lighting. Art director Albert Brenner built huge mock-up sets of areas representing the Pentagon war room, the president's White House bomb shelter, and Strategic Air Command's Omaha headquarters based on military journals, copies of *Air Force Magazine*, and interviews. The computer-generated images on SAC's control-room screen (depicting the location of bomber jets and air explosions over a map of the world) were entirely drawn by hand courtesy of former Disney cartoonist John Hubley. A flight trainer at La Guardia airport was used for cockpit filming; an oversized metal construction-site phone was used for the "hotline" conversations; and all shots of the outside of the U.S. Air Force Vindicator bombers (an invention of the novelists) were represented by a single piece of bootlegged footage of a Convair B-58 Hustler.[64]

Fail-Safe bears many similarities with Lumet's first movie, *Twelve Angry Men* (1957), an economically made (merely $343,000), tightly structured drama starring (and produced by) Hollywood heavyweight Henry Fonda. In it, Lumet used the space restrictions of the cramped setting to great advantage, generating uncommon tension from the claustrophobic confines of a jury room. *Fail-Safe* unfolds in a documentary-style format, with claustrophobic close-ups and long silences between the characters. The action takes place almost entirely in dimly lit bunkers, underground conference rooms, and aircraft cockpits. Cinematographer Gerald Hirschfield plays with light and shadow, often going for high-contrast compositions, but there is no overtly flashy camerawork. All this, allied to a tight script, lends *Fail-Safe* the look of a topical television program rather than a conventional Hollywood feature.

After introductory scenes, the story is told from four locations—SAC's underground headquarters in Omaha, the Pentagon war room, the president's White House bunker, and a Vindicator cockpit cruising into Soviet air space. It explores the deepening international crisis caused by a computer glitch in SAC's headquarters mainly through the eyes of four characters. Warren A. Black (played by the handsome, offbeat, Irish-born Dan O'Herlihy) is an Air Force general who, even before the crisis starts, has grave concerns about the superpowers' arms strategies. Like Gusev in *Nine Days in One Year*, he becomes the movie's martyr-hero who puts duty above life and love. Professor Groeteschele (the slouching, awkward-looking Walter Matthau) is Black's chief adversary, a defense analyst who believes in the rationality of nuclear computerization and in the concept of a winnable Third World War. Jack Grady (the grizzled, avuncular Edward Binns) is a jaded but loyal commander of SAC's Group Six, which mistakenly undertakes the bombing of Moscow. Finally, there is the wise and morally sound unnamed American president (Henry Fonda), who, despite being commander-in-chief, finds himself powerless in the face of a gargantuan military machine. Fonda, whose characteristically American, dignified personality helped him land the role of U.S. president several times in his career, privately shared Lumet's misgivings about their country's nuclear strategy.[65]

All these characters are finely drawn and played, but it is the chilling Groeteschele who stands out. While *Nine Days in One Year* indirectly challenged those pure scientists who were helping to make nuclear weapons, *Fail-Safe* overtly condemned the emerging new class of pseudo-scientists who were advising government on how those weapons could be used most creatively. If Gusev's character in *Nine Days in One Year* was patterned partly on Andrei Sakharov, then Groeteschele's was more obviously based on the leading U.S. "strategic analyst" of the era, Herman Kahn. By the 1960s, atomic strategy had become an arcane pursuit in the United States, dominated by a small group of civilian experts under contract to the armed services and based at semi-autonomous research institutes or at think tanks such as the RAND Corporation (which was closely tied to the Air Force). Using computer simulations, John von Neuman's game theory, and other analytical tools, these "defense intellectuals" transformed nuclear strategy into a rarified, quasi-scientific discipline. Their privileged status in academia, combined with the immense authority they wielded in high places, earned them the title "new priesthood" from their critics. Kahn, who worked for the RAND Corporation, refuted as "nonsense" the opinions of renowned Manhattan Project physicists such as Robert Oppenheimer, who for years had been campaigning about the dangers that nuclear escalation posed to humanity. Measuring the real nuclear threat and usability of weapons, Kahn argued, required newly devised "quantitative" studies performed from a "systems analysis point of view," meaning state-of-the-art scholarship that involved political, military, and strategic (rather than just technological) decisions. Kahn called this new approach "rational" and "logical," and dismissed anti-nuclear scientists as prehistoric "laymen."[66]

Groeteschele spouts Kahn's theories on the survivability and winnability of nuclear conflict almost verbatim on occasions. In his best-selling book *On Thermonuclear War,* published in 1960, Kahn had argued that *only* forty to eighty million U.S. civilians would be killed in a superpower nuclear conflict, leaving more than enough survivors to rebuild the American economy and Western "civilization." Early in the film Groeteschele amuses a late-night Washington cocktail party crowd with these sorts of figures. Later, in the Pentagon war room, as the crisis reaches its climax, he insists the government concentrate on rescuing not the people from New York but the records of American corporations from the debris of the metropolis. In his follow-up book, *Thinking the Unthinkable* (1962), Kahn had coolly discussed the possibility of nuclear automated response systems that required no human intervention. Such machinery did not in fact exist yet (and Kahn ultimately rejected their use in his book), but *Fail-Safe*'s makers found Kahn's theories barbaric and profoundly troubling. Groeteschele's philosophy is that of the survival of the fittest without the luxury of a moral dilemma. He is not insane. Instead, he is what Lumet considered that most dangerous of creatures: a civilian warmonger and sardonic monomaniac who slaps women rather than have sex with them and who would take great pleasure in personally pushing the nuclear button.

Fail-Safe's fast-paced, at times complex narrative opens in a disorientating, surrealistic fashion. It is 5:30 a.m. in New York. We see a shrouded matador flaying a wounded bull, before the words "FAIL-SAFE" are flashed up, almost subliminally and unaccompanied by credits but with a high-pitched whine instead. These broken, discordant images are part of a troubled, recurring dream. In a cold sweat, Air Force general Warren A. Black awakens

Fail-Safe: Professor Groeteschele advises Pentagon officials to order a first strike on America's mortal enemy. Courtesy of the Academy of Motion Picture Arts and Sciences (AMPAS).

and discovers, to his great relief, that he and his family are safe. But for how long, he and the audience are asking themselves?

Cut to Washington, D.C., where a tuxedoed, milk-drinking, political scientist who advises the Pentagon, Professor Groeteschele, is entertaining (or, perhaps better, educating) a small bunch of upper-class strangers at the end of a long cocktail party. An argument breaks out between the professor and a portly, inebriated gentleman over whether America's loss of some sixty million lives would be too high a price to pay in war. Groeteschele, who remains completely unflustered, believes it most certainly would not, if it saw the destruction of Soviet culture. Convicts in solitary confinement and file clerks in fireproof rooms would be the most likely Americans to survive, he predicts, in answer to a lady's question. The two groups would then fight for the remaining means of life, Groeteschele quips, with the convicts having the advantage of violence and the clerks their skills of organization. "Who do you think will win?" he asks his audience, with a wry smile.

The scene shifts to the underground control room at the heart of Strategic Air Command headquarters in Omaha. The room, like all the other places we will see in the film, is cut off from society, reminiscent of *Nine Days in One Year.* Its occupants, and the audience, feel isolated, even trapped. All chrome and black, and with a constant humming of electronic equipment in the background, the control room pulsates with technological efficiency.

Fail-Safe: The regimented and spectacularly lit control room at SAC headquarters in Omaha, Nebraska. Courtesy of Columbia Pictures/Photofest.

At SAC headquarters, General Bogan (Frank Overton) and Colonel Cascio (Fritz Weaver) are giving a visiting congressman a tour of the facilities. Pointing to a satellite image showing the exact whereabouts of every Soviet submarine in the Pacific, Bogan assures his guest that SAC's nerve center can tell the difference between a whale breaking wind and a Soviet sub blowing its tanks. The tour comes to an abrupt halt, however, when SAC detects an unidentified aircraft approaching U.S. air space. Fighter planes are deployed to investigate and, as part of the "fail-safe" system, strategic bombers constantly in the air in case of surprise attacks are dispersed to attack positions close to the borders of the Soviet Union. Each is equipped with nuclear air-to-air missiles and two twenty-megaton hydrogen bombs designed to detonate over enemy targets. The bombers, the congressman is confidently informed, have standard orders not to proceed past a certain geographical point, the fail-safe point, without receiving a special attack code.

What has seemed a potential threat turns out to be just an off-course commercial airliner, and Bogan and the others watch with relief as SAC's giant computerized screen shows the scrambled fighters return to base. Moments later, however, they notice that one set of bombers has gone beyond its fail-safe point and will soon be entering Soviet airspace. Due to a technical failure, Group Six, which consists of six Vindicator supersonic bombers, has received an attack code rather than a recall order. When its leader, Colonel Jack Grady, tries to contact Omaha for verification, he fails due to Soviet radio jamming. Grady therefore reaches the only sensible conclusion: World War III has started, and it is now his duty to deliver Group Six's deadly

Fail-Safe: Colonel Jack Grady (Edward Binns, center) whiles away the hours in Anchorage, Alaska, before his fateful mission to Moscow. Courtesy of the Academy of Motion Picture Arts and Sciences (AMPAS).

payload over its allotted target, Moscow. Henceforth he must disregard all signals to turn back, whether they be commands or entreaties, on the assumption that they will be Soviet subterfuge. This logic of nuclear war, as one pilot puts it, "eliminates the personal factor."

Meetings are quickly convened in Omaha, the White House, and the Pentagon, where military chiefs, politicians, and intellectuals grapple over what to do next. The three places are linked by an open conference line. In the Pentagon, Professor Groeteschele, the hardliners' mouthpiece, sees the accidental attack as an opportunity to end the threat of worldwide communism forever and calculates that a full-blooded first strike, forcing the Soviet Union to surrender, is the only reasonable option. General Black, the keeper of the liberal flame, argues the opposite. At an earlier briefing session, Black had declared Groeteschele's concept of limited, tactical nuclear war lunacy, arguing that the mad logic of Groeteschele's war games had only increased the complexity and power of war technology beyond humanity's power to oversee it. In order to prevent Armageddon, Black urges, the Pentagon must do everything in its power to either recall or destroy the Vindicators before they reach Moscow.

In line with procedures, the military dispatches six fighter jets to bring down the Vindicators over the Arctic Ocean. This is effectively a suicide mission, as the fighters need to travel so far they will run out of fuel in the process. The mission fails. The fighters crash into the frozen ocean, leaving the Vindicators, which are out of range of the fighters' missiles, to fly on.

The president, entombed in his spartan fallout shelter and assisted by a young interpreter, Buck (Larry Hagman), now acts decisively. He uses the newly installed hotline to inform the Soviet premier of the terrible accident that has taken place and to get his assistance in stopping Group Six, an action Groeteschele equates with treachery. Suspicious at first, the premier agrees. He lifts the jamming, enabling the president to make a personal appeal over the radio to Grady to turn back. Grady is clearly perturbed by his president's plea, but he refuses. Years of training have told him that this could be a Soviet trick, evidence even that the communists have already occupied the White House. Grady's crewmen do not bat an eyelid. Silent, dressed alike, and wearing heavy facemasks, they look more like robots than men.

Meanwhile, at SAC headquarters the tension is pushing some officers to the breaking point. General Bogan agrees fully with the president's line of action and carries out his instructions to supply Soviet military headquarters over the phone with tactical information about the Vindicators. However, Bogan's executive officer, Cascio, cracks under the strain, exposing the subjective, human element at the heart of even the most technologically sophisticated systems. An insecure character with an alcoholic background, Cascio believes SAC is falling into a Soviet trap. He rips the phone from Bogan's hand and tries to take over command of SAC, telling everyone he is acting at the behest of the White House. Confusion reigns until Cascio is arrested, but vital time has gone by.

Everything now rests on the Soviet military's ability to destroy Group Six. In the minutes that follow, SAC's giant screen shows four of the six U.S. aircraft disappear. When one of the Soviet planes is downed by a Vindicator, the control room's junior officers instinctively cheer wildly. "Quiet!" shouts Bogan, "This isn't some damned football game." With only two Vindicators remaining, it looks as though war might be averted. Then disaster strikes: Bogan tells his Soviet counterpart, Marshal Nyevsky, to ignore Plane # 6 because it is merely a support aircraft and has no bombs. However, instead of focusing all his defense corps' efforts on downing the last bomber, the suspicious Nyevsky hedges his bets and orders the Soviet aircraft to attack both U.S. planes. The screen shows the wrong, harmless plane being snuffed out.

Even a desperate, last-minute measure, which sees the Soviets fire a barrage of rockets to form a thermonuclear barrier over Moscow in the hope of knocking the low-flying Vindicator out of the sky, fails. Colonel Grady has anticipated this and, with dogged ingenuity, diverts the Soviet rockets by shooting up two missiles of his own. Similarly, a sobbing, hysterical appeal by Grady's wife over the radio to her husband to abort the mission comes to nothing. Grady is no automaton, and he is briefly caught in two minds when he hears his wife's voice, but, again, all the training manuals have told him to interpret such irregularities as Soviet tricks.

It is now only a matter of minutes till Moscow's, and the planet's, obliteration. The president has one last move, however. To prove this was not a preemptive strike, and to stop the Soviets from full-scale retaliation, the president tells the Kremlin he will order the destruction of America's most populous city, New York. At first the Soviet premier cannot believe the president's macabre tit-for-tat offer, but he eventually accepts. This has all been a terrible accident, the premier says, one beyond our control. You're wrong, the president argues, delivering a rather different message from and certainly one less sentimental than the novel's ending: "We're to blame, both of us. We let our machines get out of hand. . . . Today we had a taste of the future, Mr. Chairman. Do we learn from it or do we go on the way we have?" Walter Bernstein's words make indelible the necessity for immediately removing the barriers between the superpowers.

The mystery of the film's opening nightmare sequence is now finally explained. As the two leaders speak, General Black is orbiting New York City in a Vindicator. Earlier, over the phone, the president had asked "Blackie," an old college friend, if he remembered the Old Testament story of the sacrifice of Abraham. The president knows the general's wife and children live in New York; Black knows the First Lady happens that day to be visiting the city. The president has asked the general to carry out his last mission.

As we listen to the general's ten-second countdown to dropping the bombs over the Empire State Building, the camera cuts to a panorama from Black's scope, then to a series of ten flashes of everyday life in the city: among them, two little girls frolic on a cement city playground, a priest chats with an elderly couple outside St. Patrick's Cathedral, and two lovers embrace in Central Park. The audience is forced visually to experience the cessation of human life, as each of these flashes is then quickly played back and frozen. In the background, the faint sound of an engine's roar emerges. "The matador, the matador . . . me, me," whispers General Black, moments before he dies from a self-administered lethal injection.

Fail-Safe was the first Hollywood movie to explore seriously the chances of an accidental nuclear war. It would prove, in time, to be one of the most powerful denunciations of nuclear deterrence theory produced by any sector of the American mass media throughout the whole Cold War. Its actual impact, in terms of its effects on public attitudes toward U.S. nuclear strategy, appears to have been only slight, however. In the months following its release, *Fail-Safe* was certainly seen by far fewer people than *Nine Days in One Year* had been; in financial terms, it seems to have just about broken even. Its relative failure in this sense can be attributed to the United States having a far more crowded movie market than in the Soviet Union, which by and large meant that individual films, regardless of their quality, could soon disappear from public view. Sidney Lumet himself had a quick and easy explanation for *Fail-Safe*'s poor box office performance: Stanley Kubrick's *Dr. Strangelove.*

The timing of *Fail-Safe*'s release—in October 1964—could, in one way at least, not have been better. Nuclear safeguards were a major issue in the presidential campaign that year. At one point in the campaign, Republican candidate Barry Goldwater had controversially proposed giving NATO's supreme commander in Europe authority over tactical nuclear weapons on the field of battle, feeding liberal anxieties about military action being taken devoid of civilian control. In a notorious television ad showing a little girl plucking the petals of a daisy while a countdown proceeds in the background that leads to a mushroom cloud, the Democratic incumbent, Lyndon Johnson, implicitly accused Goldwater of being a dangerous hawk.[67]

When *Fail-Safe* opened on the big screen nationwide just one month before the election in early November, White House press secretary Bill Moyers sent Johnson an upbeat memo predicting the film "should have a pretty good impact on the campaign in our favor, since it deals with irresponsibility in the handling of nuclear weapons." This was a far cry from the Eisenhower administration's extremely hostile reaction to an earlier anti-nuclear movie, Stanley Kramer's aforementioned *On the Beach* (1959), against which the White House ran a counter-propaganda campaign. In his memoirs, Goldwater later blamed both *On the Beach* and *Fail-Safe* for fattening "the public's almost hysterical, unreasoned attitude toward nuclear war," and thereby contributing to his defeat in 1964. Johnson won by a landslide; under such circumstances it seems highly unlikely that a couple of films made that much of a difference.[68]

Fail-Safe's critical reception matched that of Burdick and Wheeler's novel in 1962. Like *Nine Days in One Year,* its politically controversial content and cinematically stylish qualities made it a critics' godsend. It was heavily reviewed, and not just by the trade press. Prominent right-wingers condemned it as "defeatist" and "peace-at-any-price propaganda." The colorful Clare Booth Luce, a former ambassador to Italy who was married to the owner of Time, Inc., the largest and most prestigious magazine publisher in the world, accused Max Youngstein of having "betrayed for gold his fellow citizens." The *Hollywood Citizen-News* struck a distinctly religious tone. It felt the movie injected doubt where there should be hope, planted seeds of suspicion where there should be faith, and tore down where it should be building up. If the characters had knelt down to pray in their hour of need, the newspaper added, the film might have been more acceptable.[69]

In contrast, the New York City–based Catholic journal *Commonweal* praised *Fail-Safe*'s "startling realism," while the National Council of Churches gave Youngstein an award for "reflecting the predicament and hope of man." Further awards came from American student bodies, the magazine *Motion Picture Exhibitor,* and the British Film Academy. Liberals in the United States and Western Europe called *Fail-Safe* "fiercely intelligent"; virtually every trade paper found it absorbing and genuinely frightening; and several critics, like the *New Republic*'s influential Stanley Kauffmann, felt the movie had outpunched the novel. Evidence that *Fail-Safe* was adopted by anti-nuclear activists can be found in Britain, where the Campaign for Nuclear Disarmament distributed leaflets outside cinemas screening the movie.[70]

Such a powerful mixture of vitriol and praise would normally give a film like *Fail-Safe* the necessary platform from which to gain further public and political purchase. This seems not to have come about mainly due to *Dr. Strangelove* having stepped on its message. Kubrick had started filming his own, black-comic vision of nuclear disaster in the autumn of 1962, some six months or so before production began on *Fail-Safe*. Kubrick's story of a demented U.S. Air Force general, Jack D. Ripper, who launches an unauthorized first-strike nuclear attack on the Soviet Union, thus triggering the Russians' "doomsday machine" that kills all life on earth, was shot for $2 million in Britain, where the director felt less constrained by U.S. officialdom. In early 1963, Kubrick and Columbia Studios, who were financing and distributing *Dr. Strangelove,* sued both Burdick and Wheeler and the makers of *Fail-Safe* for plagiarism. The lawsuit was settled out of court, with Columbia buying the distribution rights to *Fail-Safe* and acceding to Kubrick's demand that his film be released first. *Dr. Strangelove* went on general release in January 1964, nine months before *Fail-Safe,* was Columbia's top earner of that year (taking $5 million in domestic U.S. rentals alone), and was nominated for four Oscars.[71]

It can be argued (as several critics did at the time) that *Dr. Strangelove* was not as effective a warning to the public about the dangers of the bomb as *Fail-Safe,* on the basis that the message was lost amidst the audience's laughter. Kubrick's satire emphasizes the absurdity, dark humor, and even beauty he found in nuclear destruction, offering, in one historian's words, "a condescending burlesque of the ultimately terrifying subject."[72] By contrast, Lumet's semi-documentary forces audiences to confront the visual and moral results of American nuclear strategy head-on. Unlike *Dr. Strangelove,* *Fail-Safe*'s characters are not maniacs, monsters, or morons, but credible, intelligent men trying (and failing) to use their wits to correct errors in a supposedly infallible deterrence system. As the renowned British arts critic Kenneth Tynan put it in 1964, using language that inadvertently aped that spoken by Groeteschele/Kahn, *Fail-Safe* made "the *logic* of catastrophe seem much more intimate and irrefutable" than *Dr. Strangelove*.[73]

In many respects, of course, Kubrick's movie was far more creative than Lumet's, but *Dr. Strangelove's* box office, and enduring popularity, was certainly helped by the fact that it appeared in advance of *Fail-Safe*. "I knew we were dead as a movie as soon as Columbia bought us," Lumet said years later. Both movies would have worked better had their release dates been reversed, he argued; after *Dr. Strangelove* audiences found it difficult to take *Fail-Safe* seriously. Whatever the case, there is no doubt *Fail-Safe* suffered in the eyes of some critics who labeled it a "humdrum remake" of Kubrick's "instant classic."[74]

Fail-Safe soon withered in *Dr. Strangelove's* shadow before being remade, as a live television play, a decade after the Berlin Wall came down. Broadcast on CBS in April 2000 and viewed by thirty million people, the star-studded Emmy-winning teleplay was in many respects a straight period piece. It was hosted by veteran newscaster Walter Cronkite, stuck rigidly to the original film's plot, used exactly the same dialogue and sound effects in some places, and was filmed in black and white. But the teleplay was also meant as a warning about the dangers posed by nuclear proliferation in the post–Cold War era. At the end, before the credits, a simple but stark caption lists the world's nine nuclear powers, beginning with the United States and finishing with North Korea. George Clooney co-produced the teleplay, as well as starring as Colonel Grady. Clooney was then emerging as one of Hollywood's most outspoken liberals and would go on to direct or star in several other films exploring the unseemly side of America's Cold War, including *Good Night, and Good Luck* (Clooney, 2004) and *The Good German* (Steven Soderbergh, 2007).[75]

CONCLUSION

The American and Soviet film industries are conventionally believed to have followed two quite distinct and separate political trajectories during the course of the Cold War. After effectively declaring war on the United States in the late Stalin era, Soviet cinema is thought to have then largely forgotten about the Cold War, before briefly and belatedly reviving anti-American hostilities in the early 1980s. By contrast, Hollywood is thought to have maintained a steady interest in the Cold War throughout, interspersed with peaks of hyper-orthodoxy and troughs of anxiety. There seems little or no room for any overlap in this general picture, let alone scope for mutual expressions of protest.

This chapter demonstrates how inadequate the conventional outline is. The post-Stalinist Thaw in Soviet cinema not only saw a flowering of interest in the private emotions and lives of ordinary people in a purely domestic context. It also cast a fresh and critical light on the lives of those caught between the leaders and the led, of nuclear scientists, for example, whose work lay at the very heart of the Cold War. Similarly, while the early 1960s have often been identified as a high point of Hollywood Cold War disquiet, few have treated this disquiet to sustained analysis. Our examination of *Fail-Safe* shows that a small group of politically committed filmmakers, some of them members of anti-nuclear organizations, thought the time had come for Hollywood to protest the narrow-mindedness of U.S. nuclear strategy.

It is clear, therefore, that the early 1960s marks the beginning of a shift away from the black-and-white views of early Cold War cinema. Yet we should beware exaggerating that cinematic deviance. Certainly, we can already see signs of the greater latitude American filmmakers had for expressing discontent with the Cold War than did their Soviet counterparts. *Fail-Safe* represents a direct attack on one of the pillars of U.S. Cold War orthodoxy, nuclear deterrence, whereas *Nine Days in One Year*'s skepticism about atomic science is more guarded and articulated in a more oblique, "art-house" fashion. We should bear in mind, however, that *Fail-Safe* was based on a best-selling novel, and therefore pushed at an open "oppositional" door rather than kicking that door off its hinges. The filmmakers did sharpen the novel's anti-nuclear message somewhat, but they also painted a highly conservative and respectful picture of the U.S. presidency and, to an extent, the U.S. military. Would someone, we might ask, really remain as calm and rational as Henry Fonda's character in the face of nuclear Armageddon? Could General Black's equivalent in real life actually expunge his wife and family even if it did mean saving the world?

American cinema would start to ask these sorts of questions in the 1970s, as we see in the next chapter. Meanwhile, Soviet cinema in the era of Leonid Brezhnev was about to take a step in the opposite direction, back to Socialist Realism and the cult of the Great Patriotic War.

Chapter Six

Conservatism versus Anarchy

There is no more curious a period of the Cold War than the 1970s. To some observers during the early part of the decade, the conflict looked to be coming to an end. Relations between Moscow and Washington in particular grew exceedingly relaxed. In 1972, President Richard Nixon, a one-time McCarthyite, visited the USSR. A year later, Soviet leader Leonid Brezhnev, who had orchestrated the 1968 Warsaw Pact invasion of Czechoslovakia, traveled in the opposite direction. East-West détente reached its high point in 1975, when the superpowers signed historic human rights agreements in Helsinki and American Apollo and Soviet Soyuz astronauts met in space.

At the same time, the seventies saw the Cold War grow more complex and in some ways more dangerous. Western Europe carved out a semi-independent bloc for itself, led by a resurgent West Germany. Mao Tse-tung's China played East off against West by engaging in ping-pong diplomacy with Washington. Proxy wars spread further into Asia, Africa, and the Middle East. Large parts of the western world suffered financial meltdown following the 1973 oil shock. And all the while, despite historic limitation agreements, the nuclear arms race intensified and proliferated; India, for instance, proudly announced its membership of the nuclear club in 1974.

Soviet and American cinema reacted very differently to this somewhat schizophrenic international scene. By and large, Soviet filmmakers ignored it.[1] Under the so-called "period of stagnation" associated with Brezhnev, Soviet cinema took a step backward from the Thaw, ideologically and chronologically. Gone were the subtle critiques of daily life in a Cold War state, seen in movies such as *Nine Days in One Year*. In came films that contributed to Brezhnev's cult of the Great Patriotic War, or that sought to revive the military's image in Soviet society, in line with the Kremlin's determination to outspend the United States on defense.

For its part, Hollywood also disengaged from the Cold War to a degree in the 1970s. Virtually no films were made directly about the Vietnam War in the early years of the decade, for example, despite it being the most contentious of Cold War issues facing Americans. But movies about the new triangular relationship between United States, USSR, and China were produced, along with a healthy number of nuclear dramas and espionage thrillers. Though some of these movies retained elements of the 1950s Cold War view in which communists posed the greatest threat to world peace,

American filmmakers generally treated détente as offering them a greater license for inquiry. A large number of movies also chimed in with the wider sense of political disaffection and socioeconomic malaise that afflicted the United States during the 1970s, caused by Cold War and non–Cold War factors. Thus, whereas sixties films such as *Fail-Safe* had questioned how the U.S. government was conducting the Cold War, their seventies counterparts asked whether the conflict was worth fighting at all, or, indeed, what the Cold War was now all about.

This chapter examines how, having briefly converged during the early 1960s, Soviet and American Cold War cinema parted company during the 1970s. Our analysis focuses on two films that, like those examined in chapter 4, superficially might not appear to be relevant to the Cold War. The movies in question—Vladimir Rogovoy's sober family saga *Officers* (*Ofitsery*), and Woody Allen's zany comedy *Bananas*—do not seem immediately comparable either. But this is our point—to show that, at particular junctures in the Cold War, Soviet and American cinema could take off in very different directions. *Officers* demonstrates Soviet cinema's return during the 1970s to soft-style positive legitimation. *Bananas* exemplifies the soft-core anti–Cold War material several American filmmakers produced during that decade. The former was highly conservative; the latter was deeply anarchic. Despite this, the two movies had more in common than at first meets the eye.

Fathers and Sons: *Officers*

In 1971, around the time that *Officers* was released, conservative critic Aleksander Karaganov published an article entitled "Cinema in the Struggle for Social Progress" in *Soviet Screen*. This article clearly explains the context from which a throwback film like *Officers* emerged. Karaganov opened by describing the cinematic crisis in the West, a "culture" where art was losing importance. Although Western cinema was occasionally capable of producing a good film, like *They Shoot Horses, Don't They?* (Sydney Pollack, 1969), unlike Soviet cinema it was more often than not corrupted by the demand to turn a profit. Soviet cinema had many shortcomings, Karaganov noted (without naming any), but its strengths were its didacticism and social consciousness. "We believe in the possibility of educating the viewer to the communist point of view," he wrote. This "communist point of view," according to Karaganov, focused on "the struggle for a new society, a new man, an art of high ideals and high values," in which "I" and "we" are unified within the space of the "collective." Even though this mandate was specific to communist societies, Karaganov was optimistic about the possibilities for broader connections, including, but not limited to, co-productions. Soviet filmmakers, he wrote, would like to collaborate with their foreign colleagues to "defend mankind, peace, democracy, and to defend a high and truthful art."[2] Although most Soviet movies at this time deviated to one degree or another from this prescription, *Officers* was a poster film for presenting the communist worldview, Soviet style. As such, it is arguably the most valuable piece of "soft" propaganda to emerge from the 1970s.

As its title indicates, *Officers* tells a military story. Soviet cinema's heroizing of the military was not new, but it had generally been confined to war films, especially those about the Great Patriotic War. In the early 1970s, war films came to dominate the Soviet box office largely because they were often excellent treatments of a subject with built-in dramatic interest. The view they presented of life in the military was, however, extraordinary rather than ordinary.[3] Several post-Stalin films had attempted to show daily life in the military in order to emphasize its character-building, but the best of these—*The Soldier Ivan Brovkin* (*Soldat Ivan Brovkin,* Ivan Lukiansky, 1955) and *Keys from Heaven* (*Kliuchi ot neba,* Viktor Ivanov, 1965)—were comedies about hapless boys who grew to become men through military service.[4] Viewers of these two popular films likely focused more on the humorous pratfalls and shenanigans than on any underlying message about the intrinsic value of the military.

Officers (1971) was different, a multigenerational family saga that spanned the whole of Soviet history, from 1919 to 1970. It returned full-bore to the ideals of Socialist Realism and presented them without irony. Vladimir Rogovoy was an unlikely director to make such a politically significant film, one that was personally commissioned by the minister of defense, Marshal A. A. Grechko, and that scored a huge box office success, "triumphantly [going] around the whole country."[5] Rogovoy had graduated from VGIK, the state film institute, in 1950 and since 1953 he had worked for the Gorky studio, which made films primarily for younger audiences. He did not, however, begin directing until 1968. *Officers* was only his second picture.[6] It earned top box office honors in 1971, with 53.4 million viewers.[7] It also tied with the last installment of *Liberation* (*Osvobozhdenie,* 1968–71) to take first place with *Soviet Screen*'s readers for best film of the year. One of *Officers'* stars, Vasily Lanovoy (who plays second lead), was named Best Actor of the year.[8]

Generational conflict is a time-honored theme in Russian culture, famously marked by Ivan Turgenev's novel *Fathers and Sons* (*Ottsy i deti,* 1863),[9] and such conflict became a hallmark of the revolutionary movement—the radical "sons" against traditional "fathers." *Officers* puts a new spin on an old theme by rendering it "Soviet," that is, by removing most of the conflict from its story of three generations of a military family. The relative lack of conflict between parents and children is a marked departure from the spirit of late Thaw films. The movie also signals a return to the positive legitimation of a soft propaganda film like *Spring on Zarechnaya Street*. The soft approach was made possible due to détente, an "island in the stream" of Cold War tensions.[10]

Officers has a disjointed plot and is structured as a series of tableaux that are presented without any contextualizing details or voiceover narration. The expectation is that the viewer will be familiar with the history behind them, which would be true of the "fathers" watching it, but not necessarily the "sons." It begins in Moscow in 1919, during the civil war. Young Aleksei Trofimov (Georgy Yumatov) is just finishing cadet school in preparation for military service in the Red Army.[11] He happens upon a pretty young woman, Lyuba (Alina Pokrovskaya), whom he saves from thugs who are menacing her (violent street crime was a serious problem in Soviet cities during the civil war). In the next scene, they are married (there is no elaboration of the romance), and Trofimov blithely takes her with him to his first assignment, a rugged outpost in Turkestan, in the midst of the raging Basmachi Rebellion, a complex series of uprisings featuring bandits, nationalists, and Islamists. There they meet Ivan Varavva (Vasily Lanovoy), the handsome, impulsive platoon commander who will become the couple's lifelong, though often absent, friend.

After various adventures, including Lyuba's kidnapping by the Basmachi and the birth of their son Yegor in a train car, the film moves to the 1930s. Yegor has matured rapidly. About twelve years old (in the fifth form), he is enamored of little Masha Belkina and bullied by local hooligans who mock his precocious romance; there is a rather frightening scene of the bullies attacking him. Mother Lyuba has matured also. No longer a feckless girl, she is studying medicine. Trofimov is away from home more often than not and now stationed in the southeastern borderlands, helping Chinese refugees escape from the Japanese occupation of Manchuria in 1931. (Again, the viewer has to surmise that this is the historical background; there are few verbal or visual clues, thus universalizing the Soviet military's altruistic behavior.) Trofimov runs into Varavva, at this point a military intelligence officer disguised as a Chinese. Time passes. Trofimov, whose path to promotion has seemed unaccountably slow, is seeking to redress his deficiencies by taking courses at the officers' academy.

One day, while Trofimov is away, Varavva appears. En route to another posting, Varavva literally drops in (by plane) to catch a glimpse of Lyuba, whom he loves passionately but silently and chastely. The film then cuts to short scenes of the Spanish Civil War, as schematic and nearly bloodless as all of *Officers'* battle scenes. In some desultory street fighting, Trofimov is gravely wounded, shot in the back. (Given the importance of the Spanish Civil War to Soviet military mythology, it is interesting that Varavva is no-

Officers: Trofimov aids Chinese refugees. Courtesy of the Scientific Research Institute of Cinema Art (NIIK).

where to be seen.) After the Soviet withdrawal from Spain, the Trofimovs change postings again, to Lyuba's bitter disappointment. Time continues to move on rapidly, without transitions or signposts. Trofimov is at last a major. His son Yegor has obliged his father by turning to the military as his profession, becoming a student at a cadet academy. Home on a five-day leave, Yegor tells Trofimov that he needs money to depart immediately. To his mother's deep but repressed sorrow, he expects to spend his precious time with his girlfriend, Masha, rather than his family, even though his father tells him that mothers come first. This is Yegor's only small sign of youthful rebellion.

The beginning of World War II is presented matter-of-factly. Not surprisingly, the Great Patriotic War marks a turning point in the Trofimovs' lives. Lyuba, now a full-fledged physician, comes into her own as the commander of a hospital train. No longer a fluttering, complaining wife, she has become a strong, calm, capable woman, easily taking charge of a chaotic and dangerous situation. Yegor (now a soldier) and Masha (a radio operator) are killed in the war, but not before Masha has entrusted their baby son Ivan (named after Varavva) to Lyuba for safekeeping. (Lyuba urges Masha to leave the military and care for her child, but Masha does not want to let her comrades down.)

The film skips abruptly to the early Khrushchev era (although Khrushchev is never mentioned), silently passing over the difficult final years of

Officers: Vanya on detention duty. Courtesy of the Scientific Research Institute of Cinema Art (NIIK).

Stalinism, with its distrust of the military. We see the Trofimovs' grandson Vanya (the diminutive for Ivan) at about ten years old, in military school, ordered around as much by his grandfather, now Major General Trofimov, as by his academy instructors. Colonel General Varavva comes to the unnamed borderlands town to try to persuade his old friend Trofimov to take a plum posting at the military academy in Moscow. Long-suffering Lyuba, a Muscovite by birth and inclination, has longed to return there since the film's beginning. Lyuba has, however, been thoroughly coopted by the military. Trofimov, not surprisingly, refuses to go, but so does Lyuba, with only a second's hesitation. They cite their loyalty to their division, to which their dead son was attached during the war, and the viewer sees that Trofimov (unlike many real-life commanders) is exceedingly popular with his men, who are troubled by the rumors that he will be leaving them. Varavva understands and smilingly hoists his little uniformed namesake Vanya. The film ends in the present with the boy Vanya grown up, a third-generation officer, Ivan Trofimov.

As a work of cinematic art, this movie is quite unremarkable, with the exception of Mikhail Kirillov's crisp black and white cinematography.[12] If *Officers* were to be considered only for its filmic qualities, it would scarcely be worth writing about. As a sociopolitical document and a writing of Soviet history, however, it is rather more notable. Indeed, it epitomizes the ideals explicated in Aleksander Karaganov's essay and thus is a perfect example of the "positive legitimation" film that remained an important part of Soviet film propaganda throughout the Cold War.

In sociopolitical terms, *Officers* privileges military life at a key moment in the history of the Soviet Army. In terms of strength and resources, the army was at its zenith in the early 1970s. After lean years under Khrushchev, who had sought to strengthen his hand with the people by focusing on purely domestic issues, defense spending had increased by 40 percent between 1965 and 1970.[13] This reflected Brezhnev's somewhat different concerns and meant that by 1970 the army stood at five million strong. Furthermore, the army and the other armed forces enjoyed considerable political power, with representation in the Supreme Soviet, the Party Central Committee, and the Politburo.[14] The army enjoyed social status as well, with self-satisfied officers believing that service in the army ranked above service in civil institutions.[15]

But there were problems. The army was poised on the brink of a dramatic decline in status, reputation, and standard of living, and cracks in its façade were already apparent. As *Officers* demonstrates through the longevity of Varavva and Trofimov as commanders, the army high command was aging and showing no signs of retiring. (Our two heroes, generals by film's end, must be in their sixties.). This left fewer opportunities for promotion for younger officers and stymied the careers of many, leading to growing grievances. The film also reflects the fact that, according to Roger Reese, "more and more officers came from career military families," thus turning the military into a kind of caste, with a stagnant outlook, again disappointing those officers who did not hail from the privileged caste.

Officers either paints a rosy picture of other troubled areas or ignores them altogether. Housing for officers had not kept pace with recruitment. Pay was declining in real terms.[16] The hazing of recruits had become a serious problem that few officers were inclined to address; in some cases officers themselves were responsible for the hazing.[17] As the state and economy stagnated, officer prestige began to decline.[18] In short, for officers, the situation in the 1970s would gradually come to feel like a return to the Khrushchev era, when military spending took a back seat to spending for civilian needs.

Another key goal of *Officers* is to show the discipline and sacrifice of professional soldiers, along with their deep commitment to the nation (commitment to the state and Party has to be inferred). The film begins during the revolutionary years, which is appropriate given that Rogovoy wants to stress old revolutionary values, notably the value of iron-clad discipline within the fighting brotherhood of the Red Army. Trofimov (initially a love-besotted dilettante) is drawn into lifetime service for the motherland because of the character-building experiences the military profession affords him. Soon the model officer, he is completely uninterested in power or status (unlike real officers).

The most important expression of this theme comes early in the film. Trofimov has just arrived at the remote border outpost in Turkestan to which he has been assigned. It is, as noted above, the middle of the Basmachi Rebellion. The local "bandits" (as the rebels are called)[19] have just been sighted, and the troops, led by Varavva, leave the fort to engage them. Too inexperienced to be sent out (having just arrived), Trofimov is ordered to stay behind to man a machine gun turret in the fort. There he has a significant conversation with his commander.

Trofimov informs the commander that he is in the military as a "service" to his country, a service that he thinks of as temporary. After the war ends, he explains, he intends to become a teacher:

> *Commander*: How long do you plan to serve?
> *Trofimov*: Until the victory of world revolution.
> *Commander*: And then what?
> *Trofimov*: I'm going to teach.
> *Commander* (musing): You know, I've been proud of what I do my whole life. And my father was proud, and my grandfather. Others are proud of wealth or knowledge, but for us, it's this profession.
> *Trofimov*: And what is this profession?
> *Commander*: To defend the motherland. There is such a profession.[20]

The callow Trofimov mulls these words over but does not immediately understand them. As he watches the commander's quiet conviction and firm mastery over his men, however, his regard for "this profession" grows. For example, Trofimov overhears the lecture that the dashing, impulsive Varavva receives for having rushed off to engage the bandits, although he had not been given direct orders to do so. "You need to think," the commander admonishes Varavva, "not just brandish a saber." Yet the commander is decisively tough when he needs to be: immediately ordering the arrest of the sentry who fell asleep at his post, thereby making it possible for the Basmachi to kidnap Lyuba. However, Trofimov's epiphany about military service occurs when he watches the commander give up his life to save Lyuba's as they rescue her from the Basmachis. How could the young man honor this ultimate sacrifice? Trofimov vows to name his first son "Georgy"[21] after the brave and admirable commander and determines to be a soldier like him. Hence the compliment the film pays Trofimov during the scene at the

Manchurian-Soviet border, when one of his men admiringly refers to him as a "very disciplined man," is most significant. For Trofimov, as for any Socialist Realist hero, this is the highest accolade.

As noted in the discussion of *Nine Days in One Year,* sacrifice is also central to the ethos of Socialist Realism. Soldiers of Trofimov's generation, the men and women who made the Revolution, had plenty of opportunity for sacrifice. Even in peacetime, the Trofimov family is always on the move, from one frontier outpost to the next. Food and fuel are often scarce, especially during the Revolution's terrible early years. During the civil war, we see Trofimov sacrifice his officer's rations—borscht with meat—to his wife since she is nursing Yegor. (She tries to refuse, but he tells her that Varavva split his meal with him.) Determined as he is to keep his family with him, Trofimov is inevitably away for long periods on various assignments, another sacrifice for a family-oriented man. He is thereby effectively removed from supervising his son's day-to-day upbringing as a soldier-in-training. Trofimov also sacrifices friendship for the profession. He and Varavva seldom see each other across the passage of years and do not communicate in the interim as Varavva announces at their first leave-taking that he will not write. During the Spanish Civil War, we observe that Trofimov is seriously wounded because he decided to carry a wounded comrade—not even a fellow Soviet—to safety, rather than to look out for himself. Curiously, we do not witness his activities during World War II nor his reaction to the death of his son, but we assume that they were heroic in the first instance and stoic in the second.

"This profession" also eventually affects those on its periphery. The cultivated, French-speaking, Mozart-loving Muscovite Lyuba is neither stoic nor heroic—at least not at first. Giving the film a human touch (her given name "Lyubov" means love in Russian), she demonstrates how difficult military discipline and sacrifice is for ordinary mortals who have not committed themselves to military service but must stand by their men. At one point, when she suspects, correctly, that they have been reassigned again, she delivers this speech to her husband: "I've been waiting my entire life. . . . Where am I going? . . . I'm sick and tired of government-owned furniture. I want to go to Moscow. . . . I'm a human being. I must finish the institute." He strips off his shirt silently. When she sees the scars on his back, she catches her breath and asks simply, "When are we going?" "Day after tomorrow," he replies. Reserved though she is at this moment, Lyuba is certainly emotional when she learns of the death of her only child as she is routinely signing death certificates. In agony, she vainly tries to wrench the train door open, presumably to throw herself out. Yet by the end of the film, although we see her face light up when Varavva offers the Moscow posting, Lyuba knows that they must return to their division and says so immediately, with a smile and without regret. Lyuba's reeducation as a Soviet woman is at last complete, even though it took many, many years.

The Trofimovs' son Yegor, an underdeveloped character by comparison with his parents, demonstrates not only the difficulty of discipline and sacrifice in the life of a child, but also the beneficent role of the military in his maturation. Like his father at the beginning of the film, Yegor is a romantic, always pining after Masha. He is mocked and beaten by the rowdies for it; his mother chides him for his constant, undisciplined brawling, reminding him that "one should fight for the right cause." (The "right" cause is obviously not a personal one.) Masha too reproves him, for being an undisciplined, disengaged, lazy student who earns only twos (on a five-point scale). She cannot feign interest when he excitedly shows her the model tank he has been working on. Even at cadet school, although he has won a five-day leave for excellence in "combat and political studies," Yegor does not understand that his doting mother must come before a girlfriend and leaves after only a few hours to spend the rest of his precious time with Masha. But wartime brings out the best in him. Yegor sacrifices his life for the motherland. Masha does as well, even though as a new mother she could have left the service. (Both die horrible deaths, Yegor afire, Masha tortured and shot by the Germans.)

Their child, little Vanya, is a different story; and his story is one of the most interesting aspects of the film. Unlike his father and grandfather, Vanya will not be allowed to learn from his errors, nor will he experience great sacrifices. At the age of around ten, he is already in military school. Trofimov was not around enough to discipline his son consistently and is determined (on the surface, anyway) not to make the same mistake with his grandson. (Of course, although he complains about Lyuba's "softness," one must remember that Trofimov readily gave Yegor the twenty rubles he needed to go see Masha in the scene discussed above.)

When we first see the boy Vanya, Lyuba and Trofimov are arguing about him. Lyuba has slipped the child some money so that he can go to the zoo and take a taxi back to the military school before his leave expires at four o'clock. "He's not a child," Trofimov admonishes Lyuba, "but a soldier. The boy understands very well what army discipline is all about." Yet at the appointed hour, Vanya is still at the zoo and as a result gets detention and punishment detail. Lyuba insists that she and Trofimov rush to the school when she learns that Vanya's next leave has been canceled. They find him sniffling and scrubbing the stairs. "You must develop a loud commanding voice!" scolds Trofimov, as he demands an explanation. "He's a loafer," Trofimov informs his wife; "your endearments are spoiling a future officer." He forbids Lyuba from asking for a dispensation from the school's director. She defies

Officers: Generals Trofimov and Varavva reminisce. Courtesy of the Scientific Research Institute of Cinema Art (NIIK).

him and does so anyway, so that at film's end the boy has arrived for his next weekend pass, to Trofimov's consternation and Varavva's amusement. When Trofimov orders Vanya back to school, Varavva countermands Trofimov's order as his superior officer. "I don't want him to be raised as a general's grandson," Trofimov blusters. Lyuba and Varavva smile indulgently. But all is well in the end. Flash forward to the present, where Captain Ivan Trofimov is promoted to major "ahead of schedule" for his achievements as a soldier. The child has not been spoiled after all; "this profession" has made a man out of him as it had for his father and grandfather.

The vagaries of the Vanya story detract a little from the film's own iron-clad discipline in pushing its message forward. For the first time since the beginning, we see a less than admirable side of Trofimov. Although he is much loved by his men, he has turned into a petty martinet with regard to his grandson. Soviets doted on their only children, at a time when one child was the norm, at least for city dwellers. The sympathies of contemporary viewers—particularly female viewers—would have been on the side of Vanya and his grandmother, not on Trofimov's, despite the nobility of his not wanting to take advantage of his status as a general. Some viewers must have thought that it was a shame to turn a mere child into a soldier before he had had a chance to experience life. Perhaps this is the point: even childhood needs to be sacrificed on the altar of "this profession." Family values and military values are the same for Trofimov.

The emphasis of *Officers* is, therefore, on the hardship of military life, not on its benefits. The Trofimovs are never shown to be living lavishly, although by the end, with Trofimov a general, they are certainly comfortable. The hardships of military service are more than outweighed by the character-building values of discipline, sacrifice, and devotion to country. When Trofimov and Varavva meet at the end of the film, after the passage of many years, Trofimov echoes their long-dead civil war commander, "There's such a profession as defending your motherland."

And this is a motherland that has needed defending in the twentieth century, as the film shows. Yet another major goal of this picture is to present Soviet history through the lens of the military. It follows the Trofimovs through four tumultuous decades of Soviet history. In Cold War terms, it is curious that the opening scenes on the civil war focus on defending the country from the "enemy within," the Basmachi nationalists from Turkestani clans that resist Soviet authority, rather than on the foreign expeditionary forces, for example, the American invaders.[22] But this choice may be a reflection of the relative relaxation of détente in the early 1970s. In any event, *Officers* repositions the enemies of Soviet rule from the cultivated Whites and the equally "civilized" British, Americans, Czechs, and others to the "savages" of the East. The captured bandit Magolit-khan is crude and wily, brashly confident of the rightness of his cause. He informs the Soviets that there are plenty of his clansmen to replace him, reminding viewers (if they needed to be reminded) that the Soviet Union had been in ever-present danger since its inception. Furthermore, the brigade translator turns out to be a traitor in cahoots with Magolit-khan and helps organize Lyuba's kidnapping. That the USSR's long Asian borders needed to be guarded was a message with contemporary resonance, especially given the volatile relations with the Chinese (like the Sino-Soviet border disputes of 1969), and the rise of Islamist groups in neighboring countries, foreshadowing the war in Afghanistan. Soviet "civilization" confronts Eastern "barbarism."

Defense rather than offense is another theme of the film's presentation of Soviet military history, most obvious in the scenes during the Great Patriotic War. The obliqueness of these scenes seems another curious lapse, perhaps to be explained by the surfeit of World War II films at the time, particularly the gargantuan *Liberation* (mentioned in chapter 2). As already noted, Trofimov is seen fighting only once, during the Spanish Civil War, although we know that he is much decorated and has been promoted rapidly since the Great Patriotic War; this was, of course, commonplace, given the extraordinary death rate of officers as well as soldiers. Throughout the film, the Soviet military has a primarily defensive purpose, to defend the motherland, to defend peace.

The Great Patriotic War is seen, therefore, through Lyuba's eyes. As a physician, her war is not the war of fighters, but a war of the dead, dying, and wounded. She bravely organizes an evacuation of the wounded under heavy bombardment and takes up arms along with the ambulatory wounded men ("officers and communists!") as the German tanks appear on the horizon. (This is one of very few times that the word "communist" is heard in the film.) Fortunately, the beleaguered survivors are rescued by "their own," a Soviet counteroffensive. But real combat is not shown until the very end of the film, with some documentary footage of the Battle of Berlin inserted. It is only at this point that the viewer learns the terrible fates of Yegor and Masha.

As much as defense is emphasized, in accordance with Soviet Cold War rhetoric about being a peace-loving nation, *Officers'* soldiers are involved in more than purely defensive maneuvers. An important aspect of Soviet military history, according to the film, is that the Soviet army uses its military might to help other nations selflessly (painfully ironic when one remembers the Prague Spring just three years earlier). This is particularly true in the case of the Chinese refugees from the Japanese annexation of Manchuria in 1931, a conflict in which the Soviet Union officially remained neutral. As the Japanese artillery continues bombing to prevent refugees from crossing the border, Trofimov's stated concern is not for his own safety but for the needs of the refugees, who are wet and cold and need to be fed.[23] This, of course, belies the tense state of Sino-Soviet relations at the time the film was made.

Soviet intervention in Spain during the civil war was highly romanticized in the USSR for civilian consumption. *Officers* represents Soviet intervention in the conflict as an effort to help fraternal comrades, even if they were socialists, not communists, regardless of nationality, and nothing more. Certainly there was no suggestion that intervention might be interpreted as an effort to use the war as a military training ground for men who had not previously seen battle, nor as an opportunity to overcharge the Republicans for war materiel.[24] And the film makes it clear that the Soviets were acting in concert with other nations. Trofimov rescues a French soldier, thus reminding viewers that there are "brothers" even in capitalist countries. It should come as no surprise that no Americans are shown; there were limits to détente.

It is easy to understand why *Spring on Zarechnaya Street* struck such a chord with audiences in 1956, only three years after Stalin's death. It is harder to understand the enormous popularity—54 million viewers strong—of *Officers* in the more cynical 1970s, long after the hopes that surrounded Brezhnev's ascendancy had faded. In an interview, Vasily Lanovoy, who played Varavva, compared *Officers* to the classic civil war adventure *Chapaev* in terms of its impact on society.[25] While this is surely an exaggeration, one can believe

Lanovoy's assertion that the film was extremely popular with the military. He recalled that the production had been supported from the beginning by the army, receiving the imprimatur from Minister of Defense Grechko, as noted above, not to mention significant logistical support.[26] Air Force Major General N. Krasnoperov gave the film a glowing review in *Soviet Screen*, noting that he hoped the generational issues the film addressed, particularly its depiction of the wisdom of the "fathers," would make an impact on the minds of the younger generation.[27] (The problem of youth alienation, evident in the 1950s, was naturally much greater in the 1970s.) Despite (or because of) the hard work of military advisers on the film, two other reviews from military men were, however, less glowing, citing a lack of realism.[28]

It is likely that audiences were drawn to this film for reasons completely separate from its sociopolitical messages. Lanovoy cited the importance of his character's unfulfilled romance with Lyuba as a reason for the popularity of the film with the public at large, and he is surely correct. The handsome, charismatic Lanovoy, who had first come to prominence as Pavel Korchagin in the eponymous civil war film of the Thaw era, played Varavva superbly, with just the right note of wistfulness and self-sacrifice, and without descending into melodrama. Near the film's end, the Trofimovs discover to their surprise that Varavva has never married. He explains that he never found a woman like Lyuba. When Trofimov asks Varavva why he did not pursue her in the early days, Varavva jokes that he could not have competed with Trofimov, which is indeed a joke. One wonders throughout the film what attraction the glum, taciturn Trofimov holds for Lyuba. Varavva does not attempt to compete with Trofimov for Lyuba's affections out of honor and respect for his friend, thus dooming himself to a life alone. This is underscored as he walks away from the Trofimovs, a tiny, lonely figure walking up the steps of army headquarters, an enormous edifice.[29] Another sacrifice to the military.

Even though there is little doubt that the film's romantic triangle and its tale of steadfast but unrequited love was attractive to audiences, surely the film's value system, with its emphasis on character building, also appealed to them. Given the film's innate conservatism, we can expect these audiences consisted more of fathers and mothers than sons and daughters, who preferred foreign pictures, as noted in chapter 4. Each of the three main characters is honorable, disciplined, and steadfast, even with their manifest flaws, which every Socialist Realist hero (and heroine) has to have. Trofimov's flaw is his tendency toward pedantry, perhaps reflecting the teacher he thought he would be before the military captured his heart. Varavva's flaw is his dogged romanticism, so alien to the Soviet worldview. Lyuba's flaw is dreaming of Moscow, like Chekhov's three sisters, failing to be satisfied with the life she has. But all have come to terms with the lives they have made for themselves by the end. Trofimov knows his wife will moderate his relations with his grandson; Varavva will sublimate his thwarted affections in his namesake; Lyuba renounces her dream of returning to her Moscow by fully supporting her husband's desire to remain with his division.

Military films continued to be made for another fifteen years, right up to the brink of glasnost, although war films proper still dominated. Rogovoy himself directed more, including *Cadet of the Northern Fleet* (*Iunga severnogo flota*, 1973/74) and *Sailors Don't Have Questions* (*U matrosov net voprosov*, 1980/81).[30] Other military films ranged from *The Heirs of Victory* (*Nasledniki pobedy*, V. Vendelovsky and Vladimir Boikov, 1975), a film that honored "the contemporary Soviet army, which preserves and develops the traditions of the fathers, who saved the world from fascism,"[31] to those discussed in the next chapter, Mikhail Tumanishvili's Soviet naval films *Incident at Map Grid 36-80* (1982) and *Solo Voyage* (1986).

FRACTURED RELATIONSHIPS AND
SILLY DICTATORSHIPS: *Bananas*

The previous chapter demonstrated American filmmakers' greater scope for Cold War dissent compared with their Soviet counterparts during the early 1960s. In the 1970s, Hollywood's challenge to Cold War orthodoxy reached its apogee. This was partly the result of further structural changes within the film industry. These changes allowed for more movies to be made outside the major studios and they gave younger, liberal-minded directors greater freedom of expression. It also reflected the more radical political climate associated with, among other things, anti–Vietnam War demonstrations, increasing unemployment and urban crime rates, the Watergate scandal, and East-West détente.

These altered circumstances provided the opportunity and stimulus for filmmakers to launch an unprecedented assault on Cold War convention. Some movies such as Robert Altman's *M*A*S*H* (1970) and Francis Ford Coppola's *Apocalypse Now* (1979)—in direct contrast with Rogovoy's *Officers*—depicted the nation's armed forces as rowdy sexual perverts or psychopaths. Others, such as Peter Davis's Oscar-winning documentary *Hearts and Minds* (1974), accused the American government of committing genocide in Vietnam. More mainstream films, such as Sydney Pollack's espionage whodunit *Three Days of the Condor* (1975), fueled widespread fears that rogue elements within the CIA had replaced the communists as America's new "enemy within."[32]

If these movies challenged Cold War shibboleths head on, many more did so indirectly. Woody Allen's madcap comedy *Bananas* (1971), the story of a bumbling New York product tester who accidentally becomes a South

American rebel-hero, is a prime example. Like *Roman Holiday* in chapter 4 and *Officers* above, *Bananas* would not have been classified as a Cold War film by the majority of those who saw it, or as propaganda. Yet Allen's film satirized a bewildering array of institutions, groups, and personalities that for many years had been pillars of the Cold War consensus in the United States, including the FBI, CIA, judiciary, organized religion, marriage, and, significantly for our purposes, the mass media. It evened things up by also ridiculing the darlings of the liberal left, among them student rioters, feminists, and Latin-American Marxist guerrillas.

In doing so, *Bananas* reflected that strand of Cold War dissent that on the one hand condemned the U.S. government for treating the Third World as a political playground, but which, on the other hand, argued that the woolly liberals who protested about Washington's actions were mostly self-indulgent idiots. In short, the film was saying that the Cold War, and the whole political system of which it formed a central part, was now a sick joke. Revealingly, critics argued fiercely over whether *Bananas,* because of its scatter-gun humor, ought to be taken seriously, and if so what its messages were. This highlights an important point about the public's reception of unconventional films of this sort during the Cold War.

Woody Allen had total creative control over *Bananas,* something that would simply not have been permitted under Hollywood's old, collaborative studio system. This was the result of extremely generous contractual conditions with United Artists, via a deal that had been brokered by Allen's long-time partners and film producers, Charles H. Joffe and Jack Rollins. Allen co-wrote the script for *Bananas* (with an old school friend, Mickey Rose), based loosely on Richard Powell's 1966 novel *Don Quixote USA* about a naïve American Peace Corps volunteer working in the Caribbean. Allen also cast the movie, directed it, and took the lead role as nerdish product tester Fielding Mellish.[33]

The movie was shot in Deluxe color through the summer of 1970, partly in New York, the locale for virtually all of Allen's films, and partly in Puerto Rico, whose governor was offering American filmmakers tax incentives in order to boost the island's economy. *Bananas* was therefore, like *Roman Holiday* and others, another example of the U.S. film industry's exploitation of overseas facilities. The New York–based composer Marvin Hamlisch, who would go on to win a raft of Academy and Grammy Awards in the mid-1970s, supplied the music for the film, while the cartoonist Jack Davis was responsible for most of the film's art work and advertisements. Davis was best known for his work on *Mad Magazine,* which had been satirizing aspects of the Cold War since the McCarthy era. *Bananas* cost $1.7 million, and would gross an estimated $5 million at the box office.[34]

Bananas could be described at root as a romantic comedy, but any resemblance to *Roman Holiday* ends there. Before establishing his position as one of
America's best-loved comedy directors via thematically offbeat but conventionally structured hits like *Annie Hall* (1977) and *Manhattan* (1979), Woody
Allen's filmmaking style was distinctly idiosyncratic. Allen's approach in *Bananas* was typically freewheeling, or, as he liked to call it, "slapdash." The
plot is a rickety framework for his disconnected scenes, which let him do
whatever he wants whenever he wants. *Bananas* is chock full of sight gags
and one-liners, many of which were ad-libbed during shooting and have
nothing at all to do with the central situation. Together with a number of
surreal sequences, the whole piece has a formless, maniacal feel to it. Critics
saw the influence of Allen's self-confessed idols, the Marx Brothers.[35]

Bananas starts abruptly with a pre-credit sequence in the troubled Latin
American state of San Marcos, where a brutal coup d'état is about to take
place live on U.S. television. The assassination of the island's president has
been "advertised" in advance, and the famous, real-life American sportscaster
Howard Cosell is there to report it for ABC's *Wide World of Sports*. Clutch-
ing his microphone eagerly on the steps of the presidential palace, Cosell
proceeds to present the whole incident as a boxing commentary, forcing his
way through the crowd to interview the head of state as he lies dying from
gunshots ("I guess now you'll have to announce your retirement"). The new
dictator is General Vargas (Carlos Mantalban), who outlines his new policies
for the benefit of the TV audience: censorship of the press, destruction of
the opposition, and so on.

After the bullet-ridden credits, we switch to New York, where a clumsy
college dropout, Fielding Mellish (Allen), is working as a product researcher
for General Equipment. His job consists of acting as a guinea pig for the
bizarre devices invented by the company. We see him testing electrically
warmed toilet seats, coffins with piped-in music, and the new "Execusizer,"
a gym built into the desks of busy corporate heads. The latter completely
bamboozles the skinny Fielding, leaving him gasping for air on the floor.
Fielding is a shy, frustrated, lonely, accident-prone loser. In no time at all,
he is being chased by muggers on the subway and failing to make it with
various girls.

One night, however, a fresh-faced City College student activist, Nancy
(Louise Lasser, Allen's ex-wife), knocks at his apartment door. Nancy is
gathering signatures against U.S. support for the new tyrannical regime
in San Marcos. Although Nancy says she is busy with yoga classes and her
women's liberation group, Fielding persuades her to go out on a date with
him. He then even takes part in political rallies and riots just to be near
her. Nancy soon dumps Fielding, though, because of his political and sexual

Bananas: Fielding and Nancy's stuttering romance comes to an end in New York's Central Park. Courtesy of MGM/United Artists/Photofest.

immaturity. "Something is missing," she says in a sunny Central Park, trying to intellectualize the breakup.

To help get over his loss and find his true self, Fielding sets off to San Marcos, where he and Nancy had planned to vacation. In impoverished San Marcos, where each peasant has been ordered to pay the dictator his weight in horse manure, we see a captured rebel being tortured by being forced to listen to a recording of Victor Herbert's operetta *Naughty Marietta*. This prompts him to confess that the rebels are planning a revolution on the fourth of July. Fielding is invited to dine with General Vargas at the palace, but upsets the dictator by bringing the wrong-flavored cake. During the meal, Vargas explains to Fielding that he wants to keep his people safe from communism by "exterminating a few troublemakers." Vargas ignores Fielding's point that the rebels are not communists and sticks Fielding with the bill.

Later, Vargas's men try to kill Fielding, intending to blame the death of an American citizen on the revolutionaries in order to win an enormous aid package from Washington. The plan goes badly wrong, however. Fielding escapes, is kidnapped by the rebels, and then turns into one of them. Fielding trains with the rebels, learns about guns, grenades, and camouflage, and—most important for him—is seduced by the curvaceous Yolanda (*Playboy* model Natividad Abascal). Their sexual encounter is accompanied by thunderous excerpts from Tchaikovsky's *1812 Overture*. Fielding also teaches the rebels a thing or two about the American way of life. When the camp is low on food, he is sent to raid a nearby town and, with a few other men, enters a café, orders a couple of thousand sandwiches, wheelbarrows of coleslaw, and some drinks, and then has it all delivered. Eventually, Vargas is overthrown and replaced by the rebel leader, Esposito (Jacobo Morales). Vargas flees to the safety of Miami.

Once in power, Esposito goes power crazy. He proclaims that Swedish will be the state's official language, and that citizens must now change their underwear every half hour, wearing it outside their clothing so that it can easily be checked. At the request of his comrades, who regard him as an intellectual because he spent a few weeks in college, Fielding takes over as president, but it is soon apparent that San Marcos needs the support of other countries in order to prevent the island from falling prey to corrupt dictators in the future. The problem, Fielding and his close associates realize, is that the Americans think of them as communists, and the communists believe them to be American puppets. In addition, they have nothing to barter for aid except bananas. Fielding's advisers urge him to go to the United States and raise money, but he knows that, back home, his reputation as an uneducated product tester has no clout.

Fielding flies to the United States, disguised in a garish red beard. At a fund-raising dinner held in his honor, which the new San Marcos leader nearly ruins by telling jokes about incest and the loose morals of his island's women, Nancy is completely dazzled. Not recognizing that it is Fielding, she becomes infatuated with the mysterious guerrilla hero and ends up in bed with him. Meanwhile, the FBI sees through Fielding's disguise. "Do you realize what a communist missile base in San Marcos would do to us?" warns one G-man. Based on his past record as a demonstrator, Fielding is arrested as a "subversive imposter" and put on trial for conspiring to overthrow the U.S. government from without and within.

In court, where Fielding acts as his own lawyer, the witnesses against him are endless: from FBI director J. Edgar Hoover, who comes disguised as a black transvestite to confuse his enemies, to Miss America, who, after singing Verdi's aria "Caro nome" and proclaiming that "differences of opinion should be tolerated as long as they are not too different," calls Fielding "a subversive mother." While the jury passes around a joint, Fielding's own defense is brought to a halt when the judge orders him bound and gagged. As announced on the television news, after an advertisement for New Testament cigarettes (which a priest tells us have "a revolutionary incense filter"), the subversive is found guilty. The judge then suspends his jail sentence so long as Fielding promises never to move into his neighborhood.

A free man, Fielding proposes to his beloved Nancy. Their wedding night at the Royal Manhattan Hotel is broadcast for television by the same Cosell

Bananas: The new president of San Marcos tours the United States, flanked by his FBI "bodyguards." Courtesy of MGM/United Artists/Photofest.

who had reported the San Marcos coup d'état. From their spectator-filled hotel suite, Cosell breathlessly provides a play-by-play description of the under-the-bedclothes "action." After the post-coital interviews with the "contestants," Cosell says farewell: "And now they will live together happily ever after. Or maybe they won't." Shortly before the credits roll, a special news bulletin informs viewers that astronauts have landed safely on the moon and have erected the first all-Protestant cafeteria.

Like Marlen Khutisev with *Spring on Zarechnaya Street,* Woody Allen did not think of *Bananas* as an overtly political film. To him, it was a funny story that used topical political and social themes as props, much as a stand-up comic (Allen's former occupation) would pick out daily news items to highlight human foibles. Allen's politics were broadly those of the American liberal left—he had campaigned in favor of several Democratic Party presidential candidates since the mid-1950s. But his overall attitude toward politics by the early 1970s, when the director was in his mid-thirties, was "a plague on both your houses." "Political thinking throughout history has never worked," he opined. "As long as it's a question of is it going to be Democrat or Republican, Communist or whatever, as long as people delude themselves into thinking they can solve those issues they'd be happy, there's nothing going to happen."[36]

Allen had already enjoyed forays into Cold War territory before making *Bananas.* He had written and starred in a popular Broadway 1966 comic

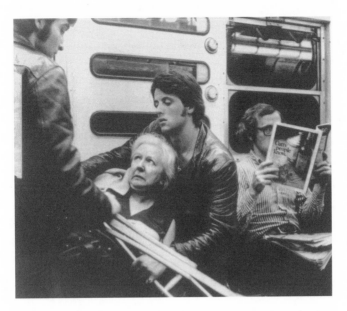

Bananas: Fielding hides behind his magazine as two muggers (one of them played by a young Sylvester Stallone, center) rob an old lady on the New York subway. Courtesy of MGM/United Artists/Photofest.

play *Don't Drink the Water,* about an American family of tourists forced to seek refuge in the U.S. embassy of a mythical Iron Curtain country after mistakenly being suspected of spying. A year later he starred in *Casino Royale* (1967), a parody of the James Bond espionage phenomenon.[37] Compared with these productions, the satiric mode of *Bananas* lends a harder edge to the comedian's well-known absurdist spirit. Although the movie is largely a farce, *Bananas* gives full voice—thematically and stylistically—to the counterculture associated with New Hollywood. Like Allen's later films (and those of his contemporaries Peter Bogdanovich and Martin Scorsese), *Bananas* parodies and distorts old movies to create a new, progressive cinema.[38]

If Rogovoy's *Officers* sought to mask emerging intergenerational conflict in the Soviet Union, Allen's *Bananas* took pleasure in fully exposing the chasm that was opening up between the young and old in early seventies America. Long-haired college students fight pitched battles with the police. An aged, out-of-touch judge pours scorn on Fielding's scruffiness and nihilism. In a news agent's store, an old lady looks on contemptuously as Fielding tries to buy a pornographic magazine concealed beneath more intellectual publications. In a subway carriage, another pensioner on crutches is tormented by two young thugs. Though Fielding tries to come to this old lady's rescue, the scene could in no way be viewed as a call for the restoration of the sort of discipline and respect promoted in *Officers*. Allen's vigilantism rebounds on him to comic effect, and the movie lionizes cowardice over bravery and heroism throughout.

Bravery and heroism is often predicated—as we saw in *Officers*—on a sense of loyalty or threat. However, there are no threats to the United States in *Bananas,* other than the phantoms dreamed up by a Middle America that is intolerant of diversity and outsiders. The only loyalty shown in the movie is that by the Establishment, whose right-wing representatives are wedded to infantile conspiracy theories. This is brought home most clearly in the scenes of Fielding's prosecution by the U.S. government on trumped-up charges of fraud, subversion, and using the word "thighs" in mixed company. Here, Allen alluded to recent examples of real-life abuses of power in the United States, most notably the politically motivated trial of the Chicago Seven—antiwar activists who were charged with conspiring to incite riots at the 1968 Democratic National Convention, and who in court pointed out the unfairness of their trial by turning it into a farce. One of them, the co-founder of the Black Panthers, Bobby Seale, was chained and gagged to silence his frequent outbursts.

Depicting J. Edgar Hoover not only as a witness to Fielding's prosecution but as an African American in drag who has been taping Fielding's dirty phone calls was, depending on one's point of view, either extremely reckless or brilliantly funny. Rumors abounded that the FBI director had spent years conducting a dirty war against civil rights leader Martin Luther King and that he was a closet homosexual. Though Hoover was in his dotage by this stage of the Cold War (dying in May 1972), he was still an extremely formidable political figure and one who did not take kindly to even humorous attacks on his image.[39]

Aiding and abetting these abuses of political power in *Bananas* is the American media. Allen would star in a later film, *The Front* (1976), that portrayed one section of the media, the 1950s Hollywood Left, as the victims of a political witch hunt. By contrast, in *Bananas,* the media are the hunters. We see U.S. television crews inciting political murder, inveigling themselves into people's private lives, and transforming even the most serious aspects of political life into entertainment for passive, voyeuristic consumers. Television's power "exposes a world," as one reviewer of *Bananas* put it, "where exploitation is everything, where taste is dead."[40] Using the celebrity sports announcer Howard Cosell at the beginning and end of the movie drew even greater attention to the media's growing invasiveness and to television's blurring of news and entertainment in particular. In the assassination scene at the film's outset, Cosell, who orders the San Marcos citizens "to make way for American TV," comes across as an arrogant Yank meddling in other people's business.[41]

One of *Bananas*' favorite targets is U.S. imperialism in Latin America. Allen's film was not the first Hollywood production to challenge Washington's long history of supporting friendly dictatorships in its backyard. And its level of protest could in no way be compared with later damning critiques like Constantin Costa-Gavras's *Missing* (1982), Roger Spottiswoode's *Under Fire* (1983), and Oliver Stone's *Salvador* (1986), set in Chile, Nicaragua, and El Salvador, respectively.[42] Yet in spoofing the CIA's reaction to Vargas's takeover in San Marcos—the agency hedges its bets by sending one contingent of American troops to fight for the dictator and another to fight against him—Allen's point was quite clear. Revelations in the press in the late 1960s had opened many Americans' eyes to the scale of U.S. intelligence activities south of the border going back over decades. These included subverting local governments if they threatened American commercial profits and even assassinating politicians who were perceived to be a danger to U.S. interests. Allen's very choice of the title for the movie (which was originally *El Weirdo*) evoked the hegemony of the United Fruit Company, a U.S. corporation long associated with neocolonialism in the region. Some viewers presumably drew links between *Bananas* and the accession to power of the prominent socialist Salvador Allende in Chile in 1970. The CIA had been conducting a semi-secret campaign against Allende since the early 1960s and was eventually complicit in his murder in 1973.[43]

Of course, *Bananas* had as much to say about the ruthless cynicism of Latin American leaders as their U.S. allies or enemies. Vargas's penchant for murdering his opponents, for cherry cake, and for sharp-suited bodyguards who wear sunglasses even indoors cannot be attributed to him simply being an American stooge. We initially sympathize with Esposito's rebels mainly due to their apparent commitment to the people. But when Esposito goes "bananas" shortly after taking power, issuing ridiculous decrees about underwear and the state's new language, he, too, becomes a figure of audience derision and living proof of the age-old axiom that absolute power corrupts absolutely. The scenes in which the revolutionaries conduct mass executions following their victory are farcical; Fielding announces numbers for the awaiting victims as though he is a deli clerk calling out to the customers. But it is nonetheless clear that the movie's message is that the political Left can be as dictatorial and corrupt as what Nancy calls the Fascist Right once they have seized the reins. It is likely many viewers would have interpreted San Marcos as a thinly veiled Cuba, whose U.S.-backed military dictator, Fulgencio Batista, was toppled by Fidel Castro in 1959. This seems not to have

Bananas: San Marcos rebel leader (and Fidel Castro lookalike) Esposito hatches a plan with his trusted comrades. Courtesy of MGM/United Artists/Photofest.

been Allen's intention, but the comparisons were inevitable given Esposito's beard, cigar, and green combat fatigues, together with Castro's political excesses in the 1960s.

Bananas also satirized those Americans who blindly, often smugly, supported the Espositos of this world. Initially, Fielding only campaigns against Vargas in order to impress Nancy and get her into bed. Because he is so goofy and fundamentally harmless, this is quite funny, but it still puts a question mark next to the motives of other political hangers-on. When Fielding then goes to San Marcos and joins the rebels, he effectively does the opposite of Trofimov in the early stages of *Officers.* Rather than defending his country against barbaric borderland bandits, Fielding becomes one of those bandits in the name of anti-imperialism. Yet even when he then usurps Esposito as leader of San Marcos's revolutionary government, Fielding has no real sense of commitment or of political reality. It is only natural, then, that he should forget about San Marcos once posing as its rebel leader has brought its rewards—sex with Nancy. *Bananas'* message here seems to be that American liberals are using Latin America as a political and sexual playground as much as the CIA and others on the U.S. political right.

Nancy herself is well meaning and sincere in her support for the San Marcos revolutionaries. However, she has none of the moral fiber or ideological fortitude shown by Lyuba in *Officers.* Nancy is flaky, lacking in self-confidence, a stereotypical pseudo-feminist hippie. She campaigns against

Vargas and is prepared to go to San Marcos to express her solidarity for the rebels. But she has no real idea who the rebels are or what they will do if they get power, largely because, though she decries its right-wing bias, she has to rely on the American media plus her college friends for her political education. Like Fielding, Nancy, too, is using revolutionary politics, to be part of the in-crowd. She is a fully paid-up member of the counterculture, complete with round, scholar's spectacles and interests (though obviously no real expertise) in metaphysics, Eastern philosophy, and free love. At the end of the film, she, too, has apparently forgotten about San Marcos, and has sold out her feminist principles by marrying Fielding.

That the two lovebirds could not only get married despite the obvious flimsiness of their relationship, but also then consummate that marriage on television, spoke volumes for the fractured nature of present-day American society. In this regard, despite its patently absurdist tone, *Bananas* carried a very different message from that of *Officers*. What holds the USSR together in Rogovoy's saga is a strong sense of family and national identity. These are completely lacking in *Bananas*. Fielding and Nancy's marriage is laughable and has no chance whatsoever of lasting as long as Trofimov and Lyuba's. Parenthood makes an appearance just once in *Bananas,* when Fielding visits his father and mother, a surgeon and a nurse, who are in the middle of conducting a hospital operation. Fielding's relationship with his parents is outlandish and utterly dysfunctional. Dr. Mellish, who is disappointed that his son has not followed him into the family business, offers no support for his son's impending trip to San Marcos and merely insists he take over the operation. It is inconceivable that Dr. and Mrs. Mellish could make the sort of sacrifices Trofimov and Lyuba have grown used to in *Officers*.

In contrast with the USSR in *Officers,* America in *Bananas* appears as a decadent, disunited nation—just as Soviet propagandists had been describing it for years. The country is at war with itself, over racial and foreign policy issues. New York, once America's beacon of vibrancy, is an unsafe, polluted mess. The strengths of American culture exhibited in *Roman Holiday*—the freedom to choose, a democratic spirit, enterprise, wealth, and glamour—have either disappeared or turned into weaknesses. What sort of society produces a combination desk and exerciser so workers can spend even longer hours on the office treadmill? Can U.S. citizens be truly happy when even those with a college education cannot communicate with one another? Americans might be free to hold religious beliefs, but who really benefits from this? Organized religion has crucified itself through commercialization. America's true gods nowadays are Mammon and TV.[44]

Bananas premiered in April 1971, a tumultuous, historic month that saw over 500,000 people march in protest against the Vietnam War in Washington and the U.S. table tennis team become the first American sports delegation to set foot in China since 1949. In such circumstances, we might have expected Woody Allen to emphasize his new movie's political relevance, but he did not. *Bananas* stands in strong contrast to *Man on a Tightrope* and *Fail-Safe* in this respect. The fact that *Bananas* did not cause any real political or cultural stir, despite its caustic targeting of numerous groups and personalities, is a measure of the greater political tolerance that existed in the United States in the 1970s compared with during the McCarthy era. It also indicates how much easier it was for filmmakers to express dissent through comedy rather than drama or documentary, not just in this period but throughout the Cold War. By way of contrast, for example, in 1974 the makers of the aforementioned anti–Vietnam War documentary, *Hearts and Minds,* were labeled propagandists, even traitors by some, on the grounds that they had used the genre to twist "reality."[45]

Woody Allen was a cult figure in American comedy in 1971 but not yet a household movie star. As a result, *Bananas'* impact was bound to be limited compared both with *Officers* in the Soviet Union and with other American movies of the era that challenged Cold War orthodoxy. *M*A*S*H,* for instance, boasted a well-known director, stars such as Donald Sutherland, and a satirical, gallows humor that was enhanced by its Korean War setting. *M*A*S*H* grossed five times as much as *Bananas* and spawned a long-running television series. *Bananas* was aimed more at a niche market, principally the young and those who were already tuned into Allen's mixture of self-effacing humor and spoofs of movie conventions. In the main, *Bananas* probably preached to the politically converted, the remainder being those traditionally drawn to farce and by reports of the movie being "scandalously funny."[46]

Whether the hip college students and others who saw *Bananas* took away any clear political messages from the film is debatable. Humor is often open to greater interpretation than drama, and Woody Allen was not one to make things any easier for audiences by providing a set of sign posts or clarifying his points through newspaper interviews. Certainly, critics did not know exactly what to make of *Bananas.* Many categorized it as innocent, knockabout fun. Others, including the National Catholic Office for Motion Pictures (formerly the Legion of Decency), warned of its subversive vulgarity.[47] The right-leaning *Motion Picture Herald* praised Allen for trying to do to Fidel Castro what Charlie Chaplin had done to Adolf Hitler in *The Great Dictator* (1940). The left-leaning *New Leader* condemned Allen for satirizing "banana republics without knowing beans about their politics." *Time* magazine thought *Bananas* was wonderfully funny and fresh but utterly incoherent politically. Judith Crist in *New York* begged to differ. The veteran critic felt *Bananas* captured the "quintessence of everyday lunacies" and was glad Allen had not indulged in "the cautious liberalism that vitiates so much of today's 'black' comedy."[48]

Notwithstanding the views of Crist and others, the Nixon administration appears not to have been unduly worried by *Bananas*. Nixon himself was an avid film fan who screened well over 500 movies at the White House, Camp David, and his various vacation homes during his presidency. Several Hollywood stars earned a place on his infamous enemies list in the early 1970s (including, as we saw in chapter 4, *Roman Holiday's* Gregory Peck), but Woody Allen was not among them.[49] This was despite the ruckus caused by an hour-long television program that Allen made for the Public Broadcasting Service in late 1971. Entitled *The Politics and Humor of Woody Allen,* it contained a fake documentary that parodied Nixon and U.S. politics generally. Allen's only truly explicit work of political satire throughout the Cold War, the program was not aired, partly due to complaints from the White House.[50]

Meanwhile, *Bananas* enjoyed a rather strange afterlife. The U.S. State Department included the movie as part of an American Humor Film Week it organized in Bucharest, Romania, in 1975. That *Bananas* was the only contemporary movie on the list—it exhibited alongside the likes of W. C. Field's *My Little Chickadee* (1940) and Buster Keaton's *The General* (1927)—testifies to Allen's growing international reputation in the mid-1970s. That Washington would countenance the official use of such a "subversive" movie behind the Iron Curtain also speaks volumes both for its greater maturity in relation to cultural diplomacy and the cinematic openness brought about by the process of East-West détente.[51]

Through the rest of the seventies and into the eighties, inspired partially by films like *Bananas,* Hollywood would continue to make movies that poked fun at the U.S. government's actions in Latin America. It is difficult to say whether these films, most of which focused on the CIA, increased American public hostility to the U.S. Cold War intelligence network. It could be argued that treating the CIA as a scapegoat for past and ongoing American misdemeanors meant wider questions about U.S. foreign policy were sidestepped. We do know, however, that, unlike *Bananas,* Washington exported none of these movies into the communist world.[52]

CONCLUSION

The Cold War was a quarter of a century old by the time *Officers* and *Bananas* appeared in 1971. The conflict had already lasted some four or five times longer than the First and Second World Wars, and was now an entry in Soviet and U.S. history books. Given the passage of time, it is not surprising that the Soviet and American film industries were out of sync in relation to the Cold War by the early 1970s, with the former exhibiting loyalty to its government and the latter opposition. Even during the six years of the Second World War, the two cinemas had never been set entirely in ideological aspic. During the decades-long Cold War, their coverage of the conflict altered according to the geopolitical, social, and cultural winds that blew through its different phases. Hollywood would always be freer to articulate public disquiet, of course, especially when, as was the case in the early 1970s, old-fashioned Cold Warriors in the American film industry were being replaced by more radically minded Young Turks.

Nothing akin to *Bananas* was or could be made in the USSR during the Cold War. Cinematic dissent was allowed, but only, as we saw in the previous chapter, in a controlled environment of cultural relaxation sanctioned by the Kremlin. Even then, Soviet filmmakers risked demotion or worse if they proposed challenging the very roots of the state's Cold War stance or ridiculing sacred institutions like the Army or KGB. In certain circumstances, Soviet films could reflect widely held social concerns—about alcoholism, delinquency, and minor corruption in Soviet institutions, for instance. But comparatively speaking, until the glasnost era, these would always be a long way short of the criticism of American culture and foreign policy seen in *Bananas.*

Woody Allen's film also points to another major difference between U.S. and Soviet Cold War cinema, one that grew more apparent as the conflict progressed. Like the vast majority of Soviet Cold War films, *Officers* looked inward, at Soviet society itself. This was because, as *Officers* amply demonstrated, the USSR remained the communist motherland throughout the conflict, deserving and demanding the peoples' devotion to service, either in or out of uniform. By contrast, *Bananas* looked both inward and outward. As well as skewering contemporary America, it cast a skeptical eye on American behavior overseas, in its southern neighborhood especially. Both superpowers were flexing their global muscles during this period of the Cold War, expanding formally and informally into Asia, Africa, the Middle East, and Latin America, but America's reach remained that much wider. This fact was reflected in how Hollywood covered the conflict, geographically and politically. Generally speaking, the more countries the United States moved into, the more disquiet American films expressed, perhaps inevitably in the aftermath of the nation's shameful defeat in Vietnam.

This chapter highlights one final point of interest. *Officers* demonstrated Soviet cinema's overall conservatism, not only politically but also artistically. A military-oriented family saga, it fell, like the vast majority of Soviet Cold War films, broadly within the genre of drama. *Bananas,* on the other hand, underlines how the Cold War made inroads into the full range of genres in American film, even madcap comedies. This may be because the Soviet authorities were the more straitlaced, leaving Soviet filmmakers with the distinct impression they were not to treat the Cold War as a subject of fun. Alternatively, it might reflect Hollywood's greater vibrancy and versatility, or greater willingness to make money out of politics. Whatever the reason, Hollywood's contribution to Cold War culture was more richly textured than that made by the Soviet film industry. The U.S. government itself seems to have recognized this by taking *Bananas* into enemy territory at the height of détente—another example, like *Roman Holiday* in the late 1950s, of the official appropriation of American screen comedy.

CHAPTER SEVEN

Last Acts

On Christmas Eve 1979, Soviet forces invaded the neighboring state of Afghanistan, a dramatic move designed in large part to reduce the perceived threat posed to the Soviet Union's southern Muslim republics by Iranian-backed Islamic radicalism. Despite the fact that over sixty American diplomats had just been taken hostage by Islamist students in Tehran, the U.S. government interpreted Moscow's actions as a newly aggressive Soviet march toward the Indian Ocean. Détente, already languishing, was now dead. One year later, on 4 November 1980, Ronald Reagan, the former Hollywood actor turned flag-bearer of the American New Right, defeated Jimmy Carter to become the fortieth president of the United States. Reagan immediately bolstered U.S. defense spending and introduced other measures that sought not merely to contain communism but to defeat it. If the start of the Cold War back in the 1940s had been slow and convoluted, its rebirth in 1979–1981 was sudden and transparent.[1]

Cinema contributed swiftly and significantly to what scholars now refer to as the second Cold War of the early to mid-1980s. It might be thought that political filmmaking had lost its luster and power by this point, given television's omnipresence in large parts of the world.[2] Compared with the 1940s and 1950s, to some extent it had. But certain movies—if they had something new to say, were entertaining and well made, or marketed aggressively (preferably all three)—could still be highly effective instruments of communication and attitude formation. This helps explain why the former U.S. secretary of state, Alexander Haig, had a hand in making *Red Dawn* (1984), a movie that warned of a Soviet-Cuban invasion of the United States. It also helps account in part for the indigenous films that were banned from Soviet screens in the early 1980s and, as discussed in chapter 2, for the tirades the Soviet film press aimed at Hollywood's "imperialist," "anti-democratic" output during the same period.[3]

During the first half of the 1980s, the Soviet and American film industries fought a propaganda battle the likes of which had not been seen for three decades. Images of peaceful coexistence and positive legitimation gave way to movies that appeared to call for, or at least to warn about, direct confrontation between the Soviet Union and United States. None of these films actually extolled the virtues of all-out nuclear war.[4] Nonetheless, through expensively produced, high-octane adventures celebrating the deadly skills of the nation's elite military units, many American films exuded hatred and took pleasure in killing the enemy, sometimes to the point of extermination. Soviet cinematic propaganda was lower key, even in its most extreme cases, but was also more schematic than at any time since the late 1940s. Because of their cartoonish characters and emphasis on action over dialogue, many such movies of this era have generally been dismissed as overly simplistic and therefore unimportant. We suggest otherwise, that these films carried considerable ideological and cultural weight.

Our final chapter contrasts the Soviet and American approaches to the second Cold War. The new breed of hyper-violent, super-patriotic combat movie produced in Hollywood is exemplified by *Rambo: First Blood Part II* (1985). Soviet cinema responded to the challenge set by Hollywood in two ways, embodied in a pair of films directed by Mikhail Tumanishvili. The more restrained and complex, and therefore more typical, example of late Soviet Cold War filmmaking is *Incident at Map Grid 36-80* (1982), but it would be a mistake to overlook *Solo Voyage* (1986), the Soviet response to films such as *Rambo,* given the Kremlin's awareness of the latter's black market popularity. Even so, as we shall see, the Soviet industry could not "out-Rambo" Hollywood. Obvious contrasts aside, *Rambo, Incident at Map Grid 36-80,* and *Solo Voyage* mark a return to face-to-face contact with the Cold War enemy.

In Defense of World Peace:
Incident at Map Grid 36-80

Given the rapprochement that the USSR had achieved with Richard Nixon in the early 1970s, Jimmy Carter had been a disappointing and even hostile American president in Soviet eyes. There is no doubt, however, that the election of Ronald Reagan significantly exacerbated tensions. A sudden burst of stridently anti-American rhetoric began to appear in the Soviet press, including the film press, after the Republican's arrival in the White House. This rhetoric (and the arms race) dramatically increased after Reagan's announcement in March 1983 of the Strategic Defense Initiative and his application of the term "evil empire" to the USSR that same month.[5] The film press was particularly annoyed that SDI was quickly dubbed "Star Wars," after what the Soviets considered the most prominent pictures in the "deplorable" series of pugnacious films that Hollywood had recently produced. *Return of the Jedi,* released in May 1983, was seen as particularly problematic.[6]

There was no question that Soviet cinema had to respond to this perceived assault, and their savior came from an improbable corner. Just as Vladimir Rogovoy had enjoyed unexpected success as a director a decade earlier with *Officers,* nothing in Mikhail Tumanishvili's prior career indicated that he would produce two major movie hits in quick succession. *Incident* at *Map Grid 36-80* took seventh place at the box office in 1982, with 33.1 million viewers,[7] considerably fewer than *Officers,* but still a hit in the days of growing disenchantment with Soviet cinema and declining movie attendance in favor of television.[8] Four years later, his second Cold War film, *Solo Voyage,* garnered the number two box office ranking with 37.8 million viewers.[9] Before turning to filmmaking, Tumanishvili had been a well-established and highly respected theater director in his native Georgia, at Tbilisi's famed Rustaveli Theater. *Incident at Map Grid 36-80* was only his second film. His screenwriter for *Incident* (and *Solo Voyage*) was Yevgeny Mesiatsev, whom the conservative Soviet critic Romil Sobolev compared to the renowned journalist, novelist, and scriptwriter Konstantin Simonov.[10] Coming from Sobolev, this was high praise indeed.

Incident at Map Grid 36-80 marked Soviet cinema's return to negative Cold War propagandizing. A suspenseful political adventure film, it is in many ways reminiscent of the Soviet film with which we began, *The Meeting on the Elbe.* Like *Elbe,* it shows the United States and the USSR in direct confrontation. However, whereas *Elbe* was relatively slow-paced, dwelling on the search for and unmasking of the Nazi Schrank, Tumanishvili's film reflects the more action-packed ethos of the early 1980s. Like *Officers, Incident* lionizes the Soviet military, focusing in this case on the navy rather than the army. Given the important role the United States and Soviet navies played in Cold War maneuverings and confrontations, and the naval buildup during the Brezhnev administration in particular, the cinematic turn to a focus on the Soviet Navy is politically significant.

In 1972, Sergei Gorshkov, who had been Admiral of the Fleet since 1956, issued a forthright declaration of the role the Soviet Navy had been assigned in achieving the nation's Cold War goals. "The Soviet Navy," he wrote, "is a powerful factor in the creation of favorable conditions for the building of Socialism and Communism, *for the active defense of peace and for strengthening international security* [emphasis added]."[11] To justify why a nation devoted to the "active defense of peace" should require a massive naval build-up, Gorshkov explained that "in their aggressive plans, the transoceanic imperialists are giving a leading role to their navies. For this reason, we too have been compelled to create a fleet capable of reliably protecting our motherland (*rodina*) and guaranteeing its state interests on the seas and oceans."[12]

Under Gorshkov's leadership, by 1968 the Soviet Navy had succeeded in achieving a formidable presence in the high seas that challenged the U.S. Navy's ability to concentrate on and control certain strategic areas.[13] By 1970, the Soviets had almost double the number of fighting ships of the U.S. Navy.[14] However, naval aviation, the subject of *Incident at Map Grid 36-80,* was a different story and occupied a different role from that in the United States. In the late 1950s, the Soviet Navy had lost its fighters and fighter bombers to the Air Defense Command. The much reduced naval air force focused on the kind of long-range air reconnaissance missions that *Incident* showcases.[15]

Incident at Map Grid 36-80 is unabashedly a genre picture, with a predictable plot standard to the adventure-suspense genre. There is conflict on the high seas, an accident that leads to the possibility of war, followed by herculean and ultimately successful efforts by the Soviets to divert the looming disaster of a probable third world war. The American and Soviet fleets, commanded by Admirals Rink and Spirin, respectively, are engaged in training exercises in the North Atlantic.[16] To complicate matters, the American fleet has a television news crew on board doing a story. Reconnaissance planes patrol the other side to spy on new ships and military hardware. (Soviet expertise in ocean surveillance and naval intelligence was held in high regard by the Americans.)[17] There is a reactor leak in the cooling compartment on an American "multipurpose" nuclear submarine loaded with sixteen cruise missiles. The American missiles, unlike those of the Soviets, are controlled not by people but by an unpredictable "Hughes computer," of which the Americans are inordinately proud but which is vulnerable to malfunction. There are shades of Sidney Lumet's *Fail-Safe* here.

A crew member sent to the reactor compartment to fix the leak becomes irradiated. Disoriented and crazed, he sends an unauthorized SOS, which the Soviet fleet picks up. (The last thing the sub captain wants is assistance from the Soviets.) Due to a computer malfunction, the missiles, seven of which are pointed at the seven Soviet ships on maneuvers, are engaged. Because no one can figure out how to reset the computer in time, two of the missiles are launched and cannot be recalled.

In the meantime, after receiving the SOS from the American crew, Soviet Admiral Spirin orders a reconnaissance plane to fly immediately to rescue the Americans as a humanitarian gesture. The problem is that the plane will not have enough fuel to accomplish this mission and return home without refueling. In full awareness of the consequences, Spirin makes a surprising decision: he orders Major Volk, the commander of the nearest available fuel transporter, to give up to the reconnaissance plane most of the fuel his own aircraft needs to return home safely. In other words, Spirin is ready to sacrifice a Soviet crew in order to save American submariners.

The American admiral is not as high-minded as his Soviet counterpart. When he learns that the Soviets are planning a rescue mission, Admiral Rink orders the submarine commander Captain Turner to prevent the boarding of the Soviet rescue team and to sink the sub as soon as practicable. This is despite the fact that the American fleet is hours away from the site, and the waters are frigid. The news crew on Rink's ship never learns of this situa-

Incident at Map Grid 36-80: The tanker crew is ready for flight. Courtesy of the Scientific Research Institute of Cinema Art (NIIK).

tion; for them it remains a routine training mission. For the Soviet viewer, this is a sign of how "real news" is kept from the American public.

In the meantime, the missiles are headed for the Soviet fleet. By keeping their weaponry in human hands, rather than turning decision making over to a computer, Spirin's men manage to intercept and explode the cruise missiles before they reach their target. World War III is thus averted, although "all [Soviet] units are ready for combat," as ordered by Admiral Spirin.

The film's attention then turns entirely to the problem of Major Volk's fuel transporter plane and crew, which coincidentally includes a general, thereby making it a more valuable commodity. The plane does indeed run out of fuel just before reaching land, but Volk's skillful flying gets everyone home safely. (Russian naval pilots were recognized for their skill in landing under difficult conditions and in "very rough country," because of the relative paucity of aircraft carriers.)[18] When their wives ask the crew how the flight was, the men blithely reply that everything was "normal," despite the fact that General Pavlov's face has been cut by broken glass as they land. (His obvious injury prompts some gentle questioning from his amused wife.) The film ends with the officers standing around the dining table toasting "our naval air force." The women are in the kitchen.

Incident at Map Grid 36-80 is an effective, if workmanlike, paean to the Soviet navy and naval aviators, but it also illustrates the Cold War divide in familiar ways. The contrasts between the American and Soviet crews are sharp, and Tumanishvili wisely takes an unusual amount of screen time to develop his Soviet characters so that the viewer cares about their fates. As a result, any viewer (even an American) would identify with the Soviets, not the Americans. The rightness of the Soviet cause is thus emphasized.

The film's hero is Major Volk (Boris Shcherbakov),[19] a capable, popular pilot approaching the age of thirty who has been passed over for promotion many times. Unknown to his wife and most of his men, all of whom worry about the way his career has stalled, there is a good reason. Eight years earlier, Volk had been in an incendiary plane explosion and was rescued by his navigator, Captain Skiba. Skiba was badly injured in the rescue effort. Volk wanted to keep Skiba on his crew, but the Ministry would allow this only if Volk flew old transport planes; Skiba could not be entrusted to serve as navigator on a new plane. Volk had, therefore, resigned himself to his current position by personal choice, not from lack of ability or administrative neglect. The issue of the overdue promotion was, however, again coming to a head. Volk's commander, General Pavlov, had offered him a new plane, told him Skiba should retire, and warned Volk that because of his age, this promotion opportunity would be his last chance to move up. The story of sacrifice for a comrade, which unfolds slowly throughout the film, is the strongest sign of Volk's superior character as a man and as an officer.

Another sign of Volk's superior character, not to mention his heroism, occurs during the refueling of the rescue plane, when he demonstrates his iron discipline. An American reconnaissance plane has been ordered to prevent the refueling in order to keep the Soviet rescue plane from getting to the submarine's crew. Major Armstrong, a pilot with whom Volk has previously had friendly conversations because they have flown the same routes over the years, pursues this task with vigor, buzzing Volk's plane at a distance of thirty, twenty-five, and finally ten meters. (Harassment of planes and ships, carried out by both sides, was a fact of life at sea during the Cold War.)[20] "The Russian kept steady," Armstrong notes to his angry superiors when he reports that the refueling occurred despite his reckless efforts. As a result of his failure to complete his deadly orders, Armstrong is instantly demoted. Nothing, not even serious harassment by a formerly friendly adversary, unnerves Volk. Nothing will prevent him from doing his duty, as ordered, no questions asked.

Finally, we see Volk's absolute poise as he flies home and, despite being out of fuel, skillfully lands his plane past the rocky coastline, thus saving the lives of a crew that was written off as lost, even by Volk himself. Although he knows that their chances of making it home safely are virtually nil and even says so to Pavlov, he does not panic. "It's our duty as defenders of our motherland," he stoically intones, although he has no idea about the circumstances behind the order to give up most of his fuel. (The viewer might wonder what Volk would have thought if he knew that their lives were put on the line to save Americans.)

Volk is not the only officer in this film who is created in the *Officers* mold. For his part, the navigator Skiba (Mikhai Volontir), who selflessly sacrificed himself for Volk years earlier, has devoted his entire life to flying to the extent that, unlike the other men, he has no wife or family. "The military is my life," he tells the crew's youngest member. "Marriage is not for flyers." Skiba further notes that "flying is a way of life, and I enjoy it." One gets the sense, however, that flying reflects more than enjoyment. Skiba's obsession for service has crowded out the "real life" that the other flyers have. Skiba is on the sidelines, witnessing their happiness, rather than participating in it. In the end, Skiba makes what is the highest sacrifice for him. He retires at the "old" age of forty-seven to release Volk from his obligation and allow the major to accept his long overdue promotion. (When Volk sharply asks General Pavlov how old he is, he receives the remarkably truthful response that age rules do not apply to generals.)

Admiral Spirin (Vladimir Sedov) and Major General Pavlov (Anatoly Kuznetsov) are also worthy officers, representing the strength, discipline, and humanity of the Soviet high command. Spirin is presented with a frightening scenario, the real possibility of war. "A disaster must be prevented at any cost," he tells his officers, when he learns that they have received an SOS from the damaged submarine. This proclamation comes despite the fact that Spirin is naturally and properly cautious of the Americans. As he tells Admiral Rink in one of their telephone conversations from their respective ships, "*In these times* [emphasis added], we shoot first and ask questions later." Yet Spirin does not shoot first, despite the American provocation, and instead sends rescuers to the Americans. When he learns that missiles are headed his way, he accepts Rink's "word as an officer" that this was a mistake caused by a faulty computer. Spirin merely orders the missiles shot down, without retaliation. Again, he is aware that a decision to go to war is in his hands, and he is determined to act decisively but calmly, not fearfully or rashly. ("The world's peace is at stake.")

Spirin's most controversial decision, of course, is to put the lives of the American submariners above the lives of his own tanker crew when he orders them to give up fuel to the rescue plane, fuel they need to return home. One of Spirin's own officers protests: "The crew is doomed if they give up their fuel. They'll die!" "There's no other way," replies Spirin. Through this tough decision, the viewer is led to understand that a Soviet commander is always thinking of the big picture, acting for the greater good of humankind, even if it means sacrificing some of his own men. Defending the motherland should not be narrowly construed. It also means defending world peace and universal brotherhood.

Spirin's air force counterpart, Pavlov, is just as steady. On a whim, General Pavlov decided to join Volk as co-pilot on their original mission, to re-fuel reconnaissance planes. It is Pavlov who receives Spirin's fatal order. Although he understands its import all too clearly, he remains expressionless as he transmits the order to Volk. All is calm. Duty is duty. Like Spirin and Volk, Pavlov never wavers.

Interestingly, with the exception of Pavlov's wife, Nadezhda ("Hope") Pavlovna, the wives seem unworthy of these men. The women are reminiscent of Lyolya in *Nine Days in One Year* and the younger Lyuba in *Officers:* they wait and resent waiting. Officers' wives are "peacetime victims," the child bride Irina, only seventeen, tells Nadezhda Pavlovna. Volkov's wife Masha nags her husband about his failure to be promoted, not letting up even after he attempts to joke it away. Significantly, her concern seems to be about herself and her own status, rather than about her husband's position and feelings. The fact that Volk has never told her about Skiba (it is Nadezhda Pavlovna who does that) perhaps indicates Volk's lack of faith in his wife's ability to understand that his honor is at stake.

Nadezhda Pavlovna serves as "mother" to the wives, just as her husband is a father figure for Volk. A traditional woman, she speaks in hoary aphorisms: "Keep a good home, and your husband will always stay around," and "Sometimes they [wives] spend their whole lives waiting." "But what about love?" asks Irina plaintively. "This [waiting] is love," Nadezhda Pavlovna sagely replies. Like a good Soviet officer, Nadezhda Pavlovna understands discipline and duty and seeks to inspire the younger women to follow her example. By telling Volk's wife the story of how he put his career aside for the sake of his comrade, the older woman subtly urges the younger to be a better, that is, a less complaining and resentful, wife.

Not surprisingly, most (but not all) of the Americans are quite different from their Soviet counterparts. Admiral Spirin is willing to sacrifice the tanker crew in order to save a greater number of lives, even if they are American lives. Admiral Rink (Omar Volmer), on the other hand, without hesitation is willing to sacrifice his own submarine crew not for some higher good, but to prevent the Soviets from boarding the ship and learning the Americans' military secrets. ("The Russians would like to have a look at our operations," he explains.) It is highly likely that the embarrassment of being "rescued" by the enemy also plays a part in his attitude. Rink does, however, keep his word to Spirin and destroys the submarine after the American sailors have been evacuated, ultimately without Soviet aid, to a fate unknown.[21]

(The Soviets estimate that humans could survive no more than twenty minutes in the icy waters. Rink's ships were eight hours away at the start of the emergency and are still hours from rescuing the submarine's crew.)

Unlike General Pavlov, Admiral Spirin, or Major Volk, the submarine's commander, Captain Turner (Paul Butkevich), lacks discipline and self-control. He panics when he learns about the reactor leak in the cooling system. He appears to have no emergency plan in place in the event of an accident and orders one man left behind in the reactor compartment to attempt a repair without proper safety equipment. First Turner says the sub must surface, but "not in front of the Russians." Then he says they should surface only in case of "extreme emergency," as though a state of emergency were not already at hand. He rushes about, sweating and shouting orders. He refuses to issue an SOS. He appears to have little idea how to use the all-important computer in his office to prevent an accident.

In contrast with the Soviet officers, Turner is casually dressed, wearing a T-shirt and baseball cap. The rest of his crew is equally scruffy-looking and clearly lacks the sobriety and integrity essential for such dangerous work. As a consequence, security on the ship is flawed. The crazed sailor Allen easily pushes aside the sentry in the supposedly secure communications room to activate an SOS, murmuring that it's "to save our souls." Allen then rows away in a lifeboat as Turner shrieks to him to come back. "Go to hell!" Allen yells defiantly. "I just took a huge dose of radiation! I switched on a permanent SOS!" Thus the only American who does the right thing is confused and dying.

The final American with a developed character is Major Armstrong (Vitautas Tomkus), pilot of one of the American reconnaissance planes. Armstrong does not take his job too seriously. We first see him gambling at cards and flying at the same time. Armstrong and Volk have formed a kind of friendship over years of patrolling the same airspace; they chat easily in English, which Volk of course speaks in contrast to Armstrong's ignorance of Russian. Armstrong informs Volk that his wife has just had a fourth baby girl. "What a nightmare!" jokes Volk in response (yet more evidence of the film's condescension toward women). They banter about how many children Armstrong is willing to have in order to secure an all-important son. (Armstrong says at least six, a number that would be quite astonishing to the Soviet urbanites who formed the bulk of moviegoers.) But when Armstrong is ordered to interfere with the refueling, he wholeheartedly and unquestioningly devotes himself to this task, to the horror of one of his juniors. "The Russians are trying to help! You know his name!" the young man cries out incredulously. No matter. For Armstrong, Volk is no longer a person, just a target.

Incident at Map Grid 36-80: Major Armstrong as automaton. Courtesy of the Scientific Research Institute of Cinema Art (NIIK).

In most respects, *Incident at Map Grid 36-80* is a true Socialist Realist film, harking back to the traditions of the late 1940s. As in *The Meeting on the Elbe,* the Soviets meet the Americans face to face, and there is no doubt who holds the moral upper hand. Like *Elbe*'s Major Kuzmin, Major Volk is a colorless, if handsome and upright, character, despite the backstory with Skiba and the presence of a wife. As in *Elbe,* there are bad Americans and very few good ones. There is "inversion" as well. Despite the spectacular disasters of the USS *Thresher* and the USS *Scorpion* in the 1960s, the Soviets had many more reactor leaks on their submarines, seven through 1982 in the Northern Fleet alone.[22]

But there are also key differences with *The Meeting on the Elbe.* The Soviets are portrayed as peace-loving, to be sure, but also as willing and ready to fight, and their fire power is displayed and used, something noticeably absent from *Elbe.* On the other hand, the Americans are negative characters but not crudely drawn cartoon villains. It was not (and is not) hard to believe that such a scenario could have occurred. Another new feature is the emphasis on military hardware, particularly American military hardware. It looks impressive, but—as in *Fail-Safe*—it does not work, whereas Soviet equipment, even the old tanker plane, functions beautifully (unlike the planes of the national airline Aeroflot, which had a dismal reputation for safety).[23] Unlike real life, the Soviet navy is in complete control of both men and materiel, and so the film may have been a successful recruiting tool. However, in case anyone doubted it, clear and present danger from the Americans remains. Admiral Rink and Captain Turner show no signs of regret and certainly no signs of learning from the experience.

Incident at Map Grid 36-80 received unusual promotion for a film of its type, a sign of its official imprimatur. It took the cover of *Art of the Cinema* in early 1983.[24] At least one Soviet critic thought it a "big step forward" for Tumanishvili in comparison to his first film.[25] Its audiences doubtless enjoyed the adventure and suspense of the film. Will the reactor explode? Will the cruise missiles reach their target? Will Volk's plane return safely? It received an 86 percent approval rating in *Soviet Screen*'s annual readers' survey, and placed eighth in a ranking from this readership of cinephiles.[26]

Tumanishvili's next Cold War film was *Solo Voyage*. Because this film represents the uneasy coexistence between the "soft" approach of *Incident at Map Grid 36-80* and the hard-charging style of the Hollywood competition, it deserves attention as well. Finished in 1985 and released in early 1986, it turned up the heat considerably from *Incident at Map Grid 36-80*. *Solo Voyage* doubtless reflects the anger that built up after Reagan announced SDI, although Reagan's rhetoric had toned down a little for his reelection campaign in 1984. It also reflects the uncertainties of the mid-1980s, by which time the Soviet Union had experienced three changes in leadership in a little less than three years. Finally, it reflects the hostility that anti-Soviet films such as *Rambo* engendered within the cinema bureaucracy, feelings that were well reflected in the cinema press, as explained in chapter 2. Nevertheless, like *Incident at Map Grid 36-80*, *Solo Voyage* emphasizes that the Soviet mission is to save world peace, not to instigate a first strike.

Even more than *Incident at Map Grid 36-80*, *Solo Voyage* is a plot-driven, action-suspense drama very much in the Hollywood style and definitely fitting the *Rambo* mold. *Solo Voyage* is, therefore, a simpler, more straightforward, and more entertaining picture than *Incident*, but also much less interesting or complex as a sociopolitical artifact. Once again, Soviet and American ships are conducting naval exercises in the same vicinity.[27] A rogue Vietnam War veteran, Hessalt, recruited by the CIA in no small part because he is a sadistic and even psychotic killer, is charged with staging an incriminating incident from a secret American nuclear base on an island. The plan is to blow up an American ocean liner, packed with 1,800 tourists, and blame it on the Soviets. The missile, again computer-controlled as in *Incident*, goes awry and explodes instead near a yacht sailed by a young American couple, Jack and Carol. (American technology apparently never works; presumably this helped allay the Soviet audiences' fears about SDI.)

With the failure of the original plan, Hessalt and his men decide to move on to their own operation. They take over the underground base from its

Solo Voyage: A psychotic Hessalt murders his servant. Courtesy of the Scientific Research Institute of Cinema Art (NIIK).

crew and prepare to launch nuclear missiles against the Soviet fleet on maneuvers. In the meantime, a solitary Soviet ship sends marines out to rescue Jack and Carol, who have unfortunately taken refuge on the same island where Hessalt and his gang are hiding out. Carol is killed in an attack by the renegades, and Jack eventually discovers, to his horror and disbelief, that her killers are his compatriots.

Back in the United States, Hessalt's handlers panic after realizing that he is out of control and about to start a world war. They decide to blow up the island themselves in order to destroy the evidence, but it will take time for the American planes to get there. In the meantime, the Soviet marines engage in a pitched battle with the renegades and manage to turn off the power to the missiles just in the nick of time, thereby averting war. The American planes sent to destroy Hessalt's team blow up an American frigate and a submarine that are in cahoots with Hessalt, and even fire a few rockets at the Soviet ship. By the end, the Soviet commander, Major Shatokhin, has been killed, and Jack understands the perfidy of the American government, which disavows knowledge of everything that has happened.

Solo Voyage's appeal to a Soviet audience is obvious apart from its anti-American message. It is action-packed, with colorful, truly evil villains whom the heroes slay with satisfying brutality. Soviet military might is unequivocal. The "unhappy ending" is softened because it is the death of only one, a selfless man and true Soviet officer who clearly had no qualms about giving up his life for his country or for human beings in distress, regardless of their nationality.[28]

Taken together, *Incident at Map Grid 36-80* and *Solo Voyage* may be seen as the swan song for the Soviet Cold War film. *Incident* is, however, a more typical example. Even though it is undeniably a piece of negative propaganda, it still bears the hallmarks of positive legitimation in the way the heroes and villains are constructed. In the end, the inherent humanity of the Soviet officers and their hope for world peace are the lasting images, not those of the flawed, though not evil, Americans. On the other hand, *Solo Voyage* ironically bears the burdens of American cinematic influences, even as it denounces Americans. The villains are cartoonish, the heroes mere sketches. Nevertheless, as we see below, compared to *Rambo* and films like it, *Solo Voyage*'s message seems almost nuanced. As in *Incident at Map Grid 36-80*, the Soviets understand that the ultimate goal is world peace, not national self-aggrandizement. Not until the end does the viewer get a sense that Major Shatokhin is also fighting for something more prosaic and personal than world peace—his homeland and the Russian way of life.

VENGEANCE AND VICTORY:
Rambo: First Blood Part II

A number of the Hollywood movies we have analyzed in our study performed relatively poorly at the box office, especially in comparison with their Soviet counterparts. This was certainly not the case with *Rambo: First Blood Part II*, however, which was the second-most-seen film in the United States in 1985. Grossing a massive $150 million domestically and $300 million worldwide, the movie attracted more viewers than *Incident at Map Grid 36-80* and *Solo Voyage* put together. In fact, on the basis of these figures, *Rambo* was, after *Top Gun* (1986), Tony Scott's paean to U.S. Naval fighter pilots, the second most popular Cold War movie to come out of Hollywood throughout the whole conflict. In total, the trilogy of Rambo films released during the Cold War (in 1982, 1985, and 1988) grossed a breathtaking $251 million domestically and $614 million worldwide. The series' phenomenal success made John Rambo, the disaffected but heroic American Vietnam War veteran played by Sylvester Stallone, the single most powerful cinematic Cold War icon in the United States, and in many other countries, too.[29]

Released in May 1985, *Rambo: First Blood Part II*, the trilogy's biggest money-spinner, quickly grew into more than just a film. This was partly due to timing. The movie capitalized on the tenth anniversary of the end of the Vietnam War and kicked off the summer season slot. It also broke the record for the greatest number of theaters in which a film had ever opened in North America (2,074), and it formed part of a new, powerful trend in Hollywood merchandising. Rambo guns, knives, bows and arrows, vitamin tablets, books, T-shirts, hats, dolls, bumper stickers, and computer games soon appeared in stores across the United States. By the end of the year a Rambo-themed nightclub had opened in Houston and "Rambo-grams" were the rage at parties across the nation. An animated children's television series, *Rambo and the Forces of Freedom,* appeared in 1986.[30]

Clever salesmanship and hype could not explain Rambo-mania by themselves, however. Cinematically, the movie provided audiences of the 1980s with the kind of no-nonsense action hero that had largely been missing from America's silver screens for a decade. Numerous commentators likened Stallone's Rambo to John Wayne, Hollywood's greatest onscreen Cold Warrior, who died in 1979. Several compared *Rambo* with Wayne's tribute to the U.S. military's efforts to save South Vietnam from communism, *The Green Berets* (1968), the only major direct-combat portrayal of Vietnam made during the war itself.[31] Politically, *Rambo* tapped into and reinforced the bullish, jingoistic mood that prevailed across large parts of the United States during the Reagan era and that made it cool again to be anticommunist, following the soft-pedal approach of the Carter years. Above everything else perhaps, "Rambo-ism" helped define a revitalized, more militant form of American patriotism and an unwillingness to remain bogged down in the depressing malaise associated with Vietnam.

From its opening pre-credit sequence, *Rambo* combines a crude 1950s form of can-do anticommunism with a New Rightist contempt for bureaucracy. The movie starts as it means to go on—with a bang. An explosion, shot in close-up, shakes the screen and sends tons of rocks flying into the air. When the boulders and dust have settled, we find ourselves not in battle but in an American penitentiary quarry. The scene might be a Soviet labor camp (or gulag), a favorite target of American Cold War propagandists since the 1940s,[32] but for the fact that the prisoners appear well fed and the sun is shining.

The camera focuses on the most handsome and imposing of the prisoners, John Rambo. Long-haired and finely chiseled, Rambo (Stallone) is doing time for having slayed a bigoted, small-town Oregon posse that had victimized him as a no-good Vietnam War veteran in *First Blood* (Ted Kotcheff, 1982). Through the barbed wire, Rambo's ex-commanding officer, Trautman (Richard Crenna), asks him if he will carry out a daring one-man mission to investigate the presence of U.S. prisoners in a mysterious area of communist Vietnam. In return, all being well, Washington will grant him a pardon. Rambo knows the area in question, as he escaped from a POW camp there in 1971, winning a Congressional Medal of Honor in the process. Being a former Green Beret, he also has the necessary expertise to em-

Rambo: First Blood Part II: Murdock orders his mercenaries to abort their helicopter rescue mission. Courtesy of Tristar Pictures/Photofest.

bark on such a dangerous mission. As the slovenly, overweight prison guards look on, Rambo has only one question, aimed more at the bureaucrats in government than at Trautman: "Do we get to win this time?"

At a high-tech U.S. command post in Thailand, Rambo receives a rankling order from Murdock (Charles Napier), a slick CIA type in charge of the covert mission. If he finds any prisoners, he must not rescue them but merely take photographs to prove they exist. Rambo parachutes into Vietnam, travels up river, and discovers POWs are indeed interned at the camp where he himself was once imprisoned. He frees one, Banks (Andy Wood), who is hardly more than a living skeleton, and gets him back to the "extraction point," the place where a helicopter is scheduled to lift Rambo out. When the approaching pilot radios the command post that Rambo has a live POW with him, Murdock orders the pilot to abort the mission—to abandon Rambo and the POW, despite knowing the two of them are surrounded by the enemy. Trautman is on the rescue helicopter and vigorously protests, but he can do nothing to help Rambo because a gun is held to his head by one of Murdock's accomplices. Trautman now realizes Rambo was never meant to succeed. Going through the motions of a search was intended to placate the public, while suppressing evidence of POWs would eliminate humiliating negotiations and reparations.

Having been captured at the extraction point, Rambo and Banks are taken back to the camp. A squad of Soviet soldiers then descends ominously from the sky aboard a phalanx of helicopters. Supplying the Vietnamese minions with arms and orders, it is clear the Russians are in charge. The Soviet chief, Lieutenant Colonel Podovsky (Steven Berkoff), sadistically interrogates Rambo to try to make him broadcast a false message to the U.S. base. "I see you are no stranger to pain," sneers Podovsky. Despite horrific torture, including being strapped, Christ-like, to an electrified bed frame, Rambo refuses to betray his compatriots; his only broadcast is to tell Murdock that he is coming to get *him*.

Helped by a beautiful Vietnamese guide masquerading as a prostitute, Co Bao (Julia Nickson), Rambo miraculously escapes, killing Podovsky's hench-man and numerous Vietnamese communists in the process. Tragically, Co is then gunned down by a North Vietnamese officer, just after she and Rambo have kissed and the American has agreed to take her over the border with him. (Unlike those who escaped communism in *Man on the Tightrope,* Co will never get to taste freedom.)

Ablaze with rage, Rambo exacts revenge. He singlehandedly destroys the camp, slays dozens of Vietnamese and Soviet communists, releases the POWs, and flies them back to the command post in a Russian helicopter after blasting Podovsky out of the sky. He then machine-guns Murdock's computers but spares the trembling *apparatchik,* warning him: "You know there's more men out there. Find them or I'll find you!" Trautman counsels Rambo against being consumed with hatred for his country. Before walking into the mythic distance, Rambo asserts: "Hate it? I'd *die* for it. . . . I want what they and every guy who came over here and spilt his guts wants . . . for our country to love us as much as we love it."

Woody Allen's *Bananas* demonstrated the greater creative control Ameri-can filmmakers could exert over their material compared with their Soviet counterparts during the Cold War, especially by the 1970s. Sylvester Stal-lone's *Rambo* underlines this important difference and shows how power-fully Hollywood's international mega-stars of the 1980s could make movies in their own image. Stallone, Arnold Schwarzenegger, Harrison Ford, Tom Cruise, and other actors levied greater financial and cultural clout than indi-vidual studios during this era. Often their image *was* the movie, potently en-hancing the commercial and political appeal of their characters' endeavors.

A journeyman actor in the early 1970s, including a role as a mugger in *Bananas,*[33] Sylvester Stallone's career was transformed after writing and star-ring in *Rocky* (1976), the Oscar-winning story of a down-and-out boxer who triumphs against heavy odds. Thanks mainly to the *Rocky* series, by the mid-1980s Stallone had become one of Hollywood's most successful star-entre-preneurs, taking personal control of his movie vehicles, frequently writing or collaborating on their scripts, and occasionally directing them. Stallone had also become—via his rags-to-riches story, his underdog persona, and his frequent patriotic statements—a byword for muscular American virtue.[34]

Stallone co-wrote *Rambo* (with James Cameron, director of the 1984 Arnold Schwarzenegger sci-fi/action hit *The Terminator*) after, he claimed, receiving an impassioned letter in July 1983 from a Virginia woman whose husband had been missing in Southeast Asia for sixteen years.[35] Stallone drastically changed *Rambo*'s original story, written by Kevin Jarre. He deleted a sidekick, thereby making Rambo more of a loner and a brave individual. He also gave Rambo a political speech at the end of the movie, wrapping his hero and other, real-life Vietnam War veterans in the American flag and calling for U.S. decisiveness overseas.[36] Like many Americans in the 1980s, Stallone believed the Vietnamese communists were holding prisoner hundreds of American military personnel classed as missing in action (MIA). This was despite the fact that Hanoi's war against the United States had officially ended in 1973, and the Pentagon had declared in 1978 that there were no American prisoners in Vietnam. "I'm convinced the MIAs are alive, living in Laos," he told the press when *Rambo* appeared. In the film, Stallone may have modeled his character partly after Bo Gritz, a former member of U.S. Special Forces who undertook a series of heavily publicized but ill-fated trips into Southeast Asia to locate and free American POWs in the early 1980s.[37]

Rambo not only popularized the "MIA myth" more powerfully than any other movie of the era,[38] but did so by telling its audience that Moscow was conspiring with the Vietnamese to keep innocent Americans in chains. On the face of it, this charge pales in significance compared with the "evidence" contained within *Incident at Map Grid 36-80* and *Solo Voyage* that the Americans might recklessly trigger a nuclear holocaust. Nevertheless, the implications of the charge were potentially endless: that Moscow had been directing Ho Chi Minh's decades-long campaign of communist expansion in Southeast Asia; that the United States should consequently have used all the weapons it had at its disposal to achieve military victory in Vietnam; that détente had been a sham on the Soviet Union's part; that, contrary to what movies like *Bananas* had been saying in the 1970s, the communist threat against the United States was real; and, indeed, that all communists were amoral hypocrites who would go to any lengths to defeat the United States and who, therefore, had to be defeated themselves using any methods necessary.[39]

Rambo's demonization of the enemy makes *Incident at Map Grid 36-80*, and even much of Hollywood's McCarthy-era Red-baiting material, look positively restrained. In contrast with *Incident* or *Solo Voyage,* it allows for no

Rambo: First Blood Part II: Colonel Podovsky's brutal sidekick, Sergeant Yushin (Vojo Goric), tortures John Rambo. Courtesy of Tristar Pictures/Photofest.

honorable opponents capable of seeing the light or who have seen the error of their ways. Rambo's guide-cum-girlfriend, Co Bao, is no ex-communist, for instance, and looks distinctly Amerasian anyway, right down to her mascara and lipstick. With the exception of Co, the North Vietnamese are sly, hunt in packs, fondle or murder women, and treat their victims as sub-humans. They hold the haggard American POWs in rat-infested tiger cages, for example, while Rambo is stripped and dunked in a leech-infested slime pit. Their Soviet overlords are cool, heartless, and expert torturers. Podovsky acts and sounds just like a Gestapo official. But even Hollywood movies of the Second World War era usually depicted dastardly Nazis as killing for a military reason. By contrast, Rambo's Soviet adversaries either do it just for fun or because they are part of a machine-like system. Their fetish for black uniforms and oversized, brutish-looking helicopter gunships reinforces the totalitarian image. Such "people" (if that is what they are) cannot be converted or saved. As death is their vocation, so death at Rambo's hands should be their reward.

Rambo's and America's other enemy, Murdock, is less evil than the communists but in many ways no less dangerous. Murdock embodies the "stinking bureaucrat" (Trautman's words) whom the New Right believed had turned the "noble cause" (Reagan's phrase) against communism in Vietnam into a humiliating quagmire by stabbing the U.S. military in the back. When we first meet him, Murdock looks like a dependable Reaganite: a photograph of the president adorns his wall, an American flag graces his desk, and (a sure sign of reactionary sympathies) a copy of the best-selling autobiography by ardent Cold Warrior G. Gordon Liddy lies conspicuously at his side. Nonetheless, Murdock thinks and acts like a Washington desk-jockey liberal. Echoing Defense Secretary Robert McNamara's notorious restrictions on the frontline fighting man's tactical options in Vietnam in the 1960s, he forbids Rambo from "engaging with the enemy" for fear of causing diplomatic and political complications.

When Rambo disobeys the order and bravely rescues a POW, thereby providing the world with living proof of communist malevolence, Murdock has no qualms whatsoever with leaving them both to die at the extraction site. In the film's most memorable cinematic moment, a dizzying aerial shot, Rambo and Banks, seconds from salvation, are left howling at an ascending helicopter as the Vietnamese communists close in from all sides. It is an extraordinary act of betrayal, one that could stand in for the many that U.S. veterans accused Washington of perpetrating during the Vietnam War, and, as one critic noted when the film was released, a scene of undeniable emotional power.[40]

Were the film to have ended at this point (unlikely as that is), *Rambo*'s message about the individual soldier, and by extension individual Americans, having fallen victim to a misguided and compromised government policy in Vietnam might have been all the more potent. However, such an ending would not have allowed Americans to indulge in a form of historical revisionism that sees the United States actually defeating the communists in Vietnam. Audiences would not have had the pleasure in seeing Rambo singlehandedly decimate the North Vietnamese and Soviet armies, thereby showing what a "free" U.S. military unencumbered by faint-hearted politicians and bureaucrats could achieve—both in the recent past and, which was more important as far as Ronald Reagan and others were concerned, in the present.

Rambo is the perfect agent of U.S. victory in Vietnam because he displays what many perceived to be peculiarly American attributes. Stallone himself saw Rambo as representative of an America that was proud and capable of standing up for "liberty, justice and freedom for all."[41] Many in the audience would surely have agreed, but there was more to his character *and* body—both of which were constructed with great care[42]—than this. Rambo's muscular physique, which enables him to withstand pain and to kill the enemy silently with his bare hands, could be said to embody the strong militaristic foreign policy position that Reagan, "the quintessential macho president," according to activist-academic John Orman, adopted in the 1980s. His perfectly toned hard body could be seen as the antithesis of

Rambo: First Blood Part II: Rambo exhibits his tender side with Vietnamese freedom-fighter Co Bao. Courtesy of Tristar Pictures/Photofest.

an American body politic that had gone soft on communism in the 1970s or had become bloated and decadent according to *Bananas*.[43]

Rambo is strong, taciturn, and fearless but, as his anguish at seeing Co die in his arms shows us, not heartless. He is, in other words, no automaton, like the communists. Rambo's Green Beret training might have turned him into what Trautman calls "a pure fighting machine," but unlike the communists he fights bravely, alone. As a clear-headed, almost spiritual maverick, he eschews the bureaucracy of warfare and the professional Cold Warrior bureaucrats on the home front. He kills for his country, not for kicks, because he and the United States have been wronged, not because they are inherently aggressive or sadistic.

Rambo is identified as half American-Indian. This enables (or allows) him to use a bow-and-arrow to gory, lethal effect and, as a racially mixed underdog, protects him against charges of American orientalism. Like the teenage American holdouts against Soviet invasion in *Red Dawn,* his hit-and-run tactics might have evoked popular images of underdog militiamen fighting for freedom against British colonialists. Alternatively, some viewers might have interpreted his tactics as a clever, American twist on the Viet Cong's own highly effective guerrilla warfare strategy—that is, giving the enemy a taste of its own medicine.[44] In contrast with the Soviet military machine, Rambo is not reliant on technology. Neither is he a prisoner of it, like the Americans

Rambo: First Blood Part II: Having landed safely in Thailand with the MIAs, Rambo has one thing left to do—destroy Murdock's bureaucracy of betrayal. Courtesy of Tristar Pictures / Photofest.

in *Incident at Map Grid 36-80* or *Fail-Safe.* "The mind is the best weapon," he tells Murdock in a room full of computers, and later we see plenty of examples of the former Green Beret's capacity for initiative and self-reliance. Yet Rambo has the technical proficiency to pilot a helicopter if necessary and is clearly not living in the dark ages.

Rambo's rugged individualism, combined with a willingness to break rules and heads, enables him to cut the Gordian knot of bureaucratic international politics. These archetypal Hollywood-hero characteristics set him apart from Major Volk in *Incident at Map Grid 36-80,* who is a colorless stoic and a conscript in an orderly, mass military state. Rambo is an outsider, a volunteer, someone who has the same devotion to duty and sacrifice as Volk, but who is able to express that devotion more freely, mentally and physically. Though he never once uses the word, freedom is central to Rambo's being. At its most basic, freedom to him means the freedom to think and, most important, to act according to natural, human instinct: in this case, to save American lives. Statecraft is for fools or cowards; action speaks louder than words, literally in Rambo's case.

In terms of its plot, *Rambo* is every bit as predictable as *Incident at Map Grid 36-80* and *Solo Voyage.* Cinematically, however, it is far more impressive and because of its higher production values was far more likely to outgun its Soviet rivals. *Rambo* is no piece of "schlock," to borrow critic Stanley

Kauffmann's word. Its taut, economical, ninety-two-minute story is, for a start, a classically structured mission adventure narrative, one that Hollywood fans had grown accustomed to over decades.[45] It was made with prime professional skills. Director George P. Cosmatos was a highly competent action-adventure expert. Buzz Feitshans, the producer, had made *First Blood, Uncommon Valor,* and *Red Dawn.* Cinematographer Jack Cardiff was an Oscar winner, as was the composer Jerry Goldsmith, who specialized in action and suspense. The special effects coordinator, Thomas Fisher, worked on all the *Rambo* films and later on blockbusters such as *True Lies* (James Cameron, 1994) and *Titanic* (James Cameron, 1997). In credibility, the action in *Rambo* is, as Kauffmann wrote in the *New Republic,* "as ludicrous as old Saturday afternoon serials." Yet "in execution," he argued, "the skills help it to skate over the incredibilities."[46]

The best skills come at a price of course, but *Rambo* could afford them. With a production budget of $28 million, it not only dwarfed *Incident at Map Grid 36-80* and *Solo Voyage,* each of which cost in the region of only $1 million.[47] It also outspent the period's other Vietnam POW rescue movies and every other Hollywood film of 1985 except, significantly, for *Rocky IV,* in which Stallone/Rocky/Rambo beats a giant robotic Soviet boxer in front of the Politburo in Moscow.[48] *Rambo*'s large coffers paid for beautiful gasoline explosions, awe-inspiring helicopter dog fights, assistance from the U.S. Navy for the construction of an authentic-looking PBR patrol boat, and the re-creation of a Vietnamese prison camp hacked out of the Mexican jungle near Acapulco.[49] The bulk of the money for *Rambo* came from Mario Kassar and Andrew Vajna, two young, foreign-born film investors who had formed the independent production company Carolco Pictures in 1976. Carolco was among the most influential global cinematic players in the 1980s and a leading producer of big-budget Hollywood action fare. Its copious body of Cold War–related material included *Iron Eagle II* (Sydney J. Furie, 1988), *Red Heat* (Walter Hill, 1988), and *Jacob's Ladder* (Adrian Lyne, 1990).[50]

Aside perhaps from persuading the Reagan administration to conduct a comprehensive search for U.S. prisoners of war in Southeast Asia, *Rambo* seems to have fulfilled just about everything its makers hoped for. It was a runaway commercial success, taking a record $20 million over the opening weekend in the United States and eventually grossing four times as much as *First Blood* worldwide. Had the R-rated *Rambo* not been restricted domestically to patrons over eighteen years of age, it would surely have been Hollywood's number one Cold War moneymaker.[51] The movie appealed to several, potentially conflicting audiences, including Vietnam War veterans, old hippies, weapons lovers, technophobes, bodybuilders, and Cold Warriors. It also bridged several popular genres: the POW/prison break film, the western, the war movie, and, with its high-tech gizmos and international action hero, the Bond film.

Rambo sparked an intense debate in the United States about the lessons of the Vietnam War, about U.S. foreign policy, and about the nature of American society as a whole. Rambo's face appeared on magazine covers across the political spectrum, primetime television news shows acknowledged the movie's social importance, and countless op-ed pieces on it appeared under the bylines of columnists from right to left. A deep fissure opened up between a liberal, vocal minority who argued the film fostered a mindless, aggressive patriotism that bordered on fascism, and a larger, more muted majority who thought the movie was simply exciting entertainment or who cheered "U-S-A" when Rambo "kicked commie butts."[52] The Vietnam Veterans Association placarded cinemas in protest at the movie's glamorizing of the war, while several commentators pointed to the striking similarities between *Rambo* (with its Aryan hero, emphasis on primal virtues, and ideology of an army undercut by the government back home) and Nazi movies of the 1930s. The *Los Angeles Herald-Examiner* reported in June 1985 that 84 percent of approximately 1,000 callers responding to the question "Is *Rambo* right about why the United States lost in Vietnam?" answered in the affirmative.[53]

The Reagan administration had not played a direct role in making *Rambo,* but it readily invoked the movie approvingly to applaud the values of loyalty, honesty, commitment, and determined action. Reagan himself used it as part of his war on what he and others on the New Right termed "Commuterrorism." "Boy, I saw *Rambo* last night," he said in July 1985 at a press conference to mark the release of American hostages held by Lebanese terrorists in Beirut. "Now I know what to do next time." Dismissed at the time as a joshing one-liner, it and other similar remarks from Reagan worried commentators who charged the former actor with habitually confusing the world depicted in the movies with the world outside it.[54] By glorifying the Vietnam War experience, *Rambo* may have increased public tolerance of U.S. military involvement elsewhere, especially in Central America, a potential base for the communist subversion or even invasion of the United States, according to the New Right. The movie was shown to U.S. troops in the Middle East to boost morale and displayed outside U.S. Army recruitment offices. *Rambo*'s success cleared the way for further "avenge-and-win" Vietnam flicks such as Gideon Amir's *POW: The Escape* (1986), while Rambo clones proliferated in Hollywood movies for the rest of the 1980s and beyond.[55] Reagan's successor, George H. W. Bush, appropriated Rambo during the 1991 Persian Gulf War. Soon after that conflict, with the Cold War now over and America's Vietnam Syndrome having been successfully kicked at last, it was clear that the character had become *the* representative of the persevering American fighter unburdened by self-doubt.[56]

Overseas, *Rambo* seems to have fared less well politically, though this is hardly surprising given the strength of anti-American feeling engendered by Reagan's rhetoric and actions in large parts of the world in the 1980s. That said, the movie broke box office records from Holland to Australia, helped by the fact that its much-derided sparse dialogue meant that the film required even less translation than an average action-adventure feature. In Syria, bizarrely, *Rambo* was dubbed in such a way as to turn the Viet Cong into Japanese and Vietnam into Burma during the Second World War. The film even played to packed houses across Southeast Asia, though it was banned in Vietnam. There was intense opposition to *Rambo* in parts of Western Europe, where it was condemned as one of the worst examples yet of Reaganite Cold War gung-hoism. Anti-nuclear campaigners demonstrating outside U.S. military bases in West Germany pasted up Rambo posters alongside signs saying, "Take the Toys from the Boys!"[57]

Behind the Iron Curtain, the Soviet government newspaper *Izvestia* condemned *Rambo* for attempting to brainwash public opinion in favor of militarist adventurism. In January 1986, Soviet artists and cultural officials could be heard attacking Rambo and Rocky as expressions of "anti-Russian phobia even more pathological than in the days of McCarthyism." "There is a new type of American hero," spat Georgy Ivanov, deputy minister of culture, "a man who kills the Reds with perverted relish." That same month, reports circulated of thousands of *Rambo* videocassettes being sold on the Soviet black market.[58] As late as 1987, a year after glasnost was introduced, *Rambo* was still being attacked for its "unfriendly" depiction of Soviets.[59]

As noted above, *Solo Voyage* opened in the USSR in February 1986, and a year later in the likes of France, Finland, Spain, and East and West Germany. Perhaps modeled on Rambo, its crazed, racist, and bloodthirsty villain, Hessalt, was the very epitome of Ivanov's New American Man. When Sylvester Stallone heard of what the U.S. press called "Russia's *Rambo*," he justifiably interpreted *Solo Voyage* as a compliment to the power and popularity of his own movie. Joking with journalists, Stallone said he would telephone the Soviets to arrange a duel between John Rambo and Major Shatokhin in what was now commonly termed the Soviet Union's own Vietnam, Afghanistan. Peter MacDonald's *Rambo III* saw the veteran helping Mujahedeen freedom fighters in the Soviet-Afghan War. The movie was released in May 1988, coincidentally the month when Moscow initiated the final withdrawal of its troops from Afghanistan.[60]

CONCLUSION

Today, the Cold War is generally categorized as an ideological struggle fought between two fundamentally opposed ideologies. In the previous chapters (especially chapter 4), we have seen how the American and Soviet film industries were more than capable of depicting the Cold War in this abstract fashion, principally by simplifying what capitalism and communism stood for. What the present chapter tells us, though, is that in seeking to understand what drove people to continue fighting the Cold War for over four decades, we overlook another, more old-fashioned -ism at our peril. American cinematic culture in particular was suffused with patriotism in the 1980s, as *Rambo: First Blood Part II* amply demonstrates. It is worth noting also that the Russians in *Incident at Map Grid 36-80* and *Solo Voyage* engage their enemy alone, as if their Warsaw Pact allies were an irrelevance. While the two Soviet films make it clear that Moscow continued to fight for the wider, international cause of "world peace," they do so by appealing, like *Rambo,* to the lowest common dominator, politically and stylistically.

It bears reemphasizing how much more restrained *Incident at Map Grid 36-80*'s (and even *Solo Voyage*'s) anti-Americanism was compared with *Rambo*'s unadulterated anti-Sovietism. This was deliberate, not accidental, a result of political and cultural calculations, not altruism. But the fact that three xenophobic military action-adventure features appeared around the same time demonstrates the degree to which our two film industries once again converged during the latter stages of the Cold War. The difference is that, unlike during the late 1940s or early 1960s, this was less by chance and more by design. As chapter 2 explained, the Soviet film industry enjoyed a love-hate relationship with Hollywood throughout the Cold War. By the 1980s, however, Soviet filmmakers had taken to mimicking American movie output on an unprecedented scale. *Solo Voyage,* a pale imitation of *Rambo,* shows not only the degree to which Hollywood influenced the Soviet film industry's agenda during this era. It also demonstrates the difficulties that Soviet cinema had in keeping up with its American counterpart. The writing appeared to be on the wall, so to speak, as far as winning the cinematic war goes.

Finally, this chapter shows that cinema had the power to influence hearts and minds right till the very end of the Cold War. *Incident at Map Grid 36-80, Solo Voyage,* and *Rambo: First Blood Part II* were among the most popular explicitly Cold War cinematic texts of the entire conflict. They demonstrate cinema's ability to reflect and shape the public's appetite for propagandistic Cold War entertainment. Together, they highlight how visceral each country's fear and hatred of the Other could still be in the 1980s. They also underline how dangerously aggressive the second Cold War was. The movies suggest the East-West conflict was finally, after all this time, about to turn hot. No one who either made or saw them could imagine that peace was just around the corner.

Conclusion

The cinematic Cold War came to an end in 1988, when Soviet cinema quietly conceded. As noted in chapter 2, this was the year that marked the formation of the American-Soviet Film Initiative and the visits of Arnold Schwarzenegger to Moscow and Elem Klimov to Los Angeles. The Hollywood film—denounced for decades—became the model for Soviet cinema to follow.[1]

As we have seen, Soviet cinema stood toe to toe with American cinema throughout the conflict, so how can the apparent victory of Hollywood in the propaganda war be explained? The historian David Caute argues that "if the West won the cultural cold war, it was more by default than by artistic achievement."[2] We offer a different interpretation of the outcome in relation to cinema.

Although there were important similarities between American and Soviet Cold War filmmaking, these similarities turned out to be less important than the differences as factors determining the results of the conflict. Both industries recognized the key role cinema could play in propagandizing the Cold War. This was most blatantly evident both in the early and late stages of the conflict, starting with the politically overt *The Meeting on the Elbe* and *Man on a Tightrope*. Both industries realized that the entertainment film was the best vehicle for political persuasion and therefore that the best cinematic propaganda was indirect, as we have seen in *Roman Holiday* and *Spring on Zarechnaya Street*. Even when film was explicitly political, as in *Fail-Safe*, it was probably still received as entertainment by the majority. Indeed, one might argue that entertainment, as much as politics, drove many Cold War scripts in both the United States and the USSR.

Both industries allowed for the possibility of dissent (*Nine Days in One Year*, *Bananas*), though, naturally, subversive messages were more overt in American film. Both industries peaked in the middle of the Cold War, primarily due to the challenges of television. Nevertheless, cinema's influence continued through to the end, fanning East-West hostilities, as pictures like *Incident at Map Grid 36-80* and *Rambo: First Blood Part II* illustrate. Both industries shared similar aims: to consolidate consensus, woo neutrals, and divide opponents. The USSR was markedly less successful in all three areas. A picture like *Officers*, for instance, surely did not succeed in weaning youth from their attachment to things Western; a life of sacrifice, including lack of material

215

goods, could not persuade neutrals of the superiority of the Soviet way of life; and the fact that *Officers* was not exported to the United States meant that it could have no impact there. Hollywood, on the other hand, enjoyed a vast distribution network and projected a sparkling lifestyle.

The differences, not surprisingly given the chasm between communism and capitalism, were manifold. Some were related to the different systems of government. Ironically, full state control proved more problematic for developing a vigorous Soviet Cold War cinema than did the state-private network in the United States. Although threats and coercion diminished after Stalin's death, the enforced compliance that we see in the Soviet system allowed for less creativity than Hollywood's striving for the middle road. (It is not surprising that the most complex Soviet picture discussed herein, *Nine Days in One Year,* had the most trouble with political watchdogs.) Moreover, Hollywood's relationship with the U.S. government was much more harmonious than was Soviet cinema's with the Soviet regime. This is most evident during the Stalin era, but conflicts between filmmakers and the state also emerged under Brezhnev, as the Thaw ended and filmmakers faced increased censorship unless their films, such as *Officers,* kept closely to the Party line. HUAC's investigations of "communists" notwithstanding, McCarthyism did not have the same impact on American film production that the *zhdanovshchina* had on Soviet film production.

Other differences stemmed from a variety of sources. The United States had not been economically damaged by World War II. The American film industry itself had thrived during that conflict, boosted by near-record levels of movie attendance. The Soviet Union, on the other hand, which engaged the bulk of the German army alone for three years, had been devastated. (The small number of films produced in the USSR in the late 1940s may explain the popularity of films like *The Meeting on the Elbe* and *The Secret Mission.*) An international cinematic juggernaut since World War I, Hollywood was better situated to engage immediately in cinematic warfare, as relatively costly pictures like *Roman Holiday* illustrate.

Some might argue that U.S. film directors were more talented than their Soviet counterparts. This is not true, but even though Soviet cinema could draw on a deep pool of native talent, as we have seen with directors like Grigory Aleksandrov, Marlen Khutsiev, and Mikhail Romm, Hollywood could attract and pay the best of the *world's* film talent, behind and in front of the screen. *Roman Holiday,* for instance, employed a first-class French-trained musical director, George Auric, and a Belgian-born leading actress, Audrey Hepburn. Jacobo Morales, who played the crazy rebel leader in *Bananas,* soon became one of Puerto Rico's most influential filmmakers. In the Englishman Jack Cardiff, *Rambo: First Blood Part II* boasted one of the best color cinematographers in the business. The American film industry also provided much better resources, technological and otherwise. These factors all combined to make Hollywood a stronger filmmaking enterprise.

Because of Hollywood's creative might, economic reach, and global popularity, Soviet cinema spent a lot of time reacting to what the American government and American cinema were saying about the USSR. The Soviet mode was, therefore, defensive rather than offensive. By contrast, Hollywood spent little time denouncing Soviet propaganda about the United States; it was a minor annoyance, not an affront to national pride. The effect was, as the film scholar Andrey Shcherbenok argues, to portray socialism as a subject of debate, rather than a self-evidently "natural" order.[3] Moreover, the Soviet film industry consistently felt inferior to Hollywood and tried to emulate Hollywood's innovations. This was despite the continual attacks on Hollywood—especially evident in the latter part of the Cold War—as a vulgar and philistine industry that sold Disneyland fantasies as a Marxian opiate for the masses.

Although events in the international arena were undeniably important factors influencing cinema (as both *The Meeting on the Elbe* and *Man on a Tightrope* demonstrate), we have shown that domestic concerns played a key role in the conflict, especially in the Soviet Union. This created one of the chief differences between Cold War cinema and, say, the cinema of World War II.[4] Films reflected domestic (political) considerations as well as the international Cold War. The Cold War was waged inside as well as between the two states/world systems, which might surprise those schooled in the "totalitarian" model of the USSR. After the early Cold War films, the "other" was often more a range of ideas within both societies, rather than a villainous foreign power. Good examples are the dissenting views about the virtues of nuclear weapons expressed in *Nine Days in One Year* and *Fail-Safe*. Most Cold War films had little opportunity to permeate the Other culture, so they essentially played out debates about the Cold War for their own audiences in their "spheres of influence." (*Incident at Map Grid 36-80* circulated on VHS in the United States as an amusing curiosity, while *First Blood* and later *Rambo: First Blood Part II* circulated in the USSR as bootlegged video, probably more for its entertainment value than its political demerits.)

As a result, the differences between the two cinemas that emanated from the persistent, systemic problems in Soviet society are especially significant. Hollywood successfully built and reinforced the American consensus about the superiority of the American way of life through commercial filmmaking; *Roman Holiday* is a shining example. Soviet cinema, on the other hand, had a much broader and more challenging mandate. It had to entertain and to *educate* not only the world but also its own population about the superiority of the Soviet way of life, a message that was difficult to sell given the "evidence" provided by Hollywood movies (even the mainly old ones in circulation on Soviet screens)—and the evidence of their own eyes about the problems in the Soviet system. Films like *Spring on Zarechnaya Street* tried to defuse these problems by dealing relatively openly with issues such as postwar housing shortages, but it is unlikely that they succeeded.

Even considering the control that the Soviet bureaucracy maintained over imports, American culture and social values had already penetrated certain segments of Soviet society prior to the Second World War, and their influence proved impossible to counter during the Cold War decades, particularly in youth culture. (This is evident as early as *The Meeting on the Elbe;* there would be no need to demonize jazz had jazz not been popular with the Soviet public.) Therefore, Soviet cinema's attention to domestic, soft propaganda makes perfect sense. It had to reinforce the ideology and "way of life" (*byt*) among its own people, a task Hollywood never really faced. This crisis of belief in the Soviet system came to full expression during the glasnost era and brought about not only the end of the Cold War but also the end of the USSR. By way of contrast, all Hollywood had to worry about, in essence, was its box office, although the demands of the market should not be underestimated.

Capitalism and democracy therefore had a distinct advantage over communism and internationalism in the public relations battle that was the cinematic Cold War. Unlike the Soviet film industry, Hollywood was not seeking to change public opinion, but rather to confirm to Americans and others that the political and economic system they had lived with for generations was (with a few modifications) the best available and what all people would want if they had a choice. Soviet filmmakers, in contrast, first had to prove their system worked, and then to persuade others to follow it as fellow travelers or convert to it as staunch communists.

Propaganda of this latter sort has historically proven to be less successful than reinforcement propaganda, and the Cold War was no exception. Propaganda works best by fortifying existing beliefs and sentiments, instead of trying to proselytize as *Officers* proselytized the virtues of lifetime military service to a public increasingly disenchanted with the military. For all these reasons, we see that the cultural Cold War was qualitatively different from the cultural competitions that accompanied the "hot" wars of the twentieth century, and as a result had different propaganda demands.

By looking inward at Soviet and American Cold War societies, this study also has sought to contrast and compare how cinema reflected and shaped Cold War mentalities and values. This can best be understood by looking at how each cinema conceptualized the Cold War. Soviet cinema conceptualized the conflict in ideological terms.[5] The Cold War was portrayed as a battle between peace and internationalism on the one hand and warmongering and capitalist materialism on the other. Whether in negative or positive propaganda, the Soviet people (with rare exceptions) were depicted as peaceful, peace-loving, and determinedly nonmaterialistic. Ideological concerns were, however, portrayed more subtly than American Cold War rhetoric about the gray, one-dimensional nature of Soviet culture would have us believe.[6] Far from tarring all Americans as villains, Major Kuzmin in *The Meeting on the Elbe* is capable of having a friendship with his U.S. counterpart, Major Hill. Tanya Levchenko and Sasha Savchenko in *Spring on Zarechnaya Street* and Dmitry Gusev in *Nine Days in One Year* are clearly unconcerned with material possessions, but they are not communist automatons. Furthermore, Gusev sees his work in nuclear physics as being explicitly defensive in nature, thus contributing to a balance of powers that will ensure peace (a point with which his antipode Ilya Kulikov disagrees). Likewise, *Officers'* Aleksei Trofimov is always shown in the defense of his country and its ideals, whether battling Basmachi rebels, patrolling the USSR's long southern borders, or fighting to save the communist cause in Spain, yet he, too, is a man with flaws. Even during the heightened tensions of the final phase of the Cold War, the Soviet military is shown extending a hand to Americans in trouble, as we see in *Incident at Map Grid 36-80* and in the undeniably hardcore propaganda hit *Solo Voyage*, through Major Shatokhin.

American cinema also conceptualized the Cold War in ideological terms, especially in the early years. Often it did so less overtly, however, and, paradoxically perhaps, therefore more effectively. By setting their stories in Europe rather than the United States, for instance, films like *Man on a Tightrope* took an indirect route to defining the Cold War in ideational ways. Nevertheless, many in the West would find these movies' expression of a binary approach to the conflict through a series of dichotomous symbols—freedom versus slavery, materialism versus poverty, democracy versus totalitarianism—easily comprehensible, even compelling. Other movies, such as *Roman Holiday*, tapped into and subtly reinforced beliefs among many in the West that personal liberties and affluence were synonymous with free-market capitalism.

From the early 1960s onward, Hollywood Cold War ideology grew more dynamic and pluralistic than its Soviet counterpart, though within limits. Pro-détente films such as *Fail-Safe* and *The Russians Are Coming, The Russians Are Coming* tended to question the means rather than the ends of U.S. foreign policy, while anarchic pictures such as *Bananas* eschewed economic or class-based readings of the Cold War in favor of cultural ones. These ways of framing ideological dissent on the big screen (and small one, for that matter)[7] might help to explain why so many Americans continued to the bitter end to view the Cold War in terms of "good" versus "evil," or at least "right" against "wrong," and to regard communism as the antithesis to the American creed. If they had not, John Rambo would likely not have even appeared onscreen in the 1980s, let alone been so wildly popular.[8]

But the Cold War was not, as many would claim, predominantly about hatred. It simply lasted too long for that to be the case. Certainly the conflict fed to a great extent on fear and ignorance; the separation of the world into two secretive blocs with a non-aligned sphere made that inevitable. Above all, however, the Cold War was inspired and then maintained—on a public level at least—by the belief that "our" values were better than "theirs," that "our" way of life was superior, that "our" version of modernity was progressive and workable. In both the Soviet Union and the United States, positive messages about "us" dominated negative messages about "them" on the silver screen.[9]

It is interesting to note that despite differing ideologies, the values presented in the films we have analyzed are essentially the same: basic human values that cut across cultures. Nobody in the Soviet films is spouting lines about the Party or the victory of the proletariat. Major Kuzmin is open, honest, friendly, but not a dupe. Sasha is both hard-working and fun-loving; an egalitarian, he does not like airs or pretense. Gusev is a stereotypical scientist, whether East or West: serious and lacking in emotional intelligence. His work is his life. Trofimov and his wife Lyuba sacrifice themselves for love of country and eschew the privileges of rank, but Lyuba is beset by doubts for much of the film. The aviators and sailors in *Incident at Map Grid 36-80* and *Solo Voyage* are altruistic to a fault, prepared to sacrifice themselves to save Americans and avert World War III, as Majors Volk and Shatokhin demonstrate.

Ironically, the majority of Americans would have admired many of these "communist" traits. Equally, many Soviet people would have been surprised by the range of values they shared with many of the leading protagonists in our Hollywood pictures. *Roman Holiday*'s Joe Bradley is open, friendly, and, in the end, altruistic and honest; his sweetheart, Princess Ann, might be a mollycoddled aristocrat but, rather like Ivan Varavva in *Officers,* she is willing to put duty before love. General Black and the U.S. president in *Fail-Safe* are exemplary military and political leaders: they remain calm and dignified under pressure, are opposed to fanatics and warmongers, and are even prepared to sacrifice loved ones for the greater good. Fielding Mellish in *Bananas* is wholly lacking in these and many other qualities, but his lovesick foolishness does have its endearing side. John Rambo is a different matter, however. His violent hatred for the enemy sets him utterly apart from Soviet military heroes like Trofimov, Volk, and even a marine leader like Shatokhin. Indeed, no Soviet film ever portrayed a heroic character like Rambo.

Russian cinema today no longer abides by such rules. Formulaic "shoot-'em-ups" starring super-patriotic, hyper-violent heroes cut straight from the Hollywood mold have been the rage for over a decade. Aleksei Balabanov's *Brother* (*Brat*, 1997) was one of the chief trendsetters of this genre and revolved around an antisemitic Chechen War veteran recruited into the post–Cold War Russian mafia. Its sequel, *Brother 2* (*Brat 2*, 2000), saw its chief protagonist battling both the Ukrainian mafia and U.S. capitalists on the streets of Chicago.[10]

Do such films form part of a new cinematic Cold War between post–Soviet Russia and the United States? Not necessarily. Russian cinema has certainly become more nationalistic over the past decade, rewriting Cold War history in the process. Since the beginning of Vladimir Putin's presidency in 2000, and continuing under his successor Dmitry Medvedev, the Kremlin has supported films championing Russia's Soviet past while at the same time resurrecting symbols of the once-despised Czarist era. Andrei Kravchuk's *The Admiral* (2008), a $20 million epic rehabilitating the life of the World War I naval hero and White Russian leader Admiral Aleksander Kolchak, was the first to canonize a figure who had fought the founders of the Soviet state.[11] But only a few of these pictures—Igor Voloshin's *Olympus Inferno* (*Olympus inferno*, 2009), a television film about the 2008 South Ossetia War, and Yury Grimov's *Strangers* (*Chuzhie*, 2009), an assault on U.S. Middle Eastern imperialism—have been explicitly anti-American.[12] In general, these chauvinistic films have served to reassure audiences tired of humiliations such as the 2000 Kursk submarine disaster, tired of the Chechnya wars, and tired of the rise of crime and poverty in the aftermath of the USSR's collapse that Russia is not on its knees.

The American film industry has, of course, offered its own interpretation of the new, post-Soviet Russia. Dyed-in-the-wool communists, crazed ex-communists, and fanatical Russian nationalists, often armed with stolen nuclear weapons, were staple Hollywood villains in the 1990s.[13] More recently, U.S. television and movies like Jeff Celentano's *Say It in Russian* and James Gray's *We Own the Night,* both released in 2007, have focused on the evils of Russian gangsterism. However, pointing the finger at an "underground" threat like the Russian mafia is quite different from alerting Americans to a state-sponsored campaign of political subversion, which was the case during the Cold War. The former is usually categorized as a crime and a job mainly for the police; the latter was an act of war and a job for the government's whole security apparatus.[14]

Instead of contributing to the much-touted new diplomatic Cold War between Washington and Moscow, the Russian and American film industries have engaged more with the defining ideological conflict of the early twenty-first century—the global War on Terror. Hollywood has dealt with this war—another unconventional, potentially open-ended conflict being fought as much in the media as militarily—from several angles. It has produced eulogies to American heroism on 9/11—Paul Greengrass's *United 93* (2006) and Oliver Stone's *World Trade Center* (2006); ridiculed President George W. Bush's claim that an "Axis of Evil" was fostering international terrorism and threatening the world with weapons of mass destruction—Michael Moore's *Fahrenheit 9/11* (2004) and Trey Parker's *Team America: World Police* (2004); prophesied terrorist attacks on Los Angeles—Lee's Tamahori's *Next* (2007) and Bryan Gunnar Cole's *Day Zero* (2007); and sought to look inside the mind of a suicide terrorist—Joseph Castelo's *War Within* (2005) and Julia Loktev's *Day Night Day Night* (2006).[15]

Rather like Soviet cinema during the Cold War, Russian filmmakers have taken a less catholic approach to the War on Terror. In line with Putin's statements that international terrorism is "the plague of the twenty-first century" and that Chechnya is on "Russia's frontline" in the war against terrorism, cinema and television have presented highly politicized images of the "Islamic threat" emanating from Russia's south. These have taken several forms, including old-fashioned combat pictures, Hollywood-style action thrillers, and shocking television news footage of the Dubrovka and Beslan sieges of 2002 and 2004.[16]

Yevgeny Lavrentiev's high-octane action romp *Countdown* (*Lichnyi nomer*, 2004) represents Russian cinema's most conspicuous contribution to the War on Terror and, for this and other reasons, seems an appropriate end point for our study. *Countdown* offers, on the one hand, a very Russian slant on international terrorism. Its chief villain is a London-based émigré (a thinly veiled attack on one of Putin's enemies, Boris Berezovsky), it centers on a Dubrovka-like theater siege in Moscow, it links Chechen rebels with Al-Qaeda, and it was partially funded by the state. On the other hand, *Countdown* highlights just how Americanized Russian cinema has become and indicates how, twenty years or so after the collapse of the Berlin Wall and despite Putin's recent efforts to revitalize his nation's film industry, the one-time "Hollywood variant" is now the cinematic norm in the former Soviet Union. Its chief protagonist, Major Aleksei Smolin (Aleksei Makarov), draws overtly on Hollywood action heroes such as *Die Hard*'s John McClane (Bruce Willis), it prioritizes special effects over plot, and the self-styled "blockbuster" cost $7 million, a reasonably high sum in Russian terms. Of greater significance, *Countdown* shows the Russian and American secret services collaborating successfully to defeat the terrorists, whose ultimate aim is to detonate a dirty bomb at a G8 summit in Rome.[17] Doubtless the American and Russian film industries will remain economic and cultural rivals for some time to come, but at the moment the two countries are allies on screen against their new, mutual international "other"—terrorism.

Notes

Introduction: Culture, Film, and the "New" Cold War History

1. For insight into how the American press made political gain out of Sin Sang-ok and Choe Eun-hui's North Korean "ordeal" immediately after their release in 1986, see *Washington Post* and *New York Times*, 15 May 1986. For the bounty report see *Los Angeles Times*, 25 July 1994. For a more considered analysis of the case see Johannes Schönherr, "A Permanent State of War: A Short History of North Korean Cinema," in *Film Out of Bounds: Essays and Interviews on Non-Mainstream Cinema Worldwide*, ed. Matthew Edwards (Jefferson, N.C.: McFarland, 2007), 135–204, and Steven Chung, "The Split Screen: Sin Sang-ok in North Korea," in *North Korea: Toward a Better Understanding*, ed. Sonia Ryang (Lanham, Md.: Lexington, 2008), 85–108. Choe Eun-hui is still alive; Sin Sang-ok died of natural causes in 2006. See obituaries in *Los Angeles Times*, 14 April 2006, and *Variety*, 24 April 2006.

2. Larry Ceplair and Steven Englund, *The Inquisition in Hollywood: Politics in the Film Community, 1930–1960* (Berkeley: University of California Press, 1979).

3. See, e.g., Sarah Davies, "Soviet Cinema and the Early Cold War: Pudovkin's *Admiral Nakhimov* in Context," *Cold War History* 4, no. 1 (October 2003): 49–70; Peter Kenez, "The Picture of the Enemy in Stalinist Films," in *Insiders and Outsiders in Russian Cinema*, ed. Stephen M. Norris and Zara M. Torlone (Bloomington: Indiana University Press, 2008), 107–111.

4. Mark Kristmanson, "Love Your Neighbour: The Royal Canadian Mounted Police and the National Film Board, 1948–53," *Film History* 10, no. 3 (1998): 254–274; Tony Shaw, *British Cinema and the Cold War: The State, Propaganda and Consensus* (London: I. B. Tauris, 2001).

5. Andrew Kelly, *Cinema and the Great War* (London: Routledge, 1997); Clayton R. Koppes and Gregory D. Black, *Hollywood Goes to War: How Politics, Profits, and Propaganda Shaped World War II Movies* (New York: Free Press, 1987); Anthony Aldgate and Jeffrey Richards, *Britain Can Take It: The British Cinema in the Second World War* (Edinburgh: Edinburgh University Press, 1994); David Welch, *Propaganda and the German Cinema* (London: I. B. Tauris, 2001); Peter B. High, *The Imperial Screen: Japanese Film Culture in the Fifteen Years' War, 1931–1945* (Madison: University of Wisconsin Press, 2003).

6. The excavation and analysis of archival materials from the Cold War's "other side" has been led by the Cold War International History Project, from the Woodrow Wilson International Center for Scholars based in Washington, D.C.: http://www.wilsoncenter.org/index.cfm?fuseaction=topics.home&topic_id=1409 (27 April 2009). On the project's findings relating to the Cuban missile crisis and Sino-Soviet-Albanian relations in particular, see http://www.wilsoncenter.org/index.cfm

?topic_id=1409&fuseaction=va2.browse&sort=Collection&item=Cuban%20 Missile%20Crisis; http://www.wilsoncenter.org/topics/pubs/CWIHPBulletin16 _p3.pdf (27 April 2009).

7. Soviet film material is also scattered in the national film archives of the former republics and satellite states. Access to sensitive Russian and Soviet film material is still subject to the vagaries of cultural politics, the whims of particular archivists, and the pressures of minuscule operating budgets. In general, there are many fewer sources—both primary and secondary—available for the study of Soviet cinema compared to Hollywood.

8. Leopoldo Nuti and Vladislav Zubok, "Ideology," in *Palgrave Advances in Cold War History*, ed. Saki Dockrill and Geraint Hughes (Basingstoke: Palgrave Macmillan, 2006), 73–110.

9. On the diplomatic historians' "cultural turn," see Thomas W. Zeiler, "The Diplomatic History Bandwagon: A State of the Field," *Journal of American History* 95, no. 4 (March 2009): 1053–1073.

10. For an excellent overview of Cold War cultural history, see Patrick Major and Rana Mitter, "Culture," in Dockrill and Hughes, *Palgrave Advances in Cold War History*, 240–262.

11. Frances Stonor Saunders, *Who Paid the Piper? The CIA and the Cultural Cold War* (London: Granta, 1999); Christopher Duggan and Christopher Wagstaff, eds., *Italy in the Cold War* (Oxford: Berg, 1995); Yoshikuni Igarashi, *Bodies of Memory: Narratives of War in Post-war Japanese Culture, 1945–1970* (Princeton, N.J.: Princeton University Press, 2000).

12. http://www.history.ac.uk/ihr/Focus/cold/articles/pittaway.html (24 April 2009); Joanna Witkowska, "Creating False Enemies: John Bull and Uncle Sam as Food for Anti-Western Propaganda in Poland," *Journal of Transatlantic Studies* 6, no. 2 (August 2008): 123–130; and in the same issue, Michel Peprnik, "The Affinity with the North American Indian in Czech Literary Discourse on the Democratic Roots of Czech National Culture," 148–157.

13. David Caute, *The Dancer Defects: The Struggle for Cultural Supremacy during the Cold War* (Oxford: Oxford University Press, 2003).

14. Though see, e.g., Jeffrey Brooks, *Thank You, Comrade Stalin! Soviet Public Culture from Revolution to Cold War* (Princeton, N.J.: Princeton University Press, 2000); special edition on "High Culture and the USSR during the Cold War," *Journal of Cold War Studies* 4, no. 1 (Winter 2002); Vladimir Pechatnov, "Exercise in Frustration: Soviet Foreign Propaganda in the Early Cold War, 1945–47," *Cold War History* 1, no. 2 (January 2001): 1–27; Eric Shiraev and Vladislav M. Zubok, *Anti-Americanism in Russia: From Stalin to Putin* (New York: Palgrave, 2000).

15. Ceplair and Englund, *The Inquisition in Hollywood;* David Caute, *The Great Fear: The Anti-Communist Purge under Truman and Eisenhower* (New York: Simon & Schuster, 1978).

16. Shaw, *British Cinema and the Cold War;* Tony Shaw, *Hollywood's Cold War* (Amherst: University of Massachusetts Press, 2007).

17. Mick Broderick, *Nuclear Movies* (Jefferson, N.C.: McFarland, 1991); Mick Broderick, *Hibakusha Cinema: Hiroshima, Nagasaki and the Nuclear Image in Japanese Film* (London: Kegan Paul, 1996).

18. Kyoko Hirano, *Mr. Smith Goes to Tokyo: Japanese Cinema under the American Occupation, 1945–1952* (Washington, D.C.: Smithsonian Institute Press, 1992).

19. Daniela Berghahn, *Hollywood behind the Wall: The Cinema of East Germany* (Manchester: Manchester University Press, 2005); Michael Chanan, *Cuban Cinema* (Minneapolis: University of Minnesota Press, 2004); Josephine Woll, *Real Images: Soviet Cinema and the Thaw* (London: I. B. Tauris, 2000).

20. On the links between the Cold War, especially nuclear weapons, and the Hollywood science-fiction boom of the 1950s, see, for instance, Joyce A. Evans, *Celluloid Mushroom Clouds: Hollywood and the Atomic Bomb* (Boulder, Colo.: Westview Press, 1998); Peter Biskind, *Seeing Is Believing: How Hollywood Taught Us to Stop Worrying and to Love the Fifties* (New York: Pantheon, 1983).

21. The semiotics of Cold War cinema, far from our own areas of expertise, still awaits its interpreter.

22. Chapter 7 alters this pattern slightly by including a longer discussion of a second Soviet film, *Solo Voyage* (*Odinochnoe plavanie*).

23. *My Son John* and *Dr. Strangelove* have been submitted to lengthy analysis. See, for instance, Stephen J. Whitfield, *The Culture of the Cold War* (Baltimore: Johns Hopkins University Press, 1996), 136–140, and John Baxter, *Stanley Kubrick: A Biography* (London: HarperCollins, 1997), 165–198. The films of Andrei Tarkovsky receive their fullest treatment in Vida T. Johnson and Graham Petrie, *The Films of Andrei Tarkovsky: A Visual Fugue* (Bloomington: Indiana University Press, 1994). For a discussion of *Liberation,* see Denise J. Youngblood, *Russian War Films: On the Cinema Front, 1914–2005* (Lawrence: University Press of Kansas, 2007), 158–162, and also on 188 for a mention of *Tehran-43*.

Part i. Introduction

1. For a recent comparative analysis of British and German film propaganda during the Second World War, see Jo Fox, *Film Propaganda in Britain and Nazi Germany: World War II Cinema* (Oxford: Berg, 2007).

2. Television and the Cold War grew simultaneously in the United States in the years following World War II. In the 1950s, the percentage of American households with TV grew from approximately 9 to 90. During the same period, weekly cinema attendance declined from approximately 60 million to 25 million. Nancy Bernhard, *U.S. Television News and Cold War Propaganda, 1947–1960* (New York: Cambridge University Press, 1999), 47; Richard Maltby, *Hollywood Cinema* (Oxford: Blackwell, 2003), 124. The decline in moviegoing came later to the USSR and was less pronounced than in the United States, in part because fewer Soviet households had television sets. In 1960 only 5 percent of the Soviet population could watch television, but by 1986 fully 93 percent of the population were viewers. Ellen Propper Mickiewicz, *Split Signals: Television and Politics in the Soviet Union* (Oxford: Oxford University Press, 1988), 3. U.S. television's role during the Cold War is a long way from being fully documented but see, for instance, Bernhard, *U.S. Television News;* Thomas Doherty, *Cold War, Cool Medium: Television, McCarthyism, and American Culture* (New York: Columbia University Press, 2003); Michael Curtin, *Redeeming the Wasteland: Television Documentary and Cold War Politics* (New Brunswick, N.J.: Rutgers University Press, 1995); and Daniel Hallin, *The "Uncensored" War: The*

Media and Vietnam (Berkeley: University of California Press, 1989). Even less work has been done on Soviet television and the Cold War, but see Mickiewicz, *Split Signals,* and Ellen Propper Mickiewicz, *Changing Channels: Television and the Struggle for Power in Russia* (Durham, N.C.: Duke University Press, 1999).

Chapter 1. American Cinema and the Cold War

1. U.S. Congress, Senate, Committee on Foreign Relations, Subcommittee on Overseas Information Programs, *Overseas Information Programs of the United States* (Washington, D.C.: Government Printing Office, 1953), pt. 2, 272.

2. William Bruce Johnson, *Miracles and Sacrilege: Roberto Rossellini, the Church, and Film Censorship in Hollywood* (Toronto: University of Toronto Press, 2008), 284.

3. Kevin Brownlow, *Behind the Mask of Innocence: Sex, Violence, Prejudice, Crime—Films of Social Conscience in the Silent Era* (Berkeley: University of California Press, 1990), 443–447.

4. Tony Shaw, *Hollywood's Cold War* (Amherst: University of Massachusetts Press, 2007), 15–27.

5. Steven J. Ross, "The Rise of Hollywood: Movies, Ideology, and Audiences in the Roaring Twenties," in *Movies and American Society,* ed. Steven J. Ross (Oxford: Blackwell, 2002), 64–97; Richard Maltby, *Harmless Entertainment: Hollywood and the Ideology of Consensus* (London: Scarecrow, 1983).

6. Clayton R. Koppes and Gregory D. Black, *Hollywood Goes to War: How Politics, Profits and Propaganda Shaped World War II Movies* (New York: Free Press, 1987), 185–221. On Sam Goldwyn's role as producer of *The North Star,* see 209–215.

7. Daniel J. Leab, "*The Iron Curtain* (1948): Hollywood's First Cold War Movie," *Historical Journal of Film, Radio and Television* 8, no. 2 (1988): 153–188.

8. See, for example, Richard Fried, *Nightmare in Red: The McCarthy Era in Perspective* (Oxford: Oxford University Press, 1991); Thomas Doherty, "Hollywood Agit-Prop: The Anti-Communist Cycle 1948–1954," *Journal of Film and Video* 40, no. 4 (1988): 15–27; Glen M. Johnson, "Sharper than an Irish Serpent's Tooth: Leo McCarey's *My Son John,*" *Journal of Popular Film and Television* 8, no. 1 (1980): 44–49.

9. Larry Ceplair and Steven Englund, *The Inquisition in Hollywood: Politics in the Film Community, 1930–1960* (Berkeley: University of California Press, 1979); Stephen J. Whitfield, *The Culture of the Cold War* (Baltimore: Johns Hopkins University Press, 1996), 127–151; Thomas Doherty, *Cold War, Cool Medium: Television, McCarthyism, and American Culture* (New York: Columbia University Press, 2003), 40–48, 251–258. The Hollywood Ten were an assorted group of screenwriters, directors, and producers imprisoned for contempt of Congress in 1950: Alvah Bessie, Herbert Biberman, Lester Cole, Edward Dmytryk, Ring Lardner Jr., John Howard Lawson, Albert Maltz, Samuel Ornitz, Adrian Scott, and Dalton Trumbo.

10. Frank Walsh, *Sin and Censorship: The Catholic Church and the Motion Picture Industry* (New Haven, Conn.: Yale University Press, 1996); Gregory D. Black, "Movies, Politics, and Censorship: The Production Code Administration and Political Censorship of Film Content," *Journal of Policy History* 3, no. 2 (1991): 95–129; Tho-

mas Doherty, *Hollywood's Censor: Joseph I. Breen and the Production Code Administration* (New York: Columbia University Press, 2007).

11. Ceplair and Englund, *The Inquisition in Hollywood,* 209–225, 258; Nora Sayre, *Running Time: Films of the Cold War* (New York: Dial, 1982), 18, 50; Lary May, *The Big Tomorrow: Hollywood and the Politics of the American Way* (Chicago: University of Chicago Press, 2000), 177, 191. Johnston was also president of the Motion Picture Export Association of America (MPEA), an MPAA agency that dealt with foreign matters.

12. Ceplair and Englund, *The Inquisition in Hollywood,* 204, 392; commentary by Peter Davis, director of the Oscar-winning documentary *Hearts and Minds* (1974), on *Hearts and Minds* DVD, MTD5206 (Metrodome, 2005).

13. John A. Noakes, "Bankers and Common Men in Bedford Falls: How the FBI Determined That *It's a Wonderful Life* was a Subversive Movie," *Film History* 10, no. 3 (1998): 311–319; Kenneth O'Reilly, *Hoover and the UnAmericans* (Philadelphia: Temple University Press, 1983), 82; Athan Theoharis, *Chasing Spies: How the FBI Failed in Counterintelligence but Promoted the Politics of McCarthyism in the Cold War Years* (Chicago: Ivan R. Dee, 2002), 155.

14. Shaw, *Hollywood's Cold War,* especially chaps. 2, 4, and 6.

15. Richard Maltby, *Hollywood Cinema* (Oxford: Blackwell, 2003),124.

16. *Variety,* 10 December 1952; http://www.imdb.com/title/tt0044750/business (12 March 2009).

17. *New York Times,* 11 June 1953; http://www.imdb.com/title/tt0046124/business (12 March 2009).

18. Doherty, "Hollywood Agit-Prop."

19. Shaw, *Hollywood's Cold War,* chap. 2.

20. Ralph Stern, "*The Big Lift* (1950): Image and Identity in Blockaded Berlin," *Cinema Journal* 46, no. 2 (Winter 2007): 66–90. On the Pentagon-Hollywood axis see Lawrence Suid, *Guts and Glory: The Making of the American Military Image in Film* (Lexington: University Press of Kentucky, 2002).

21. Daniel Leab, *I Was a Communist for the FBI* (University Park: Pennsylvania State University Press, 2000); *Time,* 29 June 1953.

22. David Eldridge, "'Dear Owen': The CIA, Luigi Luraschi and Hollywood, 1953," *Historical Journal of Film, Radio and Television* 20, no. 2 (June 2000): 182.

23. *Variety,* 24 October 1951.

24. *Los Angeles Times,* 28 January 1954; *Variety,* 11 June 1952; *Time,* 23 June 1952.

25. *Hollywood Reporter,* 28 November 1952; *New York Times,* 25 October 1952; *Variety,* 11 July 1951; *Hollywood Reporter,* 13 January 1953.

26. James M. Skinner, "Cliché and Convention in Hollywood's Cold War Anti-Communist Films," *North Dakota Quarterly* (Summer 1978): 35–40; *New York Times,* 27 June 1949.

27. *Variety,* 29 December 1949; *Hollywood Reporter,* 12 December 1955.

28. Russell E. Shain, "Hollywood's Cold War," *Journal of Popular Film* 3, no. 4 (Fall 1974): 334–350, 365–372; Robert J. Lentz, *Korean War Filmography: 91 English Language Features through 2000* (Jefferson, N.C.: McFarland, 2003).

29. *The Challenge of Ideas* is available in two parts at http://www.archive.org/ details/Challeng1961 and http://www.archive.org/details/Challeng1961_2 (12 March 2009). The movie, closely based on Frank Capra and Anatole Litvak's Second World War *Why We Fight* film, *War Comes to America* (1945), was produced by the U.S. Army Pictorial Center based in New York and hosted by Edward R. Murrow. John Wayne and Helen Hayes presented sections of it. On the U.S. Army Pictorial Center's output during the Cold War see http://www.ascendantimage. com/Army%20Pictorial%20Center/APC.htm (12 May 2009). On the War Department's seven-part *Why We Fight* series see Thomas Doherty, *Projections of War: Hollywood, American Culture and World War II* (New York: Columbia University Press, 1999), 70–78.

30. See, for example, *Anarchy USA* (1966), a seventy-eight-minute 16mm film sponsored by the John Birch Society. It argued that the civil rights movement and urban disturbances of the 1960s were evidence of a worldwide communist revolution, and that communists were planning to create an independent African American state. *Los Angeles Times*, 2 October 1967, SG1.

31. *Storm Center* was based on a true story. See Louise S. Robbins, *The Dismissal of Miss Ruth Brown: Civil Rights, Censorship, and the American Library* (Norman: University of Oklahoma Press, 2000).

32. G. Tom Poe, "Historical Spectatorship around and about Stanley Kramer's *On the Beach*," in *Hollywood Spectatorship: Changing Perceptions of Cinema Audiences*, ed. Melvyn Stokes and Richard Maltby (London: BFI, 2001), 91–102.

33. *Film Daily Year Book*, 1951, 51.

34. The following musicals were among the top ten box-office hits in the year of their release: *Annie Get Your Gun* (no. 5, 1950), *Showboat* and *An American in Paris* (no. 2 and no. 3, 1951), *White Christmas* and *The Glenn Miller Story* (no. 1 and no. 3, 1954), *Guys and Dolls* and *The King and I* (no. 1 and no. 2, 1956), and *South Pacific* (no. 7, 1958). Cobbett Steinberg, *Reel Facts* (Harmondsworth: Penguin, 1981), 434–438.

35. Peter Filene, "'Cold War Culture' Doesn't Say It All," in *Rethinking Cold War Culture*, ed. Peter J. Kuznick and James Gilbert (Washington, D.C.: Smithsonian Institution Press, 2001), 164–166.

36. Shaw, *Hollywood's Cold War*, 114–128.

37. Vladislav M. Zubok, *A Failed Empire: The Soviet Union in the Cold War from Stalin to Gorbachev* (Chapel Hill: University of North Carolina Press, 2007), 173; Diane Neumaier, ed., *Beyond Memory: Soviet Nonconformist Photography and Photo-related Works of Art* (New Brunswick, N.J.: Rutgers University Press, 2004), 187.

38. Paul Swann, "The Little State Department: Hollywood and the State Department in the Postwar World," *American Studies International* 29, no. 1 (April 1991): 2–19; Kerry Segrave, *American Films Abroad: Hollywood's Domination of the World's Movie Screens from the 1890s to the Present* (Jefferson, N.C.: McFarland, 1997).

39. Daniel J. Leab, *Orwell Subverted: The CIA and the Filming of Animal Farm* (University Park: Pennsylvania State University Press, 2007).

40. Kenneth Osgood, *Total War: Eisenhower's Secret Propaganda Battle at Home and Abroad* (Lawrence: University Press of Kansas, 2006); Melinda Schwenk, "Reforming the Negative through History: The US Information Agency and the 1957 Little

Rock Integration Crisis," *Journal of Communication Inquiry* 23, no. 3 (July 1999): 288–306.

41. Soviet-made films were largely confined to art houses in New York and Los Angeles, where they played to niche audiences comprising left-wingers and/or lovers of Russian culture. James H. Krukones, "The Unspooling of Artkino: Soviet Film Distribution in America, 1940–1975," *Historical Journal of Film, Radio and Television* 29, no. 1 (March 2009): 91–112.

42. Peter Biskind, *Easy Riders, Raging Bulls: How the Sex 'n' Drugs 'n' Rock 'n' Roll Generation Saved Hollywood* (London: Bloomsbury, 1998).

43. *The Bedford Incident* and *Dr. Strangelove* both warrant inclusion here. Despite being made in Britain, they were widely regarded as American movies, due mainly to their directors and casts. However, each movie, especially Kubrick's, has a foreign production history that sets it apart from the Hollywood norm, therefore excluding it from detailed case-study analysis in this book.

44. Matthew Frye Jacobson and Gaspar Gonzalez, *What Have They Built You to Do? The Manchurian Candidate and Cold War America* (Minneapolis: University of Minnesota Press, 2006).

45. Michael Coyne, "*Seven Days in May:* History, Prophecy and Propaganda," in *Windows on the Sixties: Exploring Key Texts of Media and Culture*, ed. Anthony Aldgate, James Chapman, and Arthur Marwick (London: I. B. Tauris, 2000), 70–90.

46. Suid, *Guts and Glory,* 242–247.

47. James Naremore, *On Kubrick* (London: BFI, 2007), 119–137.

48. Norman Jewison, *This Terrible Business Has Been Good to Me: An Autobiography* (New York: Key Porter Books, 2004), 115–132; Walter M. Mirisch, inter-office memo to Norman Jewison, 21 April 1965, and letter from Jerry Ludwig (Mirisch Corporation) to David Zeitlin (*Life*), 14 February 1966: David Zeitlin Collection, Margaret Herrick Library, Academy of Motion Picture Arts and Sciences, Los Angeles (hereafter AMPAS).

49. Maltby, *Hollywood Cinema,* 124.

50. John Huston, *An Open Book* (Cambridge, Mass.: Da Capo, 1994), 336–341; *Motion Picture Herald,* 11 February 1970.

51. Shaw, *Hollywood's Cold War,* 249–262.

52. Jeremy M. Devine, *Vietnam at 24 Frames a Second: A Critical and Thematic Analysis of over 400 Films about the Vietnam War* (Jefferson, N.C.: McFarland, 1995), 130–197.

53. Wayne J. McMullen, "*The China Syndrome:* Corruption to the Core," *Literature Film Quarterly* 23, no. 1 (1995): 55–62.

54. Michael Ryan and Douglas Kellner, *Camera Politica: The Politics and Ideology of Contemporary Hollywood Film* (Bloomington: Indiana University Press, 1988), 95–98, and Ian Scott, *American Politics in Hollywood Film* (Edinburgh: Edinburgh University Press, 2000), 119–124.

55. These include Ivan Dixon's *The Spook Who Sat by the Door* (1973), Saul Landau and Haskell Wexler's *CIA Case Officer* (1978), and Arthur Hiller's *The In-Laws* (1979).

56. Ronald Reagan, *An American Life* (London: Hutchinson, 1990), 104–125; Gary Wills, *Reagan's America: Innocents at Home* (New York: Doubleday, 1987), 246–258;

Alvin Snyder, *Warriors of Disinformation: American Propaganda, Soviet Lies and the Winning of the Cold War* (New York: Arcade, 1995).

57. See, for example, *The Osterman Weekend* (Sam Peckinpah, 1983), *The Falcon and the Snowman* (John Schlesinger, 1985), and *Spies Like Us* (John Landis, 1985), details of which can be found in William J. Palmer, *The Films of the Eighties: A Social History* (Carbondale: Southern Illinois University Press, 1993), 222–232.

58. Robert Rosenstone, *History on Film / Film on History* (London: Pearson, 2006), 97–110; Robert Brent Toplin, *History by Hollywood: The Use and Abuse of the American Past* (Chicago: University of Chicago Press, 1996), 104–124; *Los Angeles Herald-Examiner,* 10 February 1982.

59. Palmer, *Eighties,* 199–202.

60. *Films and Filming,* January 1983, 24–25; Robert Scheer, *With Enough Shovels: Reagan, Bush, and Nuclear War* (New York: Random House, 1982).

61. Frances Fitzgerald, *Way Out There in the Blue: Reagan, Star Wars and the End of the Cold War* (New York: Simon & Schuster, 2000), 74.

62. Shaw, *Hollywood's Cold War,* 9–11, 269–276; *Hollywood Reporter,* 26 September 1985; *Variety,* 23 May 1984; *Photoplay,* November 1984, 25–27.

63. *Hollywood Reporter,* 3 April 1984; *Variety,* 12 August 1987; *Photoplay,* August 1982; *Jump Cut,* April 1990; *Variety,* 21 September 1988.

64. Suid, *Guts and Glory,* 485–502; *American Film,* November 1983.

65. Devine, *Vietnam,* 219–223, 240, 266, 271–274.

66. *Variety,* 4 November 1987.

67. Shaw, *Hollywood's Cold War,* 285–292; *Variety,* 16 November 1988.

68. *Los Angeles Times,* 10 February 1988; Palmer, *Eighties,* 209.

69. *Variety,* 23 August 1989; http://www.imdb.com/title/tt0097633/ (13 March 2009).

70. Suid, *Guts and Glory,* 570–578. *The Hunt for Red October* was the sixth most popular film in the United States in 1990 and made $200 million worldwide: http://www.boxofficemojo.com/yearly/chart/?yr=1990&p=.htm (13 March 2009).

CHAPTER 2: SOVIET CINEMA AND
THE COLD WAR

1. Isaiah Berlin, "Soviet Russian Culture," in Berlin, *The Soviet Mind: Russian Culture under Communism,* ed. Henry Hardy (Washington, D.C.: Brookings Institution Press, 2004), 155.

2. The best history of Soviet cinema is Birgit Beumers, *A History of Russian Cinema* (Oxford: Berg, 2009).

3. Denise J. Youngblood, *Movies for the Masses: Popular Cinema and Soviet Society in the 1920s* (Cambridge: Cambridge University Press, 1992), chap. 3.

4. There were no American villains in Soviet cinema in the 1920s; Paul Babitsky and John Rimberg, *The Soviet Film Industry* (New York: Praeger, 1955), 223.

5. Socialist Realism, which became the state's official aesthetic doctrine in 1934, emphasized monumentalism, forward thinking, an active "positive hero" to guide the collective, and a concrete, optimistic ending.

6. For a detailed discussion, see Denise J. Youngblood, *Soviet Cinema in the Silent Era, 1918–1935* (Austin: University of Texas Press, 1991), chaps. 8–9; Peter

Kenez, *Cinema and Soviet Society, 1917–1953* (Cambridge: Cambridge University Press, 1992), chap. 5; Richard Taylor, *The Politics of the Soviet Cinema, 1917–1929* (Cambridge: Cambridge University Press, 1979), chap. 6.

7. Glavrepertkom was renamed GURK in 1933; in 1936 it became part of the All-Union Committee for the Arts and in 1938 part of the Cinema Committee structure. See Jamie Miller, *Soviet Cinema: Politics and Persuasion under Stalin* (London: I. B. Tauris, 2010), 55. Chapter 2 of Miller's book provides an invaluable discussion of the twists and turns of cinema censorship in the 1930s.

8. Babitsky and Rimberg, *Soviet Film Industry,* 33, 39. The new administration was subordinated to the All-Union Committee on Art Affairs in 1936. The many administrative changes in the 1930s are indicative of cinema's importance to the state but also of the fact that it was difficult to control.

9. See Kenez, *Cinema and Soviet Society,* chaps. 6–8.

10. Babitsky and Rimberg, *Soviet Film Industry,* 223.

11. Beumers, *History of Russian Cinema,* 101.

12. For more information on Soviet cinema during the war years, see Kenez, *Cinema and Soviet Society,* chap. 9; Denise J. Youngblood, *Russian War Films: On the Cinema Front, 1914–2005* (Lawrence: University Press of Kansas, 2007), chap. 3.

13. Valerii I. Fomin, *Kino na voine: Dokumenty, svidetelstva, kommentarii* (Moscow: Materik, 2005).

14. Some twenty American films were, however, imported by the Soviets and shown during the war. For details see Sergei Kapterev, "Illusionary Spoils: Soviet Attitudes towards American Cinema during the Early Cold War," *Kritika* 10, no. 4 (Fall 2009): 783.

15. James H. Krukones, "The Unspooling of Artkino: Soviet Film Distribution in America, 1940–1975," *Historical Journal of Film, Radio, and Television* 29, no. 1 (March 2009): 94. A few nonwar films were imported to the United States as well (94–95).

16. Mark Donskoi, "*Raduga,*" *Sovetskii ekran,* no. 3 (1969): 19.

17. Babitsky and Rimberg, *Soviet Film Industry,* 49.

18. Vladislav M. Zubok, *A Failed Empire: The Soviet Union in the Cold War from Stalin to Gorbachev* (Chapel Hill: University of North Carolina Press, 2007), 172.

19. These figures are based on *Sovetskie khudozhestvennye filmy: Annotirovannyi katalog,* vol. 3 (Moscow: Iskusstvo, 1966). See Babitsky and Rimberg, *Soviet Film Industry,* 243, for the number of copies made.

20. Val Golovskoy with John Rimberg, *Behind the Soviet Screen: The Motion Picture Industry in the USSR, 1972–1982,* trans. Steven Hill (Ann Arbor, Mich.: Ardis Publishers, 1986), 48.

21. Kapterev, "Illusionary Spoils," 783. Kapterev (790) notes that 1,531 of the trophy films were American, 906 German, 572 French, and 183 British. Kapterev (783) also sees the considerable influence of Hollywood in late Stalinist cinema.

22. For a discussion of these campaigns, see Jeffrey Brooks, *Thank You Comrade Stalin! Soviet Public Culture from Revolution to Cold War* (Princeton, N.J.: Princeton University Press, 2000), chap. 8, and Konstantin Azadovskii and Boris Egorov, "From Anti-Westernism to Anti-Semitism: Stalin and the Impact of the 'Anti-Cosmopolitan' Campaigns on Soviet Culture," *Journal of Cold War Studies* 4, no. 1 (Winter 2000): 66–80; see 68–69 in particular.

23. Azadovskii and Egorov, "From Anti-Westernism to Anti-Semitism," 77.

24. For a discussion of the problems *Admiral Nakhimov* faced on its way to the screen, see Sarah Davies, "Soviet Cinema and the Early Cold War: Pudovkin's *Admiral Nakhimov* in Context," *Cold War History* 4, no. 1 (October 2003), reprinted in *Across the Blocs: Cold War Cultural and Social History*, ed. Rana Mitter and Patrick Major (London: Frank Cass, 2004).

25. Katerina Clark and Evgeny Dobrenko, eds., with Andrei Artizov and Oleg Naumov, comps., *Soviet Culture and Power: A History in Documents, 1917–1953*, trans. Marian Schwartz (New Haven, Conn.: Yale University Press, 2007), 457.

26. Vladimir Pechatnov, "Exercise in Frustration: Soviet Foreign Propaganda in the Early Cold War, 1945–47," *Cold War History* 1, no. 2 (January 2001), esp. 7, 11, 12.

27. Ibid., 3.

28. Ibid., 2.

29. Ibid., 3.

30. Elena Zubkova, *Russia after the War: Hopes, Illusions, and Disappointments, 1945–1957*, trans. and ed. Hugh Ragsdale (Armonk, N.Y.: M. E. Sharpe, 1998), 82. Zubkova's depiction of public opinion in this period reveals a society much more dynamic than Western Cold War rhetoric allowed.

31. Pechatnov, "Exercise in Frustration," 4. On the pervasiveness of the propaganda about the inevitability of war, see also Zubkova, *Russia after the War,* 83.

32. Oleg Kovalov, "Zvezda nad stepiu: Amerika v zerkale sovetskogo kino," *Iskusstvo kino,* no. 10 (2003), http://www.kinoart.ru/magazine/10–2003/review/Kovalov0310/. "Artistic documentary" was their label at the time; *The History of Soviet Cinema* (*Istoriia sovetskogo kino*) blandly categorizes them as "films on international themes." See *Istoriia sovetskogo kino,* vol. 3, *1941–1952* (Moscow: Iskusstvo, 1975), 132.

33. Detailed plot summaries for these films may be found in David Caute, *The Dancer Defects: The Struggle for Cultural Supremacy during the Cold War* (Oxford: Oxford University Press, 2003), 132–142, 147–157.

34. Babitsky and Rimberg, *Soviet Film Industry,* 223. Just as there were no American villains in the 1920s, as noted above, there were none between 1930 and 1945, either.

35. These inversions have been noted by everyone who has written on early Soviet Cold War films since the glasnost era. Evgeny Dobrenko, however, argues that "even if we read anti-American as inverted Soviet, the suppressed complexes of the Soviet Union shine through in these films." In other words, even if the inversions were a sly trick by the filmmakers to fool the censors, the films still reveal much about the complications of Soviet life at this time. See his "Late Stalinist Cinema and the Cold War: An Equation without Unknowns," trans. Birgit Beumers, *Modern Language Review* 98, no. 4 (2003): 937.

36. *The Court of Honor* was based on a true story about a supposed cure for cancer developed by Soviet biologists that fell into American hands, known as the Kliueva-Roskin affair. See Nikolai Krementsov, "In the Shadow of the Bomb: U.S.-Soviet Biomedical Relations in the Early Cold War," *Journal of Cold War Studies* 9, no. 4 (Fall 2007): 41–67.

37. Caute, *Dancer Defects,* 117.

38. Clark and Dobrenko, *Soviet Culture and Power,* 458.

39. Dobrenko, "Late Stalinist Cinema," 944.

40. The council thought casting was too important to be left to the director and spent much time deliberating over which actors were just right. See, e.g., the discussion of casting for *The Court of Honor* in Gosfilmofond, Ministerstvo kinematografii, Sud chesti, 18 March 1948, 9ff. [hereafter GFF/Mk/Sch]. This is an example of what Clark and Dobrenko call "creative censorship" in *Soviet Culture and Power,* 447.

41. GFF/Mk, U nikh est rodina, 15 April 1948, 31[hereafter Uner]; GFF/Mk, Sekretnaia missiia [hereafter Sm], 13 July 1950, 7.

42. GFF/Mk/Sm, 5 January 1949, 24. "Our enemies shout about an iron curtain."

43. Andrey Shcherbenok, "Asymmetric Warfare: Cold War Cinema in the Soviet Union and the United States," paper presented at the conference "Dream Factory of Communism: Cultural Practices and the Memory of the Cold War," Miami University, Oxford, Ohio, 2007. http://www.units.muohio/edu/havighurstcenter/conferences/documents/shcherbenok.pdf, 6.

44. See Frank J. Coppa, "Pope Pius XII and the Cold War: The Post-war Confrontation between Catholicism and Communism," 60–66, and Peter C. Kent, "The Lonely Cold War of Pius XII," 67–76, both in *Religion and the Cold War,* ed. Diane Kirby (Houndsmills: Palgrave Macmillan, 2003).

45. GFF/Mk/Uner, 15 April 1948, 31a.

46. GFF/Mk/Uner, 15 April 1948, 25.

47. GFF/Mk/Uner, 2 January 1950, 6a.

48. GFF/Mk/Uner, 2 January 1950, 17. Scriptwriter Sergei Mikhalkov fought bitterly against the accusations. Mikhalkov, noted writer of children's books and author of the lyrics for the Soviet national anthem, was one of the few writers whose position was so secure that he could afford to do so.

49. GFF/Mk/Russkii vopros [hereafter Rv], 8 January 1948, 21.

50. GFF/Mk/Sm, 14 April 1949, 13.

51. GFF/Mk/Sm, 7 April 1949, 36.

52. GFF/Mk/Uner, 15 April 1948, 31. Evgeny Dobrenko has dubbed this the "non-meeting of new worlds"; see his "Late Stalinist Cinema," 935.

53. GFF/Mk/Sm, 7 April 1949, 36.

54. GFF/Mk/Sm, 7 April 1949, 39.

55. GFF/Mk/Uner, 10 May 1949, 6.

56. GFF/Mk/Serebristaia pyl, 5 February 1953, 16.

57. GFF/Mk/Rv, 18 September 1947, 54.

58. GFF/Mk/Rv, 18 September 1947, 54, 72.

59. GFF/Mk/Rv, 18 September 1947, 35; 8 January 1948, 14.

60. GFF/Mk/Rv, 8 January 1948, 21.

61. GFF/Mk/Sm, 7 April 1949, 48.

62. The label "positive legitimation" is borrowed from Vladimir Shlapentokh, *Soviet Public Opinion and Ideology: Mythology and Pragmatism in Interaction* (New York: Praeger, 1986), 14.

63. Babitsky and Rimberg, *Soviet Film Industry,* 51.

64. Alexander Prokhorov, "The Unknown New Wave: Soviet Cinema of the 1960s," in *Springtime for Soviet Cinema: Re/Viewing the 1960s*, ed. Alexander Prokhorov (Pittsburgh: Pittsburgh Russian Film Symposium, 2001), 7.

65. Ibid., 8. For the history of Thaw cinema, see Josephine Woll, *Real Images: Soviet Cinema and the Thaw* (London: I. B. Tauris, 2000).

66. Sergei Kapterev, *Post-Stalinist Cinema and the Russian Intelligentsia, 1953–1960: Strategies of Self-Representation, De-Stalinization, and the National Cultural Tradition* (Saarbrücken: VDM Verlag Dr. Müller, 2008), 33.

67. Prokhorov, "Unknown New Wave," 8; also based on Denise J. Youngblood's analysis of *Sovetskie khudozhestvennye filmy.*

68. Prokhorov, "Unknown New Wave," 9.

69. Other examples are *The "Colorful" Case* (*Delo "pestrykh,"* Nikolai Dostal, 1958, 33.7 million viewers), *Case No. 306* (*Delo no. 306*, Anatoly Rybakov, 1956, 33.5 million), *The Shadow by the Pier* (*Ten u pirsa*, Mikhail Viniarsky, 1955, 29.7 million), *Flight 713 Asks Permission to Land* (*713-i prosit posadku*, Grigory Nikulin, 1962, 27.9 million), *The Road* (*Doroga*, Aleksander Stolper, 1955, 25.2 million), and *The Case of Lance Corporal Kochetkov* (*Sluchai s efreiterom Kochetkovym*, Aleksander Razumnyi, 1955, 20.3 million). These films, with the exception of *Ch.P.*, are discussed in Julian Graffy, "Scant Signs of Thaw: Fear and Anxiety in the Representation of Foreigners in the Soviet Films of the Khrushchev Years," in *Russia and Its Other(s) on Film: Screening Intercultural Dialogue*, ed. Stephen Hutchings (Houndsmills: Palgrave Macmillan, 2008), 27–46. For a description of *Ch.P.*, which is based on the true story of a Soviet ship captured by the Guomindang in 1954, see Woll, *Real Images,* 95–96.

70. The film with identifiable American enemies was *The Fort in the Mountains.* See Graffy, "Scant Signs of Thaw," 30.

71. Sergei Kapterev calls the style "updated Socialist Realism," i.e., Socialist Realism + Neorealism; see Kapterev, *Post-Stalinist Cinema,* 204.

72. See Woll's analysis of these films in *Real Images,* 66–70.

73. For an excellent overview of this issue see Marsha Siefert, "From Cold War to Wary Peace: American Culture in the USSR and Russia," in *The Americanization of Europe: Culture, Diplomacy, and Anti-Americanism after 1945*, ed. Alexander Stephan (New York: Berghahn Books, 2006), 185–217; also see Richard Stites, *Russian Popular Culture: Entertainment and Society since 1900* (Cambridge: Cambridge University Press, 1992), chaps. 5–7, passim.

74. Eric Shiraev and Vladislav Zubok, *Anti-Americanism in Russia: From Stalin to Putin* (New York: Palgrave, 2000), 15. Also see Iu. Dobrokhotov, "*Rimskie kanikuly,*" *Sovetskii ekran,* no. 23 (1958): 16, for a discussion of some of the films shown in the first film exchange in the late 1950s and early 1960s. Chapter 4 in the present volume looks at this exchange in greater detail.

75. Yana Hashamova, *Pride and Panic: Russian Imagination of the West in Post-Soviet Film* (Bristol: Intellect Books, 2007), 27.

76. Joseph Brodsky, "Spoils of War," in Brodsky, *On Grief and Reason: Essays* (New York: Farrar, Straus, Giroux, 1995), 8. Other popular American films were *Stagecoach* (John Ford, 1939) and *The Roaring Twenties* (Raoul Walsh, 1939).

77. Ibid., 10.

78. Ibid., 12.

79. Alexei Yurchak, *Everything Was Forever until It Was No More: The Last Soviet Generation* (Princeton, N.J.: Princeton University Press, 2006), chap. 5, passim.

80. Kapterev, *Post-Stalinist Cinema,* 110–111.

81. Ibid., 109.

82. Sergei Dobrynin, "The Silver Curtain: Representations of the West in the Soviet Cold War Films," *History Compass* 7, no. 3 (2009): 865. Dobrynin's excellent overview mainly focuses on the films of the Brezhnev era.

83. Andrei Rogachevskii, "The Cold War Representation of the West in Russian Literature," in *Cold War Literature: Writing the Global Conflict,* ed. Andrew Hammond (London: Routledge, 2005), 41. Rogachevskii is writing about literature, of course, but his idea can apply to any aspect of post-Stalinist Soviet culture.

84. Beumers, *History of Russian Cinema,* 116.

85. Golovskoy and Rimberg, *Behind the Soviet Screen,* 23.

86. Beumers, *History of Russian Cinema,* 149. In 1973, Goskino added VNIIK, the new institute for film research, to its roster.

87. Prokhorov, "Unknown New Wave," 25. Banning, of course, continued past 1968. See Beumers, *History of Russian Cinema,* chap. 5.

88. See Valerii Fomin, *Kino i vlast: Sovetskoe kino, 1965–1985 gody: Dokumenty, svidetelstva, razmyshleniia* (Moscow: Materik, 1996). This book consists of documents and interviews on banned films, troubled productions, and so on, from which we can see the return to an obsession with minutiae.

89. Hashamova, *Pride and Panic,* 27. Dobrynin, "Silver Curtain," 868–869, interprets this neutrality more positively than we do. It is true, however, that the hero of the film, a young Russian sailor, is eventually rescued by Americans.

90. See Elena Prokhorova, "Savva Kulish, *Dead Season* (Mertvyi sezon)," *Studies in Russian and Soviet Cinema* 3, no. 1 (2009): 85–86, and Dobrynin, "Silver Curtain," 865–866. *Dead Season* earned twelfth place at the box office in 1969, with 34.5 million viewers. Sergei Zemlianukhin and Miroslava Segida, *Domashniaia sinemateka: Otechestvennoe kino, 1918–1996* (Moscow: Dubl-D, 1996), 245. The title has also been translated as *Off Season.*

91. Shcherbenok, "Asymmetric Warfare," 7.

92. Beumers, *History of Russian Cinema,* 149.

93. Charlz Khemblet [Charles Hamblet?], "Kto ubil Merilin Monro?" *Sovetskii ekran,* no. 9 (1968): 16.

94. "Konkurs-67. Itogi," *Sovetskii ekran,* no. 10 (1968): 2. There were 40,000 responses to the survey. The demographics reveal that the regular moviegoing population was urban, educated (high school and above), and young (under thirty-five), more female than male, but not out of proportion to their representation in the population. It was not unusual for American films to reach Soviet screens years and sometimes decades after their release.

95. Ellen Propper Mickiewicz's research shows the strong preference for foreign films through the last days of the USSR. *Media and the Russian Public* (New York: Praeger, 1991), 78–80. In the five years between 1965 and 1970 the availability of television sets in the USSR more than doubled. Mickiewicz, *Split Signals: Television and Politics in the Soviet Union* (Oxford: Oxford University Press, 1988), 3.

96. F. Belov, "Kak priobretaiutsia zarubezhnykh filmov," *Sovetskii ekran,* no. 6

(1972): 17. This was followed by an homage to the "progressive" Hollywood actor Marlon Brando.

97. For a discussion of the blockbuster status of *The Crew,* see Valerii Golovskoi, *Mezhdu ottepeliu i glasnostiu: Kinematograf 70-x* (Moscow: Materik, 2004); for a discussion of *Moscow Does Not Believe in Tears,* see Anna Lawton, *Kinoglasnost: Soviet Cinema in Our Time* (Cambridge: Cambridge University Press, 1992), 17–19. (The latter book was republished in 2002 by New Academia Publishing as *Before the Fall: Soviet Cinema in the Gorbachev Years.*)

98. See Paula A. Michaels, "Mikhail Kalatozov's *The Red Tent:* A Case Study in International Coproduction across the Iron Curtain," *Historical Journal of Film, Radio and Television* 26, no. 3 (August 2006): 311–325.

99. Here Japan is considered "Western" as a U.S. ally during the Cold War.

100. "Dersu Uzala," www.imdb.com.

101. The first effort at American-Soviet co-production, an adaptation of Mitchell Wilson's novel *Meeting at a Far Meridian,* failed. See Dobrynin, "Silver Curtain," 868.

102. For a full analysis of the making of this film see Tony Shaw, "Nightmare on Nevsky Prospekt," unpublished manuscript.

103. Shiraev and Zubok, *Anti-Americanism in Russia,* 16.

104. For a discussion of the cult see Nina Tumarkin, *The Living and the Dead: The Rise and Fall of the Cult of World War II in Russia* (New York: Basic Books, 1994).

105. Archie Brown, "Perestroika and the End of the Cold War," *Cold War History* 7, no. 1 (February 2007): 5.

106. See Youngblood, *Russian War Films,* chaps. 6–7.

107. Vladimir Shlapentokh notes that establishing "false explanations of negative developments in society" was as important as positive legitimation in attempting to influence Soviet public opinion. See *Soviet Public Opinion and Ideology,* 34.

108. Dobrynin, "Silver Curtain," 869.

109. Ibid.

110. See Beumers, *History of Russian Cinema,* 169–174, for a description of some of these films.

111. Tarkovsky did not formally announce that he had defected until 1984, after *Nostalgia (Nostalgiia)* had been completed. *Nostalgia* began as a Soviet-Italian co-production but Mosfilm withdrew its support.

112. Brown, "Perestroika," 6.

113. See, e.g., Iurii Kornov, "Zapreshchennye igry," *Sovetskii ekran ,* no. 7 (1978): 18, about Brooke Shields's and Jodie Foster's roles in *Pretty Baby* (Louis Malle, 1978) and *Taxi Driver* (Martin Scorsese, 1976), respectively.

114. Romil Sobolev, "Meniaiushchisia i neizmennyi," *Sovetskii ekran,* no. 14 (1975): 16–17.

115. Shlapentokh, *Soviet Public Opinion,* 14.

116. V. Baskakov, "Ekrannaia agressiia," *Iskusstvo kino,* no. 3 (1983): 114–128, esp. 123, 126. Circulation figures come from Beumers, *History of Soviet Cinema,* 149.

117. Vladimir Chernenko, "Novye modeli agressii," *Sovetskii ekran,* no. 7 (1983): 16–17.

118. I. Kokarev, "Mify i realnost," *Sovetskii ekran,* no. 13 (1983): 17.

119. Leonid Trauberg, "O korabliakh i gluptsakh," *Iskusstvo kino*, no. 12 (1983). The article is about *Ship of Fools* (Stanley Kramer, 1965).

120. Mariia Racheva, "Voennye igry" [trans. from the Bulgarian], *Sovetskii ekran*, no. 19 (1984): 18–19.

121. Nina Tsyrkun, "'Novye prava' v Gollivude," *Iskusstvo kino*, no. 2 (1984): 139.

122. Nikolai Savitskii, "Kontur triadi: Zametki o zapadnom kino 80-x," *Iskusstvo kino*, no. 8 (1986): 111.

123. Beumers, *History of Russian Cinema*, 181. In 1982, movie attendance had reached a new low: fifteen visits per year, half what it had been in the 1970s. See Nancy Condee, *The Imperial Trace: Recent Russian Cinema* (Oxford: Oxford University Press, 2009), 50.

124. Dobrynin provides a list that includes films set in other Western countries, particularly Germany, in "Silver Curtain," 872.

125. Shcherbenok disagrees with this assessment; see "Asymmetric Warfare," 7.

126. For the details, see "Alexander Godunov," *Russian Life* (July/August 2009): 23–25.

127. Viktor Demin, "Initsiativa," pt. 2, *Iskusstvo kino*, no. 1/2 (1987): 118.

128. Beumers, *History of Russian Cinema*, 186–187.

129. "Chto zh, davaite sporit!" *Sovetskii ekran*, no. 20 (1986): 19.

130. Recall from chapter 1 that Soviet audiences in special screenings had enjoyed the film, but Soviet critics never accepted it officially as a worthy American production.

131. Demin, "Initsiativa," 115, 119–120.

132. Iurii Agunov and Vladislav Orlov, "Boevaia raskraska Gollivuda—ili muzhskie prikliuchenie na Amerikanskikh maner," *Sovetskii ekran*, no. 9 (1987): 20–22.

133. Andrei Kokarev, "Iz Rossii—s liubovem," *Sovetskii ekran*, no. 13 (1988): 11–12; "ASK: Net pregrad dlia sotrudnichestva," *Iskusstvo kino* 9 (1988): 134–188; "Elem Klimov: Nash chelovek v Los-Andzhelese," *Sovetskii ekran*, no. 14 (1988): 12–14. The American-Soviet Film Initiative was founded in February 1988 by Mark Gerzon, a professional organizer of international non-profit initiatives, and Elem Klimov, the head of the Union of Cinematographers; see also Aljean Harmetz, "U.S. and Soviet Film Makers Plan Joint Ventures," *New York Times*, 7 February 1988.

134. Feliks Andreev, "SShA: Filmy, liudi, vstrechi," *Sovetskii ekran*, no. 14 (1989): 28–29.

135. E. Kartseva, "Novaia model kinematografa: gollivudskii variant," *Iskusstvo kino*, no. 9 (1988): 123–125.

CHAPTER 3. JUSTIFYING WAR

1. In other words, these are the films that directly relate to the Cold War. See chapter 2 for a discussion of other films that may also be considered part of Cold War propaganda.

2. See Stephen M. Norris and Zara M. Torlone, eds., *Insiders and Outsiders in Russian Cinema* (Bloomington: Indiana University Press, 2008), and Stephen Hutchings, ed., *Russia and Its Other(s) on Screen: Screening Intercultural Dialogue* (Houndsmills: Palgrave Macmillan, 2008), for essays discussing this issue.

3. This had been a tradition in Soviet films since *Cross and Mauser* (*Krest i mauzer,* Vladimir Gardin, 1925).

4. Grigorii Aleksandrov, *Epokha i kino* (Moscow: Izd-vo politicheskoi literatury, 1976), 251.

5. Ibid., 255.

6. *The Conspiracy of the Doomed* is set in a satellite state akin to Czechoslovakia, but rather than focusing on Soviet reconstruction it concentrates on the political infighting among native communists and the skullduggery of the Roman Catholic Church.

7. Evgeny Dobrenko, "Late Stalinist Cinema and the Cold War: An Equation without Unknowns," trans. Birgit Beumers, *Modern Languages Review* 98, no. 4 (2003): 934.

8. Aleksandrov later expressed his contempt for American movies, especially the "murder and sex" of those shown at the 1947 Venice Film Festival. See *Epokha i kino,* 245.

9. A. Mariamov, "Borba za mir," *Iskusstvo kino,* no. 2 (1949): 8.

10. Francine Hirsch, "The Soviets at Nuremberg: International Law, Propaganda, and the Making of the Postwar Order," *American Historical Review* 113, no. 3 (June 2008): 710. See also Maya Turovskaya, "Soviet Films of the Cold War," in *Stalinism and Soviet Cinema,* ed. Richard Taylor and Derek Spring (London: Routledge, 1993), 140.

11. The lyrics were by Yevgeny Dolmatovsky and Vasily Lebedev-Kumach; Aleksandrov, *Epokha i kino,* 245.

12. The name "Vladlen" is derived from "*Vlad*imir *Len*in."

13. Also rendered in English as Jeanette Sherwood.

14. Peter Kenez, *Cinema and Soviet Society, 1917–1953* (Cambridge: Cambridge University Press, 1992), 238.

15. Grigorii Aleksandrov, "Dva mira," *Ogonek,* no. 12 (1949).

16. Aleksandrov noted that he also wanted to contrast the two nations' music, setting the song "Homesickness" ("Toska po rodine") ("The Russian heart is very big / All of the Great Motherland is in it") alongside a silly ditty like "Yankee Doodle Dandy" or a religious-militaristic song like "The Battle Hymn of the Republic." See ibid., 12.

17. Aleksandrov, *Epokha i kino,* 252.

18. Historian Richard Stites recalls Soviet friends recounting the Soviet audience's applause as the black GI was dragged off, indicative of the racism in the USSR, particularly against blacks, anti-racist propaganda notwithstanding. Conversation with Denise J. Youngblood, 22 November 2008. Nevertheless, Soviet propaganda often played the race card against the United States, as seen in the film *Silvery Dust,* mentioned in chapter 2.

19. Aleksandrov, *Epokha i kino,* 256. Aleksandrov was never shy about promoting his own work, so this is undoubtedly exaggerated. Isabelle de Keghel notes that it was shown in East Germany only three months after its Soviet release. "*Meeting on the Elbe (Vstrecha na El'be):* A Visual Representation of the Incipient Cold War from a Soviet Perspective," *Cold War History* 9, no. 4 (November 2009): 466n36.

20. Gosfilmofond, Ministerstvo kinematografii, Vstrecha na Elbe [hereafter GFF/ Mk/ VE], 3 March 1949, 3, 5.

21. Ibid., 3. Keghel ties this to Andrei Zhdanov's "Two-Camp-Theory" of 1947. See her *"Meeting on the Elbe,"* 457.

22. See Elena Zubkova, *Russia after the War: Hopes, Illusions, and Disappointments, 1945–1957,* trans. and ed. Hugh Ragsdale (Armonk, N.Y.: M.E. Sharpe, 1998), 82–84.

23. Eric Shiraev and Vladislav Zubok, *Anti-Americanism in Russia: From Stalin to Putin* (New York: Palgrave, 2000), 15.

24. Soviet officials considered jazz a sinister plot by the U.S. government to break down resistance to American imperial expansion. The Soviet jazz great Eddie Rosner was arrested in 1946. Officials contrasted "lascivious" jazz-inspired modern dances like the boogie-woogie to wholesome dances like the waltz and the polka that enjoyed regime support. See S. Frederick Starr, *Red and Hot: The Fate of Jazz in the Soviet Union, 1917–1980* (New York: Oxford University Press, 1983), 209, 214, 218.

25. *Pervyi vek nashego kino: Entsiklopediia* (Moscow: Izd-vo Lokid-Press, 2006), 381.

26. GFF/Mk/VE, 20 May 1948, 3.

27. GFF/Mk/VE, 3 June 1948, 4; 18 November 1948, 6–7.

28. GFF/Mk/VE, 18 November 1948, 8a.

29. GFF/Mk/VE, 3 March 1949, 13.

30. Ibid., 28–29.

31. Ibid., 17, 20.

32. Ibid., 9.

33. Ibid., 32–33.

34. See, e.g., M. Chiaureli, "Dva mira," *Literaturnaia gazeta,* 9 March 1949, 3.

35. Vsevolod Pudovkin, *"Vstrecha na Elbe,"* *Pravda,* 10 March 1949, and Al. Abramov, *"Vstrecha na Elbe,"* *Vecherniaia Moskva,* 12 March 1949.

36. *"Vstrecha na Elbe,"* *Leningradskaia pravda,* no. 57, 10 March 1949, as excerpted in *Sovetskoe kino, 1919–1991* (Moscow: Interros, 2006).

37. See Oleg Kovalov, "Zvezda nad stepiu: Amerika v zerkale sovetskogo kino," *Iskusstvo kino,* no. 10 (2003): 11.

38. David Caute, *The Dancer Defects: The Struggle for Cultural Supremacy during the Cold War* (Oxford: Oxford University Press, 2003), 141.

39. Turovskaya, "Soviet Films of the Cold War," 141.

40. Aleksandrov, *Epokha i kino,* 250, and GFF/Mk/VE, 18 November 1948, 7.

41. Grigorii Aleksandrov, *Gody poiskov i truda* (Moscow: Soiuz kinematografistov SSSR/Biuro propagandy sovetskogo kinoiskusstva, 1975).

42. See, for example, *The Echelon* (*Eshelon,* Dmitrii Dolinin and Niiole Adomenaite, 2005) and *The Penal Battalion* (*Shtrafbat,* Nikolai Dostal, 2004).

43. Richard Bessel, *Germany 1945: From War to Peace* (New York: HarperCollins, 2009), 143–144, 159–160. According to Bessel, American transgressions included looting and the shooting of POWs.

44. In the early stages of gaining control over the new governments in Central and Eastern Europe, the Soviets sought to engineer the elections of some nonparty people, rather than native communists or socialists.

45. Norman M. Naimark, *The Russians in Germany: A History of the Soviet Zone of Occupation, 1945–1949* (Cambridge, Mass.: Belknap Press/Harvard University Press, 1995), 421.

46. See, for example, Zubkova, *Russia after the War;* Vasily Aksyonov, *In Search of Melancholy Baby,* trans. Michael Henry Heim and Antonina Bouis (New York: Random House, 1985).

47. GFF/Mk, Sekretnaia missiia [hereafter GFF/Mk/Sm], 20 July 1950, 28–29.

48. GFF/Mk/Sm, 13 July 1950, 35–36.

49. GFF/Mk/Sm, 29 September 1949, 43.

50. Ron Briley, "John Wayne and *Big Jim McLain* (1952): The Duke's Cold War Legacy," *Film & History* 3, no. 1 (2001): 28–33; *Variety*, 25 March 1953.

51. Martin Wien, *Zirkus zwischen Kunst und Kader: Das Zirkuswesen in der SBZ/DDR* (Berlin: Duncker & Humblod, 2001), 60; *New York Times*, 7 September 1952; *Time*, 8 October 1951.

52. *Lilliput*, January–February 1952, 81–104; Lew Schreiber to George Watson, 29 January 1952, *Man on a Tightrope*, Box FXLR1019, Twentieth Century-Fox Legal Files, Arts Library Special Collections, UCLA.

53. Larry Ceplair and Steven Englund, *The Inquisition in Hollywood: Politics in the Film Community, 1930–1960* (Berkeley: University of California Press, 1979), 305; *Sunday Times* (London), 24 May 1953. *There Shall Be No Night* was adapted for American television in 1957, its locale switched from Finland to Hungary in order to make it more topical. http://www.imdb.com/title/tt0595424/ (17 March 2009).

54. On Sherwood's six iterations between March and October 1952, see *Man on a Tightrope*, Core Collection Scripts, AMPAS; *Man on a Tightrope*, Box 1164, Twentieth Century-Fox Script Collection, UCLA; *Man on a Tightrope*, Folders 1–3, Twentieth Century-Fox Collection, University of Southern California.

55. On U.S. race relations as a Cold War propaganda theme see Tony Shaw, *Hollywood's Cold War* (Amherst: University of Massachusetts Press, 2007), 167–198, and Mary L. Dudziak, *Cold War Civil Rights* (Princeton, N.J.: Princeton University Press, 2000).

56. Les K. Adler and Thomas G. Paterson, "Red Fascism: The Merger of Nazi Germany and Soviet Russia in the American Image of Totalitarianism, 1930s–1950s," *American Historical Review* 75, no. 4 (April 1970): 1046–1064.

57. Thomas H. Pauly, *American Odyssey: Elia Kazan and American Culture* (Philadelphia: Temple University Press, 1983), 164; Lew Schreiber to Frank Ferguson, 28 May 1952, *Man on a Tightrope*, Elia Kazan Box FXLR1075, Twentieth Century-Fox Legal Files, UCLA.

58. Brian Neve, "Elia Kazan's First Testimony to the House Committee on Un-American Activities, Executive Session, 14 January 1952," *Historical Journal of Radio, Film and Television* 25, no. 2 (June 2005): 251–272; Elia Kazan, *A Life* (New York: Alfred A. Knopf, 1988), 468. Kazan died in 2003.

59. Kazan, *A Life*, 475–477, 481; Michel Ciment, ed., *Elia Kazan: An American Odyssey* (London: Bloomsbury, 1988), 106; Pauly, *American Odyssey*, 164.

60. R. A. Klune to Frank Ferguson, 26 July 1952, *Man on a Tightrope*, Box FXLR1019, Twentieth Century-Fox Legal Files, UCLA; *Man on a Tightrope*, press

book and marketing material, British Film Institute Library, London (hereafter BFIL).

61. *Man on a Tightrope*, press book and marketing material, BFIL; Arch Puddington, *Broadcasting Freedom: The Cold War Triumph of Radio Free Europe and Radio Liberty* (Lexington: University Press of Kentucky, 2000), ix, 20–24, 29, 44; Susan L. Carruthers, "Between Camps: Eastern Bloc 'Escapees' and Cold War Borderlands," *American Quarterly* 57, no. 3 (2005): 911–942; Michael Nelson, *War of the Black Heavens: The Battles of Western Broadcasting in the Cold War* (Syracuse: Syracuse University Press, 1997), 48.

62. Conference between Zanuck, Sherwood, Robert Jacks (producer of *Man on a Tightrope*), and Molly Mandaville, 24 July 1952, *Man on a Tightrope*, Box 1164, Twentieth Century-Fox Script Collection, UCLA; Zanuck to Kazan, 29 July 1952, *Man on a Tightrope*, Folder 2, Twentieth Century-Fox Collection, USC; Zanuck and Robert Jacks to Kazan, 14 August 1952, Folder 3, Twentieth Century-Fox Collection, USC; Brian C. Etheridge, "*The Desert Fox*, Memory Diplomacy, and the German Question in Early Cold War America," *Diplomatic History* 32, no. 2 (April 2008): 207–238. *The Desert Fox* caused a storm of protest in the United States and Western Europe for its heroic depiction of the Second World War German general Erwin Rommel. The movie was part of Hollywood's fascination with the Second World War in the 1950s, one which all but erased the Soviet Union's role in defeating fascism on the Eastern front in favor of the part played by the United States and Britain in the Pacific, North Africa, and Normandy.

63. Jeff Young, ed., *Kazan on Kazan* (London: Faber & Faber, 1999), 113; Kazan, *A Life*, 479–480; Ceplair and Englund, *The Inquisition in Hollywood*, 104, 114, 150, 193, 259, 276.

64. This is, however, after they hear a snippet from the unofficial Czech national anthem, Bedřich Smetana's "Vltava" (The Moldau), from his cycle *Má vlast* (My Country), which by this time had nationalist, anticommunist connotations.

65. Ciment, ed., *Kazan*, 107–108.

66. *Man on a Tightrope*, press book and marketing material, BFIL. This kind of publicity, so common in Hollywood, was unknown in the staid world of Soviet cinema.

67. *New York Times*, 12 June 1953; Nelson, *Black Heavens*, 67; Puddington, *Freedom*, 56–57.

68. David Lewis Hammarstrom, *Circus Rings around Russia* (Hamden, Conn.: Archon, 1983), 79–82.

69. *Los Angeles Examiner*, 2 April 1953.

70. *Time*, 27 April 1953; *Hollywood Reporter*, 1 April 1953.

71. *New York Times*, 5 June 1953.

72. *New York Times*, 27 December 1953; Lew Schreiber to Frank Ferguson, 3 December 1953, *Man on a Tightrope*, Box FXLR1019, Twentieth Century-Fox Legal Files, UCLA.

73. *Daily Worker* (London), 23 May 1953; *The Times* (London), 25 May 1953; http://www.imdb.com/title/tt0046040/awards (7 April 2008); Harry J. McIntyre to Frank Ferguson, 17 February 1953, *Man on a Tightrope*, Box FXLR1019, Twentieth Century-Fox Legal Files, UCLA.

74. *Variety*, 22 March 1961; *Motion Picture Herald*, 14 November 1962; *Hollywood Reporter*, 5 November 1985.

75. We should not underestimate the role the 1950–53 Korean War played in solidifying Cold War tensions, but it did not involve fighting directly between American and Soviet forces. On U.S. propaganda during the Korean War see Steven Casey, *Selling the Korean War: Propaganda, Politics, and Public Opinion in the United States, 1950–1953* (Oxford: Oxford University Press, 2007).

CHAPTER 4. PLEASURE VERSUS PROGRESS

1. David Caute, *The Dancer Defects: The Struggle for Cultural Supremacy during the Cold War* (Oxford: Oxford University Press, 2003); Stephen J. Whitfield, *The Culture of the Cold War* (Baltimore: Johns Hopkins University Press, 1996); Peter Kenez, *Cinema and Soviet Society, 1917–1953* (Cambridge: Cambridge University Press, 1992); Maya Turovskaya, "Soviet Films of the Cold War," in *Stalinism and Soviet Cinema*, ed. Richard Taylor and Derek Spring (London: Routledge, 1993).

2. See, for instance, Reinhold Wagnleitner, *Coca-Colonization and the Cold War: The Cultural Mission of the United States in Austria after the Second World War* (Chapel Hill: University of North Carolina Press, 1994); Frances Stonor Saunders, *Who Paid the Piper? The CIA and the Cultural Cold War* (London: Granta, 1999); Helen Laville, "'Our Country Endangered by Underwear': Fashion, Femininity, and the Seduction Narrative in *Ninotchka* and *Silk Stockings*," *Diplomatic History* 30, no. 4 (September 2006): 623–644.

3. *Story of Enterprise,* made by Fotovox, Inc., is available online at http://www.archive.org/details/Spiritof1955 (15 March 2008). For more on films like it see Rick Prelinger, *The Field Guide to Sponsored Films* (San Francisco: National Film Preservation Foundation, 2006), available at http://www.filmpreservation.org/projects/sponsored.pdf (15 March 2008).

4. Phillip L. Gianos, *Politics and Politicians in American Film* (Westport, Conn.: Praeger, 1998), 3–4.

5. David A. Cook, *A History of Narrative Film* (New York: W. W. Norton, 2004), 387–430.

6. Thomas H. Guback, "Hollywood's International Market," in *The American Film Industry* (Madison: University of Wisconsin Press, 1976), ed. Tino Balio, 387–409; Paul Swann, "The Little State Department: Hollywood and the State Department in the Post-war World," *American Studies International* 29, no. 1 (April 1991): 2–19; David Eldridge, "'Dear Owen': The CIA, Luigi Luraschi and Hollywood, 1953," *Historical Journal of Film, Radio and Television* 20, no. 2 (June 2000): 149–196.

7. Wagnleitner, *Coca-Colonization,* 230–266; Eric Johnston, "A Frontline Post," *Film Daily Year Book,* 1951, 51; Walter F. Wanger, "Donald Duck and Diplomacy," *Public Opinion Quarterly* 14, no. 3 (1950): 443–452.

8. Yale Richmond, *Cultural Exchange and the Cold War: Raising the Iron Curtain* (University Park: Pennsylvania State University Press, 2003), 129–130; Walter L. Hixson, *Parting the Curtain: Propaganda, Culture and the Cold War, 1945–1961* (Basingstoke: Macmillan, 1997), 154–156; Caute, *The Dancer Defects,* 117–118.

9. On Hepburn's career see Barry Paris, *Audrey Hepburn* (London: Orien, 1996).

10. See Dina M. Smith, "Global Cinderella: *Sabrina* (1954), Hollywood, and Postwar Internationalism," *Cinema Journal* 41, no. 2 (2002): 27–51, for more on Hepburn's international image and popular appeal. Billy Wilder's *Sabrina* was another cross-class fantasy in which Hepburn played a chauffeur's daughter over whom two wealthy American bachelors fight.

11. Steven J. Ross, "The Rise of Hollywood: Movies, Ideology, and Audiences in the Roaring Twenties," in Ross, *Movies and American Society* (Oxford: Blackwell, 2002), 64–97.

12. Emily S. Rosenberg, "'Foreign Affairs' after World War II: Connecting Sexual and International Politics," *Diplomatic History* 18, no. 1 (1994): 59–70; Smith, "Global Cinderella."

13. Peck's image as the perfect American might have been bolstered further by his outspoken criticism of the Hollywood blacklist. The actor had strong liberal democratic views and would eventually find himself on President Richard Nixon's infamous enemies list in the 1970s. Michael Freedland, *Gregory Peck: A Biography* (London: William Morrow, 1980), 86–89.

14. On Trumbo's politics and career see Peter Hansen, *Dalton Trumbo, Hollywood Rebel: A Critical Survey and Filmography* (Jefferson, N.C.: McFarland, 2007).

15. "Detailed Quick Estimate," 7 October 1949, *Roman Holiday* Budgets, f. 1, Paramount Collection, AMPAS; Joseph McBride, *Frank Capra: The Catastrophe of Success* (New York: Simon & Schuster, 1992), 552–553; Stanley Kauffmann, "Roman Holiday," *American Film* (April 1978): 67–69, 78–79.

16. Axel Madsen, *William Wyler: The Authorised Biography* (London: W. H. Allen, 1974), 286, 306; Wyler to Y. Frank Freeman, 29 December 1952, f. 349, William Wyler Collection, AMPAS.

17. *Hollywood Reporter,* 12 May 1991; *Variety,* 28 October 1991; Henry Henigson to Jack Karp, 25 September 1952, William Wyler Collection, f. 343, AMPAS; Lester Koenig to John Mock, 4 July 1952, f. 367, William Wyler Collection, AMPAS.

18. Wyler at press conference, Warner Bros. Beverly Hills Theatre, 24 February 1954, William Wyler Papers, Box 15, f.1, UCLA; Ian McLellan Hunter script, 3 March 1950, Willam Wyler Papers, Box 15, f. 13, UCLA.

19. Ben Hecht script, 5 November 1951, William Wyler Papers, Box 15, f. 12, UCLA.

20. David Ellwood, "Italian Modernisation and the Propaganda of the Marshall Plan," in *The Art of Persuasion: Political Communications in Italy from 1945 to the 1990s,* ed. Luciano Cheles and Lucio Sponza (Manchester: Manchester University Press, 2001), 23–48. For details of the ERP's film output see http://www.marshallfilms. org/ and http://www.sellingdemocracy.org (4 June 2009). On how U.S. films sold American glamour during this period, particularly in Italy, see Stephen Gundle, "Hollywood Glamour and Mass Consumption in Postwar Italy," *Journal of Cold War Studies* 4, no. 3 (Summer 2002): 95–118.

21. Tony Judt, *Postwar: A History of Europe since 1945* (London: Pimlico, 2005), 231–232; Richard Maltby, *Hollywood Cinema* (Oxford: Blackwell, 2003), 126–127, 214; Geoffrey Nowell-Smith, "Introduction," in *Hollywood and Europe: Economics,*

Culture, National Identity 1945–1995, ed. Geoffrey Nowell-Smith and Steven Ricci (London: BFI, 1998), 1–16.

22. Soon nicknamed "Hollywood on the Tiber," Cinecittà's other U.S. productions of the fifties included *Three Coins in a Fountain* (Jean Negulesco, 1954), *A Farewell to Arms* (Charles Vidor, 1957), and *Ben-Hur* (William Wyler, 1959).

23. Wyler to Don Hartman, 26 July 1952, f. 349, William Wyler Collection, AMPAS; Warren G. Harris, *Audrey Hepburn: A Biography* (New York: Simon & Schuster, 1994), 94.

24. *Motion Picture Herald*, 23 June 1951 and 8 March 1952; Jill Forbes, "Winning Hearts and Minds: The American Cinema in France 1945–49," *French Cultural Studies* 8, no. 1 (1997): 31–32; Saunders, *Who Paid the Piper?*, 289–290; Eldridge, "'Dear Owen'"; Luraschi correspondence with Joseph Breen at Production Code Administration, 24 and 29 April 1952, 1 and 7 April 1953, Production Code Administration Files, AMPAS.

25. *Hollywood Citizen-News*, 1 October 1953; *Los Angeles Examiner*, 1 October 1953; *Look*, 11 August 1953.

26. *New York Times*, 27 December 1953; *Saturday Review of Literature*, 26 December 1953; *Washington Post*, 21 December 1953; Paris, *Hepburn*, 81. Dalton Trumbo died in 1976. His original story for *Roman Holiday* was granted a special Oscar in 1993. See *Variety*, 12 May 1993.

27. Cobbett Steinberg, *Reel Facts* (Harmondsworth: Penguin, 1981), 435–436; http://www.imdb.com/title/tt0046250/business (17 March 2008); Edward Schellhorn to Stu Miller, 21 June 1955, William Wyler Papers, Box 15, f. 10, UCLA.

28. Wyler cable to Maurice Bessy, 29 June 1955, William Wyler Papers, Box 16, f. 5, UCLA; *Hollywood Reporter*, 9 September 1954.

29. Réka Buckley, "Elsa Martinelli: Italy's Audrey Hepburn," *Historical Journal of Film, Radio and Television* 26, no. 3 (August 2006): 327–340.

30. *Variety*, 9 July 1954; Madsen, *William Wyler*, 312; Harris, *Hepburn*, 102.

31. Saunders, *Who Paid the Piper?*, 289–290. On the USIA's Motion Picture Service see Wilson P. Dizard, *Inventing Public Diplomacy* (Boulder, Colo.: Lynne Rienner, 2004), 167–169.

32. Hixson, *Parting the Curtain*, 153–154.

33. Five of these movies had literary or classical pedigrees: *The Idiot* (*Idiot*, Ivan Pyryev, 1958), *Othello* (*Otello*, Sergei Yutkevich, 1955), *Don Quixote* (*Don kikhot*, Grigori Kozintsev, 1957), *And Quiet Flows the Don* (*Tikhii Don*, Sergei Gerasimov, 1957), and *Swan Lake* (*Lebedinoe ozero*, Z. Tulubeva, 1957). *Circus Stars* (*Artisty tsirka*, Leonid Kristi, 1957), a non-narrative film, belonged to the variety genre. *The Cranes Are Flying* (*Letiat zhuravli*, Mikhail Kalatozov, 1957) was one of the defining films of the Soviet cinematic Thaw, a moving drama set during the Second World War. On the failure of these films inside the United States, partly because of poor distribution and inadequate dubbing, see James H. Krukones, "The Unspooling of Artkino: Soviet Film Distribution in America, 1940–1975," *Historical Journal of Film, Radio and Television* 29, no. 1 (March 2009): 100–104.

34. *Department of State Bulletin*, 39, 3 November 1958, 696–698; Krukones,

"Artkino," 100–102; *Variety,* 5 November 1958, 14; *Newsweek,* 26 January 1959, 48; *Film Daily Year Book,* 1959, 65, 133.

35. *Sovetskii ekran,* no. 23 (1958): 16–17; *New York Times,* 22 March 1960; *Los Angeles Times,* 23 March 1960; Krukones, "Artkino," 103.

36. *Roman Holiday* evidently continued to play in the USSR for some years to come. For example, Elena Sukhorukova saw the film as a fourteen-year-old in 1976: "This film simply captivated my mother," Sukhorukova recounted thirty years later. "She in general worshipped Audrey Hepburn, simply worshipped her." Interview with historian Sudha Rajagopalan, email to Denise J. Youngblood, 31 October 2008. On how the USIA sold the image of the liberated, leisured, and fashionable American woman overseas during the 1950s, including behind the Iron Curtain, see Laura Belmonte, "A Family Affair? Gender, the US Information Agency, and Cold War Ideology, 1945–1960," in *Culture and International History,* ed. Jessica Gienow-Hecht and Frank Schumacher (New York: Berghahn, 2003), 79–93. On the representation of Soviet women in Soviet cinema in the 1950s see Lynne Attwood, *Red Women on the Silver Screen* (Pandora, London, 1993), 71–77.

37. Wyler-Balaban-Karp correspondence, 24–28 March 1960, William Wyler Papers, Box 16, f. 6, UCLA. On the Cold War role of the Voice of America, the U.S. government's official external radio (and later television) broadcasting service, see Nicholas J. Cull, *The Cold War and the United States Information Agency: American Propaganda and Public Diplomacy, 1945–1989* (Cambridge: Cambridge University Press, 2008).

38. Richmond, *Cultural Exchange,* 129–130; *Sovetskii ekran,* no. 11 (1975): 16–17.

39. Paris, *Hepburn,* 81; Andrei Gelasimov, "A Tender Age," trans. Susanna Nazarova, *Chtenia: Readings from Russia,* no. 2 (Spring 2008): 80–89. On the popular reception of Western, mainly U.S., films in Ukraine, see Sergei I. Zhuk, *Rock and Roll in the Rocket City: The West, Identity, and Ideology in Soviet Dniepropetrovsk, 1960–1985* (Baltimore: Johns Hopkins University Press, 2010).

40. Denise J. Youngblood, *Movies for the Masses: Popular Cinema and Soviet Society in the 1920s* (Cambridge: Cambridge University Press, 1992), chaps. 7–8.

41. V. Troianovskii, "Chelovek ottepeli," *Kinematograf ottepeli,* vol. 1, ed. V. Troianovskii (Moscow: Materik, 1996), 25.

42. Sergei Kapterev, *Post-Stalinist Cinema and the Russian Intelligentsia, 1953–1960: Strategies of Self-Representation, De-Stalinization, and the National Cultural Tradition* (Saarbrücken: VDM Verlag Dr. Müller, 2008), 196–201.

43. Ibid., 36.

44. That is, after Khutsiev's diploma film for the All-Union State Institute of Cinematography (VGIK), *Town Planners* (*Gradostroiteli,* 1950), on which Mironer served as co-scenarist with Khutsiev. *Kino: Entsiklopedicheskii slovar* (Moscow: Sovetskaia entsiklopediia, 1986), 474–475.

45. See *Vercherniaia Moskva,* 26 November 1956.

46. See, e.g., N. Ignateva, "Nachalo puti," *Literaturnaia gazeta,* 1 December 1956. Maya Turovskaya was the most prominent critic who emphatically dissented. Although she thought the directors showed talent, she found the characters psychologically

underdeveloped. See Troianovskii, "Chelovek ottepeli," 25. For the quotation, see *Istoriia sovetskogo kino,* vol. 4, *1952–1967* (Moscow: Iskusstvo, 1978), 150.

47. Julian Graffy, "Cinema," in *Russian Cultural Studies: An Introduction,* ed. Catriona Kelly and David Shepherd (Oxford: Oxford University Press, 1998), 183. Graffy also included *The Rumiantsev Affair (Delo Rumiantseva)* with *Spring on Zarechnaya Street* in the statement quoted.

48. Josephine Woll, "Being 20, 40 Years Later: Marlen Khutsiev's *Mne dvadstat let (I Am Twenty,* 1961)," *Kinoeye: New Perspectives on European Film* 1, no. 8 (10 December 2001), http://www.kinoeye.org/01/08/w01108.php, 2.

49. *Pervyi vek nashego kino: Entsiklopediia* (Moscow: Izd-vo Lokid-Press, 2006), 420.

50. See Tamara Eidelman, "Spring on the Silver Screen," *Chtenia: Readings from Russia,* no. 2 (Spring 2008): 112, and Marlen Khutsiev, "Ia nikogda ne delal polemicheskikh filmov," in Troianovskii, *Kinematograf ottepeli,* 191. Khutsiev mentions (191) that some of the winter scenes were filmed in Moscow as the winter in Zaporozhe that year was not wintry enough.

51. Woll, "Being 20," 2.

52. Stephen V. Bittner, *The Many Lives of Khrushchev's Thaw: Experience and Memory in Moscow's Arbat* (Ithaca, N.Y.: Cornell University Press, 2008), 50.

53. Eidelman, "Spring on the Silver Screen," 112. Unfortunately, there is no production still for this scene.

54. Julianne Fürst, "The Arrival of Spring? Changes and Continuities in Soviet Youth Culture and Policy between Stalin and Khrushchev," in *The Dilemmas of De-Stalinization: Negotiating Cultural and Social Change in the Khrushchev Era,* ed. Polly Jones (London: Routledge, 2006), 140.

55. Neya Zorkaya, *The Illustrated History of the Soviet Cinema* (New York: Hippocrene Books, 1989), 209. Maya Turovskaya agrees, and also criticizes Ivanova's acting in the role of Tanya. See Turovskaia, "Marlen Khutsiev," in *Molodye rezhissery sovetskogo kino: Sbornik statei* (Leningrad: Iskusstvo, 1962), 183.

56. Zorkaya, *Illustrated History,* 209.

57. Elena Zubkova, *Russia after the War: Hopes, Illusions, and Disappointments, 1945–1957,* trans. and ed. Hugh Ragsdale (Armonk, N.Y.: M. E. Sharpe, 1998), 176.

58. Ibid., 109.

59. S. Frederick Starr, *Red and Hot: The Fate of Jazz in the Soviet Union, 1917–1980* (New York: Oxford University Press, 1983), 237.

60. For the definitive history of Soviet jazz, see ibid.

61. Alexei Yurchak, *Everything Was Forever until It Was No More: The Last Soviet Generation* (Princeton, N.J.: Princeton University Press, 2006), 166.

62. Ibid.

63. Sergei Zemlianukhin and Miroslava Segida, comps., *Domashniaia sinemateka: Otechestvennoe kino, 1918–1996* (Moscow: Dubl-D, 1996), 278.

64. See Vasily Aksyonov's memoirs, *In Search of Melancholy Baby,* trans. Michael Henry Heim and Antonina Bouis (New York: Random House, 1985), 17–18, for his recollection of the importance of foreign movies and, 12–14, for a lively recollection of a "statenik" party.

65. Eric Shiraev and Vladislav Zubok, *Anti-Americanism in Russia: From Stalin to Putin* (New York: Palgrave, 2000), 15–17.

66. Fürst, "The Arrival of Spring," 137.

67. Julianne Fürst, "The Importance of Being Stylish: Youth, Culture, and Identity in Late Stalinism," in *Late Stalinist Russia: Society between Reconstruction and Reinvention*, ed. Fürst (London: Routledge, 2006), 211. She also notes (222) concerns about flagging attendance at events organized by factory clubs.

68. Sergei Zhuk provides important new information about Soviet youth culture during the Cold War; see "Popular Culture, Identity, and Soviet Youth in Dniepropetrovsk, 1959–84," *Carl Beck Papers in Russian & East European Studies,* no. 1906 (2008). Indian films were also extraordinarily popular. See Sudha Rajagopalan, *Leave Disco Dancer Alone! Indian Cinema and Soviet Movie-Going after Stalin* (New Delhi: Yoda Press, 2008), reprinted as *Indian Films in Soviet Cinema: The Culture of Movie-Going after Stalin* (Bloomington: Indiana University Press, 2009).

69. Zubkova, *Russia after the War,* 82.

70. *Sovetskie khudozhestvennye filmy,* vol. 3, 618.

71. "*Vesna na Zarechnoi ulitse,*" *Trud,* no. 264, 14 November 1956, as excerpted in *Sovetskoe kino, 1919–1991.*

72. Zemlianukhin and Segida, *Domashniaia sinemateka,* 62. "Best" expectations for a film's audience were a minimum of 15 million viewers. Most Soviet films were seen by 4 million or fewer. Val Golovskoy with John Rimberg, *Behind the Soviet Screen: The Motion Picture Industry in the USSR, 1972–1982,* trans. Steven Hill (Ann Arbor, Mich.: Ardis, 1986), 51. In an artistic sense, the film was noteworthy for establishing new genre conventions, e.g., a plot structured around the changing of seasons, the binary of the sensitive man and "emotionally rigid woman," and so on. See Alexander Prokhorov, "The Unknown New Wave: Soviet Cinema of the 1960s," in *Springtime for Soviet Cinema: Re/Viewing the 1960s,* ed. Prokhorov (Pittsburgh: Pittsburgh Russian Film Symposium, 2001), http://www.rusfilm.pitt.edu, 8. Prokhorov also praises Khutsiev for "abolish[ing] the primacy of the cause-and-effect narrative in Soviet film and mak[ing] individual identity both the central theme and paramount stylistic issue for films of the Soviet New Wave in general" (17).

73. For a post-Soviet Russian assessment, see Nadezhda Aleksandrova, "*Vesna na Zarechnoi ulitse,*" in *Rossiiskii illiuzion* (Moscow: Materik, 2003), 273–278.

74. "Konkurs SE—1981," *Sovetskii ekran,* no. 10 (1982): 12. *Spring on Zarechnaya Street* is frequently shown on Russian television today, and a newly remastered DVD is now available.

75. Josephine Woll, *Real Images: Soviet Cinema and the Thaw* (London: I. B. Tauris, 2001), 67. *Heights* was also the most popular of *Spring*'s successors, with 24.8 million viewers; Zemlianukhin and Segida, *Domashniaia sinemateka,* 85.

76. Woll, "Being 20," 2.

77. Ibid., 2.

78. Ibid., 2–3.

79. Ibid., 4.

80. Krukones, "The Unspooling of Artkino," 104.

CHAPTER 5: DETERRENCE AND DISSENT

1. "Liudy, filmy, fakty," *Sovetskii ekran,* no. 29 (1967): 3–4.

2. A literal translation is "Nine Days *of* One Year"; the film title has also been translated as "Nine Days of *a* Year."

3. "Konkurs 1966. Itogi," *Sovetskii ekran,* no. 1 (1967): 1–2. The ever-popular *Chapaev* concerned the exploits of the legendary commander of the Russian Civil War Vasily Ivanovich Chapaev.

4. See Ethan Pollock, *Stalin and the Soviet Science Wars* (Princeton, N.J.: Princeton University Press, 2006), 75.

5. Ibid., 215.

6. Emma Widdis examines this film in quite a different light in "Dressing the Part: Clothing Otherness in Soviet Cinema before 1953," in *Insiders and Outsiders in Russian Cinema,* ed. Stephen M. Norris and Zara M. Torlone (Bloomington: Indiana University Press, 2008), 61–64.

7. *Pyshka* is an adaptation of Guy de Maupassant's short story set during the 1870–71 Franco-Prussian War, "Boule de suif."

8. *Kino: Entsiklopedicheskii slovar* (Moscow: Sovetskaia entsiklopediia, 1986), 356–357; Neya Zorkaya, *The Illustrated History of the Soviet Cinema* (New York: Hippocrene Books, 1989), 245.

9. Quoted by Zorkaya, *Illustrated History,* 245.

10. Josephine Woll, *Real Images: Soviet Cinema and the Thaw* (London: I. B. Tauris, 2001), 127; Zorkaya, *Illustrated History,* 245.

11. Andrei Sakharov, *Memoirs,* trans. Richard Lourie (New York: Alfred A. Knopf, 1990), 144.

12. Romm jettisoned an already composed score, a brilliant move that enhanced the ascetic tone of the film; Woll, *Real Images,* 130. The artistic effect of the lack of music is noted by Tatiana Egorova in *Soviet Film Music: An Historical Survey,* trans. Tatiana A. Ganf and Natalia A. Egunova (Amsterdam: Harwood Academic, 1997), 146–147.

13. Pollock, *Stalin,* 99.

14. Ibid., 218.

15. Ibid., 100.

16. Zubkova, *Russia after the War: Hopes, Illusions, and Disappointments, 1945–1957* trans. and ed. Hugh Ragsdale (Armonk: N.Y.: M. E, Sharpe, 1998), 93.

17. Woll notes that Romm and scriptwriter Khrabovitsky were able to visit a secret facility with the help of physicists Igor Tamm and Lev Landau; *Real Images,* 128.

18. Prokhorov, "The Unknown New Wave: Soviet Cinema of the 1960s," in *Springtime for Soviet Cinema: Re/Viewing the 1960s,* ed. Alexander Prokhorov (Pittsburgh: Pittsburgh Russian Film Symposium, 2001), 18.

19. *Istoriia sovetskogo kino,* vol. 4, *1953–67* (Moscow: Iskusstvo, 1978), 91.

20. Indeed, Sergei Kapterev labels the film a Socialist Realist work, for its "monumentalism, its self-sacrificing hero, and its 'stylistic objectivism.'" See Kapterev, *Post-Stalinist Cinema and the Russian Intelligentsia, 1953–1960: Strategies of Self-Representation, De-Stalinization, and the National Cultural Tradition* (Saarbrücken: VDM Verlag Dr. Müller, 2008), 160–162.

21. Sakharov cites the similarity in their names: Gusev's name is Dmitry Andreevich, while Sakharov's is Andrei Dmitrievich; *Memoirs,* 144. This seems rather flimsy evidence, unless Romm wanted to imply that Sakharov was the father figure to Gusev. ("Andreevich" means "son of Andrei.")

22. S. Freilikh, *Mikhail Romm: Ispoved kino-rezhissera.* (Moscow: Iskusstvo, 1988), 40–41.

23. Mikhail Romm wrote that he worked the hardest on defining Kulikov's character. See *Kogda film okonchen: Govoriat rezhissery Mosfilma*. (Moscow: Iskusstvo, 1964), 128–130.

24. Woll, *Real Images,* 127.

25. Romm was particularly proud of this scene. See Romm, "Kinematograf v riadu iskusstv," *Iskusstvo kino,* no. 12 (2001), http://kinoart.ru/2001/12/6htm, 4. This is the republication of a letter to director Sergei Gerasimov dated 19 October 1971. The wall scene was also mentioned in reviews. See, e.g., Vl. Amlinskii, "Novyi film Mikhail Romma," *Sovetskaia kultura,* 2 February 1962.

26. Lev Anninskii, *Shestidesiatniki i my: Kinematograf, stavshii i ne stavshii istoriei* (Moscow: Soiuz kinematografistov SSSR, 1991), 94. His discussion of the film may be found on pp. 93–105.

27. Quoted by Woll, *Real Images,* 128.

28. Sakharov, *Memoirs,* 144.

29. Woll, *Real Images,* 129.

30. Sakharov, *Memoirs,* 144.

31. Woll, *Real Images,* 129.

32. *Pervyi vek nashego kino: Entsiklopediia* (Moscow: Izd-vo Lokid-Press, 2006), 460. *Nine Days* was one of only two films featured for 1962.

33. Woll, *Real Images,* 129.

34. See, e.g., G. Medvedeva, "30 polezhnykh metrov," *Sovetskii ekran,* no. 20 (1961): 4–5, and Evgenii Gabrilovich, "Vsego neskolko dnei," *Literaturnaia gazeta,* 27 February 1962.

35. See, e.g., the long list in *Sovetskie khudozhestvennye filmy,* vol. 4, 365–366, which is not even complete.

36. Amlinskii, "Novyi film Mikhaila Romma."

37. Nik. Kruzhkov, "Ballada o nashem sovremennike," *Ogonek,* no. 12 (March 1962): 16.

38. M. Kuznetsov, "Esli by chelovechestvo sostoialo iz Gusevykh [If humanity were constituted from Gusevs]," *Sovetskii ekran,* no. 6 (1962): 14.

39. L. Pogozheva, "Poltora chasa razmyshlenii," *Iskusstvo kino,* no. 4 (April 1962): 9; "Atomy i liudi," *Pravda,* 20 March 1962.

40. "Atomy i liudi."

41. "*Deviat dnei odnogo goda,*" *Nauka i zhizn,* no. 5 (May 1962), as excerpted in *Sovetskoe kino, 1919–1991.*

42. Kruzhkov, "Ballada o nashem sovremennike," 16.

43. Woll, *Real Images,* 132–133.

44. Quoted in ibid., 133.

45. M. Kvasnetskaia, "Dni nashei zhizni," *Komsomolskaia pravda,* 7 March 1962.

46. Sergei Zemlianukhin and Miroslava Segida, *Domashniaia sinemateka: Otechestvennoe kino, 1918–1996* (Moscow: Dubl-D, 1996), 112. The top box office draw of 1962, Gennady Kazansky and Vladimir Chebotaryov's *Amphibious Man* (*Chelovek amfibiia*), also dealt with the theme of "science and sacrifice," but in the more palatable form of science fiction. In the film, a Dr. Salvator wants to create an underwater utopia and has transplanted gills into his only child, Ikhtiander. The creepy premise

is made palatable by the beautiful tropical setting, by the idealism of the "mad scientist" Dr. Salvator, and by the fact that everyone is obviously foreign, not Soviet, and the outside world is thoroughly bourgeois. For a brief discussion of this film see Woll, *Real Images*, 125–127.

47. Zemlianukhin and Segida, *Domashniaia sinemateka*, 173. Tarkovskii's films *Andrei Rublev* (1966/71) and *Solaris* (*Soliaris*, 1972) were much less successful, with 2.9 and 10.5 million viewers, respectively. Only 277 copies of *Andrei Rublev* were printed. Zemlianukhin and Segida, *Domashniaia sinemateka*, 20, 418.

48. Zemlianukhin and Segida, *Domashniaia sinemateka,* 112, 426; James H. Krukones, "The Unspooling of Artkino: Soviet Film Distribution in America, 1940–1975," *Historical Journal of Film, Radio and Television* 29, no. 1 (March 2009): 104.

49. "Konkurs 1966. Itogi," 2, and "Liudy, filmy, fakty," 3–4.

50. In addition to works already cited, see, e.g., *Moi rezhisser Romm* (Moscow: Iskusstvo, 1993); Mark Zak, *Mikhail Romm i ego filmy* (Moscow: Iskusstvo, 1988); L. Pogozheva, *Mikhail Romm* (Moscow: Iskusstvo, 1967).

51. Rostislav Iurenev, *Kratkaia istoriia sovetskogo kino* (Moscow: Biuro propagandy sovetskogo kinoiskusstva, 1979), 203–204; Zemlianukhin and Segida, *Domashniaia sinemateka,* 161.

52. *Cue*, 10 October 1964; *Time*, 9 October 1964.

53. See, for instance, James Chapman, *Cinemas of the World* (London: Reaktion, 2003); David A. Cook, *A History of Narrative Film* (New York: W. W. Norton, 2004); Geoffrey Nowell-Smith, ed., *The Oxford History of World Cinema* (Oxford: Oxford University Press, 1997).

54. *Variety*, 3 June 1964.

55. *New Leader*, 10 December 1962. On the links between the CIA and the Congress for Cultural Freedom, the most prominent liberal intellectual and artistic movement to campaign against communism during the Cold War, see Frances Stonor Saunders, *Who Paid the Piper? The CIA and the Cultural Cold War* (London: Granta, 1999).

56. Norbert Wiener, "Some Moral and Technical Consequences of Automation," *Science* 131 (6 May 1960); W. J. Rorabaugh, *Kennedy and the Promise of the Sixties* (Cambridge: Cambridge University Press, 2002), 39.

57. John Lewis Gaddis, *We Now Know: Rethinking Cold War History* (Oxford: Oxford University Press, 1997), 273.

58. *Newsweek*, 4 March 1963; Allan Hunter, *Walter Matthau* (New York: St. Martin's, 1984), 55; *Variety*, 9 January 1963 and 3 June 1964; *Boxoffice*, 14 May 1964. The Committee for a Sane Nuclear Policy (SANE) was founded in the United States in 1957.

59. Joyce A. Evans, *Celluloid Mushroom Clouds: Hollywood and the Atomic Bomb* (Boulder, Colo.: Westview Press, 1998).

60. Lawrence Suid, *Guts and Glory: The Making of the American Military Image in Film* (Lexington: University Press of Kentucky, 2002); for discussion of Mann's *Strategic Air Command* see 220–222.

61. Jeanne Hall, "The Benefits of Hindsight: Re-visions of HUAC and the Film and Television Industries in *The Front* and *Guilty by Suspicion*," *Film Quarterly* 54, no. 2 (2001): 15–26.

62. Walter Bernstein, "Fail-Safe," 15 March 1963, Box 395, Motion Picture Scripts Collection (073), UCLA; Geoffrey M. Shurlock to Sol Schwartz, 15 April 1963, and Shurlock to M. J. Frankovich, 23 June 1964, Production Code Administration Files, AMPAS.

63. Suid, *Guts and Glory*, 235–238; *Newsday*, 7 May 1963.

64. John C. Flinn's production notes (undated), *Fail-Safe* Production Files, AMPAS; *Hollywood Citizen-News*, 26 April 1963; *Variety*, 24 April 1963; Lumet's commentary on *Fail-Safe* DVD (Sony Pictures, CDR 10252, 2007).

65. Lumet's commentary, *Fail-Safe* DVD.

66. Herman Kahn, *On Thermonuclear War* (Princeton, N.J.: Princeton University Press, 1960); Herman Kahn, *Thinking the Unthinkable* (New York: Avon Books, 1962); J. R. Newman, "Two Discussions of Thermonuclear War," *Scientific American* 204 (March 1961): 197–204.

67. Lawrence S. Wittner, *Resisting the Bomb: A History of the World Nuclear Disarmament Movement, 1954–1970* (Stanford, Calif.: Stanford University Press, 1997), 438; Barry M. Goldwater, *With No Apologies: The Personal and Political Memoirs of United States Senator Barry M. Goldwater* (New York: Morrow, 1979), 149.

68. Suid, *Guts and Glory*, 238–239; G. Tom Poe, "Historical Spectatorship around and about Stanley Kramer's *On the Beach*," in *Hollywood Spectatorship: Changing Perceptions of Cinema Audiences*, ed. Melvyn Stokes and Richard Maltby (London: BFI, 2001), 91–102.

69. *America*, 17 October 1964; *Boxoffice*, 14 May 1964; *Hollywood Citizen-News*, 16 November 1964.

70. *Commonweal*, 9 October 1964; *Boxoffice*, 29 March 1965; *Boxoffice*, 7 September 1964; http://www.imdb.com/title/tt0058083/awards (18 September 2009); *New Republic*, 12 September 1964; Campaign for Nuclear Disarmament National Council Minutes, 1–2 May 1965 and 4–5 December 1965, Modern Records Centre, University of Warwick, UK.

71. John Baxter, *Stanley Kubrick: A Biography* (London: HarperCollins, 1997), 165–198; *Film Daily*, 14 February 1963; *Variety*, 4 December 1963.

72. Frank R. Cunningham, *Sidney Lumet: Film and Literary Vision* (Lexington: University Press of Kentucky, 2001), 136–137.

73. *Observer* (London), 25 April 1965.

74. Hunter, *Walter Matthau*, 55; Lumet's commentary, *Fail-Safe* DVD; *Time*, 9 October 1964.

75. The *Fail-Safe* teleplay was directed by Stephen Frears: *Fail-Safe* DVD (Warner Bros., Z1 18653, 2000); *Film Review*, March 2006, 48–57; *Sight and Sound*, March 2007, 26–29.

CHAPTER 6: CONSERVATISM VERSUS ANARCHY

1. Exceptions are Aleksander Stefanovich's politically neutral *Dear Boy* (see chapter 2) and the anti-American *The Escape of Mr. MacKinley* (*Begstvo mistera MakKinli*, Mikhail Shveitser, 1975). See Sergei Dobrynin, "The Silver Curtain: Representations of the West in the Soviet Cold War Films," *History Compass* 7, no. 3 (2009): 870.

2. Aleksandr Karaganov, "Kino v borbe za sotsialnyi progress," *Sovetskii ekran, no.* 18 (1971): 4–5. On *They Shoot Horses, Don't They?*, a drama set around a Depression-era dance marathon and based on the book by Horace McCoy, see *Film Comment* 6, no. 4 (1970): 65–73.

3. See Denise J. Youngblood, *Russian War Films: On the Cinema Front, 1914–2005* (Lawrence: University Press of Kansas, 2007), chap. 7.

4. *Soldier Ivan Brovkin* was the most widely seen film of 1955, with 40.37 million viewers; *Keys to Heaven* drew 22.3 million. Zemlianukhin and Segida, *Domashniaia sinemateka: Otechestvennoe kino, 1918–1996* (Moscow: Dubl-D, 1996), 416, 198.

5. *Pervyi vek nashego kino: Entsiklopediia* (Moscow: Izd-vo Lokid-Press, 2006), 560.

6. "Rogovoi, Vladimir Avraamovich," in *Kino: Entsiklopedicheskii slovar* (Moscow: Sovetskaia entsiklopediia, 1986), 355.

7. Zemlianukhin and Segida, *Domashniaia sinemateka,* 313.

8. "Konkurs-71. Itogi," *Sovetskii ekran,* no. 10 (1972): 18.

9. "Deti" actually means children, not sons.

10. Harry Gelman, *The Brezhnev Politburo and the Decline of Détente* (Ithaca, N.Y.: Cornell University Press, 1984), 116.

11. "Georgii Iumatov," *Sovetskii ekran,* no. 18 (1971): 9. This article pointedly noted that Yumatov was a World War II veteran. It also reported that *Officers* was presently screening "with success."

12. Color came to predominate in Soviet cinema much, much later than in Hollywood. Even as late as 1971, the fact that *Officers* was in black and white would not have drawn much notice, and Soviet cinema was justifiably proud of the black-and-white work of its cinematographers.

13. Mike Bowker, "Brezhnev and Superpower Relations," in *Brezhnev Reconsidered,* ed. Edwin Bacon and Mark Sandle (Houndsmills: Palgrave Macmillan, 2002), 90; Roger R. Reese, *The Soviet Military Experience* (London: Routledge, 2000), 140.

14. Reese, *Soviet Military Experience,* 141, 143.

15. Roger R. Reese, *Red Commanders: A Social History of the Soviet Army Officer Corps, 1918–1991* (Lawrence: University Press of Kansas, 2005), 177.

16. Reese, *Soviet Military Experience,* 138, 143–144, 147.

17. Ibid., 149–151; Reese, *Red Commanders,* 193–195. Military hazing is called *dedovshchina* in Russian. The root word is *ded,* or grandfather, giving this practice a generational twist.

18. Reese, *Red Commanders,* 178.

19. "Bashmachi" means "bandits." This is what the Russians, and then the Soviets, dubbed nationalist and Islamist rebels in the region.

20. Soviet Air Force Major General N. Krasnoperov quoted these lines in his appreciation of the film, "Da, est takaia professiia!" *Sovetskii ekran,* no. 21 (1971): 5.

21. "Yegor" is a diminutive of "Georgy."

22. On the Basmachi Rebellion, see Alexander G. Park, *Bolshevism in Turkestan, 1917–1927* (New York: Columbia University Press, 1957), 40–42, 49–52.

23. In fact, Soviet policies were rather more self-serving. The government had actually expected the League of Nations to stop the Japanese advance. Viacheslav Molotov, chair of the Council of People's Commissars, remarked at the time: "All

this [the Japanese incursion] compels us to strengthen our vigilance as regards happenings in the Far East. We must not forget that our border lies along the Manchurian line." Quoted by Charles B. McLane, *Soviet Policy and the Chinese Communists, 1931–1946* (New York: Columbia University Press, 1958), 48.

24. See Stanley G. Payne, *The Spanish Civil War, the Soviet Union, and Communism* (New Haven, Conn.: Yale University Press, 2004).

25. Interview with Vasily Lanovoy, undated, "Dopolnitelnyi material," *Ofitsery,* Ruscico, 2000, DVD.

26. Lanovoy interview. In the Soviet system, it was impossible for a military film to be made without the military's thorough oversight, and this includes the military comedies like *Keys from Heaven.*

27. Krasnoperov, "Da, est takaia professiia!"

28. Lt. N. Cherkashin, "Eskiz sotsialnogo portreta," *Sovetskii ekran*, no 18 (1971): 4; Lt. Col. E. Bogdanov, "Neskolko pozhelanii," ibid., 4–5.

29. This scene is reminiscent of the wall scene in *Nine Days in One Year.*

30. "Rogovoi," *Kino*, 355. Neither of these films has attendance registered in Zemlianukhin and Segida's work.

31. Vladimir Ponizovskii, "Nasledniki pobedy," *Sovetskii ekran*, no. 9 (1975): 11.

32. Jeremy M. Devine, *Vietnam at 24 Frames a Second: A Critical and Thematic Analysis of over 400 Films about the Vietnam War* (Jefferson, N.C.: McFarland, 1995), 71–74, 182–195, 344–347; Tony Shaw, *Hollywood's Cold War* (Amherst: University of Massachusetts Press, 2007), 234–266.

33. *Hollywood Reporter*, 27 February 1970; John Baxter, *Woody Allen: A Biography* (New York: Carroll & Graf, 1998), 177–179.

34. Richard A. Schwartz, *Woody: From Antz to Zelig: A Reference Guide to Woody Allen's Creative Work, 1964–1998* (Westport, Conn.: Greenwood, 2000), 30; *Boxoffice*, 10 May 1971; *Los Angeles Herald-Examiner*, 12 July 1970; *Hollywood Reporter*, 25 June and 3 August 1970. On *Mad Magazine*'s skewering of so much of the Cold War consensus in the 1950s and 1960s, thereby anticipating much of what we see in *Bananas*, see Teodora Carabas, "Tales Calculated to Drive You MAD: The Debunking of Spies, Superheroes, and Cold War Rhetoric in *Mad Magazine*'s 'Spy vs Spy,'" *Journal of Popular Culture* 40, no. 1 (2007): 4–24.

35. Robert Benayoun, *The Films of Woody Allen* (New York: Harmony, 1986), 39; *Los Angeles Times*, 16 May 1971; *Films and Filming*, November 1971.

36. Stig Bjorkman, *Woody Allen on Woody Allen: In Conversation with Stig Bjorkman* (New York: Grove Press, 1993), 39; Baxter, *Woody Allen*, 194.

37. *Don't Drink the Water* was turned into a strained film, directed by Howard Morris, in 1969. See *Motion Picture Herald*, 19 November 1969. On *Casino Royale*, which had five different directors, see *Variety*, 19 April 1967.

38. On New Hollywood generally, see Peter Biskind, *Easy Riders, Raging Bulls: How the Sex 'n' Drugs 'n' Rock 'n' Roll Generation Saved Hollywood* (London: Bloomsbury, 1998).

39. For an easily accessible account of the Chicago Seven trial see *Time*, 2 March 1970, http://www.time.com/timemagazine/article/0,9171,904199–2,00 .html (3 November 2008). On the Hoover rumors see Richard Gid Powers, *Secrecy*

and Power: The Life of J. Edgar Hoover (London: Hutchinson, 1987), 171–172, 369–373.

40. *Los Angeles Herald-Examiner*, 14 May 1971.

41. Allen emphasized this media intertextuality elsewhere, including in a scene with a bogus Bob Hope acting as a decoy so government planes could bomb the rebels. Hope was an indefatigable performer in war zones and an ardent anticommunist who fully supported the U.S. war in Vietnam. Ultimately, the scene was deemed to look too much like a war documentary and, like several other sequences, was therefore left on the cutting room floor. Woody Allen and Mickey Rose, "El Weirdo AKA Bananas," January 1970, Writers Guild Foundation, Los Angeles.

42. William J. Palmer, *The Films of the Eighties: A Social History* (Carbondale: Southern Illinois University Press, 1993), 132–151.

43. Rhodri Jeffreys-Jones, *Cloak and Dagger: A History of American Secret Intelligence* (New Haven, Conn.: Yale University Press, 2002), 192, 211. One iteration of the script for *Bananas* emphasized the U.S. government's history of support for right-wing authoritarian leaders in the third world by a long scene showing Vargas attending a Dictators Convention in Chicago, then appearing on a U.S. children's television show. This scene did not appear in the final print. Woody Allen and Mickey Rose, "El Weirdo AKA Bananas," January 1970, Writers Guild Foundation, Los Angeles.

44. *Bananas'* "Execusizer" scene drew comparisons with the one in Charlie Chaplin's *Modern Times* (1936) where Chaplin's little tramp acts as the hapless guinea pig for a machine designed to feed workers without their needing to leave the production line. Chaplin had fled the United States as a suspected subversive at the height of McCarthyism and then issued a bitter critique of American culture via the British-made *A King in New York* (1957). In its portrayals of political hysteria and decadence, this film bore a number of parallels with *Bananas*. Wallace Brown, "Charles Chaplin's *A King in New York* Revisited," *Film and History* 22, no. 3 (September 1992): 88–98.

45. *National Review*, 6 June 1975, 621; *New York Times*, 23 March 1975, sec. 2, 1.

46. Cobbett Steinberg, *Reel Facts* (Harmondsworth: Penguin, 1981), 442; Richard A. Schwartz, *Cold War Culture: Media and the Arts, 1945–1990* (New York: Checkmark, 1998), 190–191; *New York Times*, 29 April 1971.

47. *Hollywood Reporter*, 28 April 1971; *Variety*, 28 April 1971; http://www.tcm.com/tcmdb/title.jsp?stid=17439&category=Notes (4 November 2008). The Legion of Decency changed its name in 1966.

48. *Motion Picture Herald*, 19 May 1971; *New Leader*, 31 May 1971; *Time*, 17 May 1971; *New York*, 3 May 1971.

49. Mark Feeney, *Nixon at the Movies: A Book about Belief* (Chicago: University of Chicago Press, 2004), xii.

50. Baxter, *Woody Allen*, 196–199.

51. U.S. Embassy, Bucharest, to USIA, Washington, 30 June 1975, Doc. No. 1975BUCHAR02916, File No. D750226–0826, United States National Archives, College Park, Maryland.

52. For a brief analysis of films like *The In-Laws* (Arthur Hiller, 1979), *Walker* (Alex Cox, 1987), and *Moon over Parador* (Paul Mazursky, 1988), plus others that featured the CIA, see Tony Shaw, "Our Man in Managua: Alex Cox, US Neo-

Imperialism and Transatlantic Cinematic Subversion in the 1980s," *Media History* 12, no. 2 (2006): 209–223, and *Films and Filming* (September 1979): 30–31, 49, and Palmer, *Eighties*, 149, 150, 222, 225–226, 229–232.

CHAPTER 7: LAST ACTS

1. Odd Arne Westad, *The Global Cold War* (Cambridge: Cambridge University Press, 2007), 316–326; S. J. Ball, *The Cold War: An International History* (London: Arnold, 1998), 186–190.

2. On television's development into a truly global cultural phenomenon by the 1980s see Anthony Smith, ed., *Television: An International History* (Oxford: Oxford University Press, 1998).

3. Tony Shaw, *Hollywood's Cold War* (Amherst: University of Massachusetts Press, 2007), 269–276. Note that the banning of indigenous films in the USSR was at its post–World War II height between 1968 and 1978.

4. The nuclear weapons issue returned to the screen in the early to mid-1980s after disappearing to an extent in the 1970s. Though one or two American movies, like *Red Dawn*, painted a sanitized picture of nuclear war, most reflected a deep sense of fear during a resurgent period in the U.S.-Soviet arms race. Even Soviet films like Konstantin Lopushansky's *Letters from a Dead Man* (*Pisma mertvogo cheloveka*, 1986) predicted nuclear catastrophe. Mick Broderick, *Nuclear Movies* (Jefferson, N.C.: McFarland, 1991), 145–191.

5. The term "evil empire" was first used at a speech before a conservative Christian group in Orlando, Florida, on March 8, 1983.

6. *Star Wars: A New Hope* (George Lucas, 1977), *The Empire Strikes Back* (Irvin Kershner, 1980), *Return of the Jedi* (Richard Marquand, 1983). See Nikolai Savitskii, "Na raznykh poliusakh: o neskolkikh amerikanskikh filmov," *Sovetskii ekran*, no. 12 (1984): 124. This article also attacked the first picture in what became the *Rambo* series, *First Blood* (Ted Kotcheff, 1982). See also Vladimir Chernenko, "Novye modeli agressii," *Sovetskii ekran*, no. 7 (1983): 17.

7. Sergei Zemlianukhin and Miroslava Segida, *Domashniaia sinemateka: Otechestvennoe kino* (Moscow: Dubl-D, 1996), 411.

8. This decline was obvious by the 1970s, when film attendance dropped by half compared to the 1960s. See *Sovetskoe kino semidesiatykh-pervoi poloviny vosmidesiatykh godov: Uchebnoe sposobie* (Moscow: VGIK, 2006), 9. As already noted, it continued to decline.

9. Zemlianukhin and Segida, *Domashniaia sinemateka*, 297. The film's title is sometimes translated as *Solitary Navigation*. In 1988, the number of viewers was reported as 40.7 million. See "Chto smotriat zriteli?" *Sovetskii ekran*, no. 9 (1988): 5.

Other examples of Cold War filmmaking at this time are three films from 1984/85: *Unmarked Freight* (*Gruz bez markirovki*, Vladimir Popkov, 35.9 million), *Can-Can in the English Garden* (*Kankan v angliiskom parke*, Valery Pidpaly, 18.3 million), and *Flight 222* (*Reis 222*, Sergei Mikaelian, 35.3 million; see chapter 2). *Unmarked Freight* tied with *Convoy* (Sam Peckinpah, 1978) as the second-ranked box office hit of 1985. See Richard Stites, *Russian Popular Culture: Entertainment and Society since 1900* (Cambridge: Cambridge University Press, 1992), 170–171, and Zemlianukhin and Segida, *Domashniaia sinemateka*, 102, 191.

10. Romil Sobolev, "Qvadrat poiska," *Iskusstvo 'kino,* no. 3 (1983): 43. This journal rarely reviewed popular films, focusing on art films and film theory. Oddly enough, *Soviet Screen* did not review either of these films, with only a brief notice in their "Coming Soon" department. See "Skoro," *Sovetskii ekran,* no. 23 (1982): 19, for an announcement of *Incident at Map Grid 36-80,* and "Skoro," *Sovetskii ekran,* no 10. (1986): 23, for an announcement of *Solo Voyage.* The oddity about the latter announcement, which appeared in May, is that the film's release date was 12 February 1986.

11. Quoted by John E. Moore, *The Soviet Navy Today* (New York: Stein & Day, 1976), 29.

12. Quoted by Bruce W. Watson, *Red Navy at Sea: Soviet Naval Operations on the High Seas, 1956–1980* (Boulder, Colo.: Westview Press, 1982), 5.

13. Ibid., 9; Donald W. Mitchell, *A History of Russian and Soviet Sea Power* (New York: Macmillan, 1976), 527.

14. Mitchell, *History of Russian and Soviet Sea Power,* 529, 535.

15. Jacob W. Kipp, "Soviet Naval Aviation," in *Soviet Naval Influence: Domestic and Foreign Dimensions,* ed. Michael MccGwire and John McDonnell (New York: Praeger Publishers, 1977), 209.

16. I have inferred that the film is situated in the North Atlantic; the film never says. For a description of these real-life exercises, see Robert G. Weinland, "The State and Future of the Soviet Navy in the North Atlantic," in MccGwire and McDonnell, *Soviet Naval Influence,* 413. On the Soviet side, this is almost certainly the Northern Fleet. Although the Baltic Fleet was in closer proximity, its ships were old and its task was limited to defending the Baltic. See Paul H. Nitze et al., *Securing the Seas: The Soviet Naval Challenge and Western Alliance Options* (Boulder, Colo.: Westview Press, 1979), 58.

17. Nitze, *Securing the Seas,* 57; Watson, *Red Navy at Sea,* 27.

18. Mitchell, *History of Russian and Soviet Sea Power,* 497.

19. "Volk" means "wolf" in Russian. Soviet naval air force officers carried army rather than navy ranks.

20. Watson, *Red Navy at Sea,* 11.

21. A loose end in the film is that the viewer never learns what happened to the Soviet rescue planes.

22. Thomas Nilsen, Igor Kudrik, Alexandr Nikitin, "The Russian Northern Fleet: Nuclear Submarine Accidents," *Bellona Report* 2, no. 96, http://spb.org.ru/bellona/ehome/russia/nfl/nf18.htm (27 August 2008). The Thresher went down in 1963 after deep-sea diving tests, at a loss of 129 men; the Scorpion disaster of 1968 is more mysterious. It is assumed that the sub and its 99-man crew were lost after an explosion of some type.

23. David R. Jones, "The Rise and Fall of Aeroflot: Civil Aviation in the Soviet Union, 1920–91," in *Russian Aviation and Air Power in the Twentieth Century,* ed. Robin Higham, John T. Greenwood, and Von Hardesty (London: Routledge, 1998), 236–238.

24. *Iskusstvo kino,* no. 3 (1983).

25. Sobolev, "Qvadrat poiska," 38.

26. "Soglasno ankete," *Sovetskii ekran,* no. 10 (1983): 1.

27. It is unclear whether the film is situated in the Pacific or the South Atlantic.

28. The ending, which appears to appeal to "Russian" rather than "Soviet" values, is the film's tiny subversive note.

29. http://www.boxofficemojo.com/movies/?id=ramb02.htm (30 January 2009); http://www.boxofficemojo.com/movies/?id=firstblood.htm (30 January 2009); http://www.boxofficemojo.com/movies/?id=ramb03.htm (30 January 2009). *Top Gun* made $176 million domestically and $353 worldwide: http://www.boxoffice mojo.com/movies/?id=topgun.htm (30 January 2009). The top-grossing American film of 1985 was Robert Zemeckis's *Back to the Future,* which made $210 million domestically and $381 million worldwide: http://www.boxofficemojo.com/ movies/?id=backtothefuture.htm (1 February 2009). According to Box Office Mojo, the average cost of an American cinema ticket in 1985 was $3.55. This roughly translates into 42 million viewers for *Rambo* domestically and 84 million worldwide. The aggregate figure for *Incident* and *Solo Voyage* is 71 million viewers.

30. *New York Times,* 17 May 1985; *Time,* 24 June 1985; *New Musical Express* (London), 10 August 1985; *Los Angeles Times,* 8 December 1985; *Hollywood Reporter,* 15 October 1985; *Los Angeles Times,* 15 November 1986.

31. *Variety,* 3 July 1985; *New Yorker,* 17 June 1985; Shaw, *Hollywood's Cold War,* 199–233. *The Green Berets* was directed by Wayne, Ray Kellogg, and Mervyn LeRoy.

32. *Silk Stockings* (Rouben Mamoulian, 1957), *The Shoes of the Fisherman* (Michael Anderson, 1968), *The Embassy* (Gordon Hessler, 1973), *The Innocent Bystanders* (Peter Collinson, 1973), and *Gulag* (Roger Young, 1984) are among the American films to feature this subject in one way or another.

33. Ironically, Woody Allen initially turned down Stallone for the mugger's role on the grounds that he did not look tough enough. Stig Bjorkman, *Woody Allen on Woody Allen: In Conversation with Stig Bjorkman* (New York: Grove Press, 1993), 93.

34. On Stallone's career and image see Frank Sanello, *Stallone: A Rocky Life* (New York: Mainstream, 1998).

35. *Time,* 24 June 1985; *Newsweek,* 23 December 1985; *Los Angeles Times,* 27 October 1985.

36. Sylvester Stallone and James Cameron, *Rambo: First Blood Part II* "Final Shooting Script," undated, American Film Institute, Los Angeles; Sylvester Stallone and James Cameron, screenplay, *Rambo: First Blood Part II,* 14 August 1984, Writers Guild Foundation, Los Angeles.

37. *Time,* 24 June 1985; Malcolm McConnell and Theodore G. Schweitzer, *Inside Hanoi's Secret Archives: Solving the MIA Mystery* (New York: Simon & Schuster, 1995), 174.

38. The MIA issue was hotly contested throughout the 1980s and beyond, but most reliable evidence suggests it was indeed a myth. Soon after the Cold War ended, in January 1993, the U.S. Senate Select Committee on POW/MIA Affairs of 1991–1993, led by Senators John Kerry, Bob Smith, and John McCain, reported there was "no compelling evidence that proves that any American remains alive in captivity in Southeast Asia." http://www.fas.org/irp/congress/1993_rpt/pow -exec.html (20 April 2008).

39. Hollywood movies released before *Rambo* that featured U.S. Vietnam War veterans trying to rescue American POWs in Southeast Asia include *Good Guys*

Wear Black (Ted Post, 1978), *Uncommon Valor* (Ted Kotcheff, 1983), *Missing in Action* (Joseph Zito, 1984), and *Missing in Action 2: The Beginning* (Lance Hool, 1985). None of these accused Moscow of complicity. Jeremy M. Devine, *Vietnam at 24 Frames a Second: A Critical and Thematic Analysis of Over 400 Films about the Vietnam War* (Jefferson, N.C.: McFarland, 1995), 119–120, 219–222.

40. Thomas Doherty, "*Rambo: First Blood Part II*," *Film Quarterly* (1 April 1986): 50–54.

41. *Mail on Sunday* (London), 25 August 1985.

42. The efforts Stallone especially put into molding Rambo's muscular stature, via weightlifting, and shaping his heroic character prior to filming are detailed in the scripts and in the *Rambo* production notes, BFIL.

43. On the relationship between "hard" bodies on screen and "hard-line" right-wing politics in the United States in the 1980s, see Susan Jeffords, *Hard Bodies: Hollywood Masculinity in the Reagan Era* (New Brunswick, N.J.: Rutgers University Press, 1994); Orman's quote is on 12.

44. It is interesting to note that the hero of the *Missing in Action* films, Braddock (played by former karate champion Chuck Norris), is half American Indian, too.

45. James Chapman argues that *Rambo* has been unfairly denigrated by critics and historians, and posits that the movie belongs to a tradition of popular cinema that exemplifies what, following Graham Dawson, we may term "the pleasure-culture of war." Chapman, *War and Film* (London: Reaktion, 2008), chap. 3.

46. *New Republic*, 1 July 1985.

47. *Newsweek*, 28 July 1986.

48. *Rocky IV* was the top moneymaker of the *Rocky* series and the only one to focus explicitly on the Cold War. It was the third-highest-grossing U.S. movie of 1985, taking $127 million domestically and $300 million worldwide: http://www.boxofficemojo.com/movies/?id=rocky4.htm (30 January 2009). See William J. Palmer, *The Films of the Eighties: A Social History* (Carbondale: Southern Illinois University Press, 1993), 218–222.

49. *Rambo* production notes, BFIL.

50. *Variety*, 16 October 1985; Palmer, *Eighties*, 213–218, 236–238; Devine, *Vietnam*, 327–331.

51. http://www.boxofficemojo.com/movies/?id=ramb02.htm (30 January 2009). *Top Gun* was rated PG-13.

52. Doherty, "*Rambo: First Blood Part II*," 50–54; *Village Voice*, 28 May 1985; *Chicago Tribune*, 27 June 1985; *Star*, 23 July 1985; *Los Angeles Times*, 25 December 1985.

53. *Los Angeles Daily News*, 25 July 1985; *Washington Post*, 22 May 1985; *Los Angeles Herald-Examiner*, 19 June 1985; *Los Angeles Daily News*, 12 July 1985.

54. Michael Rogin, *Ronald Reagan, The Movie: And Other Episodes in Political Demonology* (Berkeley: University of California Press, 1987), 7.

55. *New Musical Express* (London), 18 August 1985; Devine, *Vietnam*, 239, 321.

56. Devine, *Vietnam*, 317.

57. *Los Angeles Times*, 24 August 1985 and 6 November 1986; Chapman, *War and Film*, 178; *Time*, 24 June 1985; *Los Angeles Herald-Examiner*, 19 June 1985.

58. *Mail on Sunday* (London), 25 August 1985; *Guardian* (London), 4 January

1986; *New York Times*, 4 January 1986; email from historian Sergei Zhuk to Denise Youngblood, 11 February 2009.

59. "There is nothing friendly in Hollywood's view of our side." Iurii Agunov and Vladislav Orlov, "Boevaia raskraska Gollivuda—ili muzhskie prikliuchenie na Amerikanskikh maner," *Sovetskii ekran*, no. 9 (1987): 22.

60. *Los Angeles Times*, 3 August 1986; Palmer, *Eighties*, 213–215.

CONCLUSION

1. E. Kartseva, "Novaia model kinematografa: Gollivudski variant," *Iskusstvo kino*, no. 9 (1988): 123.

2. David Caute, *The Dancer Defects: The Struggle for Cultural Supremacy during the Cold War* (Oxford: Oxford University Press, 2003), 612.

3. Andrey Shcherbenok, "Asymmetric Warfare: Cold War Cinema in the Soviet Union and the United States," paper presented at the conference "Dream Factory of Communism: Cultural Practices and the Memory of the Cold War," Miami University, Oxford, Ohio, 2007.

4. Of course, homefront World War II films dealt with domestic issues, but the bulk of the pictures focused on the military battle front.

5. Shcherbenok, "Asymmetric Warfare."

6. Indeed, it is to be hoped that this study dispels conventional notions in the West that mainstream Soviet cinema was stiff, predictable, "black and white," and aggressively propagandistic.

7. Nancy Bernhard, *U.S. Television News and Cold War Propaganda, 1947–1960* (New York: Cambridge University Press, 1999); Michael Curtin, *Redeeming the Wasteland: Television Documentary and Cold War Politics* (New Brunswick, N.J.: Rutgers University Press, 1995); Daniel Hallin, *The "Uncensored" War: The Media and Vietnam* (Berkeley: University of California Press, 1989).

8. According to a 1983 U.S. public opinion survey, 92 percent said that in a communist country "you only hear news the government wants you to hear"; 91 percent agreed that "if you speak your mind, you risk going to jail"; and 84 percent rejected the notion that life for the average communist "is pretty much the same as in the United States." "Thus," writes John Kenneth White, "when Ronald Reagan dubbed the Soviet Union the 'evil empire,' most Americans (and many Russians) agreed with him." John Kenneth White, "Seeing Red: The Cold War and American Public Opinion," 3, paper delivered at the conference "The Power of Free Inquiry and Cold War International History," 25–26 September 1998, U.S. National Archives, College Park, Maryland: http://www.archives.gov/research/cold-war/conference/white.html (14 May 2009).

9. In the USSR, cinema's generally positive air undercut the many negative messages about the West that appeared in newspapers such as the official *Pravda* and *Izvestia* and on "wall newspapers," large public poster displays on the street and in parks, schools, and workplaces.

10. For a perceptive analysis of Balabanov's films and politics, see Nancy Condee, *The Imperial Trace: Recent Russian Cinema* (Oxford: Oxford University Press, 2009), chap. 8.

11. David MacFadyen, "Andrei Kravchuk: *The Admiral* (Admiral 2009)," *Kino-Kultura* 24 (April 2009), www.kinokultura.com/2009/24r-admiral-dmf.shtml.

12. "*Olympius Inferno,*" *Russia Today* (29 March 2009), http://www.russiatoday.com/Art_and_Fun/2009–03–29/Olympius_Inferno. Anti-Americanism is much more pronounced in other aspects of Russian life. See Cathy Young, "From Russia with Loathing," *New York Times,* 21 November 2008, www.nytimes.com/2008/11/21/opinion/21young.html?_r=2.

13. These appeared in, for instance, *Aurora: Operation Intercept* (Paul Levine, 1995), *Golden Eye* (Martin Campbell, 1986), *The Peacemaker* (Mimi Leder, 1997), and *The Saint* (Philip Noyce, 1997).

14. http://www.sayitinrussianmovie.com (20 May 2009); *Variety,* 4 June 2007.

15. *Sight and Sound* (October 2006): 20–23; *Film Review* (July 2006): 52–60; Robert Brent Toplin, *Fahrenheit 9/11: How One Film Divided a Nation* (Lawrence: University Press of Kansas, 2006); *Variety,* 18 October 2004; *Variety,* 30 April 2007; *Variety,* 14 May 2007; *Variety,* 17 October 2005; *Variety,* 5 June 2006.

16. Fyodor Bondarchuk's *Company 9* (*9-ia rota,* 2005) is putatively set in Afghanistan, although the details are more suited to the Chechen conflict; see Denise J. Youngblood, *Russian War Films: On the Cinema Front, 1914–2005* (Lawrence: University Press of Kansas, 2007), 207–208. For a Russian view of the film, which was extremely popular in the Russian Federation, see Valerii Kichin, "Po tu storonu podviga," *Rossiiskaia gazeta,* www.film.ru/article.asp?ID=4263.

17. *Guardian* (London), 15 April 2005; David MacFadyen, "Evgenii Lavrent'ev, *Countdown* (*Lichnyi nomer*) (2004)," *KinoKultura* (October 2005), http://www.kinokultura/reviews/R10–05/lichnyinomer.html. There have been four films in the *Die Hard* series, spanning twenty years (1988, 1990, 1995, and 2007).

Select Bibliography

Unpublished Material
American Film Institute, Los Angeles
Miscellaneous scripts

British Film Institute Library, London, UK (BFIL)
Miscellaneous press books, scripts, and marketing files

Gosfilmofond, Belye Stolby, Russian Federation
Ministerstvo kinematografii

*Margaret Herrick Library, Academy of Motion Picture Arts and
Sciences, Los Angeles (AMPAS)*
Miscellaneous press books, scripts, clippings files, production files, and marketing
files
Paramount and William Wyler Collections
Production Code Administration Files

Modern Records Centre, University of Warwick, Coventry, UK
Campaign for Nuclear Disarmament Archives

United States National Archives, College Park, Maryland
Record Group 59: Department of State
Record Group 306: United States Information Agency

University of California, Los Angeles (UCLA)
Motion Picture Scripts Collection
Twentieth Century-Fox Legal Files and Script Collection
William Wyler Papers

University of Southern California, Los Angeles (USC)
Twentieth Century-Fox Collection

Writers Guild Foundation, Los Angeles
Miscellaneous scripts

Published Documentary Sources

Department of State Bulletin, Vol. 39, No. 3, 1958

U.S. Congress. Senate. Committee on Foreign Relations. Subcommittee on Overseas Information Programs. *Overseas Information Programs of the United States.* Washington, D.C.: Government Printing Office, 1953.

Newspapers and Periodicals

Sources of reviews and contemporary articles can be traced through the endnotes. Where film reviews or newspaper articles are cited without a page reference, the sources are the Academy of Motion Picture Arts and Sciences clippings files or the British Film Institute microfiche collection.

Soviet Union

Komsomolskaia pravda; Literaturnaia gazeta; Ogonek; Pravda; Sovetskaia kultura; Vecherniaia Moskva.

United Kingdom

Daily Worker; Guardian; Mail on Sunday; New Musical Express; Observer; Sunday Times; The Times.

United States

America; Chicago Tribune; Commonweal; Life; Look; Los Angeles Daily News; Los Angeles Examiner; Los Angeles Herald-Examiner; Los Angeles Times; Nation; National Review; New Leader; New Republic; New York; New York Times; New Yorker; Newsday; Newsweek; Playboy; Saturday Review of Literature; Star; Time; Village Voice; Wall Street Journal; Washington Post.

Film Journals and Trade Papers

Soviet Union

Iskusstvo kino; Sovetskii ekran.

United Kingdom

Films and Filming; Sight and Sound.

United States

American Film; Boxoffice; Cineaste; Cue; Film Comment; Film Daily; Film Daily Year Book; Hollywood Citizen-News; Hollywood Reporter; Jump Cut; Motion Picture Daily; Motion Picture Exhibitor; Motion Picture Herald; Photoplay; Variety.

Books and Articles

Abramov, Al. "*Vstrecha na Elbe.*" *Vecherniaia Moskva,* 12 March 1949.

Adler, Les K., and Thomas G. Paterson. "Red Fascism: The Merger of Nazi Germany and Soviet Russia in the American Image of Totalitarianism, 1930s–1950s." *American Historical Review* 75, no. 4 (April 1970).

Agunov, Iurii, and Vladislav Orlov. "Boevaia raskraska Gollivuda—ili muzhskie prikliuchenie na Amerikanskikh maner." *Sovetskii ekran,* no. 9 (1987).

Aksyonov, Vasily. *In Search of Melancholy Baby.* Trans. Michael Henry Heim and Antonina Bouis. New York: Random House, 1985.

Aldgate, Anthony, and Jeffrey Richards. *Britain Can Take It: The British Cinema in the Second World War.* Edinburgh: Edinburgh University Press, 1994.

Aleksandrov, Grigorii. "Dva mira." *Ogonek,* no. 12 (1949).

―――. *Epokha i kino.* Moscow: Izd-vo politicheskoi literatury, 1976.

―――. *Gody poiskov i trudy.* Moscow: Soiuz kinematografistov SSSR / Biuro propagandy sovetskogo kinoiskusstva, 1975.

Aleksandrova, Nadezhda. "*Vesna na Zarechnoi ulitse.*" In *Rossiiskii illiuzion.* Moscow: Materik, 2003.

"Alexander Godunov." *Russian Life* (July / August 2009).

Amlinskii, Vl. "Novyi film Mikhail Romma." *Sovetskaia kultura,* 2 February 1962.

Andreev, Feliks. "SSHA: Filmy, liudi, vstrechi." *Sovetskii ekran,* no. 14 (1989).

Anninskii, Lev. *Shestidesiatniki i my: Kinematograf, stavshii i ne stavshii istoriei.* Moscow: Soiuz kinematografistov SSSR, 1991.

"ASK: Net pregrad dlia sotrudnichestva." *Iskusstvo kino,* no. 9 (1988).

"Atomy i liudi." *Pravda,* 20 March 1962.

Attwood, Lynne. *Red Women on the Silver Screen.* London: Pandora, 1993.

Azadovskii, Konstantin, and Boris Egorov. "From Anti-Westernism to Anti-Semitism: Stalin and the Impact of the 'Anti-Cosmopolitan' Campaigns on Soviet Culture." *Journal of Cold War Studies* 4, no. 1 (Winter 2000).

Babitsky, Paul, and John Rimberg. *The Soviet Film Industry.* New York: Praeger, 1955.

Ball, S. J. *The Cold War: An International History.* London: Arnold, 1998.

Baskakov, V. "Ekrannaia agressiia." *Iskusstvo kino,* no. 3 (1983).

Baxter, John. *Stanley Kubrick: A Biography.* London: HarperCollins, 1997.

―――. *Woody Allen: A Biography.* New York: Carroll & Graf, 1998.

Belmonte, Laura. "A Family Affair? Gender, the US Information Agency, and Cold War Ideology, 1945–1960." In *Culture and International History,* ed. Jessica Gienow-Hecht and Frank Schumacher. New York: Berghahn, 2003.

Belov, F. "Kak priobretaiutsia zarubezhnykh filmov." *Sovetskii ekran,* no. 6 (1972).

Benayoun, Robert. *The Films of Woody Allen.* New York: Harmony, 1986.

Berghahn, Daniela. *Hollywood behind the Wall: The Cinema of East Germany.* Manchester: Manchester University Press, 2005.

Berlin, Isaiah. *The Soviet Mind: Russian Culture under Communism.* Ed. Henry Hardy. Washington, D.C.: Brookings Institution Press, 2004.

Bernhard, Nancy. *U.S. Television News and Cold War Propaganda, 1947–1960.* New York: Cambridge University Press, 1999.

Bessel, Richard. *Germany 1945: From War to Peace.* New York: HarperCollins, 2009.

Beumers, Birgit. *A History of Russian Cinema.* Oxford: Berg, 2009.

Biskind, Peter. *Easy Riders, Raging Bulls: How the Sex 'n' Drugs 'n' Rock 'n' Roll Generation Saved Hollywood.* London: Bloomsbury, 1998.

―――. *Seeing Is Believing: How Hollywood Taught Us to Stop Worrying and to Love the Fifties.* New York: Pantheon, 1983.

Bittner, Stephen V. *The Many Lives of Khrushchev's Thaw: Experience and Memory in Moscow's Arbat.* Ithaca, N.Y.: Cornell University Press, 2008.

Bjorkman, Stig. *Woody Allen on Woody Allen: In Conversation with Stig Bjorkman*. New York: Grove Press, 1993.

Black, Gregory D. "Movies, Politics, and Censorship: The Production Code Administration and Political Censorship of Film Content." *Journal of Policy History* 3, no. 2 (1991).

Bogdanov, E. "Neskolko pozhelanii." *Sovetskii ekran*, no. 18 (1971).

Bowker, Mike. "Brezhnev and Superpower Relations." In *Brezhnev Reconsidered*, ed. Edwin Bacon and Mark Sandle. Houndsmills: Palgrave Macmillan, 2002.

Briley, Ron. "John Wayne and *Big Jim McLain* (1952): The Duke's Cold War Legacy." *Film & History* 3, no. 1 (2001).

Broderick, Mick. *Hibakusha Cinema: Hiroshima, Nagasaki and the Nuclear Image in Japanese Film*. London: Kegan Paul, 1996.

———. *Nuclear Movies*. Jefferson, N.C.: McFarland, 1991.

Brodsky, Joseph. "Spoils of War." In *On Grief and Reason: Essays*. New York: Farrar, Straus, Giroux, 1995.

Brooks, Jeffrey. *Thank You Comrade Stalin! Soviet Public Culture from Revolution to Cold War*. Princeton, N.J.: Princeton University Press, 2000.

Brown, Archie. "Perestroika and the End of the Cold War." *Cold War History* 7, no. 1 (February 2007).

Brown, Wallace. "Charles Chaplin's *A King in New York* Revisited." *Film and History* 22, No. 3 (September 1992)

Brownlow, Kevin. *Behind the Mask of Innocence: Sex, Violence, Prejudice, Crime—Films of Social Conscience in the Silent Era*. Berkeley: University of California Press, 1990.

Buckley, Réka. "Elsa Martinelli: Italy's Audrey Hepburn." *Historical Journal of Film, Radio and Television* 26, no. 3 (August 2006).

Carabas, Teodora. "Tales Calculated to Drive You MAD: The Debunking of Spies, Superheroes, and Cold War Rhetoric in *Mad Magazine*'s 'Spy vs. Spy.'" *Journal of Popular Culture* 40, no. 1 (2007).

Carruthers, Susan L. "Between Camps: Eastern Bloc 'Escapees' and Cold War Borderlands." *American Quarterly* 57, no. 3 (2005).

Casey, Steven. *Selling the Korean War: Propaganda, Politics, and Public Opinion in the United States, 1950–1953*. Oxford: Oxford University Press, 2007.

Caute, David. *The Dancer Defects: The Struggle for Cultural Supremacy during the Cold War*. Oxford: Oxford University Press, 2003.

———. *The Great Fear: The Anti-Communist Purge under Truman and Eisenhower*. New York: Simon & Schuster, 1978.

Ceplair, Larry, and Steven Englund. *The Inquisition in Hollywood: Politics in the Film Community, 1930–1960*. Berkeley: University of California Press, 1979.

Chanan, Michael. *Cuban Cinema*. Minneapolis: University of Minnesota Press, 2004.

Chapman, James. *Cinemas of the World*. London: Reaktion, 2003.

———. *War and Film*. London: Reaktion Books, 2008.

Cherkashin, N. "Eskiz sotsialnogo portreta." *Sovetskii ekran*, no. 18 (1971).

Chernenko, Vladimir. "Novye modeli agressii." *Sovetskii ekran*, no. 7 (1983).

Chiaureli, Mikhail. "Dva mira." *Literaturnaia gazeta*. 9 March 1949.

"Chto smotriat zriteli?" *Sovetskii ekran*, no. 9 (1988).

"Chto zh, davaite sporit!" *Sovetskii ekran*, no. 20 (1986).

Ciment, Michel, ed. *Elia Kazan: An American Odyssey*. London: Bloomsbury, 1988.

Clark, Katerina, and Evgeny Dobrenko, eds., with Andrei Artizov and Oleg Naumov, comps. *Soviet Culture and Power: A History in Documents, 1917–1953*. Trans. Marian Schwartz. New Haven, Conn.: Yale University Press, 2007.

Condee, Nancy. *The Imperial Trace: Recent Russian Cinema*. Oxford: Oxford University Press, 2009.

Cook, David A. *A History of Narrative Film*. New York: W. W. Norton, 2004.

Coppa, Frank J. "Pope Pius XII and the Cold War: The Post-war Confrontation between Catholicism and Communism." In *Religion and the Cold War*, ed. Diane Kirby. Houndsmills: Palgrave Macmillan, 2003.

Coyne, Michael. "*Seven Days in May*: History, Prophecy, and Propaganda." In *Windows on the Sixties: Exploring Key Texts of Media and Culture*, ed. Antony Aldgate, James Chapman, and Arthur Marwick. London: I. B. Tauris, 2000.

Cull, Nicholas J. *The Cold War and the United States Information Agency: American Propaganda and Public Diplomacy, 1945–1989*. Cambridge: Cambridge University Press, 2008.

Cunningham, Frank R. *Sidney Lumet: Film and Literary Vision*. Lexington: University Press of Kentucky, 2001.

Curtin, Michael. *Redeeming the Wasteland: Television Documentary and Cold War Politics*. New Brunswick, N.J.: Rutgers University Press, 1995.

Davies, Sarah. "Soviet Cinema and the Early Cold War: Pudovkin's *Admiral Nakhimov* in Context." *Cold War History* 4, no. 1 (October 2003). Reprinted in *Across the Blocs: Cold War Cultural and Social History*, ed. Rana Mitter and Patrick Major. London: Frank Cass, 2004.

Davis, Peter. Commentary on *Hearts and Minds* DVD. Criterion, 2005.

Demin, Viktor. "Initsiativa." Pt. 2. *Iskusstvo kino*, no. 1/2 (1987).

Devine, Jeremy M. *Vietnam at 24 Frames a Second: A Critical and Thematic Analysis of over 400 Films about the Vietnam War*. Jefferson, N.C.: McFarland, 1995.

Dizard, Wilson P. *Inventing Public Diplomacy*. Boulder, Colo.: Lynne Rienner, 2004.

Dobrenko, Evgeny. "Late Stalinist Cinema and the Cold War: An Equation without Unknowns." Trans. Birgit Beumers. *Modern Languages Review* 98, no. 4 (2003).

Dobrokhotov, Iu. "*Rimskie kanikuly*." *Sovetskii ekran*, no. 23 (1958).

Dobrynin, Sergei. "The Silver Curtain: Representations of the West in the Soviet Cold War Films." *History Compass* 7, no. 3 (2009).

Doherty, Thomas. *Cold War, Cool Medium: Television, McCarthyism, and American Culture*. New York: Columbia University Press, 2003.

———. "Hollywood's Agit-Prop: The Anti-Communist Cycle, 1948–1954." *Journal of Film and Video* 40, no. 4 (Fall 1988).

———. *Hollywood's Censor: Joseph I. Breen and the Production Code Administration*. New York: Columbia University Press, 2007.

———. *Projections of War: Hollywood, American Culture and World War II*. New York: Columbia University Press, 1999.

———. "*Rambo: First Blood Part II*." *Film Quarterly* (1 April 1986).

Donskoi, Mark. "*Raduga*." *Sovetskii ekran*, no. 3 (1969).

Dudziak, Mary L. *Cold War Civil Rights.* Princeton, N.J.: Princeton University Press, 2000.

Duggan, Christopher, and Christopher Wagstaff, eds. *Italy in the Cold War.* Oxford: Berg, 1995.

Egorova, Tatiana. *Soviet Film Music: An Historical Survey.* Trans. Tatiana A. Ganf and Natalia A. Egunova. Amsterdam: Harwood Academic, 1997.

Eidelman, Tamara. "Spring on the Silver Screen." *Chtenia: Readings from Russia,* no. 2 (Spring 2008).

Eldridge, David. "'Dear Owen': The CIA, Luigi Luraschi and Hollywood, 1953." *Historical Journal of Film, Radio and Television* 20, no. 2 (June 2000).

"Elem Klimov: Nash chelovek v Los-Andzhelese." *Sovetskii ekran,* no. 14 (1988).

Ellwood, David. "Italian Modernisation and the Propaganda of the Marshall Plan." In *The Art of Persuasion: Political Communications in Italy from 1945 to the 1990s,* ed. Luciano Cheles and Lucio Sponza. Manchester: Manchester University Press, 2001.

Etheridge, Brian C. "*The Desert Fox*: Memory, Diplomacy, and the German Question in Early Cold War America." *Diplomatic History* 32, no. 2 (April 2008).

Evans, Joyce A. *Celluloid Mushroom Clouds: Hollywood and the Atomic Bomb.* Boulder, Colo.: Westview Press, 1998.

Feeney, Mark. *Nixon at the Movies: A Book about Belief.* Chicago: University of Chicago Press, 2004.

Filene, Peter. "'Cold War Culture' Doesn't Say It All." In *Rethinking Cold War Culture,* ed. Peter J. Kuznick and James Gilbert. Washington, D.C.: Smithsonian Institution Press, 2001.

Fitzgerald, Frances. *Way Out There in the Blue: Reagan, Star Wars and the End of the Cold War.* New York: Simon & Schuster, 2000.

Fomin, Valerii I. *Kino i vlast: Sovetskoe kino, 1965–1985 gody: Dokumenty, svidetelstva, razmyshleniia.* Moscow: Materik, 1996.

————. *Kino na voine: Dokumenty, svidetelstva, kommentarii.* Moscow: Materik, 2005.

Forbes, Jill. "Winning Hearts and Minds: The American Cinema in France 1945–49." *French Cultural Studies* 8, no. 1 (1997): 29–40.

Fox, Jo. *Film Propaganda in Britain and Nazi Germany: World War II Cinema.* Oxford: Berg, 2007.

Freedland, Michael. *Gregory Peck: A Biography.* London: William Morrow, 1980.

Freilikh, S. *Mikhail Romm: Ispoved kino-rezhissera.* Moscow: Iskusstvo, 1988.

Fried, Richard. *Nightmare in Red: The McCarthy Era in Perspective.* Oxford: Oxford University Press, 1991.

Fürst, Julianne. "The Arrival of Spring? Changes and Continuities in Soviet Youth Culture and Policy between Stalin and Khrushchev." In *The Dilemmas of De-Stalinization: Negotiating Cultural and Social Change in the Khrushchev Era,* ed. Polly Jones. London: Routledge, 2006.

————. "The Importance of Being Stylish: Youth, Culture, and Identity in Late Stalinism." In *Late Stalinist Russia: Society between Reconstruction and Reinvention,* ed. Julianne Fürst. London: Routledge, 2006.

Gabrilovich, Evgenii. "Vsego neskolko dnei." *Literaturnaia gazeta,* 27 February 1962.

Gaddis, John Lewis. *We Now Know: Rethinking Cold War History.* Oxford: Oxford University Press, 1997.

Gelasimov, Andrei. "A Tender Age." Trans. Susanna Nazarova. *Chtenia: Readings from Russia,* no. 2 (Spring 2008).

Gelman, Harry. *The Brezhnev Politburo and the Decline of Détente.* Ithaca, N.Y.: Cornell University Press, 1984.

"Georgii Iumatov." *Sovetskii ekran,* no. 18 (1971).

Gianos, Phillip L. *Politics and Politicians in American Film.* Westport, Conn.: Praeger, 1998.

Goldwater, Barry M. *With No Apologies: The Personal and Political Memoirs of United States Senator Barry M. Goldwater.* New York: Morrow, 1979.

Golovskoi, Valerii, with John Rimberg. *Behind the Soviet Screen: The Motion Picture Industry in the USSR, 1972–1982.* Trans. Steven Hill. Ann Arbor, Mich.: Ardis, 1986.

———. *Mezhdu ottepeliu i glasnostiu: Kinematograf 70-x.* Moscow: Materik, 2004.

Golovskoy, Val. See Golovskoi, Valerii.

Graffy, Julian. "Cinema." In *Russian Cultural Studies: An Introduction,* ed. Catriona Kelly and David Shepherd. Oxford: Oxford University Press, 1998.

———. "Scant Signs of Thaw: Fear and Anxiety in the Representation of Foreigners in the Soviet Films of the Khrushchev Years." In *Russia and Its Other(s) on Film: Screening Intercultural Dialogue,* ed. Stephen Hutchings. Houndsmills: Palgrave Macmillan, 2008.

Guback, Thomas. "Hollywood's International Market." In *The American Film Industry,* ed. Tino Balio. Madison: University of Wisconsin Press, 1976.

Gundle, Stephen. "Hollywood Glamour and Mass Consumption in Postwar Italy." *Journal of Cold War Studies* 4, no. 3 (Summer 2002).

Hall, Jeanne. "The Benefits of Hindsight: Re-visions of HUAC and the Film and Television Industries in *The Front* and *Guilty by Suspicion.*" *Film Quarterly* 54, no. 2 (2001).

Hallin, Daniel. *The "Uncensored" War: The Media and Vietnam.* Berkeley: University of California Press, 1989.

Hammarstrom, David Lewis. *Circus Rings around Russia.* Hamden, Conn.: Archon, 1983.

Hansen, Peter. *Dalton Trumbo, Hollywood Rebel: A Critical Survey and Filmography.* Jefferson, N.C.: McFarland, 2007.

Harmetz, Aljean. "U.S. and Soviet Film Makers Plan Joint Ventures." *New York Times,* 7 February 1988.

Harris, Warren G. *Audrey Hepburn: A Biography.* New York: Simon & Schuster, 1994.

Hashamova, Yana. *Pride and Panic: Russian Imagination of the West in Post-Soviet Film.* Bristol: Intellect Books, 2007.

High, Peter B. *The Imperial Screen: Japanese Film Culture in the Fifteen Years' War, 1931–1945.* Madison: University of Wisconsin Press, 2003.

Higham, Robin, John T. Greenwood, and Von Hardesty, eds. *Russian Aviation and Air Power in the Twentieth Century.* London: Routledge, 1998.

Hirano, Kyoko. *Mr. Smith Goes to Tokyo: Japanese Cinema under the American Occupation, 1945–1952.* Washington, D.C.: Smithsonian Institution Press, 1992.

Hirsch, Francine. "The Soviets at Nuremberg: International Law, Propaganda, and the Making of the Postwar Order." *American Historical Review* 113, no. 3 (June 2008).

Hixson, Walter L. *Parting the Curtain: Propaganda, Culture and the Cold War, 1945–1961*. Basingstoke: Macmillan, 1997.

Hunter, Allan. *Walter Matthau*. New York: St. Martin's, 1984.

Hurd, Geoffrey, ed. *National Fictions: The Second World War in British Films and Television*. London: BFI, 1984.

Huston, John. *An Open Book*. Cambridge, Mass.: Da Capo, 1994.

Hutchings, Stephen, ed. *Russia and Its Other(s) on Screen: Screening Intercultural Dialogue*. Houndsmills: Palgrave Macmillan, 2008.

Igarashi, Yoshikuni. *Bodies of Memory: Narratives of War in Post-war Japanese Culture, 1945–1970*. Princeton, N.J.: Princeton University Press, 2000.

Ignateva, N. "Nachalo puti." *Literaturnaia gazeta*, 1 December 1956.

Istoriia sovetskogo kino. Vol. 3: *1941–1952*. Moscow: Iskusstvo, 1975.

Istoriia sovetskogo kino. Vol. 4: *1952–1967*. Moscow: Iskusstvo, 1978.

Iurenev, Rostislav. *Kratkaia istoriia sovetskogo kino*. Moscow: Biuro propagandy sovetskogo kinoiskusstva, 1979.

Jacobson, Matthew Frye, and Gaspar Gonzalez. *What Have They Built You to Do? The Manchurian Candidate and Cold War America*. Minneapolis: University of Minnesota Press, 2006.

Jeffords, Susan. *Hard Bodies: Hollywood Masculinity in the Reagan Era*. New Brunswick, N.J.: Rutgers University Press, 1994.

Jeffreys-Jones, Rhodri. *Cloak and Dagger: A History of American Secret Intelligence*. New Haven, Conn.: Yale University Press, 2002.

Jewison, Norman. *This Terrible Business Has Been Good to Me: An Autobiography*. New York: Key Porter Books, 2004.

Johnson, Glen M. "Sharper than an Irish Serpent's Tooth: Leo McCarey's *My Son John*." *Journal of Popular Film and Television* 8, no. 1 (1980).

Johnson, Vida T., and Graham Petrie. *The Films of Andrei Tarkovsky: A Visual Fugue*. Bloomington: Indiana University Press, 1994.

Johnson, William Bruce. *Miracles and Sacrilege: Roberto Rossellini, the Church, and Film Censorship in Hollywood*. Toronto: University of Toronto Press, 2008.

Johnston, Eric. "A Frontline Post." *Film Daily Yearbook* (1951).

Jones, David R. "The Rise and Fall of Aeroflot: Civil Aviation in the Soviet Union, 1920–1991." In *Russian Aviation and Air Power in the Twentieth Century*, ed. Robin Higham, John T. Greenwood, and Von Hardesty. London: Routledge, 1998.

Judt, Tony. *Postwar: A History of Europe since 1945*. London: Pimlico, 2005.

Kahn, Herman. *On Thermonuclear War*. Princeton, N.J.: Princeton University Press, 1960.

———. *Thinking the Unthinkable*. New York: Avon Books, 1962.

Kapterev, Sergei. "Illusionary Spoils: Soviet Attitudes towards American Cinema during the Early Cold War." *Kritika* 10, no. 4 (Fall 2009).

———. *Post-Stalinist Cinema and the Russian Intelligentsia, 1953–1960: Strategies of Self-Representation, De-Stalinization, and the National Cultural Tradition*. Saarbrücken: VDM Verlag Dr. Müller, 2008.

Karaganov, Aleksandr. "Kino v borbe za sotsialnyi progress." *Sovetskii ekran*, no. 18 (1971).

Kartseva, E. "Novaia model kinematografa: gollivudskii variant." *Iskusstvo kino*, no. 9 (1988).

Katz, Ephraim. *The Macmillan International Film Encyclopedia*. London: HarperCollins, 1998.

Kauffmann, Stanley. "*Roman Holiday.*" *American Film* (April 1978).

Kazan, Elia. *A Life*. New York: Alfred A. Knopf, 1988.

Kelly, Andrew. *Cinema and the Great War*. London: Routledge, 1997.

Keghel, Isabelle de. "*Meeting on the Elbe (Vstrecha na El'be):* A Visual Representation of the Incipient Cold War from a Soviet Perspective." *Cold War History* 9, no. 4 (November 2009).

Kenez, Peter. *Cinema and Soviet Society, 1917–1953*. Cambridge: Cambridge University Press, 1992.

————. "The Picture of the Enemy in Stalinist Films." In *Insiders and Outsiders in Russian Cinema*, ed. Stephen M. Norris and Zara M. Torlone. Bloomington: Indiana University Press, 2008.

Kent, Peter C. "The Lonely Cold War of Pius XII." In *Religion and the Cold War*, ed. Diane Kirby. Houndsmills: Palgrave Macmillan, 2003.

Khemblet, Charlz. "Kto ubil Merilin Monro?" *Sovetskii ekran*, no. 9 (1968).

Khutsiev, Marlen. "Ia nikogda ne delal polemicheskikh filmov." In Troianovskii, *Kinematograf ottepeli*. Vol. 1. Moscow: Materik, 1996.

Kichin, Valerii. "Po tu storonu podviga." *Rossiiskaia gazeta*. N.d. http://www.film.ru/article.asp?ID=4263.

Kino: Entsiklopedicheskii slovar. Moscow: Sovetskaia entsiklopediia, 1986.

Kipp, Jacob W. "Soviet Naval Aviation." In *Soviet Naval Influence: Domestic and Foreign Dimensions*, ed. Michael MccGwire and John McDonnell. New York: Praeger, 1977.

Kogda film okonchen: Govoriat rezhissery Mosfilma. Moscow: Iskusstvo, 1964.

Kokarev, Andrei. "Iz Rossii—s liubovem." *Sovetskii ekran*, no. 13 (1988).

Kokarev, I. "Mify i realnost," *Sovetskii ekran*, no. 13 (1983).

"Konkurs 1966. Itogi." *Sovetskii ekran*, no. 1 (1967).

"Konkurs-67. Itogi." *Sovetskii ekran*, no. 10 (1968).

"Konkurs-71. Itogi." *Sovetskii ekran*, no. 10 (1972).

"Konkurs SE—1981." *Sovetskii ekran*, no. 10 (1982).

Koppes, Clayton R., and Gregory D. Black. *Hollywood Goes to War: How Politics, Profits, and Propaganda Shaped World War II Movies*. New York: Free Press, 1987.

Kornov, Iurii. "Zapreshchennye igry." *Sovetskii ekran*, no. 7 (1978).

Kovalov, Oleg. "Zvezda nad stepiu: Amerika v zerkale sovetskogo kino." *Iskusstvo kino*, no. 10 (2003).

Krasnoperov, N. "Da, est takaia professiia!" *Sovetskii ekran*, no. 21 (1971).

Krementsov, Nikolai. "In the Shadow of the Bomb: U.S.-Soviet Biomedical Relations in the Early Cold War." *Journal of Cold War Studies* 9, no. 4 (Fall 2007).

Kristmanson, Mark. "Love Your Neighbour: The Royal Canadian Mounted Police and the National Film Board, 1948–53." *Film History* 10, no. 3 (1998).

Krukones, James H. "The Unspooling of Artkino: Soviet Film Distribution in America, 1940–1975." *Historical Journal of Film, Radio and Television* 29, no. 1 (March 2009).

Kruzhkov, Nik. "Ballada o nashem sovremennike." *Ogonek*, no. 12 (March 1962).

Kuznetsov, M. "Esli by chelovechestvo sostoialo iz Gusevykh." *Sovetskii ekran*, no. 6 (1962).

Kvasnetskaia, M. "Dni nashei zhizni." *Komsomolskaia Pravda,* 7 March 1962.

Lanovoi, Vasilii. "Dopolnitelnyi material." *Ofitsery* DVD. Ruscico, 2000.

Laville, Helen. "'Our Country Endangered by Underwear': Fashion, Femininity, and the Seduction Narrative in *Ninotchka* and *Silk Stockings*." *Diplomatic History* 30, no. 4 (September 2006).

Lawton, Anna. *Kinoglasnost: Soviet Cinema in Our Time.* Cambridge: Cambridge University Press, 1992. Reprinted as *Before the Fall: Soviet Cinema in the Gorbachev Years.* Washington, D.C.: New Academia Publishing, 2002.

Leab, Daniel J. *I Was a Communist for the FBI.* University Park: Pennsylvania State University Press, 2000.

——. "*The Iron Curtain* (1948): Hollywood's First Cold War Movies." *Historical Journal of Film, Radio and Television* 8, no. 2 (1988).

——. *Orwell Subverted: The CIA and the Filming of Animal Farm.* University Park: Pennsylvania State University Press, 2007.

Lentz, Robert J. *Korean War Filmography: 91 English Language Features through 2000.* Jefferson, N.C.: McFarland, 2003.

"Liudy, filmy, fakty." *Sovetskii ekran,* no. 29 (1967).

Lumet, Sidney. Commentary. *Fail-Safe* DVD. Sony Pictures, 2007.

MacFadyen, David. "Andrei Kravchuk: *The Admiral* (Admiral) (2008)." *KinoKultura* 24 (April 2009). http://www.kinokultura.com/2009/24r-admiral.dmf.shtml.

——. "Evgenii Lavrent'ev, *Countdown* (Lichnyi nomer) (2004), *KinoKultura* (October 2005)." www.kinokultura/reviews/R10-05/lichnyinomer.html.

Madsen, Axel. *William Wyler: The Authorised Biography.* London: W. H. Allen, 1974.

Major, Patrick, and Rana Mitter. "Culture." In *Palgrave Advances in Cold War History,* ed. Saki Dockrill and Geraint Hughes. Basingstoke: Palgrave Macmillan, 2006.

Maltby, Richard. *Harmless Entertainment: Hollywood and the Ideology of Consensus.* Metuchen, N.J.: Scarecrow Press, 1983.

——. *Hollywood Cinema.* Oxford: Blackwell, 2003.

Manvell, Roger. *Films and the Second World War.* London: A. S. Barnes, 1974.

Mariamov, A. "Borba za mir." *Iskusstvo kino,* no. 2 (1949).

May, Lary. *The Big Tomorrow: Hollywood and the Politics of the American Way.* Chicago: University of Chicago Press, 200.

McBride, Joseph. *Frank Capra: The Catastrophe of Success.* New York: Simon & Schuster, 1992.

McConnell, Malcolm, and Theodore G. Schweitzer. *Inside Hanoi's Secret Archives: Solving the MIA Mystery.* New York: Simon & Schuster, 1995.

McGilligan, Patrick, and Paul Buhle. *Tender Comrades: A Backstory of the Hollywood Blacklist.* New York: St. Martin's, 1999.

McLane, Charles B. *Soviet Policy and the Chinese Communists, 1931–1946.* New York: Columbia University Press, 1958.

McMullen, Wayne J. "*The China Syndrome*: Corruption to the Core." *Literature Film Quarterly* 23, no. 1 (1995).

Medvedeva, G. "30 polezhnykh metrov." *Sovetskii ekran*, no. 20 (1961).

Michaels, Paula A. "Mikhail Kalatozov's *The Red Tent*: A Case Study in International Coproduction across the Iron Curtain." *Historical Journal of Film, Radio and Television* 26, no. 3 (August 2006).

Mickiewicz, Ellen Propper. *Changing Channels: Television and the Struggle for Power in Russia*. Durham, N.C.: Duke University Press, 1999.

————. *Media and the Russian Public*. New York: Praeger, 1991.

————. *Split Signals: Television and Politics in the Soviet Union*. Oxford: Oxford University Press, 1988.

Miller, Jamie. *Soviet Cinema: Politics and Persuasion under Stalin*. London: I. B. Tauris, 2010.

Mitchell, Donald W. *A History of Russian and Soviet Sea Power*. New York: Macmillan, 1976.

Moi rezhisser Romm. Moscow: Iskusstvo, 1993.

Moore, John E. *The Soviet Navy Today*. New York: Stein & Day, 1976.

Munn, Michael. *Gregory Peck*. London: Robert Hale & Co., 1999.

Naimark, Norman M. *The Russians in Germany: A History of the Soviet Zone of Occupation, 1945–1949*. Cambridge, Mass.: Belknap Press, Harvard University Press, 1995.

Naremore, James. *On Kubrick*. London: BFI, 2007.

Navasky, Victor S. *Naming Names*. New York: Viking Press, 1980.

Nelson, Michael. *War of the Black Heavens: The Battles of Western Broadcasting in the Cold War*. Syracuse: Syracuse University Press, 1997.

Neumaier, Diane, ed. *Beyond Memory: Soviet Nonconformist Photography and Photo-related Works of Art*. New Brunswick, N.J.: Rutgers University Press, 2004.

Neve, Brian. "Elia Kazan's First Testimony to the House Committee on Un-American Activities, Executive Session, 14 January 1952." *Historical Journal of Film, Radio and Television* 25, no. 2 (June 2005).

Newman, J. R. "Two Discussions of Thermonuclear War." *Scientific American*, no. 204 (March 1961).

Nilsen, Thomas, Igor Kudrik, and Alexandr Nikitin. "The Russian Northern Fleet: Nuclear Submarine Accidents." *Bellona Report* 2, no. 96, http://spb/org.ru/bellona/ehome/russia/nfl/nfl18.htm.

Nitze, Paul H., et al. *Securing the Seas: The Soviet Naval Challenge and Western Alliance Options*. Boulder, Colo.: Westview Press, 1979.

Noakes, John A. "Bankers and Common Men in Bedford Falls: How the FBI Determined That *It's a Wonderful Life* Was a Subversive Movie." *Film History* 10, no. 3 (1998).

Norris, Stephen M., and Zara M. Torlone, eds. *Insiders and Outsiders in Russian Cinema*. Bloomington: Indiana University Press, 2008.

Nowell-Smith, Geoffrey, ed. *The Oxford History of World Cinema*. Oxford: Oxford University Press, 1997.

Nowell-Smith, Geoffrey, and Steven Ricci, eds. *Hollywood and Europe: Economics, Culture, National Identity 1945–1995*. London: BFI, 1998.

Nuti, Leopoldo, and Vladislav Zubok. "Ideology." In *Palgrave Advances in Cold War History*, ed. Saki Dockrill and Geraint Hughes. Basingstoke: Palgrave Macmillan, 2006.

"*Olympius inferno.*" *Russia Today* (29 March 2009). http://www.russiatoday.com/Art_and_Fun/2009-03-29/Olympius_Inferno.

O'Reilly, Kenneth. *Hoover and the UnAmericans*. Philadelphia: Temple University Press, 1983.

Osgood, Kenneth. *Total War: Eisenhower's Secret Propaganda Battle at Home and Abroad*. Lawrence: University Press of Kansas, 2006.

Palmer, William J. *The Films of the Eighties: A Social History*. Carbondale: Southern Illinois University Press, 1993.

Paris, Barry. *Audrey Hepburn*. London: Orien, 1996.

Park, Alexander G. *Bolshevism in Turkestan, 1917–1927*. New York: Columbia University Press, 1957.

Pauly, Thomas H. *American Odyssey: Elia Kazan and American Culture*. Philadelphia: Temple University Press, 1983.

Payne, Stanley G. *The Spanish Civil War, the Soviet Union, and Communism*. New Haven, Conn.: Yale University Press, 2004.

Pechatnov, Vladimir. "Exercise in Frustration: Soviet Foreign Propaganda in the Early Cold War, 1945–47." *Cold War History* 1, no. 2 (January 2001).

Peprnik, Michel. "The Affinity with the North American Indian in Czech Literary Discourse on the Democratic Roots of Czech National Culture." *Journal of Transatlantic Studies* 6, no. 2 (August 2008).

Pervyi vek nashego kino: Entsiklopediia. Moscow: Izd-vo Lokid-Press, 2006.

Poe, G. Tom. "Historical Spectatorship around and about Stanley Kramer's *On the Beach*." In *Hollywood Spectatorship: Changing Perceptions of Cinema Audiences*, ed. Melvyn Stokes and Richard Maltby. London: BFI, 2001.

Pogozheva, L. *Mikhail Romm*. Moscow: Iskusstvo, 1967.

———. "Poltora chasa razmyshlenii." *Iskusstvo kino*, no. 4 (1962).

Pollock, Ethan. *Stalin and the Soviet Science Wars*. Princeton, N.J.: Princeton University Press, 2006.

Ponizovskii, Vladimir. "Nasledniki pobedy." *Sovetskii ekran*, no. 9 (1975).

Powers, Richard Gid. *Secrecy and Power: The Life of J. Edgar Hoover*. London: Hutchinson, 1987.

Prelinger, Rick. *The Field Guide to Sponsored Films*. San Francisco: National Film Preservation Foundation, 2006.

Prokhorov, Alexander. "The Unknown New Wave: Soviet Cinema of the 1960s." In *Springtime for Soviet Cinema: Re/Viewing the 1960s*, ed. Alexander Prokhorov. Pittsburgh: Pittsburgh Russian Film Symposium, 2001.

Prokhorova, Elena. "Savva Kulish, *Dead Season* (Mertvyi sezon)." *Studies in Russian and Soviet Cinema* 3, no. 1 (2009).

Puddington, Arch. *Broadcasting Freedom: The Cold War Triumph of Radio Free Europe and Radio Liberty*. Lexington: University Press of Kentucky, 2000.

Pudovkin, Vsevolod. "*Vstrecha na Elbe*." *Pravda*, 10 March 1949.

Racheva, Mariia. "Voennye igry." *Sovetskii ekran*, no. 19 (1984).

Radosh, Ronald, and Allis Radosh. *Red Star over Hollywood: The Film Colony's Long Romance with the Left*. San Francisco: Encounter Books, 2005.

Rajagopalan, Sudha. *Leave Disco Dancer Alone! Indian Cinema and Soviet Movie-Going after Stalin*. New Delhi: Yoda Press, 2008. Reprinted as *Indian Films in Soviet Cinema: The Culture of Movie-Going after Stalin*. Bloomington: Indiana University Press, 2009.

Reagan, Ronald. *An American Life*. London: Hutchinson, 1990.

Reese, Roger R. *Red Commanders: A Social History of the Soviet Army Officer Corps, 1918–1991*. Lawrence: University Press of Kansas, 2005.

———. *The Soviet Military Experience*. London: Routledge, 2000.

Richmond, Yale. *Cultural Exchange and the Cold War: Raising the Iron Curtain*. University Park: Pennsylvania State University Press, 2003.

Robbins, Louise S. *The Dismissal of Miss Ruth Brown: Civil Rights, Censorship, and the American Library*. Norman: University of Oklahoma Press, 2000.

Rogachevskii, Andrei. "The Cold War Representation of the West in Russian Literature." In *Cold War Literature: Writing the Global Conflict*, ed. Andrew Hammond. London: Routledge, 2005.

Rogin, Michael. *Ronald Reagan, The Movie: And Other Episodes in Political Demonology*. Berkeley: University of California Press, 1987.

Romm, Mikhail. "Kinematograf v riadu iskusstv." *Iskusstvo kino*, no. 12 (2001).

Rorabaugh, W. J. *Kennedy and the Promise of the Sixties*. Cambridge: Cambridge University Press, 2002.

Rosenberg, Emily S. "'Foreign Affairs' after World War II: Connecting Sexual and International Politics." *Diplomatic History* 18, no. 1 (1994).

Rosenstone, Robert. *History on Film / Film on History*. London: Pearson, 2006.

Ross, Steven J. "The Rise of Hollywood: Movies, Ideology and Audiences in the Roaring Twenties." In *Movies and American Society*, ed. Steven J. Ross. Oxford: Blackwell, 2002.

Ryan, Michael, and Douglas Kellner. *Camera Politica: The Politics and Ideology of Contemporary Hollywood Film*. Bloomington: Indiana University Press, 1988.

Sakharov, Andrei. *Memoirs*. Trans. Richard Lourie. New York: Alfred A. Knopf, 1990.

Sanello, Frank. *Stallone: A Rocky Life*. New York: Mainstream, 1998.

Saunders, Frances Stonor. *Who Paid the Piper? The CIA and the Cultural Cold War*. London: Granta, 1999.

Savitskii, Nikolai. "Kontur triadi: Zametki o zapadnom kino 80-x." *Iskusstvo kino*, no. 8 (1986).

———. "Na raznykh poliusakh: o neskolkikh amerikanskikh filmov." *Sovetskii ekran*, no. 12 (1984).

Sayre, Nora. *Running Time: Films of the Cold War*. New York: Dial, 1982.

Scheer, Robert. *With Enough Shovels: Reagan, Bush, and Nuclear War*. New York: Random House, 1982.

Schwartz, Richard A. *Cold War Culture: Media and the Arts, 1945–1990*. New York: Checkmark, 1998.

———. *Woody: From Antz to Zelig: A Reference Guide to Woody Allen's Creative Work, 1964–1998*. Westport, Conn.: Greenwood, 2000.

Schwenk, Melinda. "Reforming the Negative through History: The US Information Agency and the 1957 Little Rock Integration Crisis." *Journal of Communication Inquiry* 23, no. 3 (July 1999).

Scott, Ian. *American Politics in Hollywood Film*. Edinburgh: Edinburgh University Press, 2000.

Segrave, Kerry. *American Films Abroad: Hollywood's Domination of the World's Movie Screens from the 1890s to the Present*. Jefferson, N.C.: McFarland, 1997.

Shain, Russell E. "Hollywood's Cold War." *Journal of Popular Film* 3, no. 4 (Fall 1974).

Shaw, Tony. *British Cinema and the Cold War: The State, Propaganda and Consensus*. London: I. B. Tauris, 2001.

———. *Hollywood's Cold War*. Amherst: University of Massachusetts Press, 2007.

———. "Our Man in Managua: Alex Cox, US Neo-Imperialism and Transatlantic Cinematic Subversion in the 1980s." *Media History* 12, no. 2, August 2006.

Shiraev, Eric, and Vladislav Zubok. *Anti-Americanism in Russia: From Stalin to Putin*. New York: Palgrave, 2000.

Shlapentokh, Vladimir. *Soviet Public Opinion and Ideology: Mythology and Pragmatism in Interaction*. New York: Praeger, 1986.

Siefert, Marsha. "From Cold War to Wary Peace: American Culture in the USSR and Russia." In *The Americanization of Europe: Culture, Diplomacy, and Anti-Americanism after 1945*, ed. Alexander Stephan. New York: Berghahn Books, 2006.

Skinner, James M. "Cliché and Convention in Hollywood's Cold War Anti-Communist Films." *North Dakota Quarterly* (Summer 1978).

Smith, Anthony, ed. *Television: An International History*. Oxford: Oxford University Press, 1998.

Smith, Dina M. "Global Cinderella: *Sabrina* (1954), Hollywood, and Postwar Internationalism." *Cinema Journal* 41, no. 2 (2003).

Snyder, Alvin. *Warriors of Disinformation: American Propaganda, Soviet Lies, and the Winning of the Cold War*. New York: Arcade, 1995.

Sobolev, Romil. "Meniaiushchisia i neizmennyi." *Sovetskii ekran*, no. 14 (1975).

———. "Qvadrat poiska." *Iskusstvo kino*, no. 3 (1983).

"Soglasno ankete." *Sovetskii ekran*, no. 10 (1983).

Sovetskie khudozhestvennye filmy: Annotirovannyi catalog. Moscow: Iskusstvo, 1961–1968.

Sovetskoe kino semidesiatykh-pervoi poloviny vosmidesiatykh godov: Uchebnoe sposobie. Moscow: VGIK, 2006.

Starr, S. Frederick. *Red and Hot: The Fate of Jazz in the Soviet Union, 1917–1980*. New York: Oxford University Press, 1983.

Steinberg, Cobbett. *Reel Facts*. Harmondsworth: Penguin, 1981.

Stern, Ralph. "*The Big Lift* (1950): Image and Identity in Blockaded Berlin." *Cinema Journal* 46, no. 2 (Winter 2007).

Stites, Richard. *Russian Popular Culture: Entertainment and Society since 1900*. Cambridge: Cambridge University Press, 1992.

Suid, Lawrence. *Guts and Glory: The Making of the American Military Image in Film*. Lexington: University Press of Kentucky, 2002.

Swann, Paul. "The Little State Department: Hollywood and the State Department in the Post-war World." *American Studies International* 29, no. 1 (April 1991).

Taylor, Richard. *Film Propaganda: Soviet Russia and Nazi Germany*. 2nd rev. ed. London: I. B. Tauris, 1998.

———. *The Politics of the Soviet Cinema, 1917–1929*. Cambridge: Cambridge University Press, 1979.

Theoharis, Athan. *Chasing Spies: How the FBI Failed in Counterintelligence but Promoted the Politics of McCarthyism in the Cold War Years*. Chicago: Ivan R. Dee, 2002.

Toplin, Robert Brent. *Fahrenheit 9/11: How One Film Divided a Nation*. Lawrence: University Press of Kansas, 2006.

———. *History by Hollywood: The Use and Abuse of the American Past*. Chicago: University of Chicago Press, 1996.

Trauberg, Leonid. "O korabliakh i gluptsakh." *Iskusstvo kino*, no. 12 (1983).

Troianovskii, V. "Chelovek ottepeli." In *Kinematograf ottepeli,* Vol. 1, ed. V. Troianovskii. Moscow: Materik, 1996.

Tsyrkun, Nina. "'Novye prava v Gollivude." *Iskusstvo kino*, no. 2 (1984).

Tumarkin, Nina. *The Living and the Dead: The Rise and Fall of the Cult of World War II in Russia*. New York: Basic Books, 1994.

Turovskaia, Maia. "Marlen Khutsiev." In *Molodye rezhissery sovetkogo kino: Sbornik statei*. Leningrad: Iskusstvo, 1962.

———. "Soviet Films of the Cold War." In *Stalinism and Soviet Cinema*, ed. Richard Taylor and Derek Spring. London: Routledge, 1993.

Vasudev, Aruna, Latika Padgaonkar, and Rashmi Doraiswamy, eds. *Being and Becoming: The Cinemas of Asia*. Delhi: Macmillan India, 2002.

Wagnleitner, Reinhold. *Coca-Colonization and the Cold War: The Cultural Mission of the United States in Austria after the Second World War*. Chapel Hill: University of North Carolina Press, 1994.

Walsh, Frank. *Sin and Censorship: The Catholic Church and the Motion Picture Industry*. New Haven, Conn.: Yale University Press, 1996.

Wanger, Walter F. "Donald Duck and Diplomacy." *Public Opinion Quarterly* 14, no. 3 (1950).

Watson, Bruce W. *Red Navy at Sea: Soviet Naval Operations on the High Seas, 1956–1980*. Boulder, Colo.: Westview Press, 1982.

Weinland, Robert G. "The State and Future of the Soviet Navy in the North Atlantic." In *Soviet Naval Influence: Domestic and Foreign Dimensions*, ed. Michael Mcc-Gwire and John McDonnell. New York: Praeger, 1977.

Welch, David. *Propaganda and the German Cinema*. London: I. B. Tauris, 2001.

Westad, Odd Arne. *The Global Cold War*. Cambridge: Cambridge University Press, 2007.

Whitfield, Stephen J. *The Culture of the Cold War*. Baltimore: Johns Hopkins University Press, 1996.

Widdis, Emma. "Dressing the Part: Clothing Otherness in Soviet Cinema before 1953." In *Insiders and Outsiders in Russian Cinema,* ed. Stephen M. Norris and Zara M. Torlone. Bloomington: Indiana University Press, 2008.

Wien, Martin. *Zirkus zwischen Kunst und Kader: Das Zirkuswesen in der SBZ/DDR*. Berlin: Duncker & Humblod, 2001.

Wiener, Norbert. "Some Moral and Technical Consequences of Automation." *Science* 131 (6 May 1960).

Wills, Gary. *Reagan's America: Innocents at Home.* New York: Doubleday, 1987.

Witkowska, Joanna. "Creating False Enemies: John Bull and Uncle Sam as Food for Anti-Western Propaganda in Poland." *Journal of Transatlantic Studies* 6, no. 2 (August 2008).

Wittner, Lawrence S. *Resisting the Bomb: A History of the World Nuclear Disarmament Movement, 1954–1970.* Stanford, Calif.: Stanford University Press, 1997.

Woll, Josephine. "Being 20, 40 Years Later: Marlen Khutsiev's *Mne dvadtsat let*" (I Am Twenty, 1961)." *Kinoeye: New Perspectives on European Film* 1, no. 8 (10 December 2001). http://www.kinoeye.org/01/08/woll08.php, 2.

————. *Real Images: Soviet Cinema and the Thaw.* London: I. B. Tauris, 2000.

Young, Cathy. "From Russia with Loathing." *New York Times,* 21 November 2008. http://www.nytimes.com/2008/11/21/opinion/21young.html?_r=2.

Young, Jeff, ed. *Kazan on Kazan.* London: Faber & Faber, 1999.

Youngblood, Denise J. *Movies for the Masses: Popular Cinema and Soviet Society in the 1920s.* Cambridge: Cambridge University Press, 1992.

————. *Russian War Films: On the Cinema Front, 1914–2005.* Lawrence: University Press of Kansas, 2007.

————. *Soviet Cinema in the Silent Era, 1918–1935.* Austin: University of Texas Press, 1991.

Yurchak, Alexei. *Everything Was Forever until It Was No More: The Last Soviet Generation.* Princeton, N.J.: Princeton University Press, 2006.

Zak, Mark. *Mikhail Romm i ego filmy.* Moscow: Iskusstvo, 1988.

Zeiler, Thomas W. "The Diplomatic History Bandwagon: A State of the Field." *Journal of American History* 95, no. 4 (March 2009).

Zemlianukhin, Sergei, and Miroslava Segida. *Domashniaia sinemateka: Otechestvennoe kino, 1918–1996.* Moscow: Dubl-D, 1996.

Zhuk, Sergei. "Popular Culture, Identity, and Soviet Youth in Dniepropetrovsk, 1959–84." *Carl Beck Papers in Russian & East European Studies,* no. 1906 (2008).

————. *Rock and Roll in the Rocket City: The West, Identity, and Ideology in Soviet Dniepropetrovsk, 1960–1985.* Baltimore: Johns Hopkins University Press, 2010.

Zorkaia, Neia. *The Illustrated History of the Soviet Cinema.* New York: Hippocrene Books, 1989.

Zubkova, Elena. *Russia after the War: Hopes, Illusions, and Disappointments, 1945–1957.* Trans. and ed. Hugh Ragsdale. Armonk, N.Y.: M. E. Sharpe, 1998.

Zubok, Vladislav M. *A Failed Empire: The Soviet Union in the Cold War from Stalin to Gorbachev.* Chapel Hill: University of North Carolina Press, 2007.

Conference Papers

Shcherbenok, Andrey. "Asymmetric Warfare: Cold War Cinema in the Soviet Union and the United States." Paper presented at the conference "Dream Factory of Communism: Cultural Practices and the Memory of the Cold War," Miami University, Oxford, Ohio, 2007. http://www.units/muohio.edu/havighurst center/conferences/documents/shcherbenok.pdf.

White, John Kenneth. "Seeing Red: The Cold War and American Public Opinion." Paper presented at the conference "The Power of Free Inquiry and Cold War International History," U.S. National Archives, 1998. http://www.archives.gov/research/cold-war/conference/white.html.

WEBSITES
http://www.archive.org
http://www.boxofficemojo.com
http://www.fas.org/irp/congress/
http://www.imdb.com
http://www.tcm.com/tcmdb/index.jsp

DVD AND VHS RECORDINGS
Deviat dnei odnogo goda. DVD. Ruscico, 2000.
Fail-Safe (1964). DVD. Sony Pictures, CDR 10252, 2007.
Fail-Safe (2000). DVD. Warner Bros., Z1 18653, 2000.
Hearts and Minds. DVD. MTD5206. Metrodome, 2005.
Incident at Map Grid 36-80. VHS. IFEX, 1983.
Odinochnoe plavanie. VHS. Krupnyi plan, 2000.
Ofitsery. DVD. Ruscico, 2000.
Vesna na Zarechnoi ulitse. DVD. SR Digital, 2002.
Vstrecha na Elbe. DVD. Retro klub, 2005.

Select Cold War Filmography

SOVIET UNION

Ch.P.: An Extraordinary Event (Chrezvychainnoe proisshestvie), 1958; A. Dovzhenko Film Studio; *dir:* Viktor Ivchenko; *scr:* Grigory Koltunov, Vitalii Kalinin, Dmitrii Kuznetsov; *cast:* Mikhail Kuznetsov, Aleksandr Anurov, Viacheslav Tikhonov, Taisiia Litvenenko, Anatolii Solovev.

The Conspiracy of the Doomed (Zagovor obrechennykh), 1950; Mosfilm; *dir:* Mikhail Kalatozov; *scr:* Nikolai Virta; *cast:* Liudmila Skopina, Pavel Kadochnikov, Vladimir Druzhinkov, Boris Sitkno, Vsevolod Aksenov.

The Court of Honor (Sud chesti), 1948; Mosfilm; *dir:* Abram Room; *scr:* Aleksandr Shtein; *cast:* Boris Chirkov, Antonina Maksimova, Evgenii Samoilov, Nikolai Annenkov, Olga Zhizneva.

Dead Season (Mertvyi sezon), 1968; Lenfilm; *dir:* Savva Kulish; *scr:* Vladimir Vladimirov (Vainshtok), Aleksandr Slepianov; *cast:* Donatas Banionis, Rolan Bykov, Sergei Kurilov, Gennadii Iukhtin, Bruno Freindlich.

The Fall of Berlin (Padenie Berlina), 1949; Mosfilm; *dir:* Mikhail Chiaureli; *scr:* Petr Pavlenko, Mikhail Chiaureli; *cast:* Mikhail Gelovani, Maksim Shtraukh, Aleksei Gribo, Nikolai Ryzhkov, Gavriil Belov.

Flight 222 (Reis 222), 1985; Lenfilm; *dir:* Sergei Mikaelian; *scr:* Sergei Mikaelian; *cast:* Larisa Poliakova, Nikolai Kochnev, Aleksandr Kolesnikov, Aleksandr Ivanov, Nikolai Aleshin.

Foreigners (Inostrantsy), 1961; Mosfilm; *dir:* Eduard Zmoiro; *scr:* Boris Laskin; *cast:* Valentin Kulik, Mariia Mironova, M. Kravchunovskaia, Aleksandr Beliavskii, Ilia Rutberg.

The Fort in the Mountains (Zastava v gorakh), 1953; Mosfilm; *dir:* Konstantin Iudin; *scr:* Mikhail Volpin, Nikolai Erdman; *cast:* Vladlen Davydov, Marina Kuznetsova, Elena Shatrova, Sergei Gruzo, Stanislav Chekan.

Game without Rules (Igra bez pravil), 1965; Sverdlovsk Film Studio; *dir:* Iaropolk Lapshin; *scr:* Lev Sheinin; *cast:* Mikhail Kuznetsov, Viktor Dobrovolskii, Tatiana Karpova, Vsevolod Iakut, Viktor Khokhriakov.

Heights (Vysota), 1957; Mosfilm; *dir:* Aleksandr Zarkhi; *scr:* Mikhail Papava; *cast:* Nikolai Rybnikov, Inna Makarova, Gennadii Karnovich-Valua, Vasilii Makarov; Mariia Strizhenova.

I Walk around Moscow (Ia shagaiu po Moskve), 1963; Mosfilm; *dir:* Georgii Danelia; *scr:* Gennadii Shpalikov; *cast:* Aleksei Loktev, Nikita Mikhalkov, Galina Polskikh, Evgenii Steblov, Rolan Bykov, Inna Churikova.

Incident at Map Grid 36-80 (Sluchai v kvadrate 36-80), 1982; Mosfilm; *dir:* Mikhail Tumanishvili; *scr:* Evgenii Mesiatsev; *cast:* Boris Shcherbakov, Mikhai Volontir, Anatolii Kuznetsov, Vladimir Sedov, Omar Volmer, Paul Butkevich.

Liberation (*Osvobozhenie*), 5 pts., 1968–1971; Mosfilm, DEFA, PRFZF, Dino de Laurentis Cinematografica; *dir:* Iurii Ozerov; *scr:* Iurii Bondarev, Oskar Kurganov, Iurii Ozerov; *cast:* Mikhail Ulianov, Vasilii Shukshin, Nikolai Olialin, Larisa Golubkina, Mikhail Nozhkin.

The Meeting on the Elbe (*Vtrecha na Elbe*), 1949; Mosfilm; *dir:* Grigorii Aleksandrov; *scr:* Tur Brothers, Lev Sheinin; *cast:* Vladlen Davydov, Konstantin Nassonov, Boris Andreev, Mikhail Nazvanov, Liubov Orlova, Faina Ranevskaia.

Neutral Waters (*Neitralnye vody*), 1968; M. Gorkii Film Studio; *dir:* Vladimir Berenshtein; *scr:* Vladimir Vendelovskii, Vasilii Solovev, Vladimir Berenshtein; *cast:* Kirill Lavrov, Vladimir Chetverikov, Gennadii Karnovich-Valua, Aleksei Ushakov, Mikhail Ianushkevich.

Nine Days in One Year (*Deviat dnei odnogo goda*), 1961 [rel. 1962]; Mosfilm; *dir:* Mikhail Romm; *scr:* Mikhail Romm, Daniil Khrabrovitskii; *cast:* Aleksei Batalov, Innokentii Smoktunovskii, Tatiana Lavrova, Nikolai Plotnikov, Evgenii Evstigneev.

Officers (*Ofitsery*), 1971; M. Gorkii Film Studio; *dir:* Vladimir Rogovoi; *scr:* Boris Vasilev, Kirill Rapoport; *cast:* Vasilii Lanovoi, Georgii Iumatov, Alina Pokrovskaia, Aleksandr Voevodin, Andrei Anisimov, Natalia Rychagova.

The Secret Mission (*Sekretnaia missiia*), 1950; Mosfilm: *dir:* Mikhail Romm; *scr:* Konstantin Isaev, Mikhail Makliarskii; *cast:* Elena Kuzmina, Nikolai Komissarov, Sergei Vecheslov, Vasilii Makarov, Aleksei Gribov.

Solo Voyage (*Odinochnoe plavanie*), 1985 [rel. 1986]; Mosfilm; *dir:* Mikhail Tumanishvili; *scr:* Evgenii Mesiatsev; *cast:* Mikhail Nozhkin, Aleksandr Fatiushin, Sergei Nasibov, Nartai Belagin, Vitalii Zikora, Arnis Litsitis.

Spring on Zarechnaya Street (*Vesna na Zarechnoi ulitse*), 1956; Odessa Film Studio; *dir:* Marlen Khutsiev, Feliks Mironer; *scr:* Feliks Mironer; *cast:* Nina Ivanova, Nikolai Rybnikov, Vladimir Guliaev, Valentina Pugacheva, Gennadii Iukhtin, Rimma Shorokhova.

UNITED STATES

Apocalypse Now, 1979; Omni Zoetrope; *dir*: Francis Ford Coppola; *prod*: Francis Ford Coppola; *scr*: Francis Ford Coppola, John Milius; *cast*: Marlon Brando, Robert Duvall, Martin Sheen, Dennis Hopper.

Bananas, 1971; Rollins & Joffe Productions; *dir*: Woody Allen; *prod*: Jack Grossberg; *scr*: Woody Allen, Mickey Rose; *cast*: Woody Allen, Louise Lasser, Carlos Montalban, Jacobo Morales.

The Big Lift, 1950; Twentieth Century-Fox; *dir*: George Seaton; *prod*: William Perlberg; *scr*: George Seaton; *cast*: Montgomery Clift, Paul Douglas, Cornell Borchers, Bruni Löbel, O. E. Hasse.

Fail-Safe, 1964; Columbia; *dir*: Sidney Lumet; *prod*: Max E. Youngstein; *scr*: Walter Bernstein; *cast*: Henry Fonda, Dan O'Herlihy, Walter Matthau, Edward Binns, Larry Hagman.

Hearts and Minds, 1974; Touchstone; *dir*: Peter Davis; *prod*: Peter Davis, Bert Schneider [documentary].

The Hunt for Red October, 1990; Paramount; *dir*: John McTiernan; *prod*: Mace Neufeld; *scr*: Larry Ferguson, Donald Stewart; *cast*: Sean Connery, Alec Baldwin, Scott Glenn, Sam Neill.

Invasion U.S.A., 1952; American Pictures; *dir*: Alfred E. Green; *prod*: Robert Zugsmith, Robert Smith; *scr*: Robert Smith; *cast*: Gerald Mohr, Peggy Castle, Dan O'Herlihy, Tom Kennedy.

The Iron Curtain, 1948; Twentieth Century-Fox; *dir*: William A. Wellman; *prod*: Sol. C. Siegel; *scr*: Milton Krims; *cast*: Dana Andrews, Gene Tierney, June Havoc, Berry Kroeger.

Man on a Tightrope, 1953; Twentieth Century-Fox; *dir*: Elia Kazan; *prod*: Robert L. Jacks; *scr*: Robert E. Sherwood; *cast*: Fredric March, Gloria Grahame, Cameron Mitchell, Terry Moore, Adolphe Menjou.

The Manchurian Candidate, 1962; M. C. Productions; *dir*: John Frankenheimer; *prod*: John Frankenheimer, George Axelrod; *scr*: George Axelrod; *cast*: Laurence Harvey, Frank Sinatra, Janet Leigh, Angela Lansbury, James Gregory.

Ninotchka, 1939; MGM; *dir*: Ernst Lubitsch; *prod*: Ernst Lubitsch, Sidney Franklin; *scr*: Charles Brackett, Billy Wilder, Walter Reisch; *cast*: Greta Garbo, Melvyn Douglas, Ina Claire, Bela Lugosi.

Rambo: First Blood Part II, 1985; Carolco; *dir*: George Pan Cosmatos; *prod*: Buzz Feitshans; *scr*: Sylvester Stallone, James Cameron; *cast*: Sylvester Stallone, Richard Crenna, Charles Napier, Julia Nickson.

Red Dawn, 1984; United Artists; *dir*: John Milius; *prod*: Buzz Feitshans, Barry Beckerman; *scr*: Kevin Reynolds, John Milius; *cast*: Patrick Swayze, C. Thomas Howell, Lea Thompson, Charlie Sheen.

Red Heat, 1988; Carolco; *dir*: Walter Hill; *prod*: Walter Hill, Gordon Carroll; *scr*: Harry Kleiner, Walter Hill, Troy Kennedy Martin; *cast*: Arnold Schwarzenegger, James Belushi, Peter Boyle, Ed O'Ross.

Roman Holiday, 1953; Paramount; *dir*: William Wyler; *prod*: William Wyler; *scr*: Ian McLellan Hunter, John Dighton; *cast*: Gregory Peck, Audrey Hepburn, Eddie Albert.

The Russians Are Coming, The Russians Are Coming, 1966; Mirisch; *dir*: Norman Jewison; *prod*: Norman Jewison; *scr*: William Rose; *cast*: Carl Reiner, Eva Marie Saint, Alan Arkin, Brian Keith.

Russkies, 1987; New Century Entertainment; *dir*: Rick Rosenthal; *prod*: Mark Levinson, Scott Rosenfelt; *scr*: Alan Jay Glueckman, Sheldon Lettich, Michael Nankin; *cast*: Whip Hubley, Peter Billingsley, Leaf Phoenix, Stefan DeSalle, Susan Walters.

Seven Days in May, 1964; Seven Arts; *dir*: John Frankenheimer; *prod*: Edward Lewis; *scr*: Rod Serling; *cast*: Burt Lancaster, Kirk Douglas, Fredric March, Ava Gardner, Edmund O'Brien.

The Ten Commandments, 1956; Paramount; *dir*: Cecil B. DeMille; *prod*: Cecil B. DeMille; *scr*: Aeneas MacKenzie, Jesse L. Lasky Jr., Jack Gariss, Fredric M. Frank; *cast*: Charlton Heston, Yul Brynner, Anne Baxter, Edward G. Robinson, Yvonne De Carlo, Debra Paget.

Three Days of the Condor, 1975; Wildwood Enterprises; *dir*: Sydney Pollack; *prod*: Stanley Schneider; *scr*: Lorenzo Semple Jr., David Rayfiel; *cast*: Robert Redford, Faye Dunaway, Cliff Robertson, Max von Sydow.

Top Gun, 1986; Paramount; *dir*: Tony Scott; *prod*: Don Simpson, Jerry Bruckheimer; *scr*: Warren Skaaren, Jim Cash, Jack Epps Jr.; *cast*: Tom Cruise, Kelly McGillis, Val Kilmer, Anthony Edwards, Tom Skerritt.

SOVIET UNION / UNITED STATES

The Blue Bird, 1976; Lenfilm, Edward Lewis Productions, Tower International, Twentieth Century-Fox; *dir*: George Cukor; *prod*: Stanley Schneider; *scr*: Alfred Hayes, Aleksei Kapler, Hugh Whitemore; *cast*: Elizabeth Taylor, Jane Fonda, Ava Gardner, Cicely Tyson, Nadezhda Pavlova, Georgii Vitsin, Margarita Terekhova, Valentina Ganibalova.

Index

Putin, Vladimir, 221, 222
Pyriev, Ivan, 48

Radio Free Europe, 86, 93, 95
Rafferty, Kevin, 33
Rafferty, Pierce, 33
Raizman, Yuly, 136
Rambo: First Blood Part II, 11, 35,
　　203(photo), 206(photo),
　　208(photo), 209(photo)
　audiences, 201, 210–211, 259n29
　box office success, 201
　budget, 210
　compared to Soviet films, 209, 213
　enemies, 205–207
　foreign showings, 212, 259n29
　hero, 202, 207–209, 220–221
　influence, 201–202
　message, 205–206, 207, 220–221
　personnel involved, 210,
　　216–217
　plot, 202–204
　production values, 209–210
　reactions to, 212
　script, 205
　social importance, 211–212
　Soviet views of, 57, 199, 212
Rambo III, 212
Rambo movies, popularity in Soviet
　Union, 190, 212
Rand, Ayn, 20
RAND Corporation, 148
Ranevskaya, Faina, 69, 140
Rassvet nad Nemanom. See *The Dawn over
　the Neman*
Reagan, Ronald
　anticommunist views, 32
　elections, 32, 190, 199
　film career, 32, 35, 211
　foreign policy, 207
　influence of films, 32–33
　Rambo and, 207, 211
　relations with Soviet Union, 56, 189,
　　190, 199
Reagan administration, 32, 33, 202, 210,
　211

Red Army, 42, 55, 68, 121. *See also*
　Soviet Army
Red Dawn, 34, 57, 189, 208
Red Heat, 35, 59
The Red Menace, 24
Reds, 33
Red Scare (1918–1920), 17
Red Scare (1950s), 85
The Red Tent (Krasnaia palatka), 53
Reed, John, 33
Reeducation films, 113, 123–124
Reese, Roger, 165
Reis 222. See Flight 222
RKO, 18
Robinson, Edward G., 93
Rocky, 34, 212
Rocky IV, 34, 35, 210, 260n48
Rogovoy (Rogovoi), Vladimir, 161, 173.
　See also *Officers*
Rollins, Jack, 174
Roman Catholic Church. *See* Catholic
　Church
Roman Holiday, 10, 100–107,
　　101(photo), 102(photo),
　　105(photo)
　box office success, 109
　budget, 108
　compared to *Spring on Zarechnaya
　　Street,* 112, 114, 124–125
　crew, 102–103, 216
　image of Western way of life, 100,
　　102–104, 111, 125
　international showings,
　　109–110, 109(photo),
　　110(photo), 112
　Italian location, 106–107, 108
　marketing, 108, 109, 110(photo)
　musical score, 105
　plot, 100–102, 104, 105
　reactions to, 108–110
　script, 105–107
　Soviet screenings, 28, 110, 111–112,
　　251n36
Romania, American Humor Film Week,
　185
Romanov, Aleksei, 51

United States film industry (*continued*)
in early Cold War (1947–1953),
19–24, 66, 81–82
end of Cold War, 35–36, 59, 215
exchanges with Soviet Union, 59
foreign locations, 27, 106–107, 108
independent filmmakers, 29, 143,
173
influence on Soviet filmmakers, 50,
52–53, 201, 213, 218
international reach, 16, 26–27, 61,
93–94, 96, 99, 107–108
liberals in, 25, 29, 31, 32, 106
in 1920s, 17–18
in 1950s and 1960s, 25–28, 29–31,
97, 99, 143
in 1970s, 28–29, 31, 159–160, 173,
185–187
in 1980s, 32–36, 56, 189–190,
204–205, 215
post–Cold War, 221
power of stars, 204–205
production values, 99, 209–210
proportion of Cold War films, 82
relations with state, 3, 15–16, 18,
19–21, 22, 27–28, 61, 216
seen as apolitical, 17, 97
studio system, 18, 29
United States Information Agency
(USIA), 28, 32, 110, 111
U.S. Navy
assistance with films, 36, 210
competition with Soviet Navy, 191
submarines, 198, 258n22
See also *Incident at Map Grid 36-80*;
Solo Voyage
Universal Studios, 18
USIA. *See* United States Information
Agency

Vajna, Andrew, 210
Vatican. *See* Catholic Church
Vesna. See *Spring*
Vesna na Zarechnoi ulitse. See *Spring on
Zarechnaya Street*

VGIK (All-Union State Institute of
Cinematography), 129, 161
Vietnam Veterans Association, 211
Vietnam War
debates on, 28, 211
films on, 31–32, 35, 159, 173, 202,
259–260n39
missing Americans, 205, 210,
259n38
protests against, 180, 183–184
revisionist views, 207
Vietnam War veterans, 57, 205, 211. See
also *Rambo*; *Solo Voyage*
Voice of America, 111
Voloshin, Igor, 221
Vstrecha na Elbe. See *The Meeting on the
Elbe*
Vyshinsky, Andrei, 45, 68
Vysota. See *Heights*

Walk East on Beacon, 22
Wanger, Walter, 99
War Comes to America, 230n29
WarGames, 33
Warner Bros., 18, 22
War on Terror, 222–223
Wars. *See specific wars*
Watergate scandal, 31
Waterloo, 53
Wayne, John, 21, 82, 202, 230n29,
259n31
Weismuller, Johnny, 24, 50, 121–122
Wellman, William, *The Iron Curtain*, 19,
81
Werker, Alfred L., *Walk East on Beacon*,
22
West Germany. *See* Germany
Wheeler, Harvey, *Fail-Safe*, 143–144,
145, 154, 155, 157
The Whip Hand, 23
White Nights, 34, 94
Wick, Charles Z., 32
Wiener, Norbert, 144
Wilder, Billy, 104, 112
Woll, Josephine, 113, 140